ALSO BY MICHAEL GOLDFARB

*Ahmad's War, Ahmad's Peace:*
*Surviving Under Saddam, Dying in the New Iraq*

# EMANCIPATION

## How Liberating Europe's Jews from the Ghetto Led to Revolution and Renaissance

# MICHAEL GOLDFARB

Simon & Schuster
NEW YORK   LONDON   TORONTO   SYDNEY

Simon & Schuster
1230 Avenue of the Americas
New York, NY 10020

First Simon & Schuster hardcover edition November 2009

SIMON & SCHUSTER and colophon are registered trademarks
of Simon & Schuster, Inc.

For information about special discounts for bulk purchases,
please contact Simon & Schuster Special Sales at
1-866-506-1949 or business@simonandschuster.com.

The Simon & Schuster Speakers Bureau can bring authors
to your live event. For more information or to book an event
contact the Simon & Schuster Speakers Bureau at
1-866-248-3049 or visit our website at www.simonspeakers.com.

DESIGNED BY KYOKO WATANABE

Manufactured in the United States of America

2 4 6 8 10 9 7 5 3 1

Library of Congress Cataloging-in-Publication Data
Goldfarb, Michael.
Emancipation : how liberating Europe's Jews from the ghetto led to revolution and renaissance /
Michael Goldfarb.
p.    cm.
1. Jews—Europe, Western—History—18th century. 2. Jews—Europe, Western—
History—19th century. 3. Jews—Emancipation—Europe, Western—History—18th century.
4. Jews—Emancipation—Europe, Western—History—19th century. 5. Jews—Cultural
assimilation—Europe, Western—History—18th century. 6. Jews—Cultural assimilation—
Europe, Western—History—19th century. 7. Haskalah—History. 8. Europe, Western—
Ethnic relations. I. Title.
DS135.E83G656 2009
305.892'40409033—dc22        2009023425
ISBN 978-1-4165-4796-9
ISBN 978-1-4391-6048-0 (ebook)

Illustration Credits: Bridgeman Art Library: 1, 2, 4, 5, 12, 13, 15, 17, 24, 25, 26, 27, 28, 29;
Wikipedia: 3, 9, 10, 11, 16; Bibliothèque nationale de France: 6; Site Internet du Judaisme
d'Alsace et de Lorraine: 7, 8; © Judisches Museum, Frankfurt am Main: 14; Jewish Museum,
Vienna: 18, 19; Hamburg Museum: 20, 21, 22; City of Frankfurt Museum: 23.

*For my daughter, Romola*

# CONTENTS

## Contents

# Contents

**emancipate**

   **verb 1**  set free, especially from legal, social, or political
   restrictions.

—*Compact Oxford English Dictionary*

What is the great task of our own age? It is emancipation.
Not only the emancipation of Irishmen, Greeks, Frankfurt Jews, West Indian Blacks, and other such oppressed
peoples, but the emancipation of the whole world . . .

—Heinrich Heine,
*The Journey from Munich to Genoa,* 1828

# EMANCIPATION

# PREFACE

FOR ALMOST HALF A MILLENNIUM, STARTING IN THE TIME OF the Black Death, the Jews of Europe lived in enforced segregation. They were sequestered in rural hamlets or locked away at night in restricted areas of towns and cities. The laws applying to them were as varied as the number of states on the continent. One of the last places to segregate its Jews was Venice. In 1516, the city-state's government ordered the seven hundred or so Jews residing there to live in a quarter locally known as the *ghèto*. Current scholarship generally agrees *ghèto* is a corruption of the Italian word for foundry. There had been a number of ironworks on the site. *Ghetto* quickly became a generic term for a place of segregation.

As centuries passed the isolation deepened. Then, in one remarkable act during the French Revolution, the Jews of France were given full citizenship. They were "emancipated." The ghetto gates were opened.

For the next century, as modern nation-states were created around the continent, the question of what to do with the Jews became intimately tangled up in the birth of each new state. Just as the question of race has had to be reanswered in each phase of America's development, the Jewish Question had to be asked and answered at each stage of European development.

It was not a smooth process. Rights were given, then taken away. But from that first action in France, Jewish Emancipation became an unstoppable force.

Something quite remarkable happened once the ghetto gates were thrown open. During the centuries of segregation Jewish community life had developed a separate existence to the surrounding society. There were points of contact in commerce and trade but the Jewish community had turned in on itself. Customs, clothes, almost all aspects of life were different inside the ghetto. Yet now, within a few short decades Jews were not only integrating but playing an increasingly important role in the life of Europe.

The transformation was startling to those who lived through it. In the early nineteenth century, Isaac D'Israeli, whose family had been expelled from Spain, lived for centuries in Venice, and then wandered north to England via the Netherlands, noted that prior to Emancipation he could count all the "Jewish men of genius or talent on his fingers . . . The previous ten centuries have not produced ten great men." But now everything was changing fast. His son, Benjamin, would become one of the great men of this new era, first as a popular novelist, then as British prime minister.

The events remain extraordinary to look back on. As he approached his ninetieth birthday, the historian Eric Hobsbawm, whose Austrian Jewish family lived the Emancipation story, wrote, "After many centuries during which the intellectual and cultural history of the world . . . could be written with little reference to the contribution of any Jews, we almost immediately enter the modern era where Jewish names are disproportionately represented."

This rapid transformation came at a heavy price. Equal rights rocked the foundations of Jewish religious practice and Jewish community life. Salo W. Baron, who was born at the end of the Emancipation era in Galicia, the easternmost extent of the Austro-Hungarian Empire, and who spent the bulk of his life writing and teaching Jewish history at Columbia University, compared "the internal crisis in Jewish life generated by the new equality with the crisis of the First Exile." He meant the first Babylonian exile, when the Temple in Jerusalem was destroyed and the city's inhabitants were marched to Babylon to hang up their harps by the riverside, sit down, and weep. The Emancipation era was an equally shattering dislocation.

In writing this book I wanted to answer two simple questions: Why? Why was there this enormous explosion of Jewish achievement, particularly in the areas of culture and intellectual life? And, what price? What was the price paid by the Jewish community and European society for the process of integrating?

These two questions had been at the back of my mind for a long time and I occasionally did some reading to look for answers. But the decision to write a book about them came out of my work as a journalist. After the attacks of September 11, 2001, I found myself reporting on radical Islam. My ears filled with the complaints of angry Muslims everywhere from Cairo to Tehran to just outside my front door in London. A year before the London bombings of 2005 I did an hour-long radio documentary on British jihadis. One of the young Muslims I interviewed was involved in a grassroots organization that held regular meetings in London's East End, once a ghetto for Jewish immigrants, now a neighborhood of Muslim immigrants mostly from Bangladesh. At these forums we debated what it meant to be a Muslim in Britain. A panel of prominent Muslims and white Britons would discuss the issues of identity and religious faith, then take questions from the floor. Almost all the queries elided into one great question: To whom did a Muslim owe first allegiance—his country or his faith? Especially when that faith posits the idea of a single nation of the Muslims.

Over and over I heard younger members of the community, most of them born in Britain, pledging allegiance to the idea of the Muslim state. Many had come to Islam in late adolescence and early adulthood. Their experience of integration and assimilation had been disappointing. Their response had been to embrace the more radical interpretation of their religion. They were Muslims first and last, and to prove they were not of the society into which they had been born, they began to make themselves outwardly different. The young men grew beards and put on traditional dress and skullcaps; the young women voluntarily wore the veil and segregated themselves from the men.

This was not unique to London's East End. It was happening in Amsterdam, Paris, and Hamburg. When the French government began to make a fuss about Muslim girls wearing the hijab to school, I knew that the laws and traditions they invoked could be traced back to statutes passed in the early days of Emancipation to hasten Jewish integration into French society. When the Dutch government passed laws giving it the right to license imams who had to prove their fluency in Dutch, it was merely dusting off a law passed by Napoleon in 1808 and applied to French rabbis, many of whom, having lived their entire lives in the ghetto, spoke virtually no French.

I realized then that it was worth going through the agony of writing a book that answered the questions "why" and "what price" because the story of Jewish Emancipation had relevance today outside the Jewish community, and not just for the developed world's immigrant Muslim communities but for other racial and ethnic minority groups in this second age of mass immigration. The story of Jewish Emancipation is not just about a religious minority's struggles to integrate, it is about a group regarded as an ethnic and racial minority fighting for its place in society.

When, early in the presidential primary campaign of 2008, some African-Americans questioned whether candidate Barack Obama was authentically black, they were raising a question that Jews raised about themselves throughout the Emancipation period (and continue to think about). Ghetto oppression had completely defined the community, so now, in an integrated world, who was authentically Jewish?

As I began researching this book, I found additional motivation for writing it. The Holocaust hangs across Jewish history like an iron curtain. It sometimes seems that the story of the Jewish community leaps from the destruction of the Second Temple by the Romans and the beginnings of the Diaspora to Kristallnacht, with only a few incidents, such as the expulsion from Spain and the mass immigration of our grandparents and great-grandparents to America, in between.

That's because the black weight of the Holocaust cut the connection to the era of Emancipation. The whole world knows the names of Marx, Freud, and Einstein but very few people have an understanding of how the process of leaving the ghetto behind shaped them.

The Holocaust also erased the memory of a great many fascinating figures who did not achieve the fame of that trio but whose lives and works were significant in their time and should be remembered now. This is particularly true of those who wrote in German. One of the main tasks I set myself was to rescue these forgotten people. I don't reclaim them for Jewish history alone. Their lives and achievements belong to the history of all men.

There is one other reason I wanted to tell this story. The Talmud tells us there are 613 *mitzvoth,* commandments mentioned in the Torah, that Jews must perform. Without violating the sanctity of the Five Books, I think there is one more: those of us born after the Holocaust have a responsibility to reclaim and retell one part of the history of our people, not just in honor of those who lived it and were murdered for it, but to help guide us to a renewed understanding of who we are.

# PART 1

# EMANCIPATION

## CHAPTER ONE

# Everything in the Universe Is Changing

Before there is revolution there is talk. Before the old regime is overthrown there must be discussion about what is to replace it.

France in the 1780s was overwhelmed with talk. Change had to come, and everybody knew it: the nobles, the peasants, the merchants, even the king himself. The country was bankrupt. Beyond the economy the whole organization of society needed modernizing, the relationship between ordinary people and their king, their church, and their laws needed to be redefined. People did not just talk about reform, they wrote pamphlets about it and formed clubs to discuss solutions. Learned societies organized essay contests to encourage debate and these contests became national forums, the place where those who wanted to step into public life could make a name for themselves.

The Royal Society of Sciences and Arts in Metz, in eastern France, was one of the foremost of these learned societies. Every two years the Metz Royal Society challenged the nation's thinkers to write on a topic of practical science and one of social philosophy. In 1783, it asked, "What are the means, compatible with good morals, to assure the upkeep of bastards and to get from them greater use for the state?" This was a critical question in a time when contraception was not practiced with the same scientific precision as today, and illegitimate births were common.

The committee choosing the subjects for the Royal Society's competitions was made up of some of the most important men in Metz. The group spent months discussing current events, trying to find a topic that was worthy of the institution and might also lead to practical solutions for serious social problems. At the end of August 1785, the local paper in Metz, *Affiches des Trois-Evêchés et Lorraine,* carried an announcement for the society's new contest. The scientific essay topic related to France's most important export product: "Is there a way to make a better wine press?" The social question was "Are there means to render the Jews more useful and happy in France?"

The committee of the Metz Royal Society could be certain of a good response to their questions. There was plenty of time for entrants to consider their arguments: the submissions weren't due until 1787. And the effort would be worth it for the winner: a prize of a gold medallion worth four hundred livres.

By making the Jews and their disposition in France the contest's subject the committee had put its finger firmly on the nation's pulse. The Jews—who they were, how to change their relationship with French society, how to "regenerate" them as a people—had become a hot topic of reformist discussion in prerevolutionary France. King Louis XVI himself had begun to take a practical interest. Jews and livestock had had to pay a poll tax when entering a new town, but the previous year the king had ruled that Jews no longer had to pay the humiliating duty.

In France, the interest in Jews was out of all proportion to their numbers. In 1785, Jews were a tiny fraction of 1 percent of the population, a little more than 40,000 out of a population of 26 million.

The average French person could go a lifetime without meeting one, knowing them only from what he heard in sermons or market gossip.

In theory, there should have been no Jews at all in France. They had been expelled from the country in 1394 by King Charles VI. But over time, as wars changed France's borders, small Jewish communities formed or were acquired in four distinct geographical locations. In the 1500s, Jews from Portugal established themselves on France's Atlantic coast in the trading cities of Bordeaux and Bayonne. At the southern end of the Rhône river around Avignon and Carpentras was an area, the Comtat Venaissin, that was nominally papal land but was considered by the French government to be part of France. There had been Jewish settlements since Roman times in the Comtat and the community continued to exist in the bureaucratic no-man's-land between the king and the pope.

Then in 1648, through the Treaty of Westphalia, France acquired new lands to the east: Metz, Alsace, and, eventually, Lorraine; and with this territory came a whole new group that doubled the number of Jews living in the kingdom. Finally, inevitably, a small group of Jews, most of them poor, had migrated to Paris from the east, where they tried to avoid the police while making ends meet in their traditional occupations: rag-picking, tinkering, and small-time moneylending.

It was the Jews from the eastern part of the country who occupied the minds of reformers. These Jews were entirely different than their more established brethren in Bordeaux and Avignon in the religious rites they followed: they were Ashkenazic; they were much poorer; and where the Jews of Bordeaux were well integrated into their communities, the Jews of the east were segregated by local law and their own customs.

The Jews of Alsace, Lorraine, and Metz were the source of national anxiety about aliens infecting the French body politic. They were also regarded as a sample group on which to test the new philosophical theories about humanity and society that were part of the age: If all men are created equal, an enlightened thinker might ask, does that mean the Jews, with their strange clothes, odd language, and, frankly, unpleasant personal habits, are our brothers as well?

It took a few months for word of the Metz Royal Society's essay topic to work its way around France. In February 1786, the *Mercure de France,* a Paris-based weekly review of arts and ideas—"fleeting pieces in verse and prose," it said on the cover—carried a long article on the subject. The author noted, "It is an astonishing spectacle, the history of this people, who from before the fall of the Roman Empire, existed in all nations of the earth but are not incorporated in them, who are strangers everywhere . . . The Jews everywhere are a people apart, a degenerate people, who have no glory, nor honor, nothing to elevate men's hearts to make them belong." He then asked, "How can you reform the moral character of this people?" Now was the time to answer that question, the anonymous author noted, because France was on the brink of a new era, an "epoch of great revolutions where everything in the universe is changing . . . opening the door to a second history for mankind."

In Paris, a Jew from Poland read the *Mercure de France* article and decided to enter the contest. In Embermenil, in eastern France, the recently appointed parish priest had already begun working on an essay. Zalkind Hourwitz and Henri Grégoire were men of the same age, from humble backgrounds, and both wanted a voice in national events that those backgrounds normally precluded. Both had already written on the subject of Jewish civil rights and had reached similar conclusions: that somehow emancipating the Jews, releasing this group from the proscriptions that kept them apart, encouraging them to integrate and become French, was a necessary step toward the modern society everyone knew had to replace the rotten ancien regime of France.

As a poor Jew living illegally in Paris, Zalkind Hourwitz's interest in civil rights was understandable, but his desire to take part in the national debate was unusual and the fact that he could reasonably expect to write a good essay was astonishing. Born in a village near Lublin in eastern Poland, Hourwitz had arrived in Paris a decade earlier, as he would later remember, with rude peasant manners and so uncultured that he thought the statues of the capital were actually alive.

His journey from the east was highly improbable and dangerous in the extreme. Everywhere along his route through Poland, Prussia, and a dozen other German-speaking principalities, Jews were subject to strict laws to keep them segregated from the rest of the population. Forbidden to be on the road after dark, Hourwitz would have been forced to find the local ghetto or Jewish hamlet for his evening's shelter and food. The one thing that might have eased the passage was the homogeneity of the Jewish world in its enforced isolation. From Lublin to Metz each isolated pocket of Jewry spoke more or less the same language, followed the same rituals, and was organized in the same way, with the ghetto or village's rabbi and its few people of wealth effectively forming a local government. The majority of the people struggled desperately to earn enough to survive and pay the taxes imposed on them by the state or the local ruling family, and all of life was circumscribed by a legal system based on the religious books, the Torah and Talmud.

Little is known of Hourwitz's early life beyond the fact that he claimed to be the son of a rabbi. When he left Lublin isn't certain, nor is his reason for leaving. Perhaps it was a scandal, or perhaps he came from a family that could give him no financial help and he faced a lifetime of poverty, without means to take a wife and have children of his own. Maybe it was a desire to break free of the enclosed world of the ghetto. Life inside the walls was as stifling to Hourwitz's individual sensibility as the laws and taxes imposed on Jews from outside by the ruling authorities. What is known is that when Hourwitz got to Paris in 1775 he spoke little French, yet within eight years he had mastered the language sufficiently well to leave his tiny room near the Temple and begin hanging around places like the Café Foy, where intellectuals and would-be revolutionaries discussed the France they wanted to create. Hourwitz felt confident enough in his new language to enter the simmering debate about Jews that was taking place in the magazines read by enlightened people.

In 1783 an anonymous letter on the subject of Jewish civil rights appeared in the *Courrier de l'Europe,* a biweekly Anglo-French magazine that had become the major forum for discussions about the American Revolution and its potential impact on European politics. The author, a gentleman from Warsaw who preferred to remain anonymous, defined what Jews as a group needed to do if they were to be considered for citizenship. First they had to act like the natives of the nations in which they lived.

"One would say to the descendants of Abraham: be French, German or Polish, cease finally to be Arabs," he wrote. Of course, they had to give up usury as a way of earning a living, and finally Jews had to "renounce those ridiculous pretensions that you are a chosen people and that you must refuse any alliance with those among whom you live in spite of yourself, for you are neither captives as in Babylon nor slaves as in Egypt."

Identifying himself as a Polish Jew, Hourwitz sent a letter to the *Courrier* in reply. Yes, he wrote, some of his coreligionists practice usury and can be unpleasant to do business with, but he then asked if one should condemn a whole group for the practices of the few: "The Polish, French, English, Irish and Portuguese, are they all responsible for the massacres and regicides committed by some scoundrels of their nation? Why not permit the same equity towards the Jews?"

Hourwitz concluded, "There is a sweet, easy and infallible means of obliging us to embrace Christianity. End our captivity by giving us all the rights of citizens."

While Zalkind Hourwitz was learning French, Henri Grégoire was already writing on the subject of Jews and their future in a new France. He was also laying the foundations for a career that would make him a major figure in the French Revolution. Henri Grégoire was born in eastern France in the village of Veho. An only child, young Grégoire possessed the easy brilliance and work ethic that charms teachers and earns someone from a modest background powerful mentors. He was awarded scholarships to various elite church schools and felt a vocation for the priesthood at an early age. The Catholic Church in France was a deeply conservative, tradition-bound institution but it did have a small liberal wing and Grégoire's career was looked after by those connected to it.

How he came to be interested in the Jewish Question is a matter of speculation. As with Zalkind Hourwitz, the story of Grégoire's early life is not known in any great detail. His family was poor and it is likely his first contact with a Jew was with the hated figure of the moneylender. In eastern France, where the future priest grew up, Jew hatred was part of the air people breathed and he certainly would have known that easy prejudice. But during his time as a scholarship boy, an old schoolmate later recalled, Grégoire himself endured discrimination from the sons of aristocrats among whom he was educated. This led to a desire to combat social injustice. In his work as a parish priest he sought to improve the situation of his parishioners on earth as well as spiritually. He set up literacy projects and encouraged experiments with modern techniques of farming. He traveled to other parishes preaching toleration for Jews.

Grégoire's personal ambition beyond the church was profound and he frequently entered literary and essay contests hoping to make his name in the wider world. In 1778 a group in Strasbourg, the Société des Philanthropes, held a contest on the Jewish Question. Grégoire entered and began working out his solution to the problem of integrating this religious and ethnic minority into the mainstream of French society. He reached similar ideas to Zalkind Hourwitz. Jews were the way they were—difficult, isolated, unwilling to step out of their culture—because of the way they were treated. Oppression had deformed them and Christians needed to examine their own behavior toward this people if the Jews were to be brought successfully into the mainstream of society. He did not keep these views to himself, and when the Jews of Lorraine were given permission to build a new synagogue in 1785, they asked Abbé Grégoire to preach a sermon at its dedication. He happily accepted.

So as they sat down to write, the two men had plenty of personal experience to bring to their essays. Beyond that Hourwitz and Grégoire had little in common but this: they were men shaped by ideas that had been developing for more than a century around Europe, ideas about religious freedom, personal liberty, and the equality of all men. These ideas had become an intellectual movement that gave a name to their time, the Age of Enlightenment. To understand the story of Jewish Emancipation, it is necessary to trace its origins in the story of the Enlightenment.

## ii.
## Enlightenment

In 1670 a book was published, in Latin, called *Tractatus Theologico-Politicus,* or *Treatise on Theology and Politics.* The place of publication was given as Hamburg, but in fact it was Amsterdam. The name of the author did not appear anywhere in the book, since he preferred anonymity.

The caution of publisher and author was understandable. The *Tractatus* was full of well-reasoned but dangerous ideas about religion and politics. The author argued that if society curbed freedom of thought and speech for religious reasons, the peace of the state would be destroyed. He stated clearly that the laws of human nature applied to every one equally and that no one group was elect. Something the author called "intellectus," meaning our ability to understand or use our reasoning power, is the best part of us, and not, by implication, our souls. Religious rituals exist to bind society together; "they have no intrinsic sanctity." So the clergy have no special political role to fill in the state, and indeed it is "disastrous to grant religious functionaries any right to concern themselves . . . with state business." Moreover, something the author calls "Democracy" is "the most natural form of state," because it is not based on coercion or fear. "In this way," the author concludes, "all remain equal . . ."

The last was a dramatically new concept. The word *democracy* in this sense had not been used by a modern philosopher. The proofs offered for these political ideas came out of a rigorous analysis of the Hebrew Bible not as revelation but as the political history of a particular group of people, the Israelites, and the man they acknowledged as their leader, Moses. To examine the holy texts using "reason" rather than accepting their inconsistencies as part of their "revealed" quality was as dangerous a thing as an intellectual could do. Miracles and the Devil were concepts with a real hold on people in the seventeenth century; they were facts of everyday life, like sunrise and sunset or the tides coming in and out. To challenge these ideas through science or mathematical logic was akin to waging war on society, and the forces of political faith had weapons with which to fight back.

It was only three and a half decades since Galileo had been shown the instruments of torture by the inquisitors of the Catholic Church and forced to renounce as heresy his proofs that the earth revolved around the sun. In the case of the *Tractatus* the heresy cut closer to the political bone. The clergy, Catholic and Protestant, sat at the right hand of Europe's rulers by dint of their unquestioned authority in interpreting scripture. This book challenged their power directly.

It didn't take long for the name of the *Tractatus*'s author to become known. The world of philosophy in the Netherlands was small and the ideas included in the book pointed to Baruch Spinoza, a Jew, as the man who wrote it. Baruch or Bento or Benedict—he was known by all three names, meaning "blessed" in Hebrew, Portuguese, and Latin—had been building a reputation as a thinker since he had run afoul of his own religious authorities. In 1656, for reasons that have never been made clear, Spinoza was excommunicated by the leaders of the Jewish community in Amsterdam.

It is hard to convey the meaning of that act of excommunication today. Its power lay less in the eternal curses called down on the head of Spinoza and more in the shunning orders to the Jewish community at large: no Jew was to speak to him or let him into their house or come within "four cubits" of him; and, most painfully, no one was to read his writing.

To be cast out in this way was more than psychologically painful, it was physically dangerous. The modern idea of the individual making his own way in the world did not exist yet. In the seventeenth century, the community was your identity and the source of protection, friendship, and security. This was doubly true for Jews who at best were merely tolerated wherever they were found. In a world where they had no citizenship and no national place of belonging, the community was the only constant in Jewish existence and so when its leaders chose to expel someone it was a sentence of living death. Excommunication was a powerful tool of coercion for maintaining community cohesion and discipline.

Even in famously liberal Amsterdam this was true. Most of the Jews living in seventeenth-century Amsterdam were fairly recent arrivals from Spain via Portugal, and all had had experience of the insecurity of Jewish existence. Their family histories for almost two centuries had been made up of coercion and flight. Forced conversions to Catholicism in Ferdinand and Isabella's Spain had not been enough to preserve their place; they had been expelled in 1492. Many of these converted Jews moved to Portugal, but eventually Portugal had forced them out as well. When the overwhelmingly Protestant Dutch provinces successfully rebelled against the Catholic Spanish toward the end of the sixteenth century, many Portuguese Jews made their way to the Netherlands. They settled in the large cities and were granted the status of "resident aliens." They organized their own synagogues, schools, and religious courts. Although they were not forced into ghettos, a kind of self-ghettoization kept the community physically close together because the daily rituals of Jewish life made it convenient for everyone to live close to the synagogue.

Spinoza was twenty-four at the time of his excommunication but he was better placed than most to survive being cast out. He had been born into one of the community's more prominent families. The Spinoza family had an import-export business that traded everywhere from North Africa to the colony of Brazil and, at the time of his banning, Baruch was the firm's manager. Cut loose from his community, but well educated and with the self-confidence gained from managing a large enterprise, Spinoza followed his curiosity.

The Jews of Amsterdam enjoyed more relaxed contact with the wider society than their coreligionists around Europe. There were non-Jews living in their neighborhood—Rembrandt's home was around the corner from the Spinoza house—and Baruch had friends outside the Jewish community. His formal Jewish schooling had ended when he began working in the family business at the age of sixteen but his interest in learning remained. Spinoza wanted to know more about science and philosophy, and since most of the important work in these areas was written in Latin, he learned that language from a former Jesuit priest who ran a school for the children of Amsterdam's wealthiest families. Spinoza then became the ex-priest's teaching assistant. The young thinker was fascinated by the social aspects of religion and spent time living in a Mennonite community that practiced an ascetic, communal form of living.

Another help to Spinoza in surviving the ban was that he lived in a time and place that understood freethinking. In the middle of the seventeenth century the Dutch were running far ahead of history. They were a trading nation, the richest in Europe, and their success in trade was connected to their form of government. Hereditary monarchs and princes ruled everywhere else, while the Dutch lived in a republic with a parliament. They were governed not by a king but by a commoner, albeit a very wealthy commoner, named Johan De Witt.

The time of De Witt's rule is still called the "Golden Age." The wealth of the world was borne to Dutch harbors by the largest merchant navy on the seas. In a time of riches, culture flourished. In their canvases Rembrandt, Vermeer, and Pieter De Hooch represented this society in minute physical and emotional detail. Holland became a center of European intellectual life. Johan De Witt, besides his commercial activities, was one of the leading practical mathematicians of the day. De Witt's example—businessman by vocation, scientist by avocation—was followed by many other members of his class, and thus science and mathematics flourished. The general acceptance of open intellectual inquiry made the country a place of refuge for European thinkers who had run afoul of their governments or ecclesiastical authorities.

But the Dutch Republic was not a one-party state. There was a monarchist party that supported the hereditary royal family, the House of Orange. This faction was backed by those who did not partake of the riches of international trade, such as the poorer artisans and farmers. It was also supported by the clergy of the Dutch Reformed Church, a strict Calvinist group, who were not so tolerant of the many dissenting sects among whom Spinoza spent so much time.

The tension between De Witt's liberal republicans and the more traditional Orange party was never far from the surface, and this, along with his own feelings about his excommunication, inspired Spinoza to write the *Tractatus Theologico-Politicus.*

By the time he sat down to work on the *Tractatus,* Spinoza had established himself in the world outside his community. He had moved from Amsterdam to Voorburg, a small town a brisk half-hour stroll from the Hague. There he lived an austere, monklike existence, earning a small living grinding and polishing lenses for telescopes, microscopes, and glasses. In the spirit of the Golden Age this work led him to scientific studies on optics and brought him into contact with well-known scientists in the Netherlands and abroad. He spent time with the Dutch astronomer Christian Huygens and corresponded regularly with members of Britain's Royal Society, including Robert Boyle. He was at the center of a group of freethinkers one degree of separation from De Witt, and the *Tractatus* was certainly meant to bolster the Republican party against the Orange party and its Calvinist contingent. Instead it became one more item in the list of charges the political enemies of De Witt were drawing up.

In the *Tractatus* Spinoza wrote, "The opponents of freedom exult because their indignation has been yielded to and because they have converted the Supreme Power to the doctrines of which they are the recognized spokesmen; they usurp His authority shamelessly."

Eventually, the opponents of De Witt, cloaked in the true Calvinist interpretation of Christianity, had their opportunity to exult. One of the iron rules of history is that small wealthy countries will be preyed on by much larger nations. In the spring of 1672, France invaded the Netherlands and was joined by England. The Dutch Republic might have survived the first onslaught but it was not big enough to fight a war on two fronts against opponents so much bigger. De Witt's authority evaporated as the struggle went from bad to worse and the Dutch turned to the Monarchist faction. Spinoza's arguments for keeping religion out of the public sphere were ignored and the embers of religious passion flared up again into political violence. First, Johan De Witt's principal aide, his brother Cornelis, was imprisoned at the Hague, tortured, and condemned to exile. When his brother Johan went to visit him a mob was allowed into the prison grounds. They set upon the brothers, mutilated them, and lynched what remained of their bodies.

Shortly after his murder a catalogue of books found in De Witt's library was published as proof that the assassinated leader was a man of debauched morals. Included in the list was the *Tractatus,* "produced by the renegade Jew from Hell in which it is demonstrated in an atheist manner that the word of God must be explained by philosophy . . ." There is no need of philosophy in the matter of God; only faith is required.

The loss of his admired political leader tore the heart of the philosopher. The murder of the De Witts brought an end to the society in which Spinoza had flourished. Now he was as isolated as those who had excommunicated him had wished, although his fame, or infamy, as the *Tractatus* was translated and published around the continent, meant that he continued to receive letters and invitations from the highest intellectual circles in Europe. The philosopher spent his days grinding lenses, then from late in the evening until the middle of the night worked on his ideas, writing books that he realized could never be published during his lifetime. It was too dangerous.

The book that occupied him most was something he had been working on for almost a decade, the *Ethics.* In the *Ethics* he went deeper into dangerous territory, creating a new definition of God that moved well beyond scripture. Spinoza conceived of God not as Michelangelo saw him, a Supreme Being who looks just like us, floating across heaven to touch life into Adam, but rather as an abstract: an indivisible substance, the only indivisible substance in the universe, a substance he identifies with nature. Over several hundred pages he proved this theory by a geometrical method of propositions and theorems. The work is dense and difficult to follow, but there are occasional flashes of prophetic light. Without meaning to, Spinoza had become a prophet, not through claiming to speak divine revelation but through reason—pure, mathematical, and dispassionate. This new definition of "nature" as identified with God would evolve in the next century and become the foundation for enlightened Christians to look at Jews with a new understanding.

Spinoza wasn't the only philosopher working with these ideas. But he was one of the first to make clear that the necessary condition for free inquiry in science and religion is a tolerance for differing points of view and that this "tolerance" should be at the core of any social contract creating a government. "The purpose of the state is not to change men from rational beings into beasts or automata, but rather that they should use their reason freely, and perform all their functions safely," he wrote. "The purpose of the state, in reality, is Freedom."

Baruch Spinoza died alone at the age of forty-four. He was never reconciled to the Jewish community. At the time of his excommunication, a friend remembered the philosopher saying, "They do not force me to do anything I would not have done of my own accord, if I did not dread scandal . . . I enter gladly on the path that is opened to me." The path took him to a place in his mind where he could live by the dictates of reason alone. There he wrote about freedom and democracy but never brought up the particular struggle of his own people to achieve rights. Yet the impact of his ideas on political thinking over the next century would make resolving the question of Jewish rights inevitable.

Upon his death, per the philosopher's instructions, the desk containing all his writing was locked. It was transported to Amsterdam, where his life's work was published posthumously. The simple way he lived his life and left it and the power of his ideas as they began to circulate combined to create a movement around his thinking. Spinoza's influence all over Europe grew rapidly. The name Spinoza became a curse and a compliment. A "Spinozist" could be a heretic, a political radical, an atheist, a Deist, a rationalist, an adherent of tolerance, an apostle of freedom. Thirty years after the philosopher's death, Jacques Basnage, a French Protestant living in exile in Holland, published a massive *History of the Jews* from the time of the destruction of the Second Temple. Spinoza was the last major figure in his book. Basnage was dismissive of Spinoza's views of God but grudgingly acknowledged his importance. "This was perhaps the first founder of a sect who did not recommend his doctrines as important truths, and that thought all religions good, and that salvation was to be had in them."

In begrudging Spinoza his place, Basnage missed the point. Those who read Spinoza avidly were not concerned about religious salvation so much as they were in creating a world where the road a person took toward salvation was his own private business, to be tolerated by the state and his neighbors.

Decade by decade, all around Europe, the ideas of the Enlightenment grew. Inexorably, new theories in philosophy, religion, politics, and economics appeared. It was a truly international movement created by men from England, the German-speaking lands, Italy, and, most of all, France. These thinkers ignored borders to engage with each other in a search to define the modern, and much of their work was a response to Spinoza.

Six years after Spinoza's death, the English philosopher John Locke took an extended vacation in Amsterdam. Locke had been caught up in political intrigues in England and fled to the Netherlands to avoid prison. While in the Dutch capital, Locke lived among those who had known Spinoza intimately and attended meetings of an informal study group that discussed Spinozist ideas. Spending time with Spinoza's old friends and listening to the stories of his life had to have left some impression on Locke as he wrote his *Letter Concerning Toleration* during his Amsterdam exile.

Spinoza's concerns were broad, he was making the general case for the freedom to think and speak and worship. Locke was more interested in defining the specific rights that a state, a commonwealth, should give its citizens when it came to religion. In the *Letter Concerning Toleration* he focused on the rights of religious minorities: "if we may openly speak the truth, as becomes one man to another, neither Pagan nor Mahometan, nor Jew, ought to be excluded from the civil rights of the commonwealth because of his religion," Locke wrote. "The Gospel commands no such thing . . . And the commonwealth, which embraces indifferently all men that are honest, peaceable, and industrious, requires it not." Civil rights for Locke means freedom of worship. "If we allow the Jews to have private houses and dwellings amongst us, why should we not allow them to have synagogues? Is their doctrine more false, their worship more abominable, or is the civil peace more endangered by their meeting in public than in their private houses?"

Toleration of the Jewish religion was just a first step in the struggle for Emancipation. Toleration of the Jewish people was a more difficult affair.

## iii.
## Toleration

> Discord is humankind's greatest evil, and toleration its
> only remedy.
>
> —Voltaire, *Philosophical Dictionary*

Toleration was the touchstone of Enlightenment. It preoccupied the philosophers, the *philosophes,* who were pledged to the movement. *Toleration* is a word with many subtle shades of meaning. *Toleration* has a golden glow when we talk about accepting someone's right to worship as they please. It implies a nobility of spirit, an open-minded gift of brotherly acceptance. But the term's origin is in the Latin word *tolerare,* meaning to endure. We speak of a person's ability to tolerate pain. There is a social meaning of toleration: think of the unpleasant spouse of a dear friend; you tolerate the spouse for the sake of friendship. The word migrated into modern use via French, where *toleration* meant permission granted by the authorities. The word's meaning here isn't a state of being open-minded and loving but rather sufferance and necessity. The full range of meanings of *tolerance* or *toleration* would come into use over the next century in relation to Jewish rights.

From Montesquieu to Jean-Jacques Rousseau, the Jews were frequently referred to by the philosophes. These were not men who knew Jews personally. They knew biblical legends and gossip from the streets. They knew the names of the Court Jews, the individuals singled out by kings and princes around the continent to raise finance for wars and provide supplies for the armies who died in them. But that was all. The Jews to them were not human beings; they were abstract ideas, symbols that could be shaped to fit their theories on the nature of man, their presence in Europe posing a two-part question that needed to be answered.

The first part of the question was religious toleration. The philosophes, having settled among themselves the question of tolerance between Catholics and Protestants, turned their minds toward the Jewish religion. Among the enlightened, the Christ-killer view of the ancient Hebrews was thrown out. Following Spinoza's lead in rational biblical analysis, Enlightenment philosophers looked at the story of the Israelites as a precursor to Christianity. In the 1720s, the French philosopher Montesquieu wrote, "The Jewish religion is an old trunk that has produced two branches that have covered the entire earth: I mean Mohammedanism and Christianity . . . It is a mother who has given birth to two daughters who have covered her with a thousand plagues."

But this new acceptance of the Jewish religion rarely was matched by acceptance of the Jews themselves, who were seen as clannish and boorish in their unwillingness to modernize and reform their religion as Christians were doing. Montesquieu directly addressed the Jews of Europe: "You live in a century in which natural enlightenment is brighter than it has ever been, in which philosophy has enlightened the minds, where the morality of your Gospel has been the best known, where the respective rights of men towards each other, the empire which one conscience has upon another, is best established. If you then revert to your ancient prejudices . . . you will have shown that you are incorrigible, incapable of any enlightenment and any instruction."

The philosophes acknowledged the necessary role of Jews in international commerce. The *Encyclopedia,* the great intellectual project of the mid-eighteenth century in France, in its entry on "Jews," concluded that the fate of all Europe is tied to them, "They are like the pegs and nails that are used in a great building and which are necessary to join all its parts." A simple observation proved the point. Spain was a great imperial power and then expelled its Jews, most of whom, like Spinoza's family, ended up in Holland. Now the Dutch were a wealthy nation and Spain, lacking commercial brilliance, was in decline.

Throughout the middle of the eighteenth century, the best-known man of Enlightenment was François-Marie Arouet, Voltaire. Partly this was because of the sheer scope and volume of his writing. He was a poet, playwright, essayist, novelist, and writer of vast numbers of letters all intended for publication. His fame around Europe was also due to the fact that he lived at one time or another in many different countries around the continent. This was because he offended so many powerful people with his pen that he had to keep on the move. After a spell in prison in his native France he fled to England, then left England for Prussia before returning to France.

In his life and writing, Voltaire summarized all the different ways in which Jews were defined by the Enlightenment. His personal contact with Jews was not happy. During his exile in London, he relied on a Jewish banker for his finance and when this man went bankrupt Voltaire found himself in dire financial straits. Later, when living in exile in

Prussia he became involved in investments with a Jewish merchant and when this business failed he ended up in a protracted and bitter lawsuit.

Despite his resentment, Jews for Voltaire had a positive use. They were a battering ram to attack his great enemy, the Catholic Church. The church via the Inquisition was to the Frenchman the chief source of superstition holding back the modernization of France and the rest of Europe. In Voltaire's view the primary victims of the Inquisition were Jews. He could write with sympathy about their sufferings, "When I see Christians cursing Jews, methinks I see children beating their fathers." He pleaded with his fellow Christians to acknowledge that Jews were their brothers, and their equals in society.

Yet Voltaire could also write, "You will only find in the Jews an ignorant and barbarous people, who for a long time have joined the most sordid avarice to the most detestable superstition and to the most invincible hatred of all peoples which tolerate and enrich them," and "Why are the Jews hated? It is the inevitable result of their laws; they either have to conquer everybody or be hated by the whole human race . . ."

Reason was the touchstone of the Enlightenment but reasoning doesn't always lead to correct analysis, especially as in Voltaire's case, when it provides a gloss for prejudice. The voice absent in all this theorizing about the Jews was the voice of the Jews themselves. One person would change that.

## CHAPTER TWO

# Hold Fast to the Religion of Your Fathers

THE COUNTERARGUMENT TO VOLTAIRE CAME IN THE SLIGHT, deformed shape of Moses Mendelssohn: philosopher, critic, and acknowledged leader of the German Enlightenment. Very few philosophers who achieve so much come out of nothing; they are part of a school or social movement. But even his contemporaries realized that Mendelssohn was unique. His life story had the romantic flow of a great novel.

Born in 1729 in Dessau, southwest of Berlin, Moses ben Mendel lived the typical ghetto life of a bright, impoverished student with all his learning bent toward mastery of the Talmud, his career path that of a rabbi, like many of his distinguished ancestors. His schooling was in Hebrew and the language he spoke at home was a form of Yiddish. In this he was no different than hundreds of bright yeshiva students in any of the Jewish communities and ghettos stretching from Germany deep into Russia.

His teacher in Dessau, Rabbi David Frankel, was one of the out-standing younger rabbis of the time, and when Frankel became chief rabbi in Berlin, Mendelssohn's life reached its first turning point. The student decided to follow his teacher to the big city. He was just fourteen years old. Shortly after the High Holidays in 1743, with no money in his pocket and rags on his feet, according to the legend, he started walking toward the Prussian capital.

Berlin was more than a hundred miles to the northeast, an epic trek for a small youth with a spinal deformity that made putting one foot in front of another very painful. The routine of the road for a Jew was arduous. When he set out in the morning he needed to know where he could find a Jewish village or ghetto before sunset. Moses could not stay in an ordinary town without paying a Jewish tax and he didn't have the money for that; also, he could only eat food that was kosher. The prospect of harassment loomed every time he encountered Christian travelers on the road. The law required a Jew to give way and the Christian could demand, "Jud mach Mores!" "Jew show your manners!" The Jew would have to remove his hat, bow, and step into muddy streets that were not paved or were covered in horse manure.

Through the autumn mud, across the flat farmland, Mendelssohn trudged until he saw the buildings of Berlin hovering over the plain. Once he reached them he had to find the Rosenthaler Gate, the one entryway to the city for Jews.

The Prussian capital in the middle of the eighteenth century was a comparatively new city of a hundred thousand people with a small community of Jews given permission to reside there. In the late seventeenth century, Jews had been expelled from Vienna. At the time, Prussia was broke and backward economically. Its king, Frederick I, decided to invite some of Vienna's wealthiest Jews to move to Berlin to provide his kingdom with a business class. Their numbers were strictly limited. In the autumn of 1747 there were 333 Jewish families and their servants and a few others to provide particular Jewish services living in Berlin, around 1,945 people altogether. There were no poor Jews allowed in the city, and the Jewish community was under strict rules to administer itself to ensure that Jews without means never made it into town.

Moses ben Mendel of Dessau found his way to the Rosenthaler

Gate, where a representative of the Jewish community decided whether to allow him to remain. Most poor, young Jews turning up there were given a bowl of soup, a place to sleep for the night, and then sent on their way the next morning. But when interrogated by the Jewish guardian of the gate, Moses of Dessau had the right name to drop: Rabbi Frankel. The rabbi vouched for him and he was allowed in. The gatekeeper's logbook for the day notes that at the Rosenthaler Gate six oxen, seven pigs, and one Jew entered the city.

With his teacher's help Moses was given lodging and a student's permit to stay in the city, and this could have been the end of the story. He might have been like so many others in that time, an impoverished student of the Talmud for the rest of his days. But in the big city the teenager was exposed to a wider knowledge than that of the yeshiva. He broke out of the ghetto of the mind, bricked in by the restrictions of language. To read more widely, within five years Moses of Dessau taught himself German, French, Greek, and Latin. He devoured contemporary enlightenment texts. The first was John Locke's *Essay Concerning Human Understanding,* which he read with a German-Latin lexicon at his elbow, translating from one newly acquired language to the next as he read.

After a few years of pure study and deep impoverishment he was offered work as a tutor to the children of Isaac Bernhard, a wealthy silk manufacturer. This work allowed him to eat regularly and gave him time to study and, once again, that might have been the end of his story. But Moses was also a companionable young man and through friendship with a few wealthy, young Berlin Jews who had contacts in the wider society, he developed a circle of acquaintances outside the Jewish community. Berlin in the middle of the eighteenth century was transforming itself into a cosmopolitan center. There was a young king on the Prussian throne, Frederick II, who was on his way to becoming Frederick the Great, and his capital was seething with new ideas. Voltaire was in residence, lending his cachet to the intellectual scene. The city's coffeehouses and chess clubs throbbed with excited discussion of Enlightenment concepts.

Moses ben Mendel, just beginning to write in German and signing his work Moses Mendelssohn, joined in this society and so arrived at the next turning point of his life: a meeting with the golden boy of Prussia's literary scene, Gotthold Ephraim Lessing. The young German was twenty-six, just a few years older than the young Jew, but already Lessing had worked for and publicly quarreled with Voltaire, established himself as one of the leading writers on the theater in German, and, most importantly, had written a play about tolerance called *The Jews.*

Lessing, the son of a Protestant pastor, and Mendelssohn, the descendant of rabbis, formed a mutual bond, and over the next decades as they met, talked, and philosophized their friendship deepened. Nothing, not even their individual growing fame, could break this bond between them, and from the very beginning of their relationship they had a cause: fighting anti-Jewish prejudice. They took the discussion about the Jews out of the coffeehouse and placed it in the pages of important German cultural magazines, with Lessing arguing for Jews to be accepted as equals and Mendelssohn defending Lessing against the attacks of Jew haters.

The men met in 1754, around the time Lessing published a selection of his theatrical writings, including his early play, *The Jews.* The young playwright had broken with a theatrical tradition going back to Marlowe and Shakespeare by creating a Jewish protagonist who is a noble, decent, heroic figure. A review of Lessing's work appeared in one of the leading cultural magazines, which took the playwright to task for creating such a character. Shouldn't plays have characters that are credible? the critic asked. Who could believe that such a thing—a noble Jew—existed? The review was unsigned, but in the small world of German letters everyone knew the author was Johann David Michaelis, one of the foremost biblical scholars in the German-speaking world. Mendelssohn was angered by the thesis of the review and upset on his new friend's behalf at the criticism. He consulted with Lessing and wrote a reply, which the playwright published in his own theatrical magazine, the *Theatrical Library.*

"How can a man in whom a sense of honesty is left have the impudence to deny a whole nation the probability of possessing a single honest man? A nation from which all the prophets and the greatest kings arose, as the author of 'The Jews' declared," Mendelssohn wrote. "Is it not enough that we have to suffer the most bitter hatred of the Christians in so many cruel ways . . . Let them continue to oppress us, let them restrict our existence among free and happy citizens . . . so long as they do not altogether deny us virtue, the only solace of hard-pressed souls, the only refuge of the forsaken."

In that time and in that kind of forum the subject of Jewish humanity had never been broached by someone who was Jewish, writing in German. The wit and controlled anger that Mendelssohn brought to his letter marked him as a stylist worth remembering.

Lessing and Mendelssohn began to dominate the intellectual scene in Frederick the Great's Prussia, Lessing through the arts and Mendelssohn through philosophical work. Essay contests were also a part of intellectual life in Prussia and the Berlin Royal Academy organized one on the rarefied topic "Whether metaphysical truths are susceptible to the same evidence as mathematical truths?" Mendelssohn entered and was declared the winner, with second place going to Immanuel Kant. The local Berlin newspaper carried the news in a terse and grudging announcement, "On Thursday the academy held its public session. The prize was awarded to the local Jew, Moses Mendelssohn, who is already sufficiently well-known by his writings."

So the Jew Moses, as he became known, entered a new phase of life. He was acknowledged as one of the foremost philosophers writing in German. His writing was eminently clear, stylistically so sophisticated that it astonished contemporaries that he had not grown up speaking German as a native language. Of Mendelssohn's contemporaries in Germany the most towering intellect belonged to Kant. The great philosopher, whose own work was bafflingly dense, acknowledged Mendelssohn's superiority as a writer. "Only few people have the good fortune to think for themselves, and, at the same time take account of the way others think so as to present the subject in a manner suited to all. There is only one Mendelssohn."

Mendelssohn worked at popularizing philosophy. Amazed that there was no good translation of Plato into German, he began translating the Greek's dialogues so that people throughout the German-speaking world could engage with classical thinking. This work might not pay his rent or feed his growing family, but he no longer had money worries because Isaac Bernhard had promoted him from tutor to his children to manager of his silk factory.

Then Mendelssohn wrote a book that elevated him to the highest rank of eighteenth-century European thinkers. His work on Plato led him to write his own version of a Socratic dialogue, in German, called *Phaedon.* In the best Enlightenment fashion, the dialogue set out to prove the immortality of the soul through reason, rather than revelation. The clarity of the thinking, the precision of the language, made the book an extraordinary success in the German-speaking world and translations soon appeared around the continent. Twenty years after he had arrived hungry and poor at Berlin's Jewish gate, Mendelssohn was regarded as a leading figure in the Enlightenment. He was a genuine celebrity in his adopted hometown, living proof that Berlin had become a rival to Paris and Vienna as a center of culture and intellectual achievement. Adding a layer to Mendelssohn's international reputation was his background. His very existence was the proof necessary for reformers to demonstrate the potential contribution Jews could make to society.

Throughout his extraordinary entry into and rise to the top of intellectual life in the German-speaking lands, Mendelssohn's Jewish identity had not been a great trouble to him. He was identified as a Jew—the French edition of *Phaedon* described the author as a "juif à Berlin," a Berlin Jew—and the fact of his Jewishness enhanced his reputation in much the same way that a century later Frederick Douglass's race enhanced his reputation as a writer on the issue of slavery. The very idea that a Jew (or an escaped African slave) could write with such eloquence was considered astonishing in and of itself, quite apart from the quality of the arguments contained in their work.

At home Mendelssohn was a practicing Jew, and in the spirit of enlightened tolerance, Lessing and the rest of his friends let that be his private business. Then it all changed.

With his sword and with his brain, Frederick the Great had turned Prussia into the most modern of the German lands. Berlin had become the place for young, talented German-speakers to migrate. Johann Kaspar Lavater was a young German Swiss on the make and followed the well-worn road to the burgeoning capital. Lavater was a theologian by academic training and a perpetual student of natural philosophy by avocation. His special area of knowledge was physiognomy, the analysis of personality from the study of a person's outward appearance, particularly the face; at the time physiognomy was considered an important branch of the new learning.

For ambitious newcomers to Berlin a meeting with the Jew Moses was a requisite for establishing serious credentials as an intellectual player. Through contacts Lavater met Mendelssohn several times and, presuming on this brief acquaintance, decided to publicly engage the philosopher in a religious debate.

Lavater translated into German a book by a French Swiss theologian named Charles Bonnet. *Palingenesis,* or *Re-Birth,* sought to make a case for Christianity beyond revelation by applying a series of logical proofs of the religion's basic tenets. Lavater dedicated his translation to Mendelssohn, but it was not done to flatter the great thinker, it was done to challenge him. The dedication began politely enough: "Most venerable Sir! I know of no better way of expressing the respect instilled into my mind by your excellent writings and your even more excellent character, which is that of an Israelite in whom there is no guile . . ."

Lavater asks Mendelssohn to read the book thoroughly, then issues a direct challenge: "I dare to ask you, before the GOD of truth, your creator and Father and mine . . . to refute it publicly in case you find the essential arguments in support of the facts of Christianity incorrect: in case however, you find them correct do what prudence, love of truth and honesty bid you to do."

What prudence, truth, and honesty were supposed to bid the philosophical Jew Moses to do was convert to Christianity.

Lavater's challenge caught the public imagination. Mendelssohn's name was known by people who were barely literate and Lavater had crudely, disingenuously put his finger on something the ordinary man on the street or the well-educated denizen of literary coffeehouses might have thought: This Jew is so much like us, so unlike the stereotype of the "guileful Israelite," why doesn't he take the final step and convert? This would become a question asked over and over again in the century to come but Mendelssohn was the first Jewish public figure to face it.

For the philosopher the Lavater challenge was a terrible event. From nothing he had created a quite remarkable life for himself. It wasn't just his achievement as an author that was now put at risk: he had a business to run and a wife and six children to provide for. He had built a unique circle of friends from all religious quarters. To create this life he had conducted himself according to a basic tenet: that a man's approach to God was a private matter and that if one person gave respect to another's different religious conviction then they could share a whole world together. Now, in the most public way this was being challenged. He had to think very carefully how to respond because if his response was taken the wrong way the life he had made for himself and his family could be destroyed. He was also keenly aware that he had become an unofficial representative of Jews throughout Prussia. What he said in reply to Lavater would have an impact on his coreligionists as well.

Mendelssohn moved deliberately. He took counsel from his friends. Everything had to be planned just so. He also had to contain his anger and disappointment. In all the years in Berlin, the philosopher's good nature had become part of his legend. Friends remarked on his ability to endure the intended and unintended insults to Jews that were part of everyday conversation in public places. The writer made his own rueful jokes about missing convivial literary dinners because of his religion's dietary laws and having to lose so many hours attending to business rather than studying and writing philosophy full-time because being Jewish meant he could not become a professor at a university. But Lavater's challenge broke his good nature. Many years previously, when the pair had first met in Mendelssohn's home, Lavater had asked his views on Christianity. The philosopher had demurred but the Swiss theologian had pressed him and Mendelssohn, off the record, expressed an admiration for Jesus as a moral—and mortal—figure. Lavater had alluded to that supposedly private conversation in his public challenge and Mendelssohn felt a great trust had been betrayed.

The challenge had been published in late summer 1769 and as the months went by the press filled with speculation about what the Jew would say in response. In November, Mendelssohn received a visit by the Prince of Brunswick, Karl Wilhelm Ferdinand, an encouragement to him and a reminder to the public of his importance as a philosopher. Finally, in late December, the reply was ready for the publisher. Written in the form of a letter, it begins with the necessary rhetoric of politeness before cutting to the chase.

"I must confess your action shocks me deeply," Mendelssohn writes, and he questions Lavater's motivations in making this public challenge. Throughout the letter Mendelssohn avoids revealing his thoughts on Christianity by telling Lavater about what being Jewish means and why he has always avoided writing about religion. "I wanted to refute the world's derogatory opinion of the Jew by righteous living," he tells Lavater, "not by pamphleteering." And he rebukes the Swiss for being unaware of how difficult it is for him and his fellow Jews to take part in this kind of study and discussion. "The civic status and position of my co-religionists are not conducive to the free development of our intellectual capacities . . . Any person who knows our plight and who has a human heart will understand more than I can possibly say here."

And, Mendelssohn points out, he has already done much thinking about his faith. "There comes a time in a man's life when he has to make up his mind about certain issues in order to be able to move on from there. This happened to me several years ago with regards to religion. I have read; I have compared; I have reflected; and I have made up my mind." He has found nothing to shake his belief in Judaism. Then he gently rebukes Lavater for even trying to convert anyone.

"It is my good fortune to count among my friends many an excellent man who is not of my faith. We love each other sincerely . . . I enjoy the pleasure of his company but at no time has my heart whispered to me, 'What a pity this beautiful soul should be lost . . .' A man will be troubled by regrets if he believes that there is no salvation outside his own church."

If Mendelssohn thought publicly answering Lavater would end the affair, he was wrong. Soon a volume putting Lavater's challenge and his response side by side was published. Then, like some blogosphere event, people with no connection to either man and no knowledge of the issue began publishing pamphlets on the affair. The controversy raged for more than a year. Ultimately Lavater got what he wanted out of it: a reputation. He published his magnum opus on physiognomy, which included a study of Mendelssohn. According to Lavater, Mendelssohn's face demonstrated a "companionable brilliance" with "piercing eyes, a man of keen taste and wide erudition."

For Mendelssohn, the affair marked a painful reversal. Although his reputation was enhanced among his colleagues, his health deteriorated badly and he began to suffer from heart palpitations and blinding headaches. He could hardly read, much less write, and had barely enough strength to run the silk factory of which he was now co-owner. His publisher was convinced the cause was the psychological stress of the Lavater affair. Mendelssohn's doctors could neither explain the cause nor offer any relief except the advice to put aside his philosophical work. For several years the philosopher did indeed put aside the rigors of abstract thinking, but he could not stop his mind from working. He turned to a social project: integrating Jews into German society. The letter to Lavater had made it clear that Mendelssohn thought it was unnecessary to become a Christian to be accorded equal respect as a human being, but to merit equal status under the law, to gain civil rights, the philosopher thought his fellow Jews had to adapt themselves to the society. This was to be done through cultural integration. Language had been Mendelssohn's entry to German culture and so he set about translating the Hebrew Bible into German. The Bible would become a lexicon to help Jews learn the language.

Now came the last twist in the story of his life. He went from being a leading German Enlightenment philosopher to the founder of a Jewish movement of self-transformation called Haskalah. Its creed was elegantly stated in a book called *Jerusalem:* "Adapt yourselves to the morals and the constitution of the land to which you have been removed; but hold fast to the religion of your fathers."

He also reached that level of fame where he became a symbol as much as a man. For the wider society, he was a symbol of the humanity that even a Jew could achieve. His old friend Lessing wrote a play about him called *Nathan the Wise,* and after initial censorship, it became a classic of the German theater. For Jews, the frail hunchback became a symbol of strength. Whenever a Jewish community was in trouble—from Zurich to Warsaw—they contacted Herr Moses and he used his reputation to help ease their situation. So when, in 1780, he received a letter from Cerf Berr, the leader of Alsace's Jewish community, asking for his help, Mendelssohn had to act.

Although there was a lot of competition for the title, Alsace was the place where life was worst for Jews in Europe. The community was strewn around Alsace's wooded hills in 182 different villages and hamlets. These places had sixty-one different owners or authorities: the king, church, or local nobility. Jews were banned from virtually every occupation and lived in the direst poverty. Their movements were tightly regulated and they were forbidden to dwell or even spend the night in Alsace's capital city, Strasbourg. Cerf Berr avoided the worst of this oppression because his family had for many decades been the chief provisioners of the French Army, and King Louis XV had granted him a letter patent, a royal decree, effectively giving Cerf Berr the rights of a citizen. But when it came to the Jews, the king's writ did not run in Strasbourg and even Cerf Berr had struggled to reside there.

Cerf Berr decided to write a "memoire," a memorandum, a petition to the king's royal council, seeking redress for all the Jews of Alsace who suffered under these terrible restrictions. After years of conducting business with the court he understood that this was the way politics was done in the Kingdom of France. But the petition's language had to be perfect; not just well reasoned, it had to have the right tone for the sensibilities of the royal councilors. The one man in Europe, Cerf Berr thought, who could write this memoire was Mendelssohn. Cerf Berr sent a letter to Berlin asking the philosopher for his help in writing this petition.

As Zalkind Hourwitz, Abbé Grégoire, and the other entrants to the Metz Royal Society's essay contest sifted through the various intellectual arguments about creating a new dispensation for France's Jews, there was one other factor they had to consider. The term *antiSemitism* had not been coined yet, so it is best to call it what it was: raw and implacable Jew hatred. In the provinces of eastern France—Alsace, Lorraine, and the city of Metz—this hatred was so profound that it threatened the cohesion of the whole society. It was born of ancient religious intolerance, ethnic prejudice, and the crude facts of economic life. Poor farmers and poor Jews were locked in a desperate struggle to earn a meager subsistence.

For peasants and small farmers working the land under feudal arrangements with big landowners, the economy was seasonal, and between planting and harvest there were frequently times when they needed to borrow money. But there were no banks. Jews were prohibited by law from owning land, from agriculture, and from joining artisans' guilds, and so had little choice for earning their living but to peddle secondhand goods, trade cattle, and lend money at interest to earn their own subsistence living. The struggle for economic survival pitted poor farmers against poor Jews.

Adding to the tension was ignorance. Unlike Mendelssohn's Berlin or Spinoza's Amsterdam, there was little friendly mingling among Jews and their neighbors. In eastern France, Jews were segregated in ghettos or in little hamlets in the forests where they lived a separate life, with their own language, laws, and customs. They had a different Sabbath. They dressed in strange baggy clothes, the men had long beards, and their diet was different. When the farmer or small artisan went to a Jewish moneylender he saw someone who was truly alien, who used French incorrectly, who spoke to his fellow Jews in an incomprehensible secret tongue, and whose records and ledgers were written in a different script. Borrowing money is always a demeaning process and that increased resentment. But it was worse when the loan came due. These small-time lenders lived on the same economic precipice as the people they made loans to and were operating with desperation when they pressed for repayment with interest.

Usury was considered a sin, which added to the peasant's sense of injustice when his loans came due. But more than that, local priests were keen to remind their parishioners of Deuteronomy's instructions to the Jews: not to lend money with interest to their brothers. That the Jews didn't charge each other interest enraged their debtors outside the community.

The degree to which the interdependence of peasants and Jewish moneylenders underpinned the economy of eastern France became apparent in 1777, when thousands of receipts, signed in Hebrew, claiming that debts to the moneylenders had been paid in full began to circulate in and around Alsace. At first it seemed a good joke on the Jews, but many of the small lenders were ruined. Then the joke turned sour because there was no longer any source of funds when farmers came looking for their seasonal loans. But the economic fate of small farmers, peasants, and artisans was of less concern to the ruling classes than the loss of tax revenue. Jews paid exorbitant taxes—protection money—to the local nobility and a variety of rich families. These taxes were critical to the nobles maintaining their own lifestyle. But with the forged receipts making it impossible to collect on their debts, the Jews could no longer pay tax.

The forces of the law were turned loose to find the source of the forgeries. Arrests were made and those accused taken to court. The ringleader of the scam was a Jew baiter with the appropriate name of Hell. The man had a fanatical hatred of Jews. In the middle of legal proceedings against him, François Hell published a pamphlet, *Observations of an Alsatian on the Current Affair of the Alsatian Jews.*

The pamphlet didn't simply recycle the old religious hatred about ritual murder and poisoning wells. It had a political dimension as well. Hell makes the point that Jews were "a nation within the nation." This phrase would be repeated over and over again in the years to come because it was at the core of the Emancipation debate: Can a Jew also be a Frenchman or a German? If an essential part of being French or German is being Christian, then the answer is no. If it means simply being a human being born in France or Germany, then the answer is yes.

Hell's answer to the question was obvious, and it was a view shared by many in Alsace. The pamphlet was widely read and the man himself became a local hero. Petitions were sent to the court and his jail sentence for masterminding the forgeries was dramatically reduced.

It was in the midst of this controversy that Cerf Berr contacted Moses Mendelssohn. The philosopher, ever attuned to the nuances of his position, realized that for a Jew to author such a petition would detract from its impact. Better to have a Christian plead the case for tolerance and equal treatment under the law for Alsatian Jews. So Mendelssohn turned to Christian Wilhelm van Dohm, a young civil servant in Berlin, who, with comments from Mendelssohn, quickly drafted the memorandum. Dohm realized that finding policy answers to the Jewish Question might help a young civil servant to a glorious career and so decided to write an expanded essay on the theme of Jewish rights. *Concerning the Amelioration of the Civil Status of the Jews,* published in

1783 in German, immediately translated into French, and smuggled into that country, shaped the terms of the Emancipation debate.

In words that might have been written by Jefferson or Madison, Dohm discusses the role of the state in guaranteeing these rights. "The great and noble business of the government is to diminish the principles of exclusion in society . . . It will have achieved its great aim when the nobleman, the peasant, the scholar, the artisan, the Christian and the Jew is most of all, a citizen."

And for those who viewed Jews as fundamentally different, incapable of reforming themselves, Dohm tells readers that "the Jew is a man more than a Jew." He writes, "Everything the Jews are blamed for is caused by the political conditions under which they now live and any other group of men, under such conditions, would be guilty of identical errors."

Dohm adds that nothing would make the Jews love the country where they are born more than the right to enjoy equal status with their Christian neighbors.

While Dohm worked on his book, in Catholic Austria the Holy Roman Emperor, Joseph II, was preparing new legislation for religious minorities. He issued the Toleranzpatent, or Edict of Toleration, in 1781. It was aimed at all non-Catholics living in Joseph's sprawling empire. Its specific clauses about the Jews gave them the right to engage in new trades and, most importantly, to attend schools and universities.

Toleration was now becoming law. The Enlightenment was ending its theoretical phase. The philosophes sought change and now the time had arrived to plan the practical steps to create tolerant societies. As they worked on their essays, the Metz contest entrants were focusing on ideas that would lead to practical success in bringing the Jews from their isolation into the mainstream of society.

## CHAPTER THREE

# The Means to Render the Jews More Useful and Happy?

THE WORDS OF JOSEPH II's EDICT OF TOLERATION, THE IDEAS in Dohm, Mendelssohn, Hell, Voltaire, Rousseau, Montesquieu, Locke, and Spinoza were hovering in the intellectual atmosphere as Zalkind Hourwitz, Abbé Grégoire, and others worked frantically on their answers to the question "What are the means to render the Jews more useful and happy in France?" The deadline for submitting the finished pieces was June 1, 1787. Hourwitz, scrambling to earn a living and making regular appearances at Paris's political and literary cafés, fell behind in his writing and took the risk of asking the Royal Society for a one-month extension. This was granted.

In Metz the essay contest was of great interest. Jews had a long and complex history in the city. There was regular and respectful contact between the Jewish community's religious and business leadership and their Christian counterparts. The "syndics," as the Jewish leaders were called, had to regularly negotiate the tax burden on their community as well as any privileges its members might be allowed in moving around the town. Relations between the ordinary people of Metz and their Hebrew neighbors, however, were not very happy.

Metz had emerged from the Middle Ages with its own governing structures still in place, and a tightly regulated Jewish community had been allowed to grow there even as expulsions were being ordered in other parts of France. The city was the site of the largest Jewish community in France. In the mid-1780s Metz had a population of 36,000, of whom 4,000 were Jews. Jews rarely made up more than 1 percent of the local population in any sizable town where they were allowed to reside but in Metz they were almost 11 percent. This changed the dynamics considerably.

The Moselle river cuts through the heart of Metz, and the Jews were forced to live in a tiny area of dank, narrow streets right along its banks. The main thoroughfare of the ghetto was locked at night. The law required Jews to wear a yellow cap in the streets, although enforcement of that particular statute had grown very lax in recent decades. Despite the restrictions and the tensions the community was stable, and over the centuries Metz had become one of the spiritual capitals of Ashkenazic Jewry. Young men traveled to the city from as far away as Lithuania to study with the famous sages of Metz and returned to the east as rabbis themselves. On his journey from Lublin, Zalkind Hourwitz spent time there.

With the wide array of special taxes they paid, Jews underpinned the entire local economy. To begin with there was the tax paid to the Duke of Brancas's family for "protection." That was a sum of 20,000 livres. There was another 7,706 livres business tax levied on the whole community. There were lesser taxes, including 450 livres for the hospital they were not allowed to use, 500 livres for lodging officers of the garrison, and 80 livres for the burial of Metz's paupers. There were twenty-nine annual taxes in all, totaling 149,625 livres, or around $283,000, levied on a community of several hundred households.

That was a lot of money for a license to live. But Metz was a garrison town, and an army presence meant business provisioning soldiers with everything from food to horses to saddles, as well as providing loans so they could visit the local taverns and brothels. But even provisioning the garrison, the community's tax bill was almost impossible to pay. The prohibitions on the ways Jews could earn a living meant they were limited in how they could raise funds, so making the Jews more "useful" was a practical question for the Royal Society to ask.

Ultimately, nine essays were submitted, four of them written by priests. One entry came from as far away as the French Caribbean island of Saint-Domingue—Haiti. Written with measures of prejudice, compassion, and ignorance, they are an accurate summary of the way the Jewish Question was discussed around the continent as the Age of Enlightenment rushed to its revolutionary conclusion.

The most direct and simple answer came from Haiti. Bruno Pic de Pere, the king's prosecutor in Haiti, wrote simply: "make them French." In five brief pages, the lawyer's essay describes Jewish life in the colony. On his island, Jews are not forced to live in ghettos but are allowed to mix and live with everyone else. As a result, Pic de Pere notes, "They are soldiers, sailors and workers like every one else and they are as generous and honest as anyone else. More important they are as likely to be regarded as French as Jews."

The views of the ordinary citizens of Metz were represented in a one-and-a-half-page memo also written by a local prosecutor. Louis-Nicolas Haillecourt was more than a lawyer, he was also related by marriage into the leadership of the city's merchant guilds. No group in French society was more fearful of Jewish rights than the guilds who enjoyed monopoly privileges on their trades. The guild members had long convinced themselves that direct competition with Jews in business would destroy their livelihoods.

Haillecourt broke down the subject this way: "If one renders them more useful, one ruins artisans and traders, to render them happier means they must be allowed to acquire (property) and in twenty years they will strip the ordinary people of every property that isn't already owned by the church." Jews were cowards, barbarians, avaricious and cruel. The prosecutor's conclusion: "It is not possible to render the Jews more happy without doing injury to Frenchmen, it is necessary to transport them en masse to the deserts of Guyana."

One other entrant echoed the Jew hatred of Haillecourt. A Benedictine monk named Dom Chais argued from scripture and from the philosophes to prove the wickedness of Jews. The blood of Christ was on their heads; this was the eternal decree of God, according to the Gospel of Matthew. Voltaire and Rousseau also made Dom Chais's case for denying Jews rights. For the monk, Voltaire described the Jews accurately when he wrote, "They are a troop of vile crooks and rogues." They could never be part of any nation other than their own because as Jean-Jacques Rousseau noted, "Moses gave the Israelites laws and customs that were designed to keep them separate."

The monk understood, however, that the question asked by the Royal Society was how to make them useful. So he suggested sending them into the countryside away from others, then giving them beehives and turning the Jews into honey makers. Honey is useful to the country, writes Dom Chais, who even provides projections on production and revenue from its sale.

Interestingly, the other Catholic prelates were much more in favor of freeing Jews from their restrictions. They saw Jews' social behavior as a direct result of the oppression they suffered. Abbé de la Lauze cut to the heart of the whole matter. The vices that we attribute to the Jews, are they an essential part of their character? he asked. Are they an effect of their particular self-government? Or are they the effect of our conduct toward them? Broadly, granting Jews equal status as citizens is the way to make them useful.

Those who took the essay question seriously all reached the same conclusion. How to achieve this quickly was the dilemma. Jews and Christians would have to give up some of their old ways to make this work. The permanent secretary of the Academy of Agriculture in Laon, a man named Valioud, argued that Jews, in order to become integrated, should be compelled to give up their traditional dress and wear the same clothes as other French people. In exchange the Church would modify its prayers so that they no longer contained harsh words about the Jews.

Zalkind Hourwitz was bursting with ideas as he wrote, far too many ideas. As a Jew, he felt the need to answer virtually every single popular prejudice against his people. He made painstaking refutations of the worst slanders, even reminding readers that eminent doctors had examined Jews and found them not to be an alien species but "men" no different than other men living in the same climate, circumcision and their different diet notwithstanding.

As a philosophe on the make he wanted to be noticed so he could give up his daily struggle as a peddler and find a nice sinecure that would allow him to write full-time. He demonstrated his erudition at every opportunity. Quotes from Plutarch, Juvenal, and Voltaire, footnotes about Molière and the Talmud, some of them in Latin, episodes from French history in the fourteenth century, none of them germane to the point—all got thrown into his essay. Hourwitz was self-taught and did not understand the rules of written rhetoric in the way the better-educated lawyers, priests, and bureaucrats who entered the contest did, and so his work seemed very scattered. Finally, he came from a long way to the east, and people there had a different way of expressing themselves in debate: irony and sarcasm trumped the formal, florid French style as a way of effectively making a point.

To begin with Hourwitz reversed the Royal Society's question in the title of his essay, "An Apology of the Jews in Response to the Question: What are the means to render the Jews more happy and useful in France?" Hourwitz answers the question in the first paragraph: "The means to make the Jews more happy and useful? Here it is, stop making them unhappy and useless; accord them, or more correctly, return to them the rights of citizens of which you deprive them, against the law of God and humanity; and against your interest."

Then he was off, praising King Louis for abolishing the poll tax, and tracing the origins of prejudice against the Jews to the ill-informed writing against them. He pointed out none too gently the absurdity of restricting Jews from society and then expecting their behavior to conform to the rules of the society from which they were banned.

Self-criticism was every bit as much a hallmark of Enlightenment discourse as ringing expressions of "Liberty, Equality, Fraternity" or "all men are created equal." The ability to acknowledge that one's critics had a point was a form of tolerance. This self-criticism wasn't always sincere but it did provide a platform for assailing an opponent's point of view. Hourwitz acknowledged that some of the criticism of his people was valid. Jews did practice usury, and, occasionally, even fraud against their Christian neighbors. But these wrongs were the product of the conditions in which Jews were forced to live. "My crimes are yours, and you punish me." And in any competition of malevolence between Jews and those who oppress them the oppressors win. He points out how many criminals there are among people who are completely free and then adds how extraordinary it is that Jews, locked away in ghettos with no freedom at all, still have "honest men" and "have not revolted or become the worst sort of thieves."

A constant argument against giving Jews the rights of citizens was that somehow their own religious law made it impossible to be fully active members of society. However, Hourwitz refuted the idea that Moses's law was somehow designed to keep the Jews apart from other nations and made it impossible for Jews to participate fully in society. Yes, there is the question of the Sabbath and other religious holidays, but look around Europe, look to other countries where Jews live with fewer restrictions, look at the Jews of Bordeaux. The law of the Talmud is not incompatible with an integrated life in the wider society.

After this summary of how the Jews came to be a problem, the essay comes to his suggestions for improving their situation. Suddenly the writing is crisp and deliberate.

1. Give them permission to acquire property; this will attach them to the country and they will no longer be regarded as strangers.

2. Allow them to practice all trades and agriculture; this will lessen the number of Jews who are peddlers who might make "mischief."
3. Allow them to take up any type of commerce; this will lead to new forms of manufacture and business.

Hourwitz then proposes official changes to Jewish life. Jews should not be allowed to use Hebrew or Yiddish in their commercial correspondence. Public schools should be opened to Jewish children so they can learn French, enlighten their conduct, and become familiar with Christians. Rabbis and the syndics should be forbidden to force Jews to keep their beards. Jews must be obligated to dress like Christians.

And finally, in court, the word *Jew* must not be used to identify someone in criminal proceedings.

To summarize, he mocked the contest's question one more time. What would the French say if the Academy of Stockholm had proposed, twelve years earlier, the following question: "Are there means for making Catholics more useful and happier in Sweden?"

But Hourwitz was not finished. He added a little coda, some moral precepts to teach Jewish and Christian children in the hopes of bringing the next generation together: all men are created by God; love your neighbor and respect your parents; Jews, Christians, and Muslims all worship one God—the difference in their faith is the way they pray to and serve Him. The brotherhood of man should be the rule. The honest man is preferable to a pious one.

He signed it, Zalkind Hourwitz, Polish Jew.

Abbé Grégoire also had a lot to say on the subject, perhaps more than the judges wanted to hear, but he said it very well by French standards. What the French consider eloquence can seem like arrogance to outsiders. A modern reader can be confused looking through Grégoire's *Essay on the Physical, Moral and Political Regeneration of the Jews.* The elegant condescension with which he writes about the Jews overshadows his profound sympathy with their plight.

He starts out trying to enlist his readers' sympathy as well. "Since the time of Vespasian, the history of the Jews offers nothing but sad scenes and bloody tragedies." The abbé then narrates a summary of the more heinous atrocities perpetrated against "this unhappy people" in the ensuing eighteen centuries.

Grégoire's purpose is to suggest how the Jews can be regenerated—revived morally, physically, and politically—and to do that he has to analyze their current state of degeneration and its causes. Jewish moral character is very poor in the abbé's analysis. They are oversexed. They reach puberty at a very precocious age. Circumcision makes the men salacious and masturbation is extremely common. "Jewesses are subject to nymphomania," he observes, "if they are forced to remain single."

But the abbé understands how this moral laxity came to engulf them: "Any people placed in the same circumstances as the Hebrews would become the same."

Next comes a look at the physical state of the Jews—in Grégoire's view, also not good. As a truly enlightened person, Grégoire was a man of science and followed avidly the new theories of physiognomy. He had become very friendly with Mendelssohn's old adversary Johann Kaspar Lavater and uses some of Lavater's analysis of Jewish features, from hooked noses to sunken eyes, to explain their craftiness and general weakness. He also notes that Jews walk a great deal as they travel from place to place peddling their wares, which gives them strong legs, but they do very little manual work, which gives them weak arms. They marry and have children too young, which also contributes to their physical degeneration.

The early start to family life also contributes to the rapid growth in the Jewish population. They are breeding rapidly. According to Grégoire, "of all men, the Jews are the most ardent to multiply." For Jews a large family is the greatest blessing of heaven. Grégoire notes that in French society a degrading love of luxury and vanity is slowing the growth of population. The abbé is saying about the Jews of the eighteenth century what many pundits in modern Europe and America say about contemporary society and Muslims: while Europeans run about spending money, consuming, having fun, and postponing having children, "they" are outbreeding us. The priest makes it clear that this status quo cannot be tolerated.

Finally, there is the degeneration of the Jews into usurers, and this must also be changed.

The onus for moral and physical regeneration is put entirely on Jews, but to enable them to be politically regenerated, the rules governing them must change, and there the burden falls on French society.

First, Grégoire recommends, allow Jews to practice other professions besides moneylending; even let them become farmers. Not all professions should be open to them, however. They can't be innkeepers, as they are in Poland, because there are too many opportunities for cheating customers in that business, nor should they be allowed to work as tax collectors or customs officers. Their moral character needs to be reformed first.

Next, there must be no more ghetto. Liberation and equality are not reasons that Grégoire offers for unlocking the gates. This is, after all, an essay of practical suggestions for regenerating a group of people. The abbé notes that physically, the ghetto is an unhealthy place where pestilential air causes epidemics. More importantly, being kept separate feeds hatred: not Christian hatred of Jews, but Jewish prejudice against Christians. The ghetto feeds many other prejudices, including a hatred of the modern. He notes that younger members of the community are desperate to learn more about Enlightenment ideas but they are unable to because they are forced to stay within a community where the old religious traditions as interpreted by the rabbis are the sole source of learning.

And here Grégoire comes to the crucial point from either side of the ghetto wall. Over the centuries of ghettoization the Jewish community had one single right: its autonomy. Kept apart, the community had its own legal system with the Talmud as law and the rabbi as judge in civil, criminal, and religious matters. From outside the ghetto wall it made the Jews look like "a nation within the nation." From inside the ghetto walls it allowed Jews to maintain order in the face of oppression as well as to hold fast to their ethnic identity as being different from other nations. After all, the dogma of Judaism is Jewish ethnicity. Jews hated the ghetto, but they were deeply ambivalent about losing their autonomy with no guarantee that the new arrangement would truly give them equality.

Grégoire insists that Jews should have total freedom of conscience to practice their religion but must submit to French civil law, not that of the Talmud. Rabbis should retain the right to rule strictly on matters of religion.

Language was Grégoire's other great passion. France is, by European standards, a vast country and there was a babel of regional dialects spoken from Brittany to Languedoc. In the decades to come Grégoire would work to standardize the French language and in the essay he makes clear that the Jewish dialect, Yiddish, would have to go. Jews would have to learn to speak French like their countrymen. Of course, they would not be educated separately; all the schools and academies would be open to them with the additional benefit that Jewish children would meet and know Christian children.

For the abbé the hoped-for outcome from granting Jews these new freedoms is this: the reform and regeneration of this people would lead to their almost inevitable conversion to Christianity, not by force, but by the logic of their position of equality.

Then Grégoire reaches his conclusion, preaching to one side of the ghetto wall and then the other. To his fellow Frenchmen he says, "The Jews are members of the universal family that would establish brotherhood among all peoples . . . For them as for us, revelation spreads its majestic sail." To the Jews he says, "Children of the same father, stripped of the pretexts for disliking your brothers, you will one day be reunited in the same fold." Then he turns back to the French: "Open up the asylums where they are forced to live and dry their tears and finally the Jew will return to the Christian his kindness and embrace him as a fellow citizen and his friend."

• • •

There was one other important entry, Claude-Antoine Thiery, a lawyer from Nancy, whose analysis of how the Jews came to be in need of regeneration is not far from those of Grégoire but who reached a much different conclusion. Like Grégoire, the lawyer was also friendly with his local Jewish syndic, Berr Isaac Berr, and clearly had taken his views on the issue of Jewish autonomy into account. So Thiery argued for the preservation of Jewish communal structures. They could live, by choice, a separate but equal existence.

And then, after all the effort expended by the entrants, the judges of the Royal Society decided that none of the essays was worthy of the prize. What the judges were after was a practical program for making the Jews useful, something that might become law. What they had received was either prejudice and easily dismissed, or pleading, or a summary of philosophical thinking about what was good or bad about this people. They felt that all the entrants had failed to come up with a practical program for increasing the usefulness of the Jews that could be turned into a coherent social policy. The chairman of the judges, Pierre-Louis Roederer, announced there would be a rerun and proposed several specific questions to be answered about whether Jewish religious law could be modified in a way that would be compatible with greater integration into French society.

Hourwitz, Grégoire, Thiery, and Dom Chais modestly reworked their essays and appended the requested answers. On August 25, 1788, the Royal Society of Sciences and Arts of Metz held its annual meeting. This time there would be a winner announced. In the morning the academy members attended a mass in memory of King Louis IX, Saint Louis. The enlightened members of the Royal Society probably didn't see the irony that on a day when a prize was to be given for an essay on making Jews more useful and happy in France they were paying religious homage to a king and saint who had on two occasions ordered the Talmud to be publicly burned in Paris.

After Mass, the permanent secretary of the Royal Society, Jean

Le Payen, announced there would be three winners: Abbé Grégoire, Claude-Antoine Thiery, and Zalkind Hourwitz. Le Payen closed his speech with a call to France's government: "The majority of the essays accuse our prejudice as being the primary cause of the Jews' vices. We have made it impossible for them to be honest: how can we run away from that? Let us be just toward them and they will become just toward us. This is the wish of humanity and all reasonable men." He concluded by urging the members of the society to demand of the government that Jews be recalled to the status of full citizenship without delay.

In the society's hall there must have been a murmur of assent. The enlightened members of the society knew that Louis XVI had appointed his special minister Chrétien de Lamoignon de Malesherbes to develop a policy for integrating Jews into wider society. Some members of the society may even have known the story of how Malesherbes was given the commission. The minister was the king's most trusted adviser and had recently enabled a change in the law giving Protestants in the Catholic kingdom full rights. That the king even considered assigning him the task indicates how important the Jewish Question had become in France. Louis said to Malesherbes, "Monsieur de Malesherbes, you became a Protestant now I wish you to become a Jew; occupy yourself with them."

The prize meant a great deal to Grégoire. In reports of the contest around Europe, his essay received the most notice and an English translation was soon published. Success meant more to Hourwitz. A position had come up in the Royal Library as head of translations. The library's manuscripts from Palestine and the Middle East needed translating into French. Hourwitz spoke and read Hebrew fluently and saw the position as a way of finally getting out of his menial peddling work. The library job was in the gift of Malesherbes. In Paris, Hourwitz organized a letter-writing campaign to the minister in hopes of gaining the job. In the spring of 1789 he got the position and so was able to give up peddling and devote himself to writing.

Grégoire also tried to make the most out of his share of the prize by contacting Malesherbes and asking if he might be allowed to dedicate the published edition of his essay to the king's minister. Malesherbes refused the honor, not out of spite but because events were moving fast and the king had to deal with more pressing issues, issues that would not be resolved short of revolution.

## CHAPTER FOUR

# No One Shall Be Troubled for His Religion

As the year 1788 dwindled away, the news of the Metz contest spread around France and the rest of Europe. Journals in Germany, Italy, and England reported on it. Within six months all three winning essays were published. People in France and around the continent—French was the language of Europe's educated elites—were able to read and discuss them.

The France in which the essays circulated was a different country from the France in which they had been written. The king was moved to reform and had decided to convene the nation's Estates General. The Estates, a kind of legislative body, hadn't met since 1614. They had been summoned out of their long retirement because France's finances were a mess: those who contributed least to the public purse enjoyed almost all the benefits of the country's wealth. This problem was reflected in the organization of the Estates General. The First Estate was the clergy. The church owned land and yet paid no tax. The Second Estate, the nobility, had its own lands and a monopoly on all public positions. They paid very little tax. The Third Estate was everybody else, and they paid the taxes that supported the first two and the king. The financial chaos was augmented by a drought, bringing the country's food production to the edge of collapse. Famine was biting at the edges of French society.

The announcement that the Estates General would be reconvened was made in August 1788, a few weeks before the Metz society announced the winners of their contest. At the beginning of 1789 the Estates General were summoned to meet at the Palace of Versailles in April. In the intervening months elections to each estate were to be held region by region. Each locality was asked to compile a "Cahier des Doléances," a list of grievances to be taken up by the assembly.

Inevitably, Abbé Grégoire decided to run for election as a representative of the First Estate, the clergy. His career to this point had seen him balancing his role as a reforming parish priest with wider political interests. He understood that the Estates General meant the door was opening to an era of reform and he wanted to bring as many changes as possible to French society before the door slammed shut. Even as he campaigned for election, he helped form a lobby for Jewish equality. On February 23, 1789, Grégoire wrote to his friend the Metz syndic Isaiah Berr Bing, urging him to launch a campaign for "emancipation." This would have to be a behind-the-scenes effort because, of course, the Jews of eastern France were not permitted to run for election to the Third Estate. But the hope was that they could at least compose their own list of grievances to be considered by the king. The Jewish leadership needed to counter what they knew was in the grievance lists prepared by representatives from Alsace, Lorraine, and Metz: requests for even greater restrictions on Jews, including the destruction of synagogues and the dispersal of Jews to other parts of the kingdom.

Cerf Berr was best placed to get a hearing from the king. As the main provisioner of the French Army he dealt with the highest levels of his government and so could write directly to the most important of Louis XVI's advisers, Minister of Finance Jacques Necker, and know the letter would be read and considered. In mid-April he contacted

Necker and asked for the Jewish community to have at least indirect representation in the Estates General. This was granted and the Jews of the east wrote a list of grievances to be presented by an elected member of the Estates. They chose Abbé Grégoire. But their list was never presented. Events moved far too quickly.

In the first week of May 1789, for the first time in more than 150 years, France's Estates General met at Versailles. Things got off to a bad start and declined rapidly from there. Political reform and noble privilege do not mingle well. From the opening session in Versailles it was clear there was no way to compromise between the two. The setting itself worked against a hopeful outcome. The Estates were to meet in the Salle des Menus Plaisirs, which means hall of small entertainments. There was double irony in that name. First, the hall was not small. It was an ornate barn with long colonnaded galleries covered with luxurious wall decorations, a constant reminder to the Third Estate of the extraordinary wealth of the royal court even as the rest of the country was struggling with bankruptcy and starvation. The second irony was that for many of the representatives attending the Estates General, redefining the nation's social contract was no light entertainment. They had arrived at Versailles in a serious mood and were in deadly earnest about what had to happen at the meeting.

From the beginning it was clear that social distinctions would continue to be observed. Members of the First and Second Estates, the clergy and the nobles, met privately and cordially with the king. Members of the Third were restricted to a formal viewing of the royal presence, forced to walk past Louis in a large hall of the palace.

The less than equal status of the Third Estate was confirmed when the king reneged on a critical promise. The Third Estate represented 90 percent of the French people. Its leaders insisted in advance that the king recognize this majority by allowing the Third more representatives than the first two estates and this Louis XVI did. The members of the Third Estate were confident this would allow them to win most decisions when put to the ballot.

But on May 5, 1789, when the Estates General met for the first time, the king's keeper of the seals, Barentin, announced that when it came time to vote on a given issue, rather than calling the roll of the entire Estates General together, each estate's vote would be tabulated separately. If, as was likely, a majority of the First and Second Estates voted one way on a question of tax reform and the Third Estate voted differently, the Third would lose two to one, even though it possessed the overall majority of votes cast. While the 1,100 members of the Estates digested this new information, they were treated to a three-hour lecture complete with all the relevant numbers on the dire state of France's finances.

When a political body comes together, the person who controls the agenda controls everything. In theory Louis and his chief ministers had this power, but they had given no thought as to how the assembly would work in this new age. Or more likely, they simply couldn't agree on how to make the body work. Louis was pulled between his court, who wanted to maintain ancient privileges, and the advice of his chief minister Jacques Necker, who was a reformer. Leaders of the Third Estate, however, were quite clear on what they wanted from this gathering: reform of the whole economic structure of the country. They set the agenda: there would be no discussion of taxation until numerical superiority was recognized and incorporated into the voting process.

So, as in America, the slide to revolution began with the subject of taxation and representation, but in France the topic had been turned into a point of parliamentary procedure. Through weeks of procedural twists and turns and speeches full of noble Enlightenment sentiments, the Third Estate dug in, demanding it be given the rights attendant on the representatives of the majority of the people, the Nation.

Tension between the Third Estate and the clergy and nobility grew. Within the first two estates, fault lines began to crack open. The clergy was divided between ordinary parish priests and the bishops. Most bishops came from aristocratic families and they tended to look down on the humble abbés and curés. Within the ranks of the aristocracy as well there was a group of reformers who rejected the sense of entitlement to which they were born.

On June 14, Grégoire decided to leave the First Estate and join the Third. Other parish priests followed him. Soon it became clear that the First and Third Estates were coming together in one group. On June 17 the members decided to rename themselves the National Assembly. On June 20, the king, now hopelessly out of control of events, decided to lock them out of the Salle des Menus Plaisirs. The Third Estate adjourned to the royal tennis court, a kind of supersized squash court. In the drafty, high-ceilinged room they dragged together some benches and arranged an area for a presiding officer. Voices echoing off the tennis court walls, they reached the decision to write a new constitution for France. They swore an oath to let no force separate them until that constitution had been written.

A new national leadership for France emerged from that tennis court. One of its central figures was Abbé Grégoire. Constitutional fever spread rapidly. A few days later, the king bowed to the inevitable and urged his loyalists in the First and Second Estates to join the National Assembly in writing a new constitution.

Before there is revolution there is talk, but by July, just a few weeks after the National Assembly invented itself, the era of talk was almost over. The *Journal de Paris* the week of July 6 carried a review of Grégoire's prize-winning Metz essay but it isn't likely that the review was read by many people. Events in Paris were coming to an unpredictable conclusion. The French people were taking away royal power in a quite spontaneous and unplanned way. Louis had dispatched troops, many of them foreign mercenaries, to surround Paris. The city seethed with rumor, excitement, and fear.

Late in the afternoon of July 12, word reached Paris that Louis had dismissed the reformer Necker. Crowds began to flock to the Palais Royal, by now the unofficial headquarters of revolution. A table in the middle of the grounds had become a public pulpit for political speeches. A young journalist with a flair for oratory, Camille Desmoulins, came out of the Café Foy, leapt onto the table, and somehow made his presence known to the throng. Brandishing a pistol, Desmoulins told them the removal of Necker was the beginning of bloody suppression and urged his fellow citizens to take up arms.

For the next day and a half, the people of Paris skirmished with the various troops of soldiers sent to contain them. They raided munitions dumps and opened up grain storehouses. Rumor ruled over them. Early on July 14 the word went around the city that the cannons mounted on the notorious Bastille prison were aimed at the Rue Saint-Antoine, a well-known revolutionary district. Crowds surged to the massive, ancient fortress. Within hours the garrison had surrendered, the handful of prisoners locked inside were released, and the commander of the fortress had his head cut off. The French Revolution had its symbolic starting point.

## ii.
## Rights of Man

After the Bastille fell, chaos reigned throughout France. The "Great Fear" swept across the country. The houses of the nobility were sacked and old scores were settled. In some places the forces of law and order no longer knew what their authority was and so were helpless.

In Alsace and Lorraine the tiny Jewish villages were under siege as debtors attacked the moneylenders. Hundreds of Jews from the Strasbourg area fled for safety up the Rhine river to Basel in Switzerland. In eastern France the forces of law and order were not so much helpless as disinterested. The Jews were not citizens, after all, so where was the obligation? The Jewish leadership, the syndics—Cerf Berr, Isaiah Berr Bing, and Berr Isaac Berr—reached out to Grégoire for help.

While the countryside was in the throes of anarchy the business of defining a new France continued at Versailles. The deputies of the National Assembly met well into the evening each day to debate a constitution. On the evening of August 3, Grégoire changed the subject. He addressed the Assembly on the plight of the Jews of the east, demanding, "as a minister of a religion that regards all men as brothers: the intervention of the Assembly's power in favor of a people outlawed and miserable."

The response was ambivalent. Other members of the Assembly demanded a factual account of events in the east before moving on Grégoire's request. But the abbé had broken the ice; the status of Jews in the new France was now on the agenda.

In these early days of the French Revolution the National Assembly had set itself the task of writing a declaration of rights. The day after Grégoire's intervention on behalf of the Jews of the east, the Assembly abolished the old feudal order. It would take months to write a new constitution so it was imperative to have some basic statement of a social contract on the rights of French citizens as a guide into the new era. "Rights are not laws," as Jérôme Pétion de Villeneuve reminded the group. "Rights are for all time and come before laws," laws such as those contained in a constitution.

There was a spontaneity to the start of the French Revolution but it did not leave the members of the National Assembly scratching their heads wondering what to do next. All those years of talking, pamphleteering, and forming clubs to discuss a new France had created a class of leaders who quickly organized committees to prepare reports on subjects the new constitution had to fix as well as draft sections of the Declaration of Rights.

Much of the initial work on the Declaration had been done before the Bastille fell by the Marquis de Lafayette, who had returned to France following his service in the American War of Independence. Thomas Jefferson was in Paris throughout this period, serving as American ambassador, and Lafayette turned his old friend into his editor. But by the time the marquis's work was put through the voluble vetting process of the National Assembly, much of his original wording didn't survive. France, members of the Assembly pointed out, was in a different situation to America. The United States inhabited a new world bounded only by ocean and virgin forest. France very much occupied an old one, stuffed with symbols of ancient privilege, surrounded by nations that were long-standing enemies, and still ruled over by a king who was, in theory, due the respect given to a sovereign.

Article I of the Declaration of the Rights of Man and of the Citizen begins, "Men are born and remain free and equal in rights." Then alluding to monarchy it continues, "Social distinctions may be founded only upon the general good." One thing the authors of the Declaration of Rights had to do similar to what happened in America was define the right of religious expression. France was an overwhelmingly Catholic country but much blood had been shed over the rights of its Protestant minority. The new document needed to codify the rights of minority faiths.

On Saturday, August 22, the debate on religion got under way. It was started by the traditionalist Bishop of Clermont. "Religion," the bishop told the Assembly, "is the eternal reason that awakens order in things. I ask, therefore, that the principles of the French constitution rest on religion as its eternal basis."

The religion the bishop had in mind was Catholicism. Monsieur de la Borde responded saying he was not interested in framing the discussion of religion in the Declaration in those terms. "Tolerance is the sentiment motivating the discussion at the moment," he told the bishop. "I don't have to recall here the blood that intolerance has spilled, the ravages it has made throughout the nation. Neutrality is without doubt the wisest course. Freedom of religion is a sacred right given to all citizens."

The chair then recognized the Count Mirabeau. The more than 1,200 members of the Assembly stopped their hustling and bustling at the back of the hall; the whispered sidebars fell silent. Mirabeau was the headline act of the National Assembly, a big-voiced speaker of unsurpassed rhetorical brilliance. One newspaper described him in full flow as "an enraged wild beast with a tiger's face." Whenever he entered the debate attention was paid.

"I haven't come to preach tolerance," he rumbled. "Unfettered freedom of religion is to my eyes a right so sacred that the word 'tolerance' appears to me a sort of tyranny; since that implies an authority that has the power to tolerate, to weigh on the freedom of thought."

The count went on, "We are making a Declaration of Rights. It is absolutely necessary that this [religion] be a right." Mirabeau offered a simple formulation for the religious section of the Declaration of the Rights of Man: "No one shall be troubled for his religion."

Mirabeau reminded the Assembly that there had always been a diversity of religious opinion and said this diversity should not be attacked. When the count finished his speech, a member of the clergy—in the hubbub that always lingered after a Mirabeau speech the stenographer recording the debate would fail to get a name—stood up and made a plea for an acceptance that there should at least be an official church in the country. This would not infringe on the tolerance of other forms of worship. The priest asked for further debate. But somewhere in the back of the hall trouble broke out and it was agreed that the discussion of religion would be put off for a day. The Assembly then turned its attention to a letter from Necker, who had been reinstated after the Bastille was overthrown, on the subject of borrowing money to keep France afloat.

The next day the discussion of religious rights continued. Mirabeau's formulation for the religion article of the Declaration was a summary of wording written by another liberal noble, the Count de Castellane: "No one shall be troubled for their religious opinions, nor harassed in exercising his form of worship."

The wording of the article was parsed. Should the Declaration's language include specific reference to forms of "worship" and other "beliefs" rather than simply "religious opinions"? Julien Maillet, from southwestern France, suggested this wording: "Since no society can exist without religion, all men have the right to live freely in their beliefs and religious opinions because what one holds in one's thoughts, God alone can judge."

Abbé d'Eymar, concerned that the role of the Catholic religion was being diminished, took the floor to introduce a motion for this sentence to be included: "It is essential and indispensable for the order of society that religion be maintained, preserved and respected."

Mirabeau, a devotee of the "natural" religion of the Enlightenment, that system of thought derived from the philosophy of Spinoza, got up and forcefully disagreed and demanded that the abbé's idea not be debated. The presiding officer denied Mirabeau's request. The count was content to make a long speech to the effect that rather than making religion a subject for the public space it should be kept a private matter. He pointed out that "each person chooses a religion that suits his passions . . . What I'm saying to you, Sirs, is that men should not carry their religion out into society."

The response from the floor: Without religion it is useless to make laws and rules. To whom do you swear a legal oath if not to God? The bishop of Autun, Talleyrand-Périgord, tried to move the debate to a different point of view. Rules concerning the practice of religion should be enshrined in the constitution but in this Declaration of Rights the religion being referred to should clearly be the Catholic Church.

Mirabeau was having none of it: "You are speaking of a dominant church. Dominant! An opinion of the majority does not have the right to dominate. It is a tyrannical word that should be banished from our legislation."

The author of the Declaration's proposed religious article, the Count de Castellane, continued this theme: "Preventing a man from offering tribute to the divinity by his own path tyrannizes the conscience; this violates the most sacred rights of man and the citizen."

Now the hall was in a clamor. It seemed like everyone wanted to make an amendment to Castellane's proposal. Order in the National Assembly was often a fragile thing but the subject of religion reduced it to a frenzy. There was complete chaos. From every side of the chamber people were demanding the floor to make new amendments. The stenographer keeping notes of the meeting for the *Moniteur Universel*—the official newspaper of the National Assembly—could hardly keep up with the shouting and noted that the motion was amended, sub-amended, divided, convoluted, twisted in a hundred ways. There was a faction that wanted to expand the meaning of *belief* beyond its religious application. Somehow an amendment relating the practice of religion to the public order was tacked on, and this amendment hinted at what was troubling so many of the delegates.

France had seen its wars of religion between Protestants and Catholics. The Catholic Church had won, and as Louis XVI sought to fix his broken kingdom he had finally extended full civil rights to Protestants. Some of the old sectarian hatred between Christians was present in the debate, but the wider concern was about the country's other religious minority, the Jews.

Eventually, the tumult subsided, and Rabaut de Saint-Etienne took the floor. Saint-Etienne was a pastor, a Protestant version of Grégoire. He believed pastoral care in this time of upheaval required the clergy to engage politically on the side of social justice. He was a veteran of the struggle for equal rights for his fellow Protestants and he now decided to do battle on behalf of Jewish equality.

His speech began with the inevitable preamble, a statement of fidelity to liberty and freedom of thought and opinion: "these freedoms live in the heart as in a sanctuary." Then he declared to the vast crowd, "The form of worship is a dogma, a dogma is an opinion, and opinions are free." And so what if someone thinks another person's belief is wrong? "Error is not a crime, so in a man's religion it must not restrict his rights."

The pastor then stopped speaking obliquely and came to his main point, calling out, "I demand liberty for a people always banned, wanderers, vagabonds on the face of the earth, this people doomed to humiliation, the Jews."

He challenged his audience. Is this done anywhere else? Are Jews granted liberty in neighboring countries? "Nation of France you don't exist to receive examples, but to give examples to others."

Then Saint-Etienne restated his theme: "I return to my principles, or rather your principles, in declaring all men are born and live free.

Have you not sanctioned the freedom of all men? . . . I demand for all non-Catholics that which you demand for yourself: equal rights, freedom of their religion, freedom of their worship, freedom to celebrate in their sacred places this worship in the certitude they will no longer be troubled for their religion . . ."

Saint-Etienne then endorsed Castellane's wording: "No one should be troubled for their religious opinions, nor harassed in exercising his form of worship."

Speaking next, the Bishop of Lydda suggested adding a qualifying clause to the article, "provided the forms of worship did not trouble public order." It isn't difficult to imagine that the bishop was referring to the fact that Jews observed a different Sabbath and that closing down their businesses on Saturday and opening them on Sunday, the Christian day of rest, might be interpreted as causing disorder. Or that the chaotic hubbub of Jews at prayer wafting out of the ghetto, another thing they were disparaged for, might be heard as disorder.

Once again chaos reigned in the chamber. After a noisy series of voice votes the bishop's amendment was added to Castellane's article so that Article X of the Declaration of the Rights of Man and of the Citizen reads: "No one should be troubled for their beliefs or their religion, nor harassed in exercising his form of worship; provided the forms of worship do not disturb public order as established by law."

The religious part of the Jewish issue was settled. The community's rights of worship were implicitly guaranteed in Article X of the Declaration but there was still the vexing question of their civil rights in French society. The moral issue of equality—Emancipation—had been turned into a political one, something to be legislated. The process by which Jews became equal citizens would be subject to the same frustrations and compromises as any other item on the legislative agenda.

## CHAPTER FIVE

# The Name of "Active Citizen"

THE VARIOUS JEWISH COMMUNITIES IN FRANCE WASTED NO time trying to influence the legislative process. The National Assembly ratified the Declaration of the Rights of Man and of the Citizen on August 26, 1789. The same day the Jews resident in Paris submitted a written address to the Assembly echoing the words of Rabaut de Saint-Etienne, asking for the same rights given to Protestants. This wasn't a spontaneous outpouring stirred by the passionate debate on the Declaration. It was the product of weeks of discussions among the leaders of the capital's Jewish community.

Paris was home to both Sephardic and Ashkenazic Jews. *Sephardic* comes from the Hebrew word for Spain and *Ashkenazic* from the Hebrew for German. The address of the Paris Jews to the National Assembly was unique because the two communities rarely worked together. Detested is not too harsh a word to describe the ill feeling between the Sephardim and Ashkenazim. The two groups lived at opposite ends of the country and this separation was maintained in Paris. The Sephardim kept their houses on the Left Bank around Saint-Germain, while the Ashkenazim stayed on the Right Bank in the area between the Place des Vosges and the Louvre, called the Marais.

The two communities were separated by more than geography. They were separated by wealth. The Sephardim of Bordeaux and Bayonne were well established in international trade and their communities were prosperous. The Ashkenazim of the east were among the poorest people in the kingdom. They had different approaches to the practice of Judaism and interpretation of the Talmud. But the key difference between the two communities ran deeper than comparative wealth and adherence to Talmudic law.

As it was for the Jews in Spinoza's Amsterdam, the history of the Jews of Bordeaux and Bayonne had been one of forced Catholic conversion and hidden Jewish practice in Spain and Portugal. In the centuries they had lived in France the "Portuguese" Jews, as they were called in official French circles, had evolved a complex wink-and-nod strategy with their Christian neighbors as they integrated and became established in their adopted cities. They were known as "New Christians" for several centuries before finally, early in the eighteenth century, being given royal letters patent acknowledging they were in fact Jewish and granting them the effective rights of citizens. The Sephardic Jews were as assimilated into the mainstream of French bourgeois society as it was possible to be at that time. They had even been invited directly to run for election to the Estates General and to submit their list of grievances.

The Sephardim were acutely aware of the precariousness of their privileges. The original laws banning Jews from living in France had never been repealed and the letters patent overriding them could be rescinded by the monarch at any time. What the Portuguese Jews didn't want was for their security to be threatened by the bad reputation of the Ashkenazic Jews as usurers and unassimilated aliens who couldn't even speak French.

The year before the overthrow of the Bastille, as the king's chief minister Malesherbes was working on the Jewish Question, he received a memorandum from Abraham Furtado and Solomon Lopes-Dubec, two leaders of the Bordeaux community, that pointed out this difference. "A Portuguese Jew is English in England and French in

France but a German Jew is a German Jew everywhere because of his customs from which he deviates rarely."

The animosity between the two groups perplexed supporters of Emancipation. Malesherbes told a story about asking the syndic of the Bordeaux Jews, David Gradis, if his religion allowed him to eat with Christians. This was an important question since one of the reasons Jews were regarded as being a "nation within the nation" was that strict observance of kosher laws meant many Jews would not share a table with other Frenchmen; they could not eat unclean food or drink un-blessed wine. This made resolving their situation difficult, Malesherbes noted, because "friendship is bound up around the glass of wine."

The syndic Gradis was a typical Bordelais, cosmopolitan, an as-similated man of the world. Could he break bread with a Christian? "Of course," he answered the king's minister. When Malesherbes put the same question to Cerf Berr, syndic of Alsace and a strictly obser-vant Jew, Cerf Berr replied, "Absolutely not."

But with the Revolution under way it was clear to the Jews living on either side of the Seine that the animosities that kept them apart needed to be set aside. Their "Address to the National Assembly" built a case from both communities for their inclusion as citizens. They pledged their patriotic allegiance: they were Frenchmen, natives of the country, faithful to the king. You can believe our word, they ex-plained, because despite our minority religious status we have always remained true to our faith. That means we are always true to our oaths of allegiance.

But their key point was the renunciation of a separate legal system for their religion. This group made clear its wish to be ruled by the same police and courts as other Frenchmen.

The spirit of the times moved the authors. In those first days of the Revolution all things were possible. A reasonable request, confidently made, had to be granted by an assembly of reasonable men: "We want to step into the place of Citizenship, to be given civil rights as an act of justice." Don't just do it for our sake, the address concludes; grant-ing this simple act of justice will set an example for all the countries of the world. For a legislative body, the National Assembly, that saw itself as the vanguard of a new era in world history it was just the right rhetorical flourish with which to finish.

Five days later the Jews of Alsace and Lorraine submitted their address. It was more explicit in its demands: the title and rights of citizenship, a declaration that Jews be permitted to live anywhere in the kingdom, the abolition of all the arbitrary taxes they paid. The final demand distinguished this submission from that of the Paris group. The Jews of eastern France asked the Assembly that they be allowed to continue in "the free exercise of our laws, rites and customs." In other words, they wanted to maintain the separate system of Talmudic law that provided the community with its cohesion.

The difference between the submissions of the Paris community and that of Alsace, Lorraine, and Metz made clear that there were actually two Emancipation debates going on. The first was legislative. The National Assembly had to decide whether to grant Jews citizenship and civil rights. The second was being conducted within the Jewish community. How much of their ghetto-grown, religious-based culture were they willing to give up to become full citizens of the new France? The first debate would take a mere two years to answer. The second would go on much longer, and not just in France but throughout the Ashkenazic world from Metz to Galicia.

## ii.
## Strategy

With the two addresses in circulation, on September 1, Abbé Grégoire asked the National Assembly to place the question of Jewish citizenship on the agenda. On September 3 the Assembly decided the time was not yet right and made the classic delaying move of all legislatures: it appointed a committee to study the situation and report back. The Assembly then turned its attention to what sort of legislature France should have: a single chamber or a bicameral setup. As the weeks went by the members moved on to other questions: what veto power the king would retain over legislation, who had authority for local government now that the old feudal order had been abolished, who was responsible for paying parish priests. A new tax system had to be invented as well because hovering over each day's discussions was financial catastrophe.

The society was being completely redesigned by the National Assembly and so the proponents of Emancipation had to fight for attention. The fact that it was discussed at all hints at a well-organized campaign to keep the subject before the legislators. The hint is all there is because the historical record is thin. But a look at how events unfolded in the first autumn and winter after the storming of the Bastille shows there was a strategy designed behind the scenes between the Jewish syndics and their friends in the National Assembly. These friends were in extremely high places. They were the liberal leadership of the Revolution.

It's not clear why these leaders took up the cause of Jewish equality. Their speeches in the National Assembly and their votes tell us much about their attitudes to the Jews but not why they were committed to Emancipation. In part it was an intellectual commitment: they were acting on abstract principles about universal brotherhood. But that doesn't explain the sincere, emotional engagement of aristocrats like Counts Mirabeau and Clermont-Tonnerre in the cause of Jewish rights.

Perhaps, like the peasants and artisans in Alsace and Lorraine, these powerful men formed their judgments based on the contact they had had with Jews. France's lower and middle classes knew the moneylenders and peddlers and were engaged in a struggle for survival with them. On the other hand, the liberal aristocrat leaders of the Revolution knew the syndics, men who carried out commissions for the highest authorities. The syndics were cultured, cosmopolitan, well-mannered. They were likable men.

Certainly they felt an intellectual affinity with modern Jewish thinkers. Mirabeau in his wanderings around Europe in the years before the Revolution had known Mendelssohn and his circle. He had even written a pamphlet on the great philosopher. Most of the Revolution's liberal leadership had knowledge of Spinoza, particularly his view of God and nature. Their own view of religion had been shaped by it. "Nature" and "natural law" were regularly invoked in their speeches. The syndics and the philosophers were the Jews the liberal leaders knew best, and that must have had something to do with their willingness to push for Jewish equality.

Throughout these early days of the Revolution, as Abbé Grégoire established himself as a leading figure in the National Assembly, Zalkind Hourwitz was experiencing the upheaval in the street. A new national guard was organized and Hourwitz joined up. The guard had plenty of work to do maintaining order in Paris. Bad harvests and a crashed financial system meant there were grain shortages in the city. No grain meant no bread and there were riots over lack of food. Occasional outbreaks of general anarchy swept the city as rumors circulated about counterrevolutionary plots. Then there were the occasional outbursts of wine-enhanced revolutionary emotion that simply got out of hand.

At the same time, Hourwitz was just getting started in his new job at the Royal Library. When he wasn't on duty with the guard, he had meetings to attend of revolutionary clubs and with his friends among the Jewish leadership.

He returned briefly to the limelight in mid-September when his name was noted in the National Assembly for a donation made to the treasury. France was so broke that the legislature had asked citizens to voluntarily give money to the government so it could continue to function. Hourwitz pledged to give a quarter of his income for the rest of his life to the country that had given him a home but not yet citizenship.

As autumn approached there was still no clear line of authority in the country. On August 26, the day the Declaration of the Rights of Man was ratified, the king had placed the Jews of France under his protection. But his word was no longer law. In Alsace and Lorraine, sporadic violence against them continued. As the High Holidays approached in the third week of September there was fear the attacks would resume. Many of those who had fled in July and August returned home for the religious festivals. For the Jew haters it was a perfect opportunity. Whole communities were reunited in one place, the synagogue. The largest synagogue was in Metz and its members feared violence.

On September 28, Count Stanislas Clermont-Tonnerre interrupted a debate on the payment of state pensions to bring to the floor a request from the Jews of Metz for protection by the National Assembly. The request was the result of behind-the-scenes lobbying by the syndics. Clermont-Tonnerre, in a brief, eloquent speech, made their case, noting that Yom Kippur was fast approaching, violence was increasing, and the Assembly needed to act without delay. "I demand . . . the Assembly place the Jewish people and their goods under the protection of the law," he concluded. "And I wish that at least they be recognized as men, even if they are not citizens; they cannot have their throats cut with impunity."

The Assembly's leaders agreed to write the letter without delay, making special note that the Declaration of the Rights of Man was a statement of universal principles and applied to every person in the world. It was quickly dispatched with the king's seal attached. A precedent had been set. A first legal right had been extended to the Jews: that of the new government's protection.

The press reported the event as earth-shattering news. The Revolution had seen an explosion in the number of newspapers published. People hungered for news of the daily debates on the constitution. The relaxation of official censorship meant it was possible to write most anything. Mirabeau started a newspaper, the *Courrier de Provence*, which reported events and advocated his positions. There were plenty of other very liberal papers, such as the *Journal de Paris* and the *Courrier de Versailles à Paris*, that took up the cause of Emancipation and kept the issue before the public in the most sympathetic light.

Supporters of Emancipation worked the process in other ways. Led by Grégoire they lobbied for a Jewish delegation to be given the opportunity to make their case directly to the National Assembly. Shortly after the September 28 vote extended government protection to them, a delegation representing the Jews of the east went to Versailles and waited to be given the chance to speak. On the evening of October 14, the delegation was invited into the opulent Salle des Menus Plaisirs and stepped to the railing where representatives of various public groups were allowed to address the legislators. Grégoire formally introduced the group to the Assembly. Their leader, the syndic of Nancy, Berr Isaac Berr, drew the text of a speech from his pocket.

"In the name of the eternal, author of all justice and truth, in the name of God who has given everyone the same rights," he began, "we come before you today to ask you to take into consideration our deplorable destiny."

A rare silence fell across the hall as reality silenced prejudice. Many in the Assembly had never encountered a Jew, and here was one whose presence belied all the stereotypes. He was clean shaven, dressed well, spoke elegant French, and made a simple and compelling case for his people.

Berr told the Assembly he would not waste their time with a long recounting of the Jews' perilous situation; those details were included in the many memoranda already submitted for their consideration. He simply wanted the Assembly to make his people's existence less miserable and requested that Jews "be regarded as brothers" and treated equally.

The president of the session, Freteau de Saint-Just, responded with a courtesy equal to Berr's and promised to take up the question during the present legislative session.

The campaign continued with Grégoire publishing a fortnight later a "Motion in Favor of the Jews." The work clarified and simplified some ideas from his Metz essay but most importantly it made explicit that Jews were natives of France and not aliens. This entitled them to full equality and all the rights of citizenship, including the right to live anywhere in the country. They should not be confined to ghettos or isolated country hamlets. The liberal press provided an echo chamber for these thoughts and the *Gazette de Paris* noted how remarkable it was that a "priest of the Gospel, a curé of the Roman church has become the defender of the Jews and put their cause before the National Assembly."

Still, a special session on the Jews continued to prove difficult to schedule. By now the factions inside the National Assembly had hardened. Sitting to the right of the Assembly's president were the ancien-regime loyalists among the clergy and the aristocrats. They were against civil rights for Jews for a combination of reasons. There was the old doctrinal reason—Jews were Christ killers who had called their crime down on the heads of their children. There was a pragmatic reason: Jews paid extortionate taxes that allowed some aristocrats to maintain their lifestyles. Then there was pure and simple Jew hatred. The right had enough legislative skill to keep a debate off the agenda.

In the middle, and veering by degrees to the left of the Assembly's president, sat Grégoire, Mirabeau, and the other leaders of the campaign for equal rights. They had to bide their time, waiting for a moment to slip the issue onto the agenda. Finally, as Christmas 1789 approached they found their opening.

The Declaration of the Rights of Man and of the Citizen was a statement of universal, inalienable principles, but "rights are not laws." Could everyone legally enjoy the civil rights of "active" citizenship, as the National Assembly's members called it? An "active" citizen—a man of twenty-five years or older who paid tax—was in theory eligible for all public employment and municipal offices. He could practice law, become a magistrate or a government bureaucrat, be elected to legislative bodies, and serve in the army. In the old regime there were some who met these qualifications but who were forbidden by law to perform these functions. Non-Catholics, actors, and public executioners were not allowed to serve in public offices. The advocates of Emancipation saw this issue as the way to sneak the discussion of Jewish rights out of committee and finally get a full debate onto the floor of the Assembly.

Late on the evening of December 21 the skirmishing began. The topic came up sideways. The law barring Protestants from the rights of "active" citizens, including the right to serve in legislative bodies, had been changed in 1787 but in many provinces of France it was ignored. Brunet de Latuque, a left-leaning lawyer, proposed that the Assembly clarify the situation by adopting a decree that any "non-Catholic" meeting the conditions of eligibility be allowed to run for election to the National Assembly. The members of the Assembly knew what this debate was really about and they began to get agitated. The ordinary citizens in the back of the hall began to get agitated as well.

By now the National Assembly had moved to Paris from the suburb of Versailles and settled into the Manège, a former riding academy, at the Tuileries Palace, adjacent to the Louvre. Throughout the Revolution, the Paris theaters remained open but the most popular show in town was the National Assembly. People flocked to watch the daily improvisational drama that was the birth of their nation. They crowded the back of the hall, poked their heads through windows, kept their ears cocked to hear what they could of the debates inside. In the chamber itself, on an elevated platform, sat whoever held the legislative body's rotating presidency, along with his secretaries. The focus of the drama was the tribune, a pulpit, from which the great set speeches were made. According to the order of the day's agenda, the president would summon a speaker who then made his way through his colleagues, ascended the steps, and faced the president. For those with an innate sense of theater it was a ritual to be milked.

The tribune was where the Revolution's stars were born. The acoustics in the halls where the Assembly met were abysmal, but the Manège was the worst. It was a long, narrow rectangle with the tribune in the middle facing the president. Speakers had to have swivel necks and voices like professional actors if they wanted their speeches to be heard around the vast space. Abbé Grégoire had that skill. He was a veteran of the pulpit and so commanded attention whenever he spoke. Mirabeau was another.

Count Clermont-Tonnerre also possessed this skill and now,

from the tribune, he tried to quickly move discussion on Brunet de Latuque's motion to a conclusion, proposing the French Constitution have a clause mandating that no active citizen meeting conditions of eligibility be excluded from public employment because of "the profession he practices or the religion he professes."

If the liberal count thought he could slip something past the Assembly's members he was wrong. "Let me ask you to be clear," said Jean-François Reubell, a lawyer from Alsace. "Are you talking about the Jews?"

"Yes," answered the count. "And I glory in the fact."

"I think of the Jews as they think of themselves. They don't think they are citizens," answered Reubell, who then turned to the rest of the Assembly. "I support Clermont-Tonnerre's amendment because they are excluded from it by the phrase active 'citizens.'"

A wave of incoherent noise swelled inside the Manège, starting with supporters of Emancipation shouting at Reubell. Partisans of the right yelled back and kept yelling. They wanted to prevent any discussion of the Jewish Question. Civility had gone to bed. It was two in the morning; exhaustion had set in. There was other practical parliamentary business to attend to so a full discussion of Clermont-Tonnerre's motion was placed on the agenda for Wednesday, December 23.

On Wednesday, after the opening business of the session—reports from the provinces on the creation of citizen militias—Count Clermont-Tonnerre was summoned to the tribune to make the case for his motion. By the standards of the Assembly, he came quickly to the point: "I have two objects to examine: exclusion because of profession, exclusion because of religion. Professions are either harmful or not. If they are, it is a crime the law can crack down on."

Clermont-Tonnerre spoke of executioners first. "Everything the law orders is good; she orders the death of a criminal, the executioner must obey the law. It is absurd that the law tell a man: do this, and if you do it you will be covered in infamy."

Then he moved on to actors. "These honest citizens present to us on the stage masterpieces of the human spirit, works full of sound philosophy, and so place these ideas in reach of all men and prepare the way to success for the revolution that we are carrying out and you would say to them . . . you are infamous?

"I condemn no man, nor proscribe any profession that the law does not expressly proscribe."

Then the count arrived at the real point of the session: Jewish civil rights. If you guarantee a man the right to worship as he pleases, can you deny him access to citizenship for exercising that right? he asked his fellow legislators. Clermont-Tonnerre reminded the Assembly again of the definition of freedom of conscience and that there should be no national religion, unless they wanted to tear up the Declaration of the Rights of Man and of the Citizen.

Then he moved on to specifics. "The reproaches against them are numerous. The worst are unjust, the others are not crimes," the count continued. "Usury, some say, is permitted by them," but so what? "These men possess only money and can do nothing but lend money because you have always forbidden them to do anything else."

But these were generalizations. It was time to stop thinking of the Jews as a group. The count called out, "We must refuse the Jews everything as a nation and grant them everything as individuals. They must become citizens . . . It is not possible to have a nation within the nation."

Alluding to the syndics, Clermont-Tonnerre reminded delegates that Jews already carried out the most important public functions, and alluding to Bordeaux Jews he reminded the Assembly that some had already run for election. Jews had joined the militias and taken up arms for the new France. "Jews are presumed citizens . . . In their requests they ask to be treated like everybody else. The law gives them that title, prejudice refuses it."

He was almost finished; he just needed to shame the Assembly to action. "You do the greatest wrong if you see the right course of action, and do not do it; if you know the truth and do not dare to speak it; because then what happens is that you place on the same throne prejudice and the law, error and reason."

The response from the right side of the chamber came from Abbé Maury. "It is impossible to employ greater talent and dialectical thinking than the previous speaker used to attack our principles," began the abbé. "So let us follow exactly the march of his reason; this is the route I trace."

And this the abbé proceeded to do, starting with the rights of executioners. Executioners being excluded from citizenship isn't prejudice, he explained. Cold-blooded killing of their fellow men is a choice and it attaches to their souls. As for actors, good moral behavior is the first law, and actors violate this law with their licentious behavior.

"Let us move on to an object of discussion more dignified for this assembly," the abbé continued. "I observe the word 'Jew' is not the name of a sect, but that of a nation, which has its law that it always follows and that it would continue to follow. To call the Jews citizens would be the same as, without letters of naturalization and without their ceasing to be English or Danish, allowing the English and Danish to become French."

Maury was the anti-Grégoire. They were roughly the same age and from approximately the same kind of background. They had both risen through the church on the basis of their writings and acknowledged brilliance in the pulpit. But where Grégoire had become the champion of society's excluded—Jews and the African slaves being worked to death in the French colony of Haiti—Maury had become the champion of ancien regime privileges. He was one of the most articulate blockers of progress in the National Assembly. And where Grégoire frequently reminded people of the almost two millennia of oppression and exclusion Jews had suffered, Maury now told the Assembly that the two millennia of tribulations they had endured was their own fault. Wherever they settled, the Jews never mingled with others. They always excluded themselves.

The reasons he offered for this exclusion were a catalogue of the old prejudices. "They" only traffic in money. "They" have a horror of getting their hands dirty in agriculture. It has always been this way, according to Maury, even in the times of King David and Solomon.

Why do "they" avoid this labor? Well, "they" have all those religious holidays. There is the Sabbath, "a really terrible day," in the abbé's words, an excuse for all manner of shirking. In addition to the Sabbath, they have fifty-six more religious festivals than Christians. How could they plant and bring in a crop with so many days off?

"Can you make them into soldiers?" he asked. "I don't know any general in the world who would wish to command an army of Jews on their Sabbath. They never fight on that day.

"Would you let them be artisans? Their many religious festivals and the Sabbath are insurmountable obstacles."

On and on he spoke. If they are allowed to own property in Alsace, within a month they will own half the province. There is an inherent threat to civil order in allowing Jews out of their ghettos, because the people in Alsace already have a profound, uncontrollable hatred of them. For the Jews' own safety they must remain in the ghetto. "They must not be persecuted: they are men, they are our brothers; and anathema to anyone who speaks of them intolerantly . . . They have been placed under your protection as individuals, not as Frenchmen, seeing that they must never be citizens."

Maury finished by clarifying a point. In speaking about one religious minority, he didn't want to confuse them with France's other minority, the Protestants. They are Christians after all, and should have the same rights as Catholics.

Maximilien Robespierre was recognized by the chair and attacked Maury's basic assertions: "You say things about the Jews that are infinitely exaggerated and often contradicted by history. Jews are born in the degradation you have plunged them into. I think you cannot deprive any individual of any class the sacred rights given to all men."

"The Jews have, without doubt, grievances that need to be redressed," responded La Fare, bishop of Nancy. "They should be given protection, security and liberty; but would you admit into the family a tribe that is a stranger to you? Who never cease to turn their eyes to another country and aspire to leave the land that supports them?"

Then there are the more than one hundred days a year they do no work at all as they celebrate their religious festivals.

The bishop took up Abbé Maury's point about the Jews' safety in Alsace and Lorraine and added into it the idea that public order in those provinces could not be guaranteed if the motion passed, so great was the hatred of Jews: "A decree giving Jews the rights of citizens would ignite a conflagration." Let's not consider the Jewish Question in this way, the bishop suggested. Let's form a committee to look at all laws concerning them.

"It is absolutely necessary to take part," shouted a voice over on the left side of the chamber. Adrien Duport could not contain himself. "If some nation came and mixed with us, and if it demanded for its individual members the right of French citizens wouldn't you welcome this request? The Jewish nation is precisely in this case."

Duport was yet another of the renegade aristocrats among the Revolution's leaders. He had founded one of the main clubs where revolutionary talk flourished—Hourwitz had sent him a copy of his Metz essay there and Duport had read it with interest. Since the establishment of the constitutional National Assembly he had established himself as a legislative organizer of the left. Duport had an idea for moving the vote on civil rights past the blockers over on the right side. He proposed a change in wording to Clermont-Tonnerre's original motion. "Let's simply reinforce the principle," he suggested, "without mentioning form of worship or profession." His amendment called for any person born in France to be given citizenship and eligibility for public offices. Clermont-Tonnerre happily accepted the change.

As the debate rocked back and forth, between speakers from the left side of the Assembly and those of the right, it became clear that what was at stake was more than the rights of a tiny, despised minority. The Jewish Question was now part of the deeper ideological struggle between conservatives and radicals over the role of religion in the new France. The radical left wanted the church to have no political role in the state, while the hard-liners on the right wanted to preserve the Catholic Church's place at the heart of government as well as guarantee that the taxpayer would pay its priests' salaries. Both sides wanted to win this point for their own sake, to confirm their power in the Assembly.

In the corridors outside the chamber the anti-Emancipation forces vigorously lobbied delegates. Inside the chamber their rhetoric grew more heated. "Jews have the ability to take over everything," declaimed the Bishop of Nancy. "If we give them rights then doubtless the day will come when they demand a Jew be named a bishop."

"This is a death warrant," roared Reubell. That was too much for many in the Assembly, who shouted back at the lawyer from Alsace until he could no longer be heard.

Calling out above the din someone demanded a vote. It was late. There were more than eight hundred members of the Assembly still present so the president ordered a simple stand-up, sit-down vote on Duport's amendment. Those in favor were called on to stand. But the vote was too close for the chair to clearly state if it had passed or not. The Manège was in an uproar. Those in favor were called on to rise again. Once more the chair could not tell which side had won. Reluctantly, amid the din, a roll call vote was conducted. One by one, names were called out and the votes recorded. In the best of circumstances calling a roll of eight hundred names would have taken a long time; in these circumstances it seemed endless. Finally, by a vote of 408 to 403, Duport's amendment was defeated. The legislators then went to bed. It was three-thirty in the morning.

If the weary participants thought that the discussion was over they were wrong. When they struggled back to the chamber a few hours later they still had to discuss Brunet de Latuque's original motion on equal rights for all active citizens. The tumult resumed. The actors of the Comédie Française presented a letter that was read into the record. Abbé Maury shouted, "This is the ultimate obscenity, that actors should be allowed to correspond directly with the Assembly." Jean-Nicolas Desmeunier, president of the session, called Maury to order, a polite way of telling him to shut up.

The actors were quickly forgotten as Reubell resumed his ranting against the Jews. The Bishop of Clermont, always reasonable even when aiding prejudice, referred to the previous evening's rejection of Duport's amendment. It was clear the Assembly felt there was no problem with guaranteeing Protestants equal rights with Catholics but they did not feel these rights should be extended to Jews. Why not take the Jews out of the equation and put it to a vote? So an amendment to Latuque's motion was agreed. The wording was changed from "non-Catholics" to "non-Catholic Christians" being guaranteed the rights of active citizens.

Clermont-Tonnerre and others demanded more discussion about Jewish rights. But overnight something had changed in the liberal camp. The defeat of Duport's motion, close as it was, made clear the votes did not yet exist to grant Jews full civil rights. Albert de Beaumetz, a liberal aristocrat, proposed a way out of the impasse. Have a vote on the rights of Protestants, actors, and executioners and add an amendment to the present motion noting the Jews' desire to be considered full citizens, eligible for all municipal offices. "It is necessary before pronouncing on this long suffering people," he argued, "to know at what price it wished to obtain its liberty and, finally, if it is worthy of receiving it."

Beaumetz's amendment stated clearly that the current vote should not prejudice a future decision on their request.

Finally, Mirabeau stood up to speak. After the vote in the early hours, the leaders of Paris's Jews had hastily dashed off another letter to the Assembly urging the group to "consult its accustomed justice," ignore the blandishments of some members, and reverse their decision. The count read parts of their letter into the record but it was merely a gesture of goodwill. Mirabeau understood the meaning of the previous evening's roll call. There simply weren't enough votes to pass legislation granting Jews equal rights. In his big, growling voice Mirabeau reluctantly endorsed Beaumetz's amendment to Latuque's motion. The National Assembly voted in favor of it and the king immediately signed it into law.

• • •

One voice missing from these pre-Christmas debates was that of Grégoire. Ironically, his constant proselytizing for Emancipation had made him a liability to the cause. The right-wing press had taken to calling him Rabbi Grégoire, and that was the kindest thing they had to say about him. The abbé's participation might have inflamed even greater anti-Jewish sentiments. So he stayed silent.

## iii.
## Divided

The defeat of Duport's amendment and the Assembly's decision to delay any decision on civil rights cracked the thin veneer of unity between the Sephardic and Ashkenazic communities. From the beginning of the Revolution the Sephardim in Bordeaux, Bayonne, Avignon, and Paris had feared that the desire of the Ashkenazim in Alsace and Lorraine to maintain communal autonomy would be a roadblock to full equality. Back in August they had written to Grégoire noting this. Now, as the Bordeaux syndics looked at the reports of the debate, they knew this had been a reason for the defeat, perhaps not the main one, but a useful cover for the hatred motivating the anti-Emancipation vote. They decided the time had come to go it alone.

These "Portuguese" Jews' existing royal letters patent effectively gave them the rights of active citizens. On December 31 they submitted an address to the constitution committee of the National Assembly asking that it recognize this fact. The committee assigned the Bishop of Autun, Talleyrand, to read it and report back.

As the weeks passed the liberal Paris press kept the Jewish Question alive. In the defeat of one battle at the National Assembly the newspapers saw the glimmering of a victory for the whole campaign. The liberal newspapers had long identified the right-wing clergy as blockers of revolutionary progress on a wide range of issues. But even with the extra weapon of blind prejudice in their hands, the clergy had only narrowly won on this vote. The lesson the papers took from this was that the right did not possess the strength to undo the Revolution. So they continued to campaign for Jewish rights, hoping to get another chance to challenge the clergy and this time defeat them.

The *Chronique de Paris* chose the week after the vote to run a review of Zalkind Hourwitz's Metz essay. Though the essay had been published more than six months previously, the paper's editors urged their readers to buy it, read it, and learn for themselves how little separated them from their Jewish brothers.

Behind the scenes, the syndics of Alsace and Lorraine, determined not to be left behind by the Bordeaux Jews, organized an intense lobbying campaign. The most eloquent of them, Berr Isaac Berr, wrote directly to Abbé Maury asking him to consider whether his positions made sense in the modern world. It was a fruitless exercise. The abbé would not change his mind. The leaders consulted with a young lawyer named Jacques Godard about writing a legal brief to present to the National Assembly in the hopes of keeping their request for equal rights alive. They held increasingly fraught meetings with the Sephardic syndics to argue for a united front. Finally, they begged Talleyrand to postpone his report until Godard's brief was ready. The bishop would not.

On January 28, Talleyrand ascended the tribune and presented his report to the National Assembly on the request of the Bordeaux Jews. Talleyrand, like many senior churchmen, had been born into a noble family. He was more aristocrat than bishop and more liberal than most who came from his background. His committee had decided that based on the fact that every French king for two hundred and fifty years had issued letters patent stating they should be "treated and regarded" like all other subjects born in France, the Jews of Bordeaux, as well as those of Bayonne and Avignon, could continue to enjoy their long-standing privileges. That wasn't a terribly controversial conclusion to reach. But what Talleyrand said to end his presentation was. He added, "The constitutional committee, without prejudging the wider question of the state of the Jews in general," had decided the Bordeaux Jews were "active citizens."

Uproar returned to the Manège. Reubell was recognized by the chair but before he could begin to spout his usual litany of hatred he was shouted down. Those speakers who managed to make themselves heard did not have time to orate with the same elegance as those who took part in the December debate. The crowd was too unruly, and besides, the issue here wasn't the grand philosophy of equality, fraternity, and civil rights but whether old royal letters patent would have meaning in the new constitutional monarchy the Assembly was trying to build. The Assembly demanded the letters patent be read out loud. They were.

Abbé Maury then weighed in. He was in a difficult position. As a staunch royalist he did not want to rescind letters patent granted by the king; on the other hand he understood that if these documents were interpreted as giving the rights of "active citizens" to one group of Jews it would open the door for the same rights to eventually be extended to all of them.

Suddenly, the precise wording of the motion overwhelmed the legislators. Specificity became the theme. How many Jews are we allowing to be active citizens? Is this an amendment just for those of Bordeaux? What about Bayonne? Avignon? Dozens of amendments to Talleyrand's simple motion were proposed, involving such minute changes of language that only a lawyer could understand their import. The National Assembly had more than its share of them. Lost in the flurry of activity was any sense of the larger, moral question about the rights of the human beings whose future was being subamended and turned into legal clauses.

Finally, Abbé Grégoire joined the debate. He demanded the decree apply to all "Portuguese, Spanish and Avignonnais" Jews. Then he added, "As for the German Jews, I demand an adjournment to a fixed date when I propose to refute the false reasoning of Abbé Maury."

Now it was time to put the various amendments to the vote. The decision on each amendment was accompanied by massive disruption as the right side of the Assembly tried to force a suspension of the session. They failed. The Assembly was on the verge of becoming a mob when Raymond de Sèze, a representative from Bordeaux, proposed a vote on the key issue, demanding for his Jewish constituents the "rights of active citizens."

It was December all over again. Those in favor were called on to stand. The result was unclear. Again those in favor were called on to stand. Still unclear. A roll call was demanded. The voice of the secretary calling out names was drowned out by shouting originating from the right side of the chamber as anti-Emancipation delegates tried to prevent a vote. They almost succeeded. Amid the noise, an accurate count was almost impossible to keep. Time was lost while the president repeatedly tried to bring the Assembly to order. The spectators at the back of the Manège joined in the screaming. The roll call was started twenty times and completely disrupted by the right wing, until finally, the president of the session, the left-winger Guy-Jean Target, told them forcefully the vote would go ahead no matter how hard they tried to stop it.

In the chaos, small groups from the right side began to leave the chamber. They hoped to end the session simply by walking out on it. The tactic didn't work. Fewer than half the members of the Assembly ultimately answered the roll call but the motion was passed, 373 to 225. The rights of the Bordeaux Jews as active citizens were confirmed.

The same day, Berr Isaac Berr, Cerf Berr, and other syndics from Alsace and Lorraine submitted their petition. "Our principal demands are the same as those of the Bordeaux Jews," the legal brief stated. "The difference is they asked to conserve [rights], we ask to gain them." The petition ran to 107 pages when it was printed. It attempted, yet again, to answer all the charges against Jews as aliens in the French body politic, unworthy of equal rights.

But it was a wasted effort. The arguments in favor of civil rights for their community had been made many times and made eloquently. If their advocates inside the Assembly hadn't convinced the other deputies by now with reason and appeals to their better angels, they never would. There would be no single moment when the Assembly rose on a tide of fraternal goodwill and embraced their long-suffering neighbors as equals. The success of the Bordeaux Jews showed that gaining civil rights, Emancipation, and release from the ghetto would be a process of individual groups of Jews chipping away at prejudice to win their citizenship in the new France.

## iv.
# A Long Campaign

Zalkind Hourwitz was enraged and despondent. He had ardently embraced the Revolution. Hourwitz had been among the first to join the newly formed national guard and had even published an article on maintaining password security among its units in Paris. But the debates and decisions made in the National Assembly in December and January had shown him he was willing to die for a country that would not grant him the basic rights of a citizen.

In the *Chronique de Paris,* one of several newspapers he wrote for regularly, he published a lengthy letter on his situation. As a guardsman he had pledged his fidelity to the new France, but to what end? "With the oath I have taken, I have promised to uphold a constitution which has as its foundation the Rights of Man. Yet that very same constitution deprives the Rights of Man to all men who pray to the Supreme Being in Hebrew, and who are born outside of Bordeaux and Avignon."

He might have turned his back on the whole revolutionary process and lived inside his "nation within the nation," but he could not and would not go back into the ghetto world and submit to what he considered the tyranny of the rabbis. Zalkind Hourwitz was a rebel son of the world of Ashkenaz and lived in the same precarious zone of isolated individualism as Spinoza had.

His temperament did not permit him to be a leader. Even his friends noted that the bitterness and irony in his writing was an extension of his personality. He was not an easy man to like, much less follow. But he was a man of tremendous energy, an organizer and proselytizer, so Hourwitz threw himself into political organizing in Paris. Luckily for him, Paris, then as now, saw itself as the vanguard of France; its residents were radical and keen to drive the Revolution forward. Thus his message found a responsive audience.

On January 28, and not by coincidence, as the National Assembly tore itself apart deciding the fate of the Bordeaux Jews, the Commune, the revolutionary city government of Paris, met to discuss the rights of the capital's Jews.

As the syndics from the east were at the Manège placing their latest petition before the Assembly, the man who helped them write it, Jacques Godard, was with Zalkind Hourwitz at the Hotel de Ville, the city hall, making a lengthy presentation to the Commune's general assembly on the subject. Over the previous month it had become clear to Hourwitz and Godard that Emancipation would be a piecemeal process. Paris was already inclined to grant rights to the Jews so the pair organized a campaign to get the city's government to give Jews active citizenship. If the capital's government did this, they reasoned, it would force the National Assembly to do the same.

As Godard began his address, he pointed to a delegation of the city's Ashkenazic Jews who were in attendance. They were led by Hourwitz. By now Hourwitz was well-known in the city. The Metz victory had made him almost famous. His work in the national guard brought him face to face with a wide range of people who might not read the newspapers but who warmed to his ardent revolutionary views. Godard reminded the Commune's official that of the five hundred Jews in Paris, one hundred had already joined the guard. What greater proof is required of this people's fidelity to France and her revolution, the lawyer asked? He asked that the Commune recognize Hourwitz and his comrades' rights to active citizenship.

The president of the Commune was a liberal clergyman, Abbé Mulot, who was fulsome in his praise for the project. Paris was divided into districts and the Commune decided to let each district have a vote on the issue, with a report on the result sent to the National Assembly.

For the next three weeks, in the bitter winter weather, Hourwitz and Godard toured each of Paris's sixty districts rallying support for Jewish rights. Even as he went to meeting after meeting, Hourwitz kept a stream of articles flowing to the local papers. By the time the campaign was over only one of the city's districts had refused to endorse Jewish rights.

Buoyed by this endorsement, a delegation from the Commune appeared before the National Assembly on February 25 to report on the Paris districts' desire that the capital's Jews be given the same rights as those of Bordeaux, Bayonne, and Avignon. But Hourwitz and Godard, like Parisians to this day, overestimated the importance of the capital in shaping the nation's policies. Their presentation was received cordially, but then the Assembly passed on to other business without giving it a second thought.

Emancipation didn't completely disappear from the agenda. About once a month someone would bring up the Jews. Maury or Reubell would make a short, sarcastic speech, and with a collective shrug the Assembly would move on to another question.

Hourwitz carried on his campaign with his pen. He publicly challenged Maury to reconcile his bigotry with his faith: "I can only explain your conduct by assuming that you are ignorant of the principles of your religion. Learn them. They reduce themselves to the following: love your neighbor as yourself, your country more than your private gain and consider as a brother, Zalkind Hourwitz, Jew."

Maury did not reply.

There was a moment in July 1790 when the Jewish issue forced its way onto the Assembly's agenda and another little piece of the ghetto wall was chipped away. Taxation obsessed the writers of the French Constitution. Public finances had precipitated the Revolution and so building a new regime meant constant discussion about who was now going to pay the bills. Setting a uniform tax code was easier said than done. In Metz, the Duke of Brancas lived well on the "protection" tax paid to him by the city's Jews. That sort of special levy had no place in the new regime, first of all because it was unfair to the national treasury, and second because in the new regime the state provided protection for all people living within its boundaries, not local aristocrats.

A committee of the National Assembly presented a report urging the abolition of the Brancas tax as well as all other taxes on Jews for "the right to live, protection and tolerance" anywhere else in France. The report was accepted by an almost unanimous voice vote. The sole dissent came from Jean-François Reubell. The lawyer from Alsace was one of the oddest birds in the Assembly. He was a radical, a member of the Jacobin club, and sat on the left of the Assembly. His Jacobin colleagues, such as Robespierre, were among the most forceful advocates for Jewish equality, yet Reubell remained the most bigoted and hate-filled opponent of Emancipation. But he was far from a stupid man. He was a lawyer of considerable legal skill and was able to find in any language aimed at ameliorating the Jews' condition the threat of a precedent that would lead to greater rights for this group he so hated.

Before the decree could be read into the record, he asked for the right to put forward a question: If the Jews were no longer going to pay this special tax, what tax would they pay? They would pay the same taxes as other citizens, came the answer from a Monsieur DuPont. The speaker had fallen into Reubell's lawyerly trap. The Jews are not citizens, so why should they pay? If you let them pay the same tax as everyone else, aren't you de facto giving them citizenship? was the point Reubell was making.

By now Reubell's constant harping on about the Jews had alienated the Assembly and the decree was passed. But in a perverse way, Reubell was right: another step toward equality had been granted to the Jews of the east. They now had the right to pay the same taxes as everyone else in France.

Months passed and then a year was gone. The task of writing the constitution was coming to an end. The process, begun in revolutionary optimism, had devolved into a strained, faction-ridden slog. Mirabeau was dead, and many aristocrats had fled the country and were agitating for a war on France to overthrow the Revolution. The king was now living under house arrest at the Tuileries.

Finally, on September 3, 1791, the Assembly presented the new Constitution of France to its king. The document's first guarantee was "all citizens are admissible to offices and employments, without any distinction other than virtue and talents."

There remained some weeks of legislative business tying up loose ends before the constitutional Assembly dissolved itself so a new legislative Assembly could be elected. On September 27, with no preamble, Adrien Duport asked for the floor and gave a brief speech: "I believe freedom of worship does not allow for any distinction in political rights among citizens because of their beliefs. The question of the Jews was adjourned . . . I demand that adjournment be revoked and, as a consequence, it be decided that the Jews of France enjoy the rights of active citizens." The National Assembly must issue a decree to that effect, Duport said.

Duport was a skilled legislative tactician. He understood there was no time left. Assembly members' attention was elsewhere and the fate of the Jews of the east was too important an issue to leave unresolved. Now was the time to quickly push full Emancipation over the finish line. After Duport finished his speech there was a loud round of cheering and calls for an immediate vote.

Reubell, shaken, overtaken by surprise, tried to intervene to demand a full debate. A supporter of Duport, Michel de Saint-Jean-d'Angely, asked the chair to call Reubell and anyone else to order who spoke against the motion, "since to speak against it is to speak against the constitution itself."

Duport's motion passed by a wide margin.

But legislating away prejudice is never so simple. The next day, as part of the Assembly's usual opening business, a vote to approve of the minutes of the previous session, including the endorsement of Duport's motion, was brought to the floor. The Prince de Broglie demanded the right to speak. Before the minutes were endorsed he insisted on an amendment to the decree moved by Duport. All citizens had to take an oath of loyalty, and therefore the law should state, said Broglie, that when a Jew takes the oath it should be considered a formal renunciation of his adherence to Jewish communal law. The legislators, keen to get on with the day's work, hastily agreed.

Then Reubell jumped in. He had another amendment. The Jews of Alsace must provide a thorough accounting of the money owed them, and the local authorities should have the authority to decide how much of the money would be paid. This amendment was added. Then another deputy, Dubois-Crancé, demanded that on the same principle all Negroes be regarded as free citizens when they enter France. This was also added to Duport's motion. Finally, with the burden of a few extra words, Duport's motion passed once more. The National Assembly decreed that all the Jews of France now had equal rights to active citizenship. They were emancipated.

It was too much for Reubell, who stood up again to demand the right to speak. One of his colleagues on the left couldn't take it anymore and reached over, clapped his hand across the lawyer's mouth, and shoved him back into his seat.

That night, Berr Isaac Berr wrote a letter to his coreligionists. From a distance of centuries and with knowledge of how much struggle and horror lay ahead, it is hard to see the process of legislating Emancipation as anything other than grudging. But for the syndic of Nancy, who had worked so hard behind the scenes, and who knew well the men inside the Assembly on both sides of the issue, it was a day when finally everything seemed possible. Berr was proud of his country and focused happily on the future. He savored his new title, "Citizen," with the same relish as if he had been made a duke. He called his message: "Letter of a Citizen, member of the former Jewish community of Lorraine, to his Brothers on the occasion of the right of active Citizen being rendered to Jews by the decree of 28 September 1791."

Citizens of the same country, no longer a separate community, it was time to make up for eighteen hundred years of separate second-class status wherever they had lived, he told his confreres. Berr began by thanking God for the happy change he had wrought: "The name of 'active citizen' that we have obtained is without contradiction the most precious quality a man can possess in a free country."

Despite the intent behind it, Berr urged his fellows to take the citizenship oath. He invoked Mendelssohn and encouraged them to study the language and customs of their fellow Frenchmen. He outlined a broad program that would lead to assimilation without surrendering their Jewish religious identity. Don't lose a minute, let the work begin, the syndic wrote. He signed the letter, "A Jew, Active Citizen."

## v.
## Terror

The Emancipation decree was one of the last acts of the National Assembly. The constitution the deputies had labored over for two years would not last long. Pressures from without and within were twisting the Revolution in a new direction. First, the king lost his head and then the radicals seized control. The fight between the left and the right over the power of the church was no longer a parliamentary one with Jewish rights as a proxy battleground. The fight was real and bloody and heads were rolling.

The radical left waged war on organized religion. Abbé Maury fled for his life before he could be dragged to the guillotine. The Protestant pastor and the early proponent of Jewish rights, Rabaut de Saint-Etienne, was not so lucky. The Jacobins seized the nation's churches, emptied them of their precious ornaments, and turned the buildings into Temples of Reason, where, in a gross perversion of Spinoza, nature and natural religion were worshipped. Jews were equal citizens now, so their synagogues were similarly desecrated. The synagogue in Metz was turned into a barn and its grounds became a pasture for the animals kept there.

Grégoire, by now the bishop of Blois, survived the Reign of Terror.

So did Zalkind Hourwitz. However, there is no record that they ever met. The pair wrote voluminously, yet never mentioned the other. Still, they must have encountered each other and been friends. Paris was not that big and they were involved in many of the same activities and knew the same people. But it is possible they did not have much conversation when they did meet. They worked at opposite ends of the political world: Hourwitz in the street and Grégoire in the highest reaches of the government. Perhaps there was lingering rivalry over the Metz contest; sharing first place is not an easy thing to do. Perhaps Hourwitz took Grégoire to task for some of his more egregious comments about Jews, such as the one about Jewesses being inclined to nymphomania. Perhaps Grégoire took offense at the sarcastic way in which the criticism had been offered.

Emancipation survived the Terror as well. It would be one of the ideals exported as the Revolution became subsumed by the genius and mania of the next great figure that emerged from its cauldron: Napoleon Bonaparte.

## CHAPTER SIX

# I Shall Maintain
# Your Freedom

IN THE GHETTO OF ANCONA, A PORT CITY ON THE ADRIATIC coast of Italy, the Jews knew their liberation was at hand and they were afraid. For months Napoleon Bonaparte and his army had been rampaging through the north, bringing the French Revolution to Italy. In Turin and Milan, Napoleon had battered open the ghetto gates.

Now, in early 1797, the general was approaching Ancona. As news of Napoleon's conquering army spread, the citizens of the principalities and medieval towns of Italy turned on the small number of Jews in their midst with fury. In Ancona, the violence was murderous. The city was part of the Papal States, a belt of central Italy controlled by the Vatican. The French Army's assault on Ancona was a direct attack on the pope. Mobs attacked the city's Jews so they barricaded themselves behind the ghetto gates at the bottom of the Via Astagna and waited in fear for their liberation.

Ancona sits on a steep knob of land that juts into the warm, placid Adriatic Sea. The topography creates a sheltered harbor for ships, and for centuries Ancona had been a major trading center. For Napoleon,

Ancona was a strategic prize, a mere ten days sailing to Constantinople. So he sat with his army in the miserable, rainy February weather and slowly strangled the city's resistance. It would fall, no doubt, like a tree to a blunt ax, but there would be no glory. The general wrote to his wife, Josephine, that he had never been "so bored as by this sorry campaign."

In Ancona, there was a sizable Jewish community engaged in trade from one end of the Mediterranean to the other. The ghetto was the typical, formless warren of narrow lanes laced around one proper street, the Via Astagna, running uphill from the port. The restrictions on its inhabitants were severe. Men were forced to wear a yellow badge on their caps to distinguish them even further from their neighbors.

By late February, Napoleon's troops had taken the city. A detachment of mostly Jewish soldiers was sent to the Via Astagna and went to work demolishing the ghetto gates. When the gates were gone they marched up the empty street. Slowly people began to come out and look at the soldiers. A soldier called out in Hebrew to one of the gawkers, "Come here." A gasp of surprise went through the growing crowd. "You Jewish?"

"Yes."

Jewish soldiers, in the uniform of France, a Christian country? Yes, one of the duties of "active citizenship" of a country is military service. It was too much for the ghetto's residents to comprehend. There was more chatter in Hebrew, then a soldier reached over and took the yellow badge off one of the ghetto dweller's caps, removed the red, white, and blue revolutionary cockade from his own hat and placed it where the badge had been. Another soldier repeated the gesture and then another. The Jews of Ancona were emancipated.

When the dust had settled, the bloodlust of the Terror satisfied and the last head cut off, France had found itself short of leaders. Someone with ambition and talent could rise quickly. In 1795, Napoleon Bonaparte, a young artillery commander on the make, put down a riot in Paris with particularly bloody efficiency. For this success, he was given command of the nation's southern army. France, a republic now, had enemies all around, and just over the Alps on the Italian peninsula the enemy was Austria. Italy in the eighteenth century was a collection of diverse city-states and principalities. In the northern part of the country many of these entities were controlled by what was left of the Holy Roman Empire, run by the Habsburgs, the royal family of Austria. In 1796, Napoleon decided to take the fight to them.

His daring military strategies brought immediate success. No less electrifying to the rest of Europe was the way he imposed his political will on the areas he conquered. A steady stream of directives issued from his command, reorganizing these territories on the principles of the Revolution, including the rights of man. It was as if Napoleon had memorized Rabaut de Saint-Etienne's declaration of 1789, "Nation of France you don't exist to receive examples, but to give examples to others."

After conquering the northern part of the peninsula he turned south into Tuscany and then turned his attention to the Papal States. The Revolution still regarded the church as its enemy and Napoleon wanted to bring the church to heel.

After liberating Ancona he turned to Rome. There the Jews were trapped in a ghetto in the marshy area between the Tiber and the Capitoline Hill. French troops once again tore down the doors and in a public ceremony planted a "Liberty Tree" in the piazza outside the synagogue. Then Napoleon turned north again and marched toward Venice, where the word *ghetto* was first used, and allowed its Jews out. In nearby Padua, he forced the city fathers themselves to tear down the ghetto doors and burn them. Then he ordered a declaration posted around the city: "First, the Hebrews are at liberty to live in any street they please. Second, the barbarous and meaningless name of Ghetto, which designates the street which they have been inhabiting hitherto, shall be substituted by that of Via Libera."

By now he was known among Italy's Jews as the Chelek Tov, Hebrew for "good part" or Bonaparte. They drank to his health and offered prayers for him. They sent delegations to his headquarters in

Milan with gifts and he sent them caring messages, such as "You are free men, you are free men . . . I shall maintain your freedom. Be strong, don't fear and don't worry."

It wasn't just in Italy that Jewish communities were liberated and granted their rights. Austria's tentacles reached across Europe, and when its rulers sued for peace in Italy Napoleon drove a hard bargain. He swapped Venice—he didn't need its port, he had Ancona—for control of Austrian territory in northern Europe. The west bank of the Rhine and the Low Countries were ceded to France by Austria and the Jews in those territories received their civil rights.

## ii.
## Jerusalem

With Italy conquered, in midsummer of 1798 Napoleon set sail for Egypt. There were strategic reasons for this—control of the eastern Mediterranean, a direct blow to the Ottoman Empire—but also psychological ones. Napoleon was not humble about his ability and the success he had enjoyed in Italy reinforced his self-belief. He had done what Hannibal had not, brought Rome to heel, and now he would follow in Alexander the Great's footsteps: conquer Egypt and then look even farther east to India.

The campaign in Egypt initially went as well as the one in Italy had. In a matter of weeks his army marched from Alexandria to take Cairo at the Battle of the Pyramids. As in Italy he was hoping to bring modern principles of political organization to the country. Napoleon summoned the leaders of Egypt's Jewish community and appointed two high priests; he gave them wide authority to reorganize their community. The use of the biblical term *high priest* rather than *rabbi* was intentional. Napoleon had answered the Jewish Question for himself. In his view the Jews were a nation as much as a religious group. In biblical times, when they had their own country the Israelites' senior clergy were called high priests rather than rabbis. Now they were stateless but he was convinced they could be allies in his conquest of the region, perhaps by holding out to the region's Jews the prospects of being restored as rulers of Palestine, the Holy Land long under the rule of the Ottoman Empire.

Then things began to go wrong. An English fleet arrived under the command of Admiral Horatio Nelson and defeated Napoleon's navy at the Battle of the Nile. In Damascus, an army was raised to retake Egypt from the European interloper, so the general decided to march into Palestine to meet it head-on. And it was along the Mediterranean coast of Palestine that the general's extraordinary three-year run of success ground to a halt. At the gates of Acre, his army got bogged down in a long siege.

In addition to his brilliance on the battlefield and his energy as an organizer, Napoleon was a relentless propagandizer. He made sure that news of his achievements reached France via the pages of the *Moniteur Universel* newspaper. His letters and proclamations were frequently published there. On May 22, 1799, the *Moniteur* ran a short news item datelined Constantinople: "News of a proclamation of General Bonaparte to Jews in which he calls on them to rally to his colors and raise up the walls of Jerusalem."

Napoleon was not a Zionist before the word had been invented. The proclamation was another example of the conqueror as political organizer. The man only expected success and the political officers on his staff always had directives and proclamations prepared in advance wherever he went so as to bring order quickly out of the chaos of conquest. Anticipating victory, it suited him to have local Jews as his allies, so he published the proclamation.

But nothing ever came of the call for a return to Jerusalem. Napoleon was forced to withdraw militarily from Palestine without entering the holy city. Then, for political reasons, he had to leave Egypt. France was a mess again. In the decade since the overthrow of the Bastille there had been four legislative bodies and one bloody Reign of Terror. The country was becoming ungovernable; certainly it was not capable of maintaining order in the territories Napoleon had conquered in Italy. The general needed to go home and sort out the domestic chaos.

## iii.
## The Great Sanhedrin

Like the passing of the seasons, a rhythm settled across Europe of war, truce, treaty. Each treaty brought France more territory, and as lands fell under French control the ghetto gates were thrown open.

Napoleon changed with these repeated cycles. He went from republican servant of the Revolution to consul to emperor. France loved him, Europe feared him. He became used to having his way. Now he was fed up with the Jews.

In late 1805 he defeated the combined armies of Austria and Russia at the Battle of Austerlitz. As he made a triumphal return back to France he passed through Alsace. Stopping in Strasbourg, he heard endless complaints about the Jews. The grumbling was on the old themes: Jewish usurers extorted interest from the peasants; the Jews refused to integrate, and instead maintained their own customs and laws. The leaders of Alsace and Lorraine wanted new laws imposed on the Jews to control what they considered their rapacity.

The emperor was troubled by all this. It was fifteen years since the National Assembly had granted the Jews their full civil rights. The hope had been that the community would cease to be a separate nation within the nation. Even in the view of supporters like Grégoire and the writers of the *Mercure de France,* this had not happened yet. Now Napoleon wanted to know why the Jews, as he saw it, had failed to integrate.

It wasn't entirely true, of course. Young French Jews had entered the schools and were being educated side by side with their Christian counterparts but the seeds of that contact had yet to bear fruit. Jews continued to lend money at interest, particularly in Alsace. Many had taken advantage of their new right to own property and had replaced the feudal overseers as the local landlords. Finally, as France lurched from revolutionary crisis to crisis, it was often unclear who was in control of law and order. In the absence of this, the Ashkenazic rabbis maintained legal authority within the community. This gave some credence to the old "nation within the nation" charge. So the emperor decided the time had come to bring administration of the Jewish religion under the auspices of the French government.

There was a precedent for this state interference in religious affairs. In 1801 Napoleon had reorganized the relationship between revolutionary France and the Catholic Church. The "Concordat" acknowledged that Catholicism was the majority religion in France—without infringing the rights of other religions. The French government reserved the right to appoint bishops and to otherwise organize the church's relationship with the state. The Protestant religion had also been brought under the government's wing.

Now Napoleon decided to do the same thing with the Jewish religion. The syndics and rabbis were not averse to this, since it would put their religion on equal bureaucratic footing with their Christian counterparts. But first the emperor had a few questions he wanted answered about Jewish religious practice and how it influenced the customs of Jewish society. In the summer of 1806, he summoned an "Assembly of Notables" from the community and presented them twelve questions. In February 1807 they reconvened with their answers. Napoleon renamed the group the "Great Sanhedrin." It suited the emperor's ego to claim he had reconvened a body that had not existed since the Roman emperor Titus had destroyed the Second Temple.

The twelve questions the seventy-one men of the Sanhedrin had to answer show how little France's rulers had learned about the community in the previous two decades. The first question was "Are Jews allowed to have several wives?" and the next few questions related to marriage and divorce, critically, "Can Jewesses marry Christians?" and vice versa.

Then came questions on patriotism, among others: "In the eyes of the Jews, are Frenchmen their brothers or strangers?" "Jews born in

France and treated by law as citizens: do they regard France as their country? Do they feel obligated to defend her? Are they obliged to follow her laws and the civil code?"

There were factual inquiries about the role of the rabbis in enforcing law inside the community, and then the concluding questions: "Does Jewish law prohibit usury with their brothers?" "Does it prohibit or permit usury with strangers?"

There was nothing new in these inquiries. It was as if all the questions asked and answered by the Metz essays of Grégoire and Hourwitz were being rehashed not for a gold prize but so that a bureaucratic system could be put in place.

The Sanhedrin convened in the Salle Saint-Jean at the Hotel de Ville. The questions may have been demeaning but the room where the deliberations took place was suitably grand, with exceptionally high ceilings supported by rows of classical columns. The group sat at a vast hemispherical table. The Great Sanhedrin was comprised of the syndics and main rabbis. France had gone through revolution, terror, and imperial conquest but the leadership of the Jewish community remained unchanged. Berr Isaac Berr was there, among others who had attended sessions of the National Assembly back in 1789. Berr's son Michel was also a member. Those who had died since the Emancipation debates, such as Cerf Berr, were also represented by their sons. The drive for Emancipation had always been an initiative of this hierarchy; they were not surrendering their seats at the high table now. Zalkind Hourwitz was not there, although he hovered in the background. Over the decades he had offended too many of those seated around the table and he was not invited. However, he was not a man to take part in this kind of assembly even if he had been asked.

The members of the Sanhedrin took their work seriously and the answers provided to the emperor were straightforward and backed by biblical citations.

On the questions related to marriage they were quick to point out that regardless of polygamy being permitted in biblical times, the community tried always to conform to the customs and morals of the countries where they lived, so there was no polygamy. As for divorce, they desired to establish a harmonization between religious law and the French Civil Code. In the case of intermarriage they parsed the difference, saying a marriage between a Jew and a Christian under the Civil Code would be legal under the Civil Code even if it weren't recognized by Jewish religious authorities.

The questions of patriotism were all answered unambiguously. Those born in France and Italy were regarded as citizens and they owed the state all the duties of citizens: defending it and obeying its laws. The questions on who controlled the organization of Jewish worship were deferred. Unlike the Catholic Church, there was no clear hierarchy, so a committee was appointed to make suggestions on establishing a bureaucratic process of appointing rabbis.

The critical questions for Napoleon, however, referred to the way members of the community earned their money. There was nothing in the Bible prohibiting Jews from any profession or craft, the leaders assured the emperor. As for usury, the controversy stemmed from a mistranslation of a Hebrew word in chapter 23, verse 19 of Deuteronomy. When an individual in the community needs a loan as a form of charity it is forbidden to take interest. This is the origin of the charge that Jews don't charge each other interest on loans. But there is a difference between that charitable act and a commercial transaction. The Holy Book clearly states that a person can charge anyone a "legitimate" rate of interest in business. Usury is frowned on for all. The state, the Sanhedrin suggested, should fix an interest rate that is fair to both lender and borrower.

With the answers in hand, Napoleon and his ministers went away to formulate a policy. On March 17, 1808, three decrees regulating Jewish life were announced. A charitable view of them is that they were intended to force the pace of integration and assimilation; a more realistic assessment is that they were intended to put the community on notice that the rights they had been given could also be taken away.

First, the Jewish religion, like the Protestant religion, would be organized into a series of administrative bodies called "consistories." The consistories would train and appoint rabbis and organize how they would be paid. Unlike the Christian clergy, the state would not pay their salaries. The Jews would have to dig into their own pockets to pay their ministers. They were given a decade to ensure that all rabbis learn to speak French. The consistories were also charged with teaching Jews patriotism and useful trades.

The next decree related to repayment of debts to Jews. Many classes of debts were declared null and void. Napoleon's intention was to force Jews out of moneylending and into other forms of employment. But he undercut that intention by including a rule that Jews entering business would have to buy an annual license to operate it. No other group in society had to pay this fee. The era of Jewish special taxes was supposed to have ended with the Emancipation decree of September 1791, now it had been reborn.

Inevitably, the Portuguese Jews were exempted from this decree.

Finally, Jews were not permitted to hire a replacement when they were called up for military service . . . a common practice among the French who could afford it.

The community was shocked and disappointed and quickly these ordinances became known as the "Infamous Decrees." The only bright spot was that they were made subject to review in ten years' time: the hope was held out that by then the community would be thoroughly assimilated and these "infamous" restrictions would no longer be necessary.

In July one more decree was published. It concerned names. Jews throughout the French Empire were given three months to take a traditional family name and first name and register it with the authorities. The Jewish tradition on naming did not include this kind of last name. A person was given a first name and used his father's first name as his or her identification, such as Moses ben Mendel, which means Moses son of Mendel. Sometimes in lieu of a father's name a person might use the place he was from as a second name, as in Moses of Dessau. The decree required the end of this practice. To make sure the names didn't sound too Jewish, it was forbidden to select a family name from the Bible or from the name of the town where the person resided, such as the villages and hamlets in Alsace where only Jews lived.

While the syndics and rabbis debated their answers and Napoleon's Council of State prepared its decrees, the expansion of the French Empire eastward continued. By conquest and by treaty Napoleon brought Emancipation to the heartland of Ashkenazic Jewry: Prussia, northern Germany, Poland, all the way to the borders of Russia. For the Jews of these territories Napoleon was not the man behind the Infamous Decrees but a hero.

Years later, the poet Heinrich Heine, the son of a wealthy Jewish family in Düsseldorf, would remember the arrival of Napoleon's army in his hometown. "I went and stood outside the front door and watched the French troops marching in, the joyful nation of glory that went through the world with music and song." And then came Napoleon himself, in Heine's memory: "The shuddering trees bent forward as he passed, the sunbeams trembled with timorous curiosity through the green foliage, and in the blue sky a golden star could be seen floating . . . a smile that warmed and reassured every heart was hovering about his lips—and yet we knew that these lips had only to whistle and the whole of the clergy would sink into silence—these lips had only to whistle and the entire Holy Roman Empire would dance."

The monarchs of the continent feared the drive for Emancipation. As the Great Sanhedrin prepared to meet an invitation had been extended to all the Jewish communities of Europe to send representatives to Paris for the conclave. The Austrian emperor Franz I wrote to his ambassador in Paris, Prince Metternich, for an assessment of the situation. Metternich tried to allay his fears. "The impulse has been given," he wrote. "The Israelites of all the lands have their eyes turned to the messiah who seems to free them from the yoke." But he added that Napoleon's intention was not to free all the Jews of Europe but to make them feel that "France is their Fatherland." In his exile, Napoleon himself would later remember that was his intention. He wanted to make France a magnet for Jews, so the nation would have the benefit of their talents.

In every direction that Napoleon expanded the French Empire, Emancipation was thrown up like a bow wave. Laws restricting Jews were eased even where the French did not take over the organization of government. By 1812, Prussian Jews had been given full citizenship and so lived with fewer restrictions than those of France. Russia's Tsar Alexander I had planned a massive transfer of Jews deeper into the Pale of Settlement but postponed the move for fear of encouraging Russian Jews to look to Napoleon for aid. Napoleon may have begun his conquests convinced he was spreading the principles of liberty, but conquering in the name of freedom rarely wins the gratitude of the people whose land has been trampled on. Napoleon was hated. He was called the Corsican Monster, the Poisoner, and a hundred other epithets in the newspapers of the time. He was the Antichrist who revived the Sanhedrin, the council that had tried and condemned Jesus to death. The Jews and their Emancipation were completely identified with Napoleon, and as ordinary people in the countries he had conquered dreamed of his end, they also dreamed of an end to Jewish rights.

# PART 2

# REFORMATION

CHAPTER SEVEN

# It Is Hateful to Be a Jewess

FINALLY, THE EMPEROR WAS DEFEATED AND BANISHED TO ELBA. In the autumn of 1814, representatives of the hereditary rulers of Europe gathered in Vienna to negotiate a treaty that would redraw the map of the continent, restore the monarchs' authority, and bury forever the egalitarian nonsense of the French Revolution.

The assembled diplomats and aristocrats were determined to celebrate and the Congress of Vienna became more famous for its parties than its plenary sessions. It was at sumptuous dinners and balls that the real work was done. There were many delegates to the Congress but only a handful were in a position to influence its deliberations: Prince Klemens Wenzel von Metternich of Austria; Robert Stewart, Viscount Castlereagh and Arthur Wellesley, Duke of Wellington from Great Britain; Prince Karl August von Hardenberg from Prussia; Karl Robert Vasilyevich, Count Nesselrode from Russia; and Charles Maurice Talleyrand-Périgord, no longer the bishop of Autun, but still a prince, representing the restored monarchy in France. These were men who understood that decisions about the future shape of Europe could be made in salubrious surroundings . . . and Vienna did not lack for grand houses.

Palais Arnstein, at Hoher Markt 1, was a favorite meeting place. It was the home of Baron Nathan von Arnstein, the foremost banker in Vienna, known as the "first baron of the Old Testament." In addition to his extraordinary skill in finance he was blessed with a good marriage. His wife, Fanny, originally from Berlin, was considered the finest hostess in the city. If you were important or lucky enough to be invited to one of these soirees then an evening to remember was in store. All twenty-seven windows of the massive town house would be ablaze with candles and torches, spilling light into the old marketplace as your carriage pulled up. Fanny von Arnstein knew how to entertain. The food and wine would be first-rate. The music would be the best. This was Vienna, music capital of the world, and the von Arnsteins had been great patrons of Mozart and continued to support other composers.

The conversation would be excellent as well. Fanny von Arnstein had the gift of bringing people with complementary interests together to talk and had a circle of women friends equally skilled at the art whom she could deploy around the room. Each of them was educated, witty, and entirely relaxed in the company of great men. They were all daughters of privilege and they were all Jewish. Dorothea von Schlegel, daughter of Moses Mendelssohn, was among them.

In Paris, when Napoleon was at the height of his power, this kind of gathering was not possible. Jews may have been legally emancipated in France but French society was not open to them. But in the German-speaking lands, social emancipation among the upper stratas of society was well under way. Fanny and her rich friends had been holding soirees in Berlin for more than two decades. They had made their homes a pleasant, neutral territory where the rigid structures of Prussian society could be forgotten. These Jewesses' background excluded them from that society and so they created one of their own. Noblemen and poets, soldiers and philosophers, men who might never meet anywhere else could get to know one another and discuss the future of their own nation, in light of the titanic events unfolding in France. Now, with all the power brokers of Europe in residence in Vienna, these women could bring together Metternich, Talleyrand, Wellington, and their senior officials for the same kind of social evenings.

A guest at the Arnsteins' would notice the women coming together from time to time throughout the evening to gossip, to exchange bits of information. If the guest was truly observant he would notice over in a corner of the ballroom one of Fanny's friends observing the scene with the intensity of a novelist making mental notes and what one admirer recalled was a "trace of endured suffering" at the edges of her face. Her name was Rahel Varnhagen von Ense, née Levin. Her husband was a diplomatic press attaché in the Prussian delegation. Later Rahel Varnhagen wrote of the great men laughing and flirting and generally acting like masters of the universe, "They wished to stop the world . . . and lead it back where it pleased them."

But they couldn't lead it all the way back. Not everything Napoleon did could be undone. Before the former emperor conquered Europe there had been more than 333 German territories. Thus Metternich and his fellow delegates decided to use the Napoleonic conquest as an opportunity to streamline the German-speaking world into thirty-nine entities that formed a loose German Confederation with Austria and Prussia as the most powerful members.

What to do about the Jews was another question. There was still a great confusion of rules applying to them. While Napoleon held sway, French emancipatory rules had been imposed and in some places voluntarily embraced in much of Germany. In Prussia, the community had been fully emancipated in 1812 and had greater rights than their coreligionists in France. In Austria, they lived within the extremely limited terms of the thirty-year-old Edict of Toleration. Baron von Arnstein rented his magnificent palace because Jews were still forbidden to own property in Vienna. Princes Metternich and Hardenberg were favorably disposed toward Jewish rights. They enjoyed the company of Fanny and the other Jewish hostesses. But most of the local politicians in areas where Napoleon had emancipated Jews were anxious to impose restrictions on them again.

When it came to the status of the Jews, the leaders of the congress—like the leaders of France's National Assembly—found themselves negotiating over minute bits of language in the treaty. As it was in France two decades previously, representatives of various Jewish communities lobbied behind the scenes for their cause. But as the congress wore on into 1815, a more pressing matter came. Napoleon had returned to France from Elba and was once again waging war. Wellington, who had been negotiating for Britain in Vienna, went back to his troops to prepare for the final confrontation. On June 8 the Treaty of Vienna was hastily agreed. Ten days later Wellington defeated Napoleon at Waterloo.

The treaty gave its German signatories the power to return Jews to the status quo before Napoleon. In the Papal States the ghetto gates were reerected and the Jews forced behind them. Poland was dismembered. Its eastern territories containing the populous heartland of the Ashkenazic world were assigned to Russia. The Jews' story in these territories would not be Emancipation but emigration en masse at the end of the century to the Americas, Palestine, and South Africa. In the German-speaking lands, Jew haters congratulated themselves that they had so confused the treaty's wording that citizenship was off the agenda, lost in the shadow of ambivalent diplomatic language.

## ii.
## Self-emancipation

What the Jew haters could not understand was that while legal emancipation had been checked, social emancipation was now an unstoppable force in European society. It was unstoppable because Jews, particularly in Germany, were emancipating themselves.

Just as Emancipation in France was pushed for by the syndics, so in Germany this social emancipation was pressed forward by the wealthy members of the community, those who already had close contact with the wider society. At the beginning of the nineteenth century these wealthy folk represented no more than 1 or 2 percent of the community. There was an additional 20 percent who possessed enough capital to be merchants rather than peddlers. The rest struggled. The poorest 10 percent of the community were beggars wandering the countryside without official status or protection, the wretched of Europe's earth.

Another similarity with France was that the obsession with Jews in the German-speaking world was out of all proportion to their numbers. Because of the fragmented nature of Germany itself, accurate population data from the early nineteenth century does not exist, but Jews were never more than 1 percent of the overall population in the German lands. Yet they were the subject of a complex web of laws and restrictions. If Germany was divided into more than 330 political entities before Napoleon, there was almost as much variation in the way Jews lived and the rules they lived under.

At one extreme was the key trading city of Frankfurt am Main, where three thousand Jews lived in a traditional ghetto: a single, dank street about three hundred and fifty yards long and fifteen to twenty feet wide. The gates at either end of this Judengasse were locked at night and on Sundays. At the other end of the spectrum was Berlin, where there was no ghetto at all. However, like the overwhelming majority of Germans at the time, Jews lived in small towns and villages. In some market towns they might make up as much as half of the population, while in other places of similar size there were no more than a few Jewish families. In some towns there were good social relations between the two communities, but in others there was total segregation and dislike.

There is no way to generalize about the Jewish community's attitudes to Germany in this time. In some places the community embraced Napoleon. In 1809 a small riot occurred when the synagogue in Trier put out special decorations to mark the emperor's birthday. In other places, young Jews joined the army and fought to throw the French off German soil.

Nor is there a generalization to make about German attitudes to Jews. Like every aspect of life in the German-speaking world, opinions were changing against a background of political chaos and constant warfare.

It was against this background that the wealthier members of the community, particularly in Berlin, began a project of religious and social reformation in the hope that a modern kind of Jew would be able to take part in society, even if the laws of that society discriminated against him.

In some ways this project began before the French Revolution. Even before he published his book *Jerusalem,* Moses Mendelssohn had urged his people everywhere to adapt to the customs of the countries where they found themselves. This adaptation included learning the local language. Mendelssohn's circle of friends in Berlin, led by the lawyer David Friedländer and the banker Daniel Itzig, father of Fanny von Arnstein, opened the Berlin Jewish Free School in 1781 to put Mendelssohn's theories into practice. At the Free School their sons learned Hebrew and German, as well as sciences. They also studied practical subjects like accountancy so that they could find useful work in society. Their daughters were educated at home but it was an education that went way beyond learning to be dutiful homemakers and helpmeets to their husbands. The young women learned German and also French, the international language of society and science. They were encouraged to read and think for themselves.

Mendelssohn's circle provided a milieu for their children to have contact with people from outside the community. As they reached young adulthood they were completely comfortable in a mixed society and the women especially began to play a leading role in Berlin's intellectual and social life.

Much of this social reformation's success was possible because Berlin itself had evolved. There was a growing understanding of the contribution made to the city's culture by this small minority and that its sensitivities should be acknowledged. In 1788, at a performance of *The Merchant of Venice* at the National Theater, an actor came out before the curtain went up and apologized for the way Shakespeare portrayed Jews in his play.

Throughout Germany, among the educated classes, a new idea had taken hold: *Bildung*. The word's meaning is difficult to express in English but it means a self-transformation, self-realization—not in a self-help book or psychotherapeutic way, but through a process of constant education and continual refinement of the senses. The word was closely associated with the novels of Johann Wolfgang von Goethe but it was also used by Mendelssohn. Learning how to be sociable in non-Jewish society was part of the educational process. For Mendelssohn's children and the children of his Jewish contemporaries in Berlin, *Bildung* became a social code and the foundation of the salons. By the 1790s, while Paris's Jews, active citizens, were negotiating the dangers of the Reign of Terror, Berlin's Jews, with extremely limited rights, were engaged in a remarkable form of integration: the Jewish salon. There were nine regular salons in Berlin by the middle of the 1790s. The first was set up by Henriette Herz, whose husband, Markus, was a brilliant philosopher. He was a disciple of Mendelssohn and had been a favorite pupil of Immanuel Kant. But because he was Jewish there was no possibility of an academic career. Herz had studied medicine and earned his living as a physician. Henriette's salon grew out of informal philosophical talks given by her husband. Mendelssohn's oldest daughter, Brendel, held a salon where Jews and Christians met in a forerunner of today's book groups.

Each of the salons had its own particular character. The one that met on the top floor of the jeweller Levin Markus's house in the Jägerstrasse was the most intensely intellectual. This reflected the forceful character and interests of Markus's daughter Rahel.

She was not beautiful, not in her own estimation nor that of others who knew her. Those who wrote about her—as many of those who attended the salon did—struggled to find the specific words to describe her physically. This was hard because she seems to have been average in every way: medium height, medium weight, pleasing enough to look at but not ravishingly beautiful. Yet she was a charismatic presence even when she was silent; no one listened to another person talk with such intensity. She had an orchestra conductor's sense for the rhythm and shape of conversation: when to interrupt, when to warm up a topic, when to tone it down. This was combined with a journalist's skill at asking the right question. Rahel was not above flattering the important men who came to the top floor of her late father's house, but flattery was not the reason her salon succeeded. The hostess possessed the gift of words herself. She was born a little too soon to become a full-time author; that career was not open yet to women in most places and certainly not to a Berlin Jewess. So Rahel poured her intelligence, sensibility, and extraordinary talent with words into the conversation that made her salon famous.

There was a full cross-section of society found there. Prince Louis Ferdinand, nephew of Frederick the Great, attended, as did Prince Radziwill, scion of the greatest land-owning family of Eastern Europe. The poet Friedrich von Schlegel attended as did the educator Wilhelm von Humboldt. The philosopher and theologian Friedrich Schleiermacher came from time to time. These were the most important intellectuals in Berlin. Then there were visitors to the Prussian capital who dropped in to meet the famous Rahel, such as the French author Germaine de Staël. There were less important people to be found at Rahel's salon as well: actors and painters, civil servants and diplomats, all drawn to the mini social revolution happening on the top floor of the house on the Jagerstrasse.

For its time, Rahel's idea of "sociability" really was a revolutionary concept. In the late eighteenth century, Prussian social hierarchies were rigid. Princes knew princes, diplomats knew diplomats, the bourgeois knew the bourgeois. Their wives knew each other and, more importantly, knew their place. But at Rahel's and the other salons all these distinctions were put aside.

Princes Louis Ferdinand and Radziwill might have discussed Goethe's latest novel but wouldn't ordinarily have been discussing it over tea in the attic of a Jewish jeweller's house with an actor or an opera singer, or government functionary. Here there were no ancient rules of correct behavior to reinforce social distinctions. There was freedom to speak one's mind, to become better acquainted, human being to human being, with fellow citizens. It was all very democratic, a practical expression of *Bildung*. Schleiermacher used the salon as the basis for his own philosophical speculations on the importance of "sociability" in creating the good society.

But the sociable democracy being lived in Rahel's attic room was a one-way street. There was no reciprocity. She might not be a traditional Jew anymore, but she was certainly not considered by her guests to be a German, either. Part of the success of the salons came out of the opportunity it gave the men who attended to experience the exotic without having to travel very far. Jewesses were seen as Asian, African, or Arab, anything but German. They were rumored to be free sexually. Goethe had written about how pretty the Jewish girls in his hometown of Frankfurt were and how much they seemed to like flirting with Christian boys.

Scandal was one of the reasons Rahel was not invited to the palaces of her princely visitors nor even to the homes of her civil servant and philosopher friends. Approaching thirty, she had never been married and her love affairs were well-known. But the main reason, she knew, was her background.

"Just as I was born," she wrote to David Veit, a member of the same close-knit Jewish society in which she had grown up, "some otherworldly being, plunged a dagger into my heart with these words on it. 'Yes, have sensibility, see the world as few see it, be great and noble, nor will I take from you the faculty of eternal thinking. But I add one more thing: Be a Jewess!' and now my life is a slow bleeding to death."

Rahel was not just a gifted conversationalist, she was also a prodigious letter writer. She wrote to friends, family, and lovers, signing many of them "J-J Rahel," the J-J standing for one of her heroes, Jean-Jacques Rousseau. The style of the letters is conversational, modern, and reading them is like eavesdropping on a tête-à-tête in the attic. The woman wrote voluminously about everything, but the great theme of these letters is that of Jewish identity. Her friend Veit wrote back, "It is doubtful anyone has ever written more pitifully and truthfully about Jews than you." Rahel was grateful for her friend's empathy and wrote to him that "only the galley slaves recognize each other." She constantly wondered who she was, what this in-between identity she found herself living meant. In a segregated society, forced to live inside a ghetto, this would not have been a question but now it assailed her. She was a member of the first generation who faced this dilemma.

There was a chasm between the Jewish life she lived in Berlin and that of other places in the Ashkenazic world. During the 1790s she made a comic visit to wealthy relatives who lived in the eastern city of Breslau, where she experienced ghetto life firsthand. Moneyed folks lived cheek-by-jowl with peasants, as livestock wandered the ghetto's street. She was awakened early in the morning by the noise of prayer at the synagogue next door. How is this life related to mine? she wondered.

For a century a tiny minority of Jews in the German-speaking lands had been elevated from the ghetto and allowed to serve local princes as "Court Jews." They were like Daedalus and Icarus, given special wings to fly above their fellows while in this case performing financial services for their royal benefactors. Occasionally, some, like Icarus, flew too close to the sun and crashed and burned. So for all the wealth and luxury these Court Jews provided for their families there was always an underlying insecurity to the life.

But in Berlin, particularly after Mendelssohn, that insecurity was receding. The philosopher's children and the tight circle of their friends had done, without benefit of legislation, what Abbé Grégoire hoped French Jews would do: regenerate themselves. Now this gilded group faced a new reality. German society was not changing to welcome them. Of all the children of this generation Rahel was the one to articulate the dilemma of those who had been encouraged to leave tradition behind but had yet to find acceptance as Germans. Many of the women she grew up with got around the problem by converting to Christianity and marrying noblemen. They brought big dowries and their husbands brought social legitimacy to their relationships.

Rahel was not capable of so basic a compromise. For years she remained in the no-man's-land familiar to all members of minorities who are trying to integrate and assimilate: you are neither of your own culture nor accepted in the majority culture. You are always trying to get people from the majority to simply hear and see you as an individual human being, not as some preconceived idea of what a Jew (or an African-American or a Hispanic) is. She wrote to a friend, Rebecca Friedländer, "How horrid it is always to have to legitimize yourself! That's why it is hateful to be a Jewess." She formulated an ideal solution to her identity problem: if Jews assimilated and then a classless society could be created, inevitably people would view one another simply as human beings.

She loved Goethe and was regarded as instrumental in creating an appreciative audience for him in Berlin. Rahel saw herself living out a life story as tragic as that of the author's most famous creation, young Werther. Yet she never doubted her own abilities. "I am as unique as the greatest manifestation of this earth. The greatest artist, philosopher, poet is not above me. We are of the same element, the same rank, and we belong together." But her egotism struck some of her regular guests as being out of place in a Jewish woman. Wilhelm von Humboldt, who would go on to found the University of Berlin, wrote, "She has bothered me, what to do with the Jewish mademoiselle? She is convinced that she is the wittiest, most intellectual woman on earth . . ." Humboldt supported the idea of political emancipation of Jews but could not begin to understand the powerful inner forces that drive an outsider who wants to assimilate into a society. Rahel saw herself in a perpetual fight against the circumstances of her birth: "I shall never accept that I am a schlemiel and a Jewess."

Eventually, she found an answer to her dilemma through the love of a younger man and conversion to Christianity. Rahel was well into her thirties when Karl August Varnhagen von Ense began to attend the salon. Varnhagen was fourteen years younger than she. The young man had had a ragtag life with every attempt to settle down uprooted by war. The only stability he had known was working as a tutor in wealthy Jewish families. The age difference didn't matter to him; he fell quickly and profoundly in love.

By the time they met, Rahel had had her heart broken very badly on two separate occasions and was in no hurry to risk that pain again, especially with someone fourteen years younger and with no prospects. But the world was in upheaval. Napoleon was tromping around the German-speaking world. Varnhagen joined the army, rose through the ranks, and found himself seconded to the diplomatic corps. After a six-year courtship, in 1814 Rahel agreed to marry him. She was forty-three, he was twenty-nine. A few days before the ceremony, she converted and wrote of the pastor who christened her, "He received me as if Spinoza himself wanted to be baptized; so crushed was he with honor." Her baptismal name was Friederike but she was always known as Rahel.

Rahel was the last of her circle to convert. Conversion had been the demand made on Moses Mendelssohn by Johann Kaspar Lavater and he eloquently refused. After his death, five of his six children became Christians. If they had been as gifted and intellectually honest as Rahel they might have left behind letters offering some psychological insight as to why. But it seems they converted for mundane reasons. They did it for the sake of business and they did it for the sake of love. Mendelssohn was an enlightened man in many ways but a traditionalist when it came to being a father. Shortly before his death he had arranged a marriage for his oldest daughter, Brendel, to a man twenty years her senior. She bore her husband two children but it was a loveless relationship. At the salons she met the poet Friedrich von Schlegel. They fell passionately in love and she moved in with him. The scandal was enormous. She was eventually divorced by her husband, then converted, choosing Dorothea as her new name.

Baptism became a regular occurrence among wealthy, younger Jews. "Processing past the font" to become Christian was the wink-and-nod gesture necessary to gain the practical benefits of integration: a civil service job or membership in a club where business connections could be made. Conversion became so common in the larger German cities that the Jewish community's leaders, particularly those who followed the ideas of Mendelssohn, became alarmed. This had not been the intention of the great philosopher when he started the Jewish enlightenment movement called Haskalah. His friends and followers began to work out a program of religious reform, building on the philosopher's writings on Judaism. Mendelssohn was already known as the German Socrates; now his followers turned him into the Jewish Luther.

The first step in the campaign for religious reform was to break the grip of the rabbis on the community. To them Mendelssohn's work had been evil. No matter that he was an observant Orthodox Jew. He had translated the Torah into German! It should only be read in the language in which God gave it to Israel. To the rabbis this act was a sin that placed the philosopher and his followers outside the true Jewish community.

It was not an easy battle to wage. The self-emancipation going on in Germany was primarily a project of the wealthiest 1 percent of Jews, those whose usefulness to the state had earned them not just money but special protected status. For the ghetto dwellers, the poor artisans, peddlers, and moneylenders, the hold of rabbinical Judaism was very strong. Their ability to excommunicate was as powerful a tool for maintaining community order as it had been more than a century before, when the anathema had been pronounced on Spinoza.

Finding a way to reach out to the wider community was difficult. A wealthy Berliner like David Friedländer could sarcastically describe rabbis three thousand years after the "granting of the Torah" as being obsessed with questions such as "If a person eats a mere crumb of food, is he required to say a blessing before and after putting it in his mouth?" rather than giving modern moral instruction based on Torah principles. This misguided rabbinical leadership, in his view, would lead the next generation to convert in even greater numbers. But Friedländer lacked the common touch to communicate these thoughts to the wider community.

The rabbis pushed against modernization with equal rhetorical force, sometimes from beyond the grave. A leading rabbi of the early nineteenth century, Moses Sofer, left instructions for his children and followers in his will: "Avoid the pernicious company of these evil-doers, the innovators who have removed themselves from God and his law! Touch not the books of Moses Mendelssohn."

But ongoing social emancipation and events outside the ghetto wall would ultimately wear down rabbinical authority.

## CHAPTER EIGHT

# Israel Must Be Exemplary for All Peoples

THE GHETTO WORLD AT THE END OF THE EIGHTEENTH CEN-
tury was not an isolation ward. It was a segregated society, but
those who lived in it were not completely cut off from outside devel-
opments. Its men had to travel to earn their living. The muddy roads
of Germany and central Europe were filled with peddlers and small
traders walking from place to place, selling goods, then buying other
stuff to trade elsewhere. Even if the travelers had to stay in ghettos or
segregated villages when on the road, it was impossible not to hear
about new ideas circulating in the wider world.

Word of the new learning going on in Berlin and Paris began to
challenge the centuries-old Jewish ways of life. A steady trickle of
young men wanted to find out more about enlightenment. Zalkind
Hourwitz was an early example. Solomon Maimon was another, and
without him there would be virtually no record of ghetto life—and
the role of religion and rabbis in it—in the Ashkenazic heartland
at the beginning of the Emancipation era. His autobiography is a
neglected classic, a book that might have been written by Laurence

Sterne, if *Tristram Shandy*'s author had read the complete works of Philip Roth.

Maimon was born in the mid-1750s in Polish Lithuania. Through the business ineptitude of his father, Maimon's family was on a rapid slide from respectability to impoverishment and Solomon quickly became their hope. He was precociously brilliant and became a local celebrity, the boy who could dispute Talmud with the elders. By the age of eleven he was acknowledged as a rabbi. His father saw in him prospects for a good match. A wealthy family would surely want such a brilliant son-in-law. There would be a fine dowry as well as a cash present for the father for arranging the marriage. Solomon's father overdid it and managed to get his son betrothed to two young girls at the same time. Solomon ended up with only one of them. So, still just eleven, he acquired a wife and the mother-in-law from hell. Maimon became a father himself at the age of fourteen.

All the while he secretly read books of science, and found his community's ways of understanding the world challenged. This wasn't just a spiritual challenge. Inside the ghetto the Torah, the first five books of the Bible, and the Talmud, thousands of pages of commentaries on the laws contained in the Torah, were the constitution and legal code of the community; in lieu of an actual country of their own, the Talmud especially became the Jewish homeland. In the country of Talmud, the highest honor went to those who could master its intricacies. The books were the basis of education. Young boys learned to read and write by memorizing them. They learned how to reason by using the logical system of rabbinical debate included in the Talmud's pages, called in Yiddish *pilpul*. The highest level of Talmudic study, wrote Maimon, was eternal dispute over its meaning, "without end or aim."

Most of the Talmud was written in Babylon in the first centuries after the Jews were driven out of Palestine by the Romans. Initially, its creators' purpose was to put in writing for the Diaspora the oral traditions that had been part of religious life in Palestine. By the middle of the eighteenth century, however, the Talmud had become a tool for the rabbis not only to enforce community discipline and cohesion but to cement their own privileged position as judge and jury within it. Daily life inside the ghetto was focused on the hundreds of rituals prescribed in these books as interpreted by the rabbis. Maimon thought his fellow rabbis were a "perpetual aristocracy under the appearance of a theocracy." In the centuries of ghettoization this aristocracy had been unchallenged and its position was unassailable from within the community.

Solomon was desperate to liberate himself from the constrictions the Talmud placed on his own mind and community. He also wanted to escape his horrendous arranged marriage. So he decided to go to Berlin. The idea of Germany had shimmered its way into ghetto life in Lithuania, the way the idea of America would a century later. It was a place where a Jew could learn freely and make his own way. Maimon knew little about Berlin except it was the home of Mendelssohn and other Jews who seemed to be modern. Berlin was the place for him.

He convinced a pious Jewish merchant to help him travel to the Prussian capital so he could learn medicine and help support his family. Then he stole away from his wife and mother-in-law. The merchant booked him passage on a ship through the Baltic Sea to the German coast and after six weeks of wandering through the countryside with little money and no change of clothes, Maimon re-created Mendelssohn's arrival in Berlin. Hungry and tired, dressed in rags, he went to the Rosenthaler Gate and waited in the little hut where Jews were interviewed by their community's representative. When the time came, Solomon, as Mendelssohn had, declared he wanted to study. Then he went a little further. Maimon explained to the representative he was already a rabbi and then, assuming his inquisitor was a man of enlightenment like Mendelssohn, chattered on about some of his more radical interpretations of the Talmud. The Berliner nodded cordially and went away. But it turned out the fellow assessing Maimon's suitability was a traditionalist and was appalled by Solomon's opinions. He told the guardian of the gate, under no circumstances let the young man in. The guardian escorted Maimon outside the gatehouse and stood there waiting for him to depart. Maimon took a few steps and collapsed, wailing inconsolably. He later remembered, "It was a Sunday and many people went, as usual, to walk outside of the city. Most of them turned aside from a whining worm like me." He was taken back into the gatehouse and allowed to sleep the night. The next day he was sent out into the world.

Maimon, like Rahel, had entered no-man's-land. To tear himself out of his community's grasp in Poland had taken an astonishing amount of will and psychological energy. There was simply no way back. Who he was, where he belonged, at that moment were unanswerable questions. So he wandered the German countryside in rags, begging for food, and only after a chance meeting with someone who knew him from Poland did his life improve. Eventually, he would return to Berlin, be taken under Mendelssohn's wing, and gain recognition as a philosopher. Immanuel Kant considered him the most capable popularizer of his masterwork, the *Critique of Pure Reason,* and said so in writing. Kant's writing is dense, his meanings difficult to tease out, but Maimon had trained from an early age in Talmudic dispute "without end" and so was able to find the key to understanding and explaining the book.

His brilliance in Kant interpretation was important in the liberal Jewish community in Berlin. Kant, the person and his philosophy, loomed over men like David Friedländer and Daniel Itzig, as well as the women holding salons. In the Age of Enlightenment philosophers were public figures. For the self-emancipators of Berlin, practitioners of *Bildung,* it was important that Jews be conversant with the latest philosophical ideas. It was proof of their ability to engage with modern "German" thinking. Kant and Mendelssohn had enjoyed a friendship of equals. Markus Herz and now Solomon Maimon had been publicly praised by the great man.

The philosophy of Kant, particularly his views on what constituted true religious expression, was also important to reformers. Kant, who favored Jewish Emancipation, was highly critical of the Jewish faith.

He did not consider Judaism to be a religion at all; rather he saw it as a set of rules adopted by a certain group of people, who had remained remarkably faithful to them despite persecution. For Kant, religion was not about adherence to doctrine and rules but a universal impulse that arose from a pure moral idealism. That view suited the reformers. Judaism was criticized everywhere for its particularism: a person was either born into the tribe and followed its rituals or not. In an age of enlightened universalism, Kant's views pointed the way to a new ethos to underpin the religion.

## ii.
## New Rituals

Time and Napoleon proved to be as effective at advancing religious reform as the wealthy friends of Mendelssohn were. Throughout the last decades of the eighteenth century, Jewish free schools similar to the one in Berlin had opened in Frankfurt, Dessau, Hamburg, and other large communities in north Germany. More and more children outside the charmed circle of Berlin's elite learned to speak German and studied secular subjects. By the middle of the first decade of the nineteenth century, a generation of middle-class children had come of age educated for the modern world. In Germany's Jewish population, middle-class meant the nonpeddling class and represented perhaps a fifth of the community. Still, the gap between them and the Talmud-dominated ghetto society grew wider. Meanwhile, campaign by campaign, Napoleon was conquering the German-speaking lands and freeing Jews from restrictive laws. This created opportunities to move freely and mingle more easily with others.

In 1806 a new Jewish magazine appeared in Germany, called *Sulamith*. Its mission statement could not have been clearer. The magazine was being published "to sort out truth from falsehood, reality from illusion, the useful from the corrupt. It wants to enlighten the Jewish nation about itself." What made *Sulamith* immediately interesting was that it was written in German. There had been other Jewish magazines published in recent decades but they had been written in Hebrew. A generation after Mendelssohn had translated the Torah into German, the philosopher's hope of helping his community learn the local language had succeeded. There were enough German-speakers (and readers) to support a monthly aimed at their concerns. *Sulamith* took it for granted that those who read it were well on the way to reform. The editors also wanted the magazine to become a forum for discussion of Emancipation with the wider community. Christians contributed to the magazine as well.

The Jewish Reformation was inspired not by theology but by a desire to break the hold of the rabbis over the community so that Jews could more easily integrate into the day-to-day life of Germany. The first battles of the reformation were not fought over matters of doctrine but over questions of style. Jewish prayer seemed formless. People worshipped at their own pace and in their own way, some silently rocking back and forth, others crying out at the top of their voices. A cantor occasionally chanted out bits and pieces of scripture or a prescribed prayer but there was no liturgy, no organized call-and-response praying between minister and congregation as there was in Christian churches. For reformers this pious chaos reflected badly on their community. Outsiders saw the synagogue not as a "house of God but a madhouse or a saloon."

The reformers wanted to reinvent the religious service to make it more like the Christian service. The idea was to bring order into worship and rid Judaism of the endless petty ceremonies that had been tacked onto it over the centuries. To build up support for this idea, *Sulamith* published a column called "Gallery of Harmful Abuses, Rude Improprieties and Absurd Ceremonies among the Jews."

Most of all, the reformation called for sermons similar to the ones heard in churches. At that point, rabbinical talks during service were focused on textual interpretations in the narrowest sense. The rabbi would take a tiny slice of Talmud and explicate it, quoting the accumulated commentaries of almost two millennia. To reformers the purpose of these disquisitions seemed primarily to be about keeping the community focused on how much more the rabbi knew about the Talmud than they did. The reformers, however, wanted rabbis to preach homilies about modern life, to find new ways of interpreting the Torah and Talmud so that the books could be used as guides to the modern era.

Over the next decade, as the reformation spread, other things would change. The interior layout of the synagogue was redesigned. Traditionally the altar, or bimah, was in the center of the room. The Torah, kept in an ark placed along the synagogue wall closest to Jerusalem, would be laid out on the bimah during a service and people could move around this space reading the week's portion, praying over the sacred scroll. The reformers moved the bimah to the wall of the synagogue as in ordinary churches.

Everything was up for redefinition, including the term by which the people would be known. Like the word *Negro* during the civil rights era in the 1960s, the word *Jew* fell out of favor. It was associated with the restrictions of the past. It was also a pejorative term, used as a curse. The Emancipation era called for a new designation for the group. "Israelite" became the community's preferred form of reference throughout Europe, although "Hebrew" and "follower of Moses" were also acceptable.

*Sulamith* was headquartered in Dessau, Moses Mendelssohn's birthplace. The city had long been a center for Hebrew publishing. By the time the magazine was founded the city had been made part of the Kingdom of Westphalia. This kingdom was an administrative invention of Napoleon, created out of conquered bits of Germany and handed to his brother Jérôme for safekeeping.

Jérôme organized his kingdom along French bureaucratic principles and set up a Jewish consistory system to administer the religion. He appointed a reformer, Israel Jacobson, as its leader. Sermons as part of synagogue worship were made a legal requirement. Jacobson built a new synagogue in Cassel with a completely reformed service. There was a choir and organ interludes to accompany silent prayer. The rabbi dressed in robes similar to those of a Lutheran pastor. The sermon and some prayers were offered in German.

*Sulamith* became a propagandizer for these changes in religious observance and linked them to a program of Abbé Grégoire's favorite word, *regeneration*. The leaders of the nascent Jewish Reformation in Germany were in many ways following the program for change outlined in Grégoire's and Zalkind Hourwitz's Metz essays. The magazine published articles reminding readers of the agricultural heritage of the Israelites and urged them to leave behind peddling and moneylending and return to their traditional employments as described in the Bible.

In 1810, Jacobson built a new place of worship in the town of Seesen. He did not call it a "house of prayer" or a "house of learning" or "synagogue," the common names given to these spaces. Israel Jacobson called this new building a "Temple." This was the single most dramatic innovation the reformers made. The Temple had been in Jerusalem. It had been destroyed twice. Its second destruction, by the Roman emperor Titus, had heralded eighteen hundred years of Diaspora. Traditions that had grown in those centuries of wandering and oppression said the Temple could only be rebuilt in Jerusalem. What the reformers were saying by calling their building a Temple was, the wandering is over, Germany is our home now.

*Sulamith*'s contributors and the leaders of the Westphalian consistory were voluntarily doing what Napoleon demanded of the Great Sanhedrin. In the Jewish community and the wider world, Emancipation and Reformation became closely linked with Napoleon's name. Yet, outside Italy, resistance to Napoleon and these French ideas was profound on both sides of the ghetto wall.

In 1811, as Napoleon marched east through the Ashkenazic heartland into Russia, Rabbi Shneur Zalman, founder of Lubavitcher Hasidism, found his sleep troubled. What should his people do? Should they aid the French Army against their oppressor, Tsar Alexander I? The answer, he wrote, came to him in a dream: "If Bonaparte wins, wealth will increase in Israel, and the glory of Israel will be raised, but the heart of Israel will be separated and estranged from their Father in Heaven. But if our Lord Alexander should win, even though poverty will increase in Israel and its glory be lowered, the hearts of Israel will be bound, fastened and tied to their Father in Heaven." Very few Jews in Russia helped the French.

As armies in the German-speaking world were formed for the final battles against Napoleon, Jews joined up to fight the emperor. Rahel wrote, "Just God, how easy and natural it is to love one's fatherland, if only it loves you back a little."

For decades after Napoleon's final defeat, the legal situation of Jews throughout the German lands changed constantly. But the confusion about legal rights did not stop the push from within the widening middle class of the community for religious reformation. In 1815 a Reform temple opened in Berlin, followed in 1819 by one in Hamburg. Volumes of collected sermons of various Reform rabbis and laymen were published and read avidly.

The Reformation began to spread. In France, Olry Terquem was the kind of new Jewish citizen Grégoire and Mirabeau dreamed of. Terquem had been among the first generation after the Revolution to be educated side by side with other young Frenchmen in the newly formed elite Grandes Ecoles. He studied mathematics at the Ecole Polytechnique—a kind of state-funded MIT—and later published groundbreaking work in geometry. Then, fired by patriotism, he decided to serve his country by joining the army and applied this geometrical expertise to the artillery corps. His textbook on arcs of fire became a standard reference.

In his spare time, under the pen name Tsarphati—Hebrew for "France"—he wrote a series of essays beginning in 1821. He urged his coreligionists to reform. "Religion is immutable in its esssence, worship is by nature variable," he wrote. "The style of worship varies depending on the climate, customs and politics of the country." He added, "It is in the interest of France, not Palestine, that we should govern our affairs." There were very few aspects of religious practice that Tsarphati failed to address. Move the Sabbath to Sunday, why not? It is the day of rest, why not observe it on the same day of the week as the majority culture? Terquem was particularly exercised by the views of women that were part of Jewish life. He was insulted by the daily prayer men uttered thanking God for making them members of the stronger sex, as well as the Talmudic observation that when a son is born it is a blessing and when a daughter is born it is a curse. He called for leaving the old prejudices against women behind as a major step in creating a modern Jewish ethos.

Traditional rabbis fought back. They quoted a midrash, or commentary, of the Talmud that explained God had decided Israel deserved salvation at the time of the Exodus because the nation had not let go of three fundamental aspects of their identity: their names, their clothes, and their language. Throughout millennia of Diaspora, fidelity to this outward display of difference had not changed despite persecution. Now the Reformation demanded Jews divest themselves of all three. This was a "perversion" of Judaism.

After the founding of the New Israelite Temple in Hamburg, the Hamburg Rabbinical Court solicited opinions from colleagues around the Ashkenazic world about Reform worship, then issued their judgment. "It is forbidden to change the worship customary in Israel" was the first declaration. "It is forbidden to pray in any language other than the Holy tongue" was the next. Finally, it was forbidden to play music in the synagogue on the Sabbath—even if the organist was not a Jew.

The reforming Rabbi of Livorno, the most important center of Jewish learning in Italy, responded by asking a Talmudic question: "If one is allowed to play a musical instrument at a wedding, should it not be allowed to do the same for the honor of God?"

The answer from the traditionalists was that the community was still mourning the destruction of the Second Temple and Jerusalem and that there should be no musical praising of God until the Jews are restored to both.

The reformers began to refer to traditionalists as Orthodox Jews. The traditionalists disliked the name. For them there was only Judaism and the reformers were apostates from it. But the designation "Orthodox" stuck.

With the form of worship changed reformers slowly turned their attention to religious belief. Judaism has very little dogma to dispute. The core of the religion is the people, a group chosen by the one God to follow his laws and commandments as laid out in the Torah. But what did it mean to be "chosen" in this new era? In the centuries of ghetto life the idea of being "chosen" made the isolation a little more bearable. Jews embraced the fact that they were different from the wider society because of the simple fact that they had been chosen and the others hadn't. On either side of the ghetto wall, chosenness had underpinned the idea that Jews were a separate nation, an alien tribe marking time in a foreign country until they could return to their homeland. When the Hamburg Rabbinical Court wrote that it was forbidden to change the form of worship "in" Israel, its members were emphasizing that outsiders' view. Inside the ghetto was Israel. But now the ghettos were opening up, restrictions on movement were easing, and integration with or without the benefits of civil rights was becoming common.

Without a plan or a single guiding influence, reformers modernized the idea of being "chosen" into an idea of mission. The words of the prophet Isaiah shaped the concept. The children of Israel would be a "light unto the nations." One reforming rabbi, Mendel Hess, put it this way: "As previously through its teaching [and] now through its example, Israel must be exemplary for all peoples, must reach the highest rung on the ladder of moral perfection."

Everything modern in 1820 was contained in Hess's definition of Jewish mission. *Bildung*, universal principles of brotherhood, and Kantian idealism were perfectly mixed with the idea of the people as "chosen." Mission became a signpost for Emancipation. It pointed back to the origins of Jews as a people given a special covenant by God and it pointed forward to a world in which this unique relationship would be demonstrated through example and achievement. The sense of mission became subsumed into Jewish life. It became part of the atmosphere of Jewish homes. As the nineteenth century went on, the sense of mission became an important support to the community's rapid achievements in education and business. Mission would also provide psychological armor against the occasionally violent frustrations and disappointments of the struggle for civil rights in the German-speaking lands.

## CHAPTER NINE

# Incite the People to Terror

AT SUNRISE ON THE MORNING OF OCTOBER 18, 1817, THE bells rang out in the town of Eisenach, in the heart of Germany. Hundreds of students from every university in the German-speaking lands hurriedly dressed in black uniforms and assembled in the town square. They were members of patriotic fraternities called Burschen-schaften. The young men stared up at a fog-shrouded ridge rearing up over the town and watched the morning mist roll away, revealing a medieval castle, the Wartburg, crowning the ridgeline.

Forming up in procession, two by two, they marched toward the castle, waving banners of black, red, and gold while singing songs that glorified the German fatherland. Each step was heavy with the symbolism of the day. It was the fourth anniversary of the Battle of Leipzig, when Napoleon had finally been driven from German soil. It was also the three-hundredth anniversary year of Martin Luther nailing his Ninety-Five Theses to Wittenberg Cathedral's door, thus sparking the Protestant Reformation. Luther had lived at the Wart-burg while translating the New Testament into German.

The procession took two hours and when the students arrived at the massive, gabled building they took their places in the Knights'

Hall to hear speeches and pious calls for freedom and rights. They banqueted in the hall where in medieval times the Teutonic Knights had feasted. They made toasts and pledged allegiance to an unreal German past and dedicated their lives to create the single German Reich in the future. The students then returned to the town for a church service.

As the sun set they climbed another ridge by torchlight. Then, in a final act of symbolism, they ended their celebration of resurgent German nationalism by building a bonfire and throwing books they deemed un-German into it. Into the flames went history books these *Burschen* (young students) deemed disrespectful to the German *Volk;* in went a copy of the Code Napoleon, the laws that the emperor had imposed on much of the German-speaking world, guaranteeing the rights of all citizens, including Jews; in went a copy of *Germanomania* by the Jewish reformer Saul Ascher, a pamphlet that dissected with acerbic wit the pretensions of the nationalists.

At the same time as the Jewish Reformation was changing forever what it meant to be Jewish, Germans were having their own identity crisis. Just as the Jews did not have their own country, neither did the Germans. They had kingdoms, confederations, principalities, duchies, free cities—but they had no single political state called Germany. In the absence of a single political entity by which they could define themselves, people began to identify themselves through a single cultural entity: a mythic Germanness. This German culture's origins were in an idealized, Christian Middle Ages. It was a world of Teutonic Knights doing heroic deeds in Germany's dark forests and endless wooded hills. Martin Luther was the real-life hero of this movement, the great man who had changed the destiny of Europe. This mythic land was a place of turbulent soul as opposed to reason. Reason was the foundation of Enlightenment and Enlightenment was something French. The German people, the *Volk,* had a different spirit.

Of course, it wasn't true that the Enlightenment was exclusively French. It was an international movement. Kant and Mendelssohn were hardly French in their approach to philosophical problems. But that didn't matter to a student of Kant's named Johann Gottfried von Herder. He was convinced that two important concepts were being ignored by his professor in the search for the universal ideas at the core of humanity.

The first concept was the individual character of different groups of people. For Herder this uniqueness was a product of the land a people inhabited, its physical shape and climate, as well as ties of kinship. Blood and soil bound a nation together. Herder coined the term *nationalism*. The nation's deepest manifestation was language. Words and grammar shaped the way a group of people thought. Herder, an ordained pastor, pointed specifically to the Jews. They hadn't had their own country for almost two thousand years and yet they maintained a national identity expressed through Hebrew.

Herder fixed on language in part as a reaction to the dominance of French as the international language of the day. Frederick the Great spoke French at court. What was wrong with Germans speaking their own language? Herder wondered. Besides, French could not begin to express the uniquely German way of thinking that came out of the physical land where Germans lived.

The second concept was the role of emotion in human life. Enlightenment thinkers such as Kant and Mendelssohn were all about reasoning stripped of the entanglements of emotion. Not Herder. In his view, poets through their feelings, rather than philosophers through their abstract rationality, expressed a nation's soul. The poets forged language. They created the myths and folk tales that gave life to a *Volk*. A national state, with borders and a government, was not necessary to define a people. The poetry, the language, the stories were the essential elements of nationhood. A movement grew around these ideas and it was called Romanticism.

Herder's ideas permeated intellectual life in the fragmented world of Germany in the late eighteenth and early nineteenth centuries. Collections of German fairy tales and folk songs began to appear, like those written by the Brothers Grimm. Herder's concepts were discussed avidly in Rahel Varnhagen's attic room by the intellectuals who visited with her.

Herder wrote vast amounts and his books didn't require the brilliance of a Solomon Maimon to be understood. They were open to a wide range of interpretation. Pastor Herder had been a strong systematic thinker but he had extolled the subjective and emotional as a way of finding truth. Younger Germans brought their own subjectivity to interpreting his writing and they were far less systematic. The philosopher wrote on many subjects but with the French Army conquering their land, students focused on Herder's ideas of nationalism and the German *Volk* and interpreted them in the narrowest possible way. Herder's idea of nationalism didn't elevate one people above another, it was a way of understanding the differences between groups. But those who came after him saw no reason for restraint. The *Volk* had qualities that were superior to other nations.

By the time Napoleon had been defeated and the Treaty of Vienna had redrawn the boundaries of the German-speaking lands, an emotional patriotism had taken hold of a new generation of professors. Some had fought the French, and all had experienced the humiliation of being conquered. They indoctrinated their students in a strident nationalism. These professors lectured on the incompatibility of French rationalism and "Jewish intellectualism" with the true German mind. The concept of emancipation was rejected out of hand. "To be emancipated means to be taken out of the hand of tradition, authority, stability," wrote Jakob Fries, a leading nationalist philosopher. "It means becoming an alien to one's heritage."

These professors influenced a generation. One student of the time wrote of the Enlightenment, "Those ideas have poisoned the Germanic soul, our rivers and our forests, our youth and our spirit." Another noted that the soul of the *Volk* would never again be weakened by the "typical dangerous, treacherous inventions of the 'Jew Rousseau' in which every stranger, every foreigner, every alien, and, of course, every Jew, is entitled to take part [in German national life], simply by claiming his so called natural rights . . . They may be natural to unnatural rationalists and Jews, however they are certainly not inscribed in the hearts of our nature, of our fields, our flowers, our birds, our skies . . ."

These attitudes were taking hold just as the first generation of Jews educated in German began entering the universities in large numbers. The universities became the place where Emancipation and nationalism came into conflict. Student life revolved around clubs, societies, and fraternities. When the wars ended many young veterans from middle-class and noble backgrounds resumed their higher education and became avid followers of nationalist professors. In 1815, at the University of Jena, where Jakob Fries lectured, the first Burschenschaft, or youth association, was formed. It was dedicated to patriotism and creating a united, Christian Germany.

Almost overnight, there were Burschenschaften everywhere. They dominated student life. These fraternities very quickly became more than social clubs; they became active political associations, the core of a movement for a united Germany. Most Jews attending the universities were filled with nationalist ideas as well. They came from that section of the community that had socially emancipated itself and thought of themselves as German. It was a rational point of view: most of their families had been living in the German-speaking lands for centuries. They were living a modern life and nationalism offered a hope of a Germany that fit the times, a place where all the old medieval political entities were integrated into a new whole. At some universities Jewish students were initially allowed to join the Burschenschaften. But by the time of the Wartburg rally they had been banned from the groups.

A week after Wartburg, one student at Jena wrote home, "Never in my life have I been asked so often, so intensively, so persistently about my being a Jew. Some pitied me for being doomed to be a Jew, others accused me, some insulted me. Oh how deeply, I was disappointed, how deeply wounded, frustrated, humiliated." The young man, whose name we don't know, confessed to bewilderment. He too had thought he was part of a generation renewing "the Germanic man . . . and national unity."

The refusal to allow Jews to join was not violent. At one level it was like the social exclusion that continues today in America, where Jews are simply not invited to pledge certain fraternities. But at another level this was an early demonstration of an insurmountable resistance on the part of some Germans to accepting Jews into their national fold.

There was one exception to this sad story. A month after the Wartburg rally, the philosopher Georg Wilhelm Friedrich Hegel took up a lectureship at the University of Heidelberg. By this point in his career, Hegel had replaced Kant as the acknowledged leader of German philosophy. This carried weight inside and outside the university communities. Hegel had had enough of the willful misinterpretation of Herder's ideas by his colleagues. The philosopher was particularly angered by the way they had indoctrinated students into this irrational, exclusionary nationalism. That had never been Herder's intention at all. Hegel's initial lectures at Heidelberg were on his book, *Elements of the Philosophy of Right*. In that book he made clear that though he thought little of Judaism as a religion this had nothing to do with the rights owed to Jews as individuals. "A man counts as a man in view of his manhood alone, not because he is a Jew, Catholic, Protestant," he wrote. Later in the book he adds, "To exclude the Jews from civil rights . . . would be to confirm the isolation for which they have been reproached."

Shortly after Hegel gave these lectures, a motion was put before the Heidelberg Burschenschaft for allowing Jews to join. There was heated debate and by a vote of 80 to 36, Jews were admitted to the fraternity. The motion had initially been put forward by one of Hegel's favorite students. The decision split the fraternity and a breakaway Burschenschaft was formed. A few months later one of those who left the fraternity, a fellow named Asverus, wrote of the "Jewish-infested" group that is now "well-founded on the ideas of universality and pure rationality." In other words, his former comrades had become very French in their principles.

So, as in France during the Revolution, Jews became an important reference point in defining what the new nation and society would be. It was a profound irony that in France the argument against Emancipation was that Jews were too particular—the nation within the nation—and so could never be French, while in Germany the argument was that they represented the "French" idea of universal brotherhood and so could never be German.

The Burschenschaften became increasingly influential in the wider society. Newspapers took up the nationalist ideology and wrote editorials condemning the idea of Emancipation. As their influence grew, the societies became more and more radical in their agitation. This alarmed the authorities. The Treaty of Vienna had created a German Confederation with Austria's Prince Metternich effectively acting as chief executive. There was long-simmering resentment between Prussia and the northern German states and Austria. Its origins were ancient, tied to the old wars of religion between the Protestant north and Catholic Austria. But there was now an overlay of naked political rivalry between Berlin and Vienna. Metternich looked on with alarm at the Luther-idolizing students' increasing influence. The Burschenschaften looked on the prince with undisguised contempt. Inevitably, the movement became violent.

August von Kotzebue was one of those writers who enjoy fame and success in their own lifetime but whose work simply leaves no impression on history. Kotzebue was best known in Germany as a playwright but he also wrote satirical essays and dabbled in history. Among the books burned at Wartburg was his history of the German people.

On the morning of March 23, 1819, a young man named Karl Ludwig Sand knocked at the door of Kotzebue's home in Mannheim, not far from Heidelberg. The playwright was not in but Sand seemed pleasant enough and was invited to come back that afternoon when Kotzebue was expected to be at home. Sand, a member of the Burschenschaften at Jena, was on a suicide mission. On his way to Mannheim, the young man had stopped at Wartburg Castle and renewed his vows to fight the enemies of the fatherland. Sand returned to Kotzebue's home that afternoon and cursing him as a traitor, stabbed the playwright to death, then went outside and turned the knife on himself in front of a crowd that had been drawn to the house by the screams from within. Sand failed to kill himself. The following year the state finished the job for him. He was beheaded.

In the interim, the murder had given Metternich the pretext he needed to clamp down on the universities and curb freedom of expression. In August 1819, he issued the Carlsbad Decrees, which shut down the fraternities and imposed heavy restrictions on free speech, including press censorship.

Within days rioting aimed at Jews began. The violence started in Würzburg in Bavaria, and traveling faster than the speed of news in those pretelegraph times, it spread northward all the way to Hamburg. In each town, the rioters took to the streets shouting "Hep! Hep!" The origin of the phrase is still debated. Some historians link "Hep! Hep!" to the Crusades. H-E-P is an acronym for *Hierosolyma est perdita,* or "Jerusalem is lost," a Crusader battle-cry. Others say it was a typical sheepherders' cry and it was being used to herd Jews out of the towns.

The riots came as a shock. For several centuries outbreaks of violent Jew hatred had been almost unknown in Germany, but now, out of nowhere and with no single cause they erupted everywhere.

Given the speed and the fact that each riot seemed to follow a similar pattern, it is possible they may have been part of a well-planned campaign by the Burschenschaften to kill two birds with one stone: start a revolution by creating civil unrest while choosing as victims of the unrest the hated Jews. It is also possible that economic conditions had something to do with it. Victory over Napoleon had not brought a peace dividend to ordinary citizens. Not for the first time, and certainly not for the last, the end of a war had led to a depressed economy. Perhaps it was just easy to vent frustration about the state of society on the weakest members of the group. Finally, Jewish Emancipation continued to be debated in nationalist terms and there remained resentments among ordinary people that this group who had been segregated were now allowed into public spaces like parks from which they had been forbidden. Perhaps the rioters thought they could force Jews to resegregate themselves through violence. For whatever reason, the Hep! Hep! riots went on for almost two months. Then just as suddenly as they had started, they stopped.

Rahel Varnhagen was not surprised by the Hep! Hep! riots. Her brother, Ludwig Robert, had been an eyewitness to the rioting in Karlsruhe in the southwest near the Rhine and had written to her describing the violence. Rahel wrote back, "I know my country, alas! An unfortunate Cassandra! For three years I have been saying: The Jews are going to be assaulted." Just in case her brother thought she was exaggerating, Rahel swore to him she had witnesses to that statement.

Rahel's claim to have prophesied the riots is believable. She knew the nationalist ideology inside out. Her salon had been a hothouse for Romantic ideas. She could trace the evolution of German Romanticism from a literary movement to personal code of conduct to political ideology by observing the changes in the behavior of people who visited her attic room. Old friends, liberal in every aspect of their sensibility, lost any sense of decency when it came to discussing Jews. She watched men of reason who grew up with a skeptical view of organized religion become pious and devoted to the idealized and, in Rahel's view, hypocritical Christianity of Germany's imagined, glorious Middle Ages. Some of her regulars had invented the Romantic myths that they now believed to be facts.

This was "our crowd," she wrote in despair to her brother. She knew where their views must inevitably lead. "Terror," she wrote her brother. "Incite the people to the only terror they can still be provoked into, because they remember it was permitted in olden times! the Pogrom!"

Throughout this time of Jewish Reformation and German identity crisis, Rahel had traveled, following her husband, Karl August, on various diplomatic postings. She liked the wandering life. Rahel felt being in motion allowed her true self to surface. She wrote to a friend, Rebecca Friedländer, "Man is 'himself' only abroad; at home he must represent his past, [and] in the present that becomes a mask, heavy to carry and obscuring the face."

On the road, she didn't feel like the "Jewish mademoiselle"; she could simply be the practitioner of *Bildung*, refining her inner self through the kind of experience travel affords, building to a new level of intellectual knowledge and understanding of the world. Away from Berlin she could challenge herself to step outside the comfortable routines of life. As Prussia rose up against Napoleon in 1813, like many other well-to-do Berliners she fled to Prague. As Prussian forces began to push Napoleon out of central Europe, Prague became the place where wounded German soldiers were brought. There were no hospital facilities for them, so Rahel organized the nursing care for the wounded, and raised funds from wealthy friends to provide them with shelter. It was a huge undertaking for someone who had done nothing more taxing in her life than organize the tea and cakes to be served at her salon.

But eventually the wandering came to an end. Karl August's career stalled. In 1819 they returned to Berlin and moved into a grand apartment on the appropriately named Französische Strasse, or French Street. Karl August devoted himself to literary criticism and building up the legend of his wife. Rahel put on her mask of salon hostess and the weekly get-togethers resumed. Against the background of the Hep! Hep! riots it seems an extraordinary thing to do, but that was the nature of life in Germany at that time. Confusion was the norm. After the violence and repression, life simply carried on. But not entirely as before. Germany's identity crisis would simmer for decades. The question of whether its Jewish population could become part of that identity remained unanswered.

Baruch Spinosa fameux Philosophe natif
d'Amsterdam il fut d'abort Juif de Religion il
se separa de la communion Judaique et professa
depuis ouvertement l'Atheisme. mort a la Haye
en 1677. age denviron 44 ans.

Auteur d'un dangereux sistème.
Spinosa n'a que trop répandu son erreur.
Mais voyez l'Univers, et sondez vous vous même,
Vous connoitrez un Créateur.

1. Baruch de Spinoza. Excommunicated by Amsterdam's Jewish leadership, Spinoza became one of the founding thinkers of the modern era. This is a fanciful French portrait from the eighteenth century, by which time the philosopher's name had become both a curse and a compliment.

2. Berlin's Rosenthaler Gate at the end of the eighteenth century. Jews hoping to enter the city were interrogated in the hut next to the gate by representatives of the Jewish community before being allowed in. Moses Mendelssohn gained entry; Solomon Maimon did not.

3.
Moses Mendelssohn discussing religion with Johan Caspar Lavatar while Gotthold Lessing looks on. This is a romanticized version of history as imagined by Daniel Moritz Oppenheim, leading painter of the Jewish bourgeoisie in the mid-nineteenth century.

**4.**
Abbé Gregoire, co-winner of the Metz Essay contest, Jacobin priest, driving force in the first fight for Jewish Emancipation.

**5.**
Honoré Gabriel Riqueti, Comte de Mirabeau. Brilliant orator and leading voice in the National Assembly for Jewish Rights.

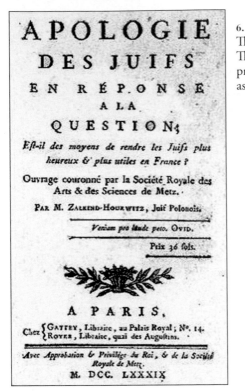

# APOLOGIE
## DES JUIFS
### EN RÉPONSE
#### A LA
## QUESTION;

*Est-il des moyens de rendre les Juifs plus heureux & plus utiles en France ?*

Ouvrage couronné par la Société Royale des Arts & des Sciences de Metz.

Par M. Zalkind-Hourwitz, Juif Polonois.

*Veniam pro laude peto.* Ovid.

Prix 36 sols.

## A PARIS,

Chez { Gattey, Libraire, au Palais Royal; N°. 14.
{ Royer, Libraire, quai des Augustins.

*Avec Approbation & Privilège du Roi, & de la Société Royale de Metz.*

M. DCC. LXXXIX.

6.
There is no portrait of Zalkind Hourwitz. This is the cover of the first edition of his prize-winning Metz Essay, identifying him as a Polish Jew.

7.
Cerf Berr, provisioner to the French Army, leader of France's Ashkenazic Jews at the time of the Revolution.

8.
Berr Isaac Berr, syndic of Nancy. He wrote to his fellow citizens upon their Emancipation, "The name of active citizen that we have obtained is without contradiction the most precious quality a man can possess in a free country."

9. "Napoleon the Great Restores Jewish Worship" by François Louis Couché. The image is a bit of propaganda and a bit of flattery. The emperor loved to project himself as a ruler to compare with the great leaders of antiquity, and he hoped that by being seen as the liberator of European Jews, he would attract their talents to France.

10.
Rahel Varnhagen von Ense, Berlin Salon Hostess. Her "magical, mystical smile" was a guiding light for Heinrich Heine and Ludwig Börne.

11.
Ludwig Börne—lawyer by training, journalist by necessity, friend and rival of Heinrich Heine. Börne's "Letters from Paris" after the 1830 revolution inspired generations of German radicals of all stripes. Sigmund Freud had a complete set of his works.

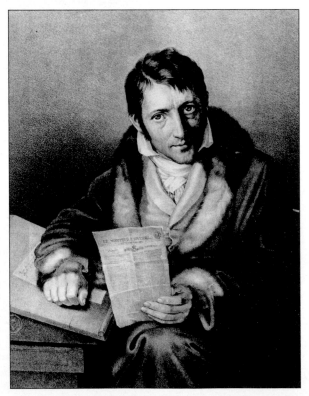

**12.**
Heinrich Heine—first genius of the Emancipation era and one of the most influential German writers of the nineteenth century. This portrait, like the one of Börne, was painted by Moritz Daniel Oppenheim, a contemporary of the pair, who specialized in depictions of Jewish life amid the rapid changes brought about by Emancipation.

**13.**
"The Lorelei," Heine's poem of love and national longing, became woven into German culture and consciousness as this cover of the December 1899 edition of *Jugend,* or *Youth,* magazine devoted to the work of the poet demonstrates.

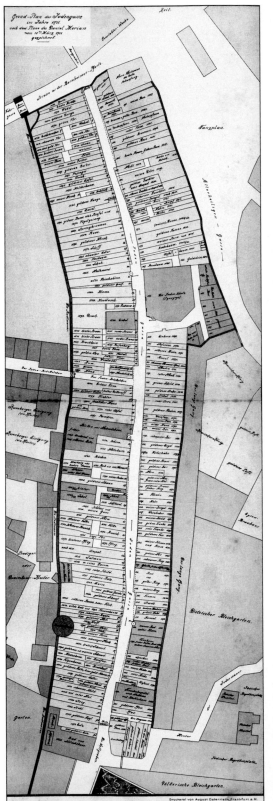

**14.**
A land registry map of the houses along the Frankfurt ghetto's only street, the Judengasse. It was dark and dank, and Jews were locked into the Judengasse at night and on weekends. By the time of Emancipation, the street was home to remarkable talents including Börne and the Rothschild family.

**15.**
The Rothschild family at prayer. The secret of Mayer Amschel Rothschild and his sons' success was family togetherness. This included strict observance of Jewish rituals at a time when many other wealthy Jews were converting. Even after his family became rich, the elder Rothschild and his wife never left the Judengasse.

**16.**
Moses Hess—Marx and Engels nicknamed him the "Communist Rabbi." He was the first political thinker to call for the establishment of a Jewish state in Palestine.

**17.**
The illustrated calling card of Karl Marx from the 1850s.

18.
Vienna's Rabbi Isaac Noah Mannheimer. At the ecumenical funeral in Vienna for the dead of March 13, 1848, he delivered the eulogy for the Jews buried in a common grave with their Catholic and Protestant brothers. He told the thousands of mourners, "Do not begrudge it that those who have fought the same battle with you, a hard battle, should live with you on the same earth, free and untroubled as yourselves."

19.
The lyrics of "The University," the anthem of the 1848 Revolution in Vienna. It was written by Ludwig August Frankl, after students seized control of Vienna following the massacre of March 13. At the bottom it proclaims it was not censored. Free speech and freedom of the press had been one of the main demands of the students. The sheet was handed out to the thousands of mourners who attended.

## Die Univerſität.

Was kommt heran mit kühnem Gange?
Die Waffe blinkt, die Fahne weht,
Es naht mit hellem Trommelklange
Die Univerſität.

Die Stunde iſt des Lichts gekommen;
Was wir erſehnt, umſonſt erſteht,
Im jungen Herzen iſt's entglommen
Der Univerſität!

Das freie Wort, das ſie gefangen,
Seit Joſeph, arg verhöhnt, geſchmäht,
Vorkämpfend ſprengte ſeine Spangen
Die Univerſität.

Zugleich erwacht's mit Lerchenliedern,
Horcht, wie es dythirambiſch geht!
Und wie die Herzen ſich erwidern:
Hoch die Univerſität.

Und wendet ihr euch zu den bleichen
Gefallnen Freiheitsopfern, ſeht:
Bezahlt hat mit den erſten Leichen
Die Univerſität.

Doch wird dereinſt die Nachwelt blättern,
Im Buche der Geſchichte ſteht
Die lichte That, mit goldnen Lettern:
Die Univerſität.

Während des Wachſtehens geſchrieben von

Ludw. Aug. Frankl.

Erſtes cenſurfreies Blatt
aus der Joſef Stöckholzer von Hirſchfeld'ſchen Buchdruckerei.

**20.**

Gabriel Riesser, lawyer and editor of *Der Jude*. This portrait was made at the time of the ill-fated Frankfurt Parliament, which he served as vice-president and primary author of the Constitution for a united Germany presented to Prussian King Frederick William IV.

Verfaſſunggebende deutſche National-Verſammlung,

in der Paulskirche zu Frankfurt ¾.

21. Saint Paul's Church in Frankfurt, where the Parliament met.

22. A cartoon in a Hamburg paper shows Riesser crashing through the last barrier to become the first Jewish judge in Germany.

23. "There's only one baptism that confers nationality: this is the baptism of blood in the common struggle for freedom and Fatherland." Gabriel Riesser's words underscore the willingness of many Jews to fight for Prussia and then Germany. Here, Jewish soldiers pray before a battle during the Franco-Prussian War of 1870.

24.
Sigmund Freud, age 8, with his father, Jacob. Freud had a hard time reconciling himself to the elder man's confessed passivity in the face of anti-Semites.

25.
Sigmund Freud in 1900, the year *The Interpretation of Dreams* was published.

26.
Gustav Mahler in 1897, the year he became conductor of the Vienna State Opera.

27.
Arthur Schnitzler, playwright, novelist, critic, physician, and touchstone of cultural life in fin de siècle Vienna.

28. The front page of *l'Aurore,* January 13, 1898, with Emile Zola's open letter to France's president, accusing the army general staff of a cover-up in the Dreyfus case. Zola's intention was to provoke a libel suit. He succeeded.

29. Alfred Dreyfus, at the ceremony reinstating him to the French Army, July 21, 1906. For the Emancipated Jews of Europe, the end of the Dreyfus affair marked what they thought was the end of political anti-Semitism. They had entered, in Stefan Zweig's words, a "golden age of security."

## CHAPTER TEN

# I Try to Tell My Grief and It All Becomes Comic

IN THE EARLY SPRING OF 1821 A YOUNG MAN BEGAN VISITING Rahel's salon. He said he was a poet and his appearance and demeanor certainly fit the romantic poet image. He was small and thin with a full-flowing mane of dark blond hair. The young man had a febrile temperament: quick to love, quicker to quarrel. Unlike a lot of people who aspire to the title of poet he had actually published verse, and the poems had attracted critical attention, some of it quite positive. He signed his work H. Heine. The "H" stood for Harry, a very Jewish name, and that part of his identity was something he did not want to emphasize. The young man didn't want readers and critics to think of him as a Jewish poet. He simply wanted to be known as a "poet."

In his desire to be taken as he was, without reference to his politics or religion, Rahel immediately recognized in Heine one of her fellow "galley slaves." Heine saw on Rahel's face "that well-known mysteriously melancholy, rationally mystical smile." From that look the young poet knew she had long walked the road he was now on:

looking for acceptance as an individual in German society, suffering humiliation because of an unavoidable fact of birth. The road led into the heart of no-man's-land. But Heine was not prepared to stop there; he was armed and ready to fight his way out. Although from different generations—Rahel was fifty and Harry Heine was almost twenty-five—they were instantly, intellectually smitten.

Poetry was not what brought Heine to the Prussian capital. The writer was there to study law. It was his third stop on a grand tour of German universities, pursuing his degree. As his poetry gained a following, word of the life he had led at his various alma maters trailed after him. He had fought a saber duel at Bonn to avenge an insult. He had been suspended from Göttingen before he could fight another. Stories like this burnished his reputation among younger German readers.

Heine was born in 1797 in Düsseldorf, a pleasant, provincial town fanned out along a bend on the Rhine. At the time, the Rhine was Germany's main industrial highway and the docks in Düsseldorf provided the town its livelihood. Heine's father, Samson, imported textiles from Britain. The family was well-to-do but there were larger sums of money hovering in the background. Both his parents had phenomenally wealthy relations, so their firstborn child, Harry, was raised with a sense of princely entitlement.

The Judaism Heine grew up with was a forerunner of the assimilated Judaism of today. It was not a Judaism of religious observance beyond Passover and perhaps the High Holidays. Heine learned just enough Hebrew to recite prayers on those occasions. His father's orthodoxy was slowly eroding and his mother no longer practiced the faith, so the religion of the Heine home was more a Judaism of food: traditional Sabbath meals and the Passover seder. It was also a Judaism of the family, in which two generations of assimilation had not led to a diminishing of the importance of parents, uncles, and cousins as a social network.

Heine's Jewishness was an entirely different matter from his Judaism. Working out what being Jewish meant personally, how much it shaped his identity and his poetic soul would be a recurrent theme in his life and work. But because his family was not really of the ghetto, his boyhood and teenage years were more typical of any young middle-class German son in the first decades of the nineteenth century. Napoleon was an overriding presence. The constant changing of borders led to a sense of insecurity and a longing for some firm national identity.

By the time he was ready for school, Düsseldorf was under Napoleonic control, and so Heine's parents sent him to a French academy where the teachers were priests. The principal came from the Abbé Grégoire branch of Catholicism, and he introduced Heine to Enlightenment thinkers. But a life of the mind was not immediately on the young man's horizon. His schooling done at the age of seventeen, it was time to earn a living. He headed to Hamburg to visit his astonishingly rich uncle, Salomon Heine. Hamburg, situated on the North Sea coast, was Germany's great port city and Salomon was its wealthiest banker.

Two things happened in Hamburg that would shape the young poet's life. Heine fell in love with his uncle's oldest daughter, Amalie, and she rejected him. Then his uncle set him up in the import-export business and Heine quickly went bankrupt. His broken heart would provide early inspiration for his poetry. The business failure convinced uncle Salomon that the only hope that his nephew would ever support himself lay in his getting a professional degree. So in 1819 he agreed to finance Heine's legal studies, thus putting the writer on the path to Berlin and his meeting with Rahel.

When Heine first walked into Rahel's salon he was going through a double-edged identity crisis that had been building for several years. On the one hand he was no different than other young Germans of his generation. He dreamt the dream of a single German state and was not clear what form it should take. He had thrown himself into student life at Bonn and joined in the patriotic activities that continued despite the Carlsbad Decrees. Just a few months after Metternich had brought those laws into effect, and weeks after the Hep! Hep! riots had ended, he had taken part in a torchlight celebration of the victory over the French at Leipzig.

The other part of his crisis came out of his Jewishness. Despite demonstrating his German nationalist fervor, he encountered discrimination because he was a Jew. The duel he had fought at Bonn was over an anti-Jewish insult. At Göttingen he had briefly been a member of a Burschenschaft before being removed because of his religion. The duel he was prevented from fighting there was also provoked by a Jew-hating insult. For someone who had no knowledge of the ghetto as a place or a mind-set, these experiences must have confused as much as hurt.

There were other things perplexing Heine. The politics of the German-speaking world at this time were extremely muddled. Modern labels like liberal and conservative almost have no meaning in describing them. The student groups, despite their blatant racism, showy Christian piety, and coarse nationalism, were seen as fighting for "liberal" causes like self-determination and free speech. But the Burschenschaften despised the progressive fight for Emancipation, considering it a Napoleonic idea. Yet a conservative like Prince Metternich favored Jewish civil rights but was also against self-determination and the creation of a single German state. Like most young Germans, Heine despised Metternich, but he could not join in his fellow students' hatred of Napoleon, the Jewish emancipator. He was faced with the puzzling reality that the German part of him desired a single German state but on the critical issue of Emancipation the politician who would most aid him as a Jew, Metternich, was the man preventing the creation of that state.

A final layer of personal confusion came from the reception Heine's poetry received. He had mastered the principles of German Romantic theory with ease. He had grown up reading folktales and knew those stories better than he knew the stories of the Hebrew Bible. The folk songs of the Rhine were an essential part of the music of his boyhood. Heine had taken that aspect of Romantic writing and married it to his own precisely metered memories of bitterness and longing from Amalie's rejection of him. His success as a young German poet had been immediate, yet at the university he was rejected as a Jew.

He brought these wounds and confusion into Rahel's salon. He also brought his talent. She challenged him as a writer. Rahel had known many brilliant thinkers during her life and knew what made them tick. She saw that Heine's facility with verse was potentially a trap so she challenged him to use that ability to do more than write moony love lyrics. Her husband, Karl August, echoed his wife's words and was instrumental in widening the number of publications where his poetry appeared. Karl August also helped him find a publisher to put out a collected edition of the poems he had already written. Heine began to rework the early verse for this collection, sanding away the cheap, adolescent sentiment.

But Heine needed more than Rahel's conversation to help him deal with the Jewish part of his identity crisis. He needed to learn more than she knew about Judaism. So he joined a new club. In the wake of the Hep! Hep! riots a group of younger Jewish intellectuals had founded the Society for the Culture and Science of the Jews. Their idea was to push reform and self-emancipation by "scientifically" studying the culture and history of their community. Their method owed much to Hegel, who had replaced Kant as the philosopher to be venerated among the younger generation. Hegel's great work as a thinker was an attempt to define scientific laws for the study of history. By 1821, the philosopher had moved on from Heidelberg University to Berlin, and Heine spent more time studying with him than reading law textbooks. It was inevitable that Heine would join the society.

The poet had a prickly relationship with his fellow members. That was typical. He had difficult relationships with most people in his life. He was extraordinarily competitive intellectually. Most of those involved in the society were serious scholars with fluency in biblical languages and an academic knowledge of religious texts. Heine simply didn't know those things and wasn't interested in learning them. What he knew was poetry. He may have been confused about the Jewish part of his identity but he was very clear about his calling as a writer. Heine was certain that the truth of history was not to be found via "scientific" laws but in the distilled visions of poets. "History is not falsified by poets," he wrote. "They faithfully convey its meaning even when they invent figures and incidents."

The poet's involvement with the Society for the Culture and Science of the Jews was that of an infatuated lover. He was passionately in love with the idea of knowing more about Judaism and his identity as a Jew. When the society set up a Hebrew school Heine volunteered to teach there a few hours a week.

But eventually the infatuation ended. Whether it was because the group had become involved in the American Mordecai Manuel Noah's bizarre scheme to set up a Jewish state on Grand Island in the Niagara River called Ararat, or because he couldn't read one more of the obscure, learned papers written by his colleagues, Heine left the society. Like a disappointed lover Heine dumped his friends with verbal abuse. He blasted their reforming ideas. "We no longer have the strength to wear a beard, to fast, to hate and to endure out of hate. That is the motive of our Reformation."

His biting words might have wounded his colleagues more if he had ever really been an observant Jew.

## ii.
## Identity and Poetry

For two years, Heine lived an astonishingly intense life in Berlin. Besides the Society and the hours he spent with Rahel reworking his early poems for publication and attending the lectures of Hegel and others, he wrote several columns for a provincial German newspaper and still managed to have time for becoming involved with inappropriate women.

Meanwhile, he continued to use his writing as a way to resolve the paradoxes and "craziness" of his Jewishness. He finished a verse drama called *Almansor*. Set in medieval Spain, its hero, Almansor, is a Moor who has been forced to flee his home rather than convert to Christianity. He leaves behind Zuleima, the Christian woman he loves. Later he returns and finds that she is about to be forced to marry a Spaniard. He helps her escape and together they flee to the countryside. But they are pursued and in the end the couple leap to their deaths rather than submit to prejudice.

The hero may be a Muslim but he is clearly a surrogate for Heine. Medieval Spain was for the poet and his colleagues in the Society for the Culture and Science of the Jews the place and time of greatest importance in their people's history in Europe. In Spain, the Sephardic Jews had achieved wealth and learning even while they were beset by the same dilemmas faced by the self-emancipated Jews of Germany. The most important of these dilemmas was conversion. The group admired the solution the Sephardic Jews came up with: public conversion while privately holding on to Judaism and Jewishness.

*Almansor* is shot through with allusions to the situation of Jews in Germany. The author might have had the burning of Jewish books and the Code Napoleon at the Wartburg fresh in his mind when he has Almansor tell his friend Hassan about Christians burning the Quran in the marketplace of Granada. Hassan prophesies, "Where men burn books / They will burn people also in the end."

Heine found the courage not to use a surrogate in a poem called "Donna Clara," a tale of the remorseless seduction of a rich Christian girl by a mysterious guitar-playing knight. Eventually, the knight leads her from her father's hall into the darkest recesses of the palace garden, where,

> . . . *the breezes kiss them fondly*
> *Roses greet them as in fables.*
> *Roses greet them as in fables*
> *Bringing messages of passion.*

As the seduction continues, four-line stanza by four-line stanza, Donna Clara spouts out Jew hatred. The mysterious knight asks why the maiden is blushing and she tells him insects are biting her and she hates them "like a bunch of long-nosed Jew boys." She pledges her heart to the mysterious knight in the name of her savior, whom "God-accursed Jewry" murdered. Through the whining litany her resistance weakens and she finally succumbs to the roses' message of passion. After their lovemaking young Donna Clara asks the mysterious knight his name.

> *I, Senora, your beloved,*
> *Am the son of the distinguished*
> *Eminent and learned Rabbi*
> *Israel of Saragossa.*

The poem is far from Heine's best work but for its time the audacity is breathtaking: a Jewish poet writes of seducing a Christian girl as an act of revenge. Men have been lynched for less. Perhaps the poem didn't get Heine into that kind of trouble because people read the poem in a different way. Heine's best friend in the society was Moses Moser. Heine showed him the work and assured him the character of Donna Clara with her constant refrain of Judeophobia was based on someone he had seduced in Berlin. Moser told him the character and the poem made him laugh. Heine admitted he hadn't been trying to be funny and then explained, "I try to tell my grief and it all becomes comic." No one has ever distilled the essence of modern Jewish writing so clearly.

In the depths of his Jewish identity crisis he traveled east to the Polish lands Prussia had acquired via the Treaty of Vienna. In the vicinity of Posen, modern Poznan, he found himself overwhelmed by the poverty and isolation in which his coreligionists lived. Rahel had made a similar journey to visit relatives many years before and had been appalled by what she saw. Her folks were wealthy, yet they lived with animals grazing in their yard and the streets of the little Jewish village where they had to walk were ankle deep in mud and filth. Heine also found the poverty and isolation repulsive but he felt something else gnaw at him—admiration. The life these Jews continued to live seemed more authentic. In his eyes they made no compromises to get a little approval and acceptance, nor did they require hours of scientific study to find out more about themselves. They knew and accepted who they were.

He longed for that kind of clarity about his Jewishness in the life he led in Berlin. He and Rahel often joked about the poor ghetto Jews. They told their stories like a couple of Borscht Belt comedians, using Yiddish accents to mock their unsophisticated cousins. As they sat in Rahel's grand Berlin apartment drinking tea and munching cakes, telling jokes helped ease the feeling of dislocation and what he would later describe as the pain of Jewishness, "the thousand-year-old family affliction . . . incurable, deep-seated hurt." They were of these people yet had nothing in common with them. Rahel found the connection a burden, but at this point in his life Harry Heine did not. He wrote, "The Polish Jew with his filthy fur hat, his infested beard, garlic-laden breath, and his jargon is dearer to me than many a German Jew in all the majesty of his government bonds."

He began work on a novel, to be called "The Rabbi of Bacharach." The novel's setup is melodramatic. At a Passover seder at the Rabbi's home in Bacharach, a town in the wine country along the west bank of the Rhine, two strangers arrive. "Let all who are hungry come and eat, let all who are needy come and celebrate the Passover with us," are the words of the seder and so the two strangers are invited to join the feast. During the meal, the Rabbi feels something at his feet, and when he looks under the table he sees the corpse of a child. Suddenly, the Rabbi realizes that the two guests have somehow smuggled the corpse into his home so they can accuse him of ritually murdering a Christian and using the dead child's blood in making the Passover matzo. The Rabbi takes his wife and flees.

Like many poets Heine found writing fiction difficult. He worked on the story in fits and starts, then would return to verse.

While exploring his Jewish identity in his work, the writer did not abandon the German sources of his art. At the same time he was working on *Almansor* and "The Rabbi of Bacharach" he wrote the poem that defined him as a great German poet.

A short distance north of Bacharach, the Rhine narrows and twists past a four-hundred-foot-high cliff jutting into the river. The river's massive waterflow is constricted there, causing dangerous currents. Rapids and shoals at the foot of the cliff make it the most hazardous stretch of the Rhine and it has been the scene of many accidents. The rock is called Lorelei and over centuries, legends about the place grew up. In 1801, one of Rahel's friends, Clemens Brentano, invented a story in which a maiden, a siren whose spirit lived in the rock, lured riverboatmen to their deaths. Brentano's story was part of the Romantic project of creating German national myths. Now Heine decided to go Rahel's old friend one better.

> *I do not know what it means that*
> *I am so sadly inclined;*
> *There is an old tale and its scenes that*
> *will not depart from my mind.*
>
> *The air is cool and darkling,*
> *And peaceful flows the Rhine;*
> *The mountain top is sparkling,*
> *The setting sunbeams shine.*
>
> *The fairest maid is reclining;*
> *In wondrous beauty there*
> *Her golden jewels are shining,*
> *She combs her golden hair.*
>
> *With a gold comb she is combing,*
> *And sings a song so free,*
> *It casts a spell on the gloaming,*
> *A magical melody.*
>
> *The boatman listens and o'er him*
> *wild-aching passions roll;*

*He sees but the maiden before him,*
*he sees not a reef or a shoal.*

*I think, at last the wave swallows*
*The boat and boatman's cry;*
*And this is the fate that follows*
*The song of the Lorelei.*

The rhyming quatrains are simple enough and the poem could be read as a clever rendering of an old myth. But that is not how it was received at the time. It was a poem that worked on several levels. It was a perfect expression of romantic longing for love, a desire that can drive a man to his death. But "Die Lorelei" ("The Lorelei") was also read as an allegory for the frustration of German national aspiration, with the boatman looking heavenward for something that is not there, a dream figure, and being dragged down to his death by the power of the Rhine, the artery that gives the German nation its life.

Heine's work became the most famous poem of this era, when young Germans were struggling with their own national identity crisis. Like the poems of his contemporaries Keats and Shelley, Heine's work captured the spirit of his generation. "Die Lorelei" instantly became part of Germany's literary canon. It was committed to memory. The poem was set to music by Robert Schumann, Franz Liszt, and, over time, dozens of others. Well into the twentieth century, German students still memorized the piece. This presented the Nazis with a dilemma when they came to power. As a solution, they had the textbooks with the poem in it reprinted. Heine's name was removed and the new textbooks said the poem's author was "unknown."

In the midst of this creative activity Heine's first collection of poems appeared. Although they seem dated and coy now, the love poems were seen in their time as being too full of realistic feelings. Older critics scoffed at their lack of elevated sentiment. Poetry was supposed to ennoble the reader with a worshipful feeling. It was supposed to follow "classical" and "ideal" forms. Goethe was the model to be emulated. But the leading critic of the younger generation, Karl Immerman, praised the poet for putting his "heart and soul" before his readers. "He must have felt and lived the context of his poems," Immerman wrote. "He possesses the spirit of youth which is a lot in an era when people are born old."

Other critics saw in Heine's poems and the tales of how he lived his life an echo of Lord Byron. The poet was happy at first to encourage that opinion, even though the pair had very little in common. The comparison helped Heine build a Europe-wide reputation.

He was now the rebel poet of Germany. How much the rebellion came from his despair over the state of Germany and how much came from his frustration and anger at the discrimination he experienced as a Jew can never be quantified. But in his work they were linked. He was trying desperately to synthesize these two parallel identities through poetry. Heine was the great genius of the first emancipated generation of Jews, and every genius is unique. But the conditions in which Heine's talent developed would be the same for all the members of his community in the century to come. The state of Germany and their changing status within it, their twin ways of experiencing society and the constant effort to balance these often irreconcilable aspects of their lives would mark generation after generation of Jews. The desperate search for synthesis would create many more rebel thinkers.

## iii.
## Identity and Travel

Then it was time for Heine to leave Berlin. Year by year, the dead weight of Metternich's repressive laws stifled expression and provided cover for increasing authoritarianism.

Heine had grown up as emancipatory laws were enacted, but now he watched as bit by bit they were being undone in Prussia. Jewish and Christian children were forbidden to be educated together; Jews were banned from holding high rank in the army; they were forbidden to hold academic posts at public universities.

None of these changes provoked much of a stir in Berlin. The Prussian capital, once a center of Enlightenment and radical new ideas, had now become conservative, the middle classes having made their accommodations with the political realities of the era. There was a collective shrug among the elites, a sense that the return of discrimination was no big deal; it was, perhaps, even necessary. A dullness fell over the city. Even Rahel remarked on it. Identity crisis explored but unresolved, it was time for Heine to move on. He made his farewell to Rahel in person and then in writing. "You did as much in the years 1822 and 1823, when you treated me, a sick, bitter, morose, poetical and insufferable creature, with a tact and kindliness which I certainly never deserved in this world . . ."

Rahel and Karl August Varnhagen von Ense were a blessing for Heine that followed him everywhere. They provided him with a network of friends and professional contacts around Germany and later in France. Karl August wrote reviews in the most important journals praising the writer. Heine's life would lead him into exile but even when far away they were his touchstone.

From within, from without Heine was squeezed by the pressure of the worlds he came from. From within, there was the fact of his background. He was not observant and never had been. He wanted to break free of the tentacles of the Jewish community but couldn't. Without the largesse of uncle Salomon there would be no money to live on.

From without, he was a product of a society in transition with little sense of what the future should be and no plan for how to create one.

Within himself he had a secure knowledge of his gifts as a poet and writer, but the outside world required him to earn a living. And his writing was not yet providing money. So, in his late twenties, still unable to support himself, he moved back in with his parents. It was humiliating but there was humiliation all around. His father's business had gone bust and so his parents had left Düsseldorf for a quiet retirement in reduced circumstances in Lüneburg. The writer worked at his poetry and prepared *Almansor* and another verse play for publication. But Lüneburg bored Heine to tears. Constantly having to explain why he wasn't earning a proper living didn't make life pleasant, either. He moved on to Hamburg, where he managed to fall in love with Amalie's little sister, Therese, with the same lack of success he experienced a decade earlier. His heart wounded again, he went to Therese's father, Salomon, and asked for money to see him through one more year of law school. Check in hand, the poet returned to Göttingen.

He approached his studies with a bit more vigor, and since he could see the end of his legal education coming he decided to take a little vacation. Walking tours were the popular form of recreation in Germany then, and Heine decided to take a brisk meander through the Harz Mountains. The mountains, humpbacked ridges folding in on themselves, are densely forested. The population is sparse and centered around the silver mines burrowed into the hills. The Harz were a popular place for the middle class to get away from it all. In 1825 tourism was sufficiently established that there were inns catering to walkers. Heine visited the mines and the summit of the tallest peak, the Brocken.

The long walk cleared his mind. When he returned to Göttingen he was invigorated and began to write about the places he had seen and people he had met. Suddenly, in his work, everything clicked. In the framework of writing about a journey he could express everything that was happening inside himself. If something he saw or felt in the forests or on top of a hill inspired him, he could churn out a poem and include it in the account of his travels. He could turn features of Germany's natural world into symbols of contemporary German politics. With secret police and censorship all around he had to be one step ahead, and so these travel stories became a clever way of slipping his political ideas past the government into print. In writing about his travels he found his own unique voice, the voice where tragic stories end up making people laugh. It was a very contemporary voice where the rules of formal, literary style went out the window. His readers felt as if they were seated with Heine in a tavern having a beer and he was telling them the story face-to-face.

He finished *The Harz Journey* and sent it off to a magazine to be published. Then he resumed his legal studies. It was as if Bob Dylan while writing and recording his early works like "Blowin' in the Wind" was also attending law school. But Heine's family remained insistent that he finish the degree. They were conventional middle-class people and simply could not understand his compulsion to write. If Harry had to be a poet, then the law degree was supposed to provide a way to support the literature habit.

But the rules on Jews practicing law had changed in the six years he had been chasing the degree. They were now forbidden from the profession. Heine himself thought he might get an appointment to a university, a tenured sinecure. But now Jews were banned from teaching at universities. The simplest thing to do, the practical way to get around the restriction was to convert. With graduation approaching the subject was brought up by his parents and uncle Salomon.

Heine and his family had long arguments about conversion. His parents didn't mind. The Jews of medieval Spain converted and privately held on to their culture and faith. It could be done in modern Germany. Rahel had converted. Her brother, the playwright Ludwig Robert, with whom Heine had become very friendly, had done so. Mendelssohn's children had become Christians and their grandchildren, among them the composer Felix, had been happy to stay within the Christian community. But Heine resisted. He was a German. Why should the law deny him his rights because he had also been born a Jew? His hero Almansor had leapt to his death rather than succumb to the intolerance of Christians. Almansor was his idealized vision of himself. He would stand up to this idiotic prejudice. Somewhere in the back of his mind must have been the image of the authentic Jews of Poznan living out their impoverished fate, not compromising themselves by seeking crumbs of approval from the religious majority.

For months the discussions in the Heine family went on. As his final exams approached, the reality of building a career that would support his writing weighed more and more heavily on the poet. Finally, he caved in. In June 1825, he was baptized in the Lutheran Church in Lüneburg as Christian Johann Heinrich Heine (Heinrich being the German rendering of Harry). Heine usually wrote about everything that happened in his life. But this hurt too much. He could only write in a letter that the baptismal ceremony was his "ticket of admission to European culture." A month later he passed, with no great distinction, his final examination and added the title of Doctor of Laws to his new name.

The conversion charade fooled no one. If anything it called attention to his true origins. Now those critics who didn't like his writing began to make note of Heine's religion. Previously they had attacked his verse for breaking classical rules; now, increasingly it was his Jewishness that they found fault with. They detected an Israelite style in his poems' "brazenness" and caustic "wit."

Heine wrote to his old friend Moser, "I am now hated by Christian and Jew. I regret very much that I had myself baptized, I cannot see that things have gone better for me since then, on the contrary, I have had nothing but misfortune." The misfortune extended to his creative work. He gave up work on "The Rabbi of Bacharach" and never finished it.

## CHAPTER ELEVEN

# Since I Was Born a Slave
# I Love Freedom More
# than You Do

Heinrich Heine wasn't the only one of his high-achieving contemporaries to succumb to pragmatism and convert. Within months, the president of the Society for the Culture and Science of the Jews, Eduard Gans, followed Heine to the baptismal font. They were the same age but unlike the poet, Gans was a brilliant scholar and had acquired the reputation as Hegel's foremost pupil. At the time he set up the society, Gans had already earned his doctorate and had published groundbreaking work finding practical applications for Hegelian theories of right and history in German law. Yet Gans could not find full-time work because of his origins. A professorship would be his if he became Christian. Within a year of his baptism he was on the faculty in Berlin.

Ludwig Börne, né Löb Baruch, was one of the leading political journalists of the German-speaking world. A decade older than Heine, Börne had had a more thorough personal experience of emancipation and discrimination. He had been born behind the locked gates of the Frankfurt ghetto, the Judengasse. He remembered the place having "A darkness prevailing there that calls to mind the ten plagues of Egypt." His father was a wealthy banker and sent young Löb away from the ghetto shortly after his bar mitzvah, first to study at a gymnasium, then to Berlin to study medicine. Ultimately Börne decided to study law and administration. By the time he took his degree, under the influence of Napoleon, emancipatory laws had been passed in Frankfurt and he became a civil servant, working with the police. After Napoleon's defeat, the old restrictions were reinstated and Börne was forced to resign.

He turned to journalism. In the Emancipation era in Germany, writing and editing newspapers became the logical career choice for many young Jewish men educated in the law but banned from practicing the profession. Löb Baruch was the first to walk that path. But it wasn't a clean decision. The prospect of regaining his government job was enticing. Conversion was the price. In 1818 he made his visit to the font and became Ludwig Börne. In the end, he decided to stick with journalism. New technology—industrial-scale printing—increasing literacy, and burgeoning nationalism were creating a vast new audience for political opinion. Journals to satisfy that audience were popping up everywhere. Börne started one.

Gans, Börne, and Heine all knew each other. By now the idea of Emancipation had spread beyond Berlin but most of its adherents still came from the small number of wealthy and upper-middle-class Jews living in Germany's cities or larger towns. They represented a small portion of the community. In the 1820s the overwhelming majority of Jews still lived in rural towns and villages.

The three men came from this urban background. They shared social networks. Börne and Gans also attended Rahel's and other Jewish salons. What is remarkable about them is that even though they were a tiny minority of a tiny minority, they very quickly were key opinion formers of the entire German-speaking world. Heine did it through verse and his prose experiments; Gans through legal writings; Börne through journalism.

## ii.
## Words as Weapons

Dr. Heinrich Heine was almost thirty and still living on the charity of his family. He was Germany's Byron but he was broke. Despite his conversion there was no academic appointment coming his way. Thus he followed Börne's lead into journalism. His first travel writing had been popular, so he continued to take short journeys and write about the places he visited in the press.

There was another reason for his wandering. He wrote to his friend Moses Moser in July 1826, "I feel the urge to say goodbye to the German fatherland. It's not because I have a particular desire to tramp around the world: what drives me away is the torment of the situation in which I now find myself. The mark of the Jew can never be washed off."

At the same time he put together a collection of all the verse he had published so far. *The Book of Songs* was published in 1827, his thirtieth year.

The title was an accurate description of what the reader would find inside. Heine's poems are lyrics without music. Indeed, their musical potential entranced the composers among his readers. Franz Schubert was the first among them to write down the musical notes that would fit the verbal counterpoint of pain and wit that made Heine's lyrics so popular. Schubert was the same age as Heine, precocious in his genius like the poet, and equally productive. Heine had redefined the style of Romantic verse. Schubert had almost single-handedly invented its musical equivalent: the lied, or art song. He set hundreds of German poems to music. Schubert had been playing around with setting Heine's work to music for a while, but shortly after *The Book of Songs* appeared he began in earnest.

He set six poems to music in a manuscript called "Swan Song." It was discovered among his papers when he died in 1828. Among musicians Schubert was an acknowledged genius at the time of his death but not widely known by the general public. But dying tragically young and neglected quickly increased the public's interest in his work. Heine's fame rose to new levels as the "Swan Song" quickly became seen as the final musical testament of the composer.

Other composers soon emulated Schubert's interest in Heine. Felix Mendelssohn, Moses Mendelssohn's grandson, and Robert Schumann were among them. But even as these songs were enhancing his fame Heine was leaving verse behind.

Not every generation gets to make a revolution and change the world. Heine's was one of these and he knew it: there was still no constitution, no freedom, no single Germany. The writer moved on from his Jewish identity crisis and began to grapple with the German one. This was easier said than done, as censorship made overt political writing impossible. But messages could be hidden inside his travel writing.

Heine went to England and hated his time there. He wrote with ironic scorn about the climate, the manners of the English, and the appalling speed at which industrialization was turning the country upside down.

But he also had time to think hard about Germany: "When the fatherland faded from my eyes I found it again in my heart." On the other side of the water he was able to see his fellow Germans more clearly. Unlike the English, words like *freedom* and *equality* have little meaning for Germans, he writes. "They are a speculative race, ideologists, prophets and after-thinkers, dreamers who only live in the past and in the future, and who have no present."

The Englishman loves liberty the way he loves his lawfully wedded wife: as a piece of property, Heine finds. The Frenchman loves liberty the way he loves his brand-new bride: "He burns for her . . . [and] he will fight for her to the death." The German, on the other hand, "loves liberty as though she were his old grandmother."

Ludwig Börne used theater reviewing to the same purpose Heine used travel writing. It was a camouflage for writing about deeper subjects,

subjects that might get you arrested and your work banned by the censors. It was easy to write critically about the foibles and prejudices of the ruling elites in the German states under the guise of reviewing productions of historical dramas by Schiller, or contemporary drawing room comedies. He could dismiss a shoddy production as wasting everyone's time and make it at the same time a call to political action when telling his readers not to bother to go see a play because "these are times when constitutions are being written, parliaments being summoned. We all have our hands full!"

Inevitably the two became friends, or as friendly as Heine would allow himself to be with someone who was clearly a rival for the public's attention. But at the beginning of their acquaintance they had a lot in common. Through the influence of Rahel they studied the new political theories coming from Paris, such as the utopian socialism of Count Henri de Saint-Simon.

This primitive socialism shaped Heine and Börne's vision of a united Germany freed from the malingering vestiges of feudalism. It would be an emancipated nation, a beacon of the old universal ideals that had been discredited because Napoleon had tried to impose them by conquest. Emancipation became their byword and their mission.

Together they made rhetorical war on the symbols of the stultified German nation. Goethe, still alive and working, was an early target. They attacked Goethe because the great writer, through no choice of his own, had been turned into a symbol of conservative classicism, a huge stick with which to beat the younger writers. Heine and Börne saw their own work relentlessly criticized for breaking classical rules. The pair didn't write novels or poetry in the classic form, the critics noted, like Goethe and Schiller, who are our very best Germans. The younger men wrote disposable things like letters from abroad, theater reviews, and poems about sex. Heine and Börne demanded that people stop looking backward and embrace something new whether it was in art or politics.

This seems like so much aesthetic hot air, but for Heine, Börne, and other mostly younger educated Germans this was deadly serious stuff. There was no Germany, just the idea of being German. There was increasingly strict censorship of the political press and so their political arguments for a united nation had to take place in the abstract world of artistic ideas.

In this fight Heine and Börne took on the role played by Mirabeau and the other pamphleteers in the years before the French Revolution. But Germany in the 1820s was not the same as France in the 1780s. Most Germans were not prepared to embrace change, as the French had been on the eve of their revolution. Nor were they going to be chivvied into demanding unification and equal rights by men who used language the way Heine and Börne did. Wit was their weapon of choice. They made jokes!!

They poked fun at windbag literary critics and laughed at the stereotypical German, who went along with the rules and the status quo. But Heine and Börne were equal-opportunity offenders. For every insult to their fellow Germans, unwilling to stand up and fight for their rights, they doled out one to the Jews, who were not integrating fast enough and so still lived up to the Jew haters' worst stereotypes about them. In the dour world of Prussian discourse this called attention to itself. There was something alien about wit to the blood-and-soil German nationalist. Heine and Börne might have been baptized but their wit gave them away. What German makes a joke? their critics asked. The jokes proved they were still Jewish. Wit became part of the Jewish stereotype like a big nose and skill in business.

Pamphlets were written about Jewish wit. Inevitably Jewish writers responded to them wittily. Moritz Saphir, another theater critic, acknowledged the nationalists were absolutely correct in their analysis. "It is indeed striking that Jews have appropriated wit almost as exclusively as they have trade," he wrote. "Why? Censorship circumcises humor almost everywhere it appears so humor considers itself a Jew. The consummately tragic destiny of this nation is the mother of its wit."

Three decades later, English novelist George Eliot devoted an essay to Heine's wit. She defined it as "Reasoning raised to a higher power."

One colleague of Börne's, Wolfgang Menzel, a leading literary historian, explained to the public why Börne wrote about Germans in his cutting, sarcastic way. Menzel theorized that his friend had been scarred forever by the abuse heaped on him as a boy by Christian children in Frankfurt. Menzel noted that Börne had written with mocking despair that despite his conversion his passport had been issued to a "Frankfurt Jew." Börne replied, "I have never, not even in the noblest sense, thought about revenge for past humiliation. And what could I have done via the printed word?" He went on to ironically point out that compared to the rights other European peoples were enjoying, everyone in Germany was in the same boat as the Jews: oppressed, denied political representation, suffering from a bewildering array of restrictive laws. "Is not Germany the ghetto of Europe? Does not every German wear a yellow star on his hat? . . . Are not the people of Frankfurt, my former masters, in the same position as the Jews of yore? Had my heart ever thirsted for revenge it would now be completely inebriated."

Börne had long left Judaism behind but he understood that there was a link between the status of Jews in the German lands and the creation of a single, modern German state. Justice for the minority meant equal rights for all.

# iii.
# Reporting the Revolution

By 1828, Heine was truly famous, but money remained a problem. The author showed the same business skill in managing his writing career as he had in the import-export business. He needed a job and asked Karl August Varnhagen von Ense to write Germany's foremost publisher, J. F. Cotta, on his behalf. Cotta published both Goethe and Schiller and to work for the firm was to join the establishment. With baptismal certificate and Byronic status in hand, Heine met with Cotta. The company was keen to join the journalism boom and was setting up a new weekly called the *New World Political Annals.* Heine was appointed editor and moved to Cotta's headquarters in Munich.

It didn't take long for Cotta and Heine to mutually realize that editing was not a good fit. The publisher decided to send his famous new signing back out on the road. The demand for Heine's travel writing was high. Where to go was the question. Goethe had written a famous travelogue about Italy. Heine, always on the lookout for an opportunity to try and knock that living icon off his pedestal, decided to head over the Alps and write a better book about Italy than the greatest German writer of all time had.

Once again travel deepened his imagination. For Heine, reconciling Napoleon the conqueror of Germany with Napoleon the liberator of the Jews and the oppressed had been an almost impossible conundrum. He and Börne argued about it. The latter was a German patriot when it came to the question of Napoleon. He abhorred the emperor's work. Heine's view was more complicated. What happens to the ideal of Emancipation if there is no great man to spread it? Somewhere along the road over the Alps he resolved the question.

In *The Journey from Munich to Genoa,* he invents a scene. Dr. Heine finds himself riding in a stagecoach, and as it crosses an open plain in northern Italy the guard calls down to the passengers, "We are on the battlefield of Marengo." Marengo was the scene of Napoleon's greatest victory in Italy. For Heine this is where it all started to go wrong. Marengo was where the seeds of egotism were planted that grew into Napoleon's imperial delusion. This place was where the betrayal of freedom and democratic ideals began. But looking out over Marengo, three decades after the battle, Heine has an epiphany. History has come to a new age. The nationalism that separated Europeans is fading. From country to country the same questions are being asked about justice and equality. Heine had the greatest gift of poets, the gift of prophecy, and in this imagined scene his vision is full of optimism.

"Gradually, day by day, foolish national prejudices are disappearing; all harsh differentiations are lost in the generality of European civilization. There are no more nations in Europe only parties; and it is marvellous to see how these parties, for all their varying coloration recognize one another and how they understand one another, despite many differences in language. Our age hastens towards its great task.

"But what is the great task of our own age? It is emancipation. Not only the emancipation of Irishmen, Greeks, Frankfurt Jews, West Indian Blacks and other such oppressed peoples but the emancipation of the whole world . . ."

Heine was a man of letters, a poet, essayist, journalist. He was not as keen a political theorist as Börne but he understood just as clearly that Emancipation could not just be about Jews or any particular group gaining equal rights. It had to be a universal mission on behalf of all the oppressed people of the world.

The 1820s meandered to a close in the German-speaking lands. The society remained ill defined and backward compared to the rest of Europe. The industrial revolution was well under way in Britain and France, but not in Germany. The movement for national unity was split between the blood-and-soil Romantics and liberal modernists, and the split was in turn exploited by censors and secret police keeping a tight lid on political activity. Torpor surrounded the society, and Heine and Börne were floating listlessly in it. Then in the summer of 1830 came a revolutionary explosion that rocked Europe. Once again, it happened in France. For three days in July, Parisians rebelled against new censorship laws imposed by King Charles X. He was forced to abdicate and a constitutional monarchy was established.

Ludwig Börne raced off to Paris to report on events. Perhaps he could stir up his fellow Germans to act. Heine, typically, was traveling, spending the summer on an island in the North Sea off the German coast. By the time news of the revolution reached him it was over and the new French Constitution was in place. No matter. Heine set off immediately to join Börne in the French capital.

Neither Börne nor Heine would ever leave the city. They went to report on events for Germans. They hoped to use their writing to proselytize for change in their homeland. But they stayed because both men found that Paris was a place where they could be German. In Germany they would always be Jews.

Both sent dispatches in the form of letters back to German newspapers on the political changes in France and what they might mean for Germany. Börne's letters in particular gained him a wide new readership. In time, his collected *Letters from Paris* became a classic text of German liberalism. He could write things from Paris secure in the knowledge that he wouldn't be arrested. He became bolder. "When I say that all our various German governments have gone crazy, I mean it in the medical sense." What makes them crazy, according to Börne, is their obsession with the dark side of the French Revolution, which blinds them to the many good ideas that motivated it. "How sad! for when governments take leave of their senses, it's the sane who get locked up."

Over the Rhine, in Germany, Börne and Heine inspired a literary movement among the coming generation of liberal writers. "Young Germany" echoed the sentiments of Börne's and Heine's dispatches from Paris. For those who agreed with them the two authors were exemplary Germans. However, conservative nationalists answered back. They referred to Young Germany as Young Israel. The critics seemed incapable of writing about Heine's or Börne's ideas without referring to their Jewish origins, as if that explained everything about their attacks on "good" Germans and their beloved status quo: fragmented, semifeudal states, and lack of basic freedoms such as freedom of speech and the press. Börne finally had to answer.

"It is miraculous! Certain people object to my being a Jew; others forgive me; still others even praise me for it; but everybody remembers it," he wrote in an article for the *Augsburg Allgemeine Zeitung* or *Augsburg General Gazette*. "No, that I was born a Jew has never made me bitter against the Germans and has never distorted my perspective. I would not be worthy of the sunlight if I repaid with ingratitude the grace which God had bestowed upon me by making me a German and Jew at the same time.

"I am well aware of the value of my unearned fortune, my being both a German and Jew. Thus being able to strive for German virtues without having to share any German faults."

Börne acknowledged that his ghetto birth had shaped his politics. "Yes, since I was born a slave I love freedom more than you do . . . Yes, since I was not born in a fatherland I wish for a fatherland more passionately than you do."

He ended his letter with a missionary's zeal, urging his German antagonists to follow the lead of assimilated Jews and liberate themselves from the constrictions of the past.

For Heine life in Paris was sweet. The city was the epicenter of European culture and Heine's reputation as the voice of young Germany preceded him. He was immediately taken up by the city's glitterati. Victor Hugo and George Sand treated him as an equal. Despite the fact he was still living on an allowance from uncle Salomon he managed to find a way to hang out with aristocrats and the superrich, particularly Baron James de Rothschild. Börne spent his time exploring the new socialist ideas bubbling in the corners of the city. While Heine reveled, Börne became more and more serious about inventing a political program that would inspire a revolution.

That they would fall out was inevitable. Börne was a political polemicist searching for a system to change society, but Heine was an artist; the ideal society for him was one in which he could be left alone to write in perfect freedom. For him political writing was metaphorical. He was always willing to fight a duel and thought of himself as a soldier. Heine asked that at his death, mourners lay a sword on his coffin, not a poet's laurel wreath, because he had been a "good soldier in the fight for the Emancipation of mankind." Börne was dismissive. Heine was "a boy chasing butterflies on the battlefield while bloodshed rages all around."

Börne was brilliant but Heine was a genius. In the end that destroyed their relationship, but not before they had crossed together out of no-man's-land and established a place for their writing inside the mainstream of German and European society. Just as importantly, they also established a place for self-emancipated Jews, converts or not, inside European culture. Börne's *Letters from Paris* would inspire liberal politics in the German-speaking lands for decades. Heine's influence could be seen in the aphoristic brilliance of Friedrich Nietzsche as well as in his disdain for classical rules in writing his philosophy. The poet's work provided the inspiration and plot lines for two early operas of that arch Jew hater Richard Wagner: *The Flying Dutchman* and *Tannhäuser*.

## iv.
## A New Voice

While Heine luxuriated in his fame and his feuds in Paris, back in Hamburg a different voice entered the Emancipation debate. Gabriel Riesser was a decade younger than Heine and that decade made a huge difference. Riesser didn't see that paying the price of admission to European culture—either through baptism or self-denial—had helped individual Jews like Heine, Börne, or Rahel to acceptance. He decided it was time to fight back on home territory.

Riesser, like Heine and Eduard Gans, had trained in the law. Baptism would have opened the door to a good living as a lawyer or a university professor, but he simply could not bring himself to do it. He wasn't particularly observant, although both his grandfathers had been rabbis and he was a member of the Reform temple in Hamburg. It was the principle of basic civil rights he was fighting for and he couldn't make that argument convincingly from the halfway house of conversion. It was all well and good to write glowingly about universal emancipation from Paris but Riesser was convinced that it was the specific legal case for Jewish Emancipation in the German lands that needed to be made.

The young lawyer began his public fight in 1831. In the Grand Duchy of Baden, changes to the laws regulating Jewish life were being debated by the local parliament, the Diet. These changes would allow

Jews the right to serve in the legislature, sit as judges, and have full rights in the civic life of the province.

This was nitty-gritty legislation, not some theoretical discussion about rights. The debate echoed everything that had been heard in France four decades previously. Those against granting full civil rights trotted out the old arguments. The Jews were a separate nation living within the nation and so couldn't be citizens. They needed to forsake those aspects of their faith that marked them out as separate: change the day they observe the Sabbath, end circumcision, forgo religious marriage contracts. As proof of this change they needed to convert to Christianity.

Riesser published a pamphlet, an amicus brief, countering all those arguments with lawyerly logic and an advocate's rhetoric. The key point is that conversion should be no guarantee of German nationality. In his view this turns "a religious act into a political one." Riesser concludes, "There is only one baptism that confers nationality: this is the baptism of blood in the common struggle for freedom and fatherland!" Many Jews had fought against Napoleon in the Wars of Liberation. Their blood sacrifice had earned their community equal rights.

His eloquence failed to sway the Baden legislators, but Riesser had found a theme that he would never let go. Emancipation could not be purchased by conversion; social acceptance could not be gained by hiding who you were. He started a magazine and left no doubt who it was for and what it was about when he decided to call it *Der Jude,* or *The Jew.* The title was a red flag to the German community and to his own, which had been desperately trying to get the word *Jew* taken out of circulation. *Israelite* was the polite term now. *Jew* was only used by Judeophobes and self-haters, never in polite society. Riesser said no to that kind of thinking. He asked readers if they thought by changing the name *Jew* to something more acceptable to society they would avoid injustice and hatred.

"Vain hope! Believe me, hatred will find its man, just like the Angel of Death. It shall recognize him through a thousand favorable names."

Despite a small inheritance and living modestly, Riesser needed to work to pay for his proselytizing. Unable to practice law, he became a financial journalist. *Der Jude* appeared occasionally, when he had the time to write and the money to publish it. It was an extremely useful way to think through his own political program and proselytize for it. The conclusion he reached by 1835 was that the question of Jewish rights was inseparable from the question of German unification: "Offer me with one hand Emancipation, my most profound wish, and with the other hand the beautiful dream of German political unity and freedom and I would without hesitation choose the latter; because I have the strongest and deepest belief that it must include the former."

Another decade of stultification would have to pass before Riesser, and others, would have the chance to fight for that choice.

## CHAPTER TWELVE

# Let the Rothschilds
# Sanctify Themselves.
# Let Them Speak to Kings

I N THE EARLY SPRING OF 1840, THE JEWS OF DAMASCUS SENT A letter to their brethren in Constantinople to tell them of their state of misery and outline its cause. "On the first day of Adar [February] there disappeared from Damascus a priest who with his servant had dwelt forty years in the city . . . The day following there came people to the Jewish quarter to look for him . . . They seized a Jewish barber, telling him he must know all about the matter, and took him to the governor who on hearing the accusation immediately ordered him to receive five hundred lashes."

The reality of what was happening in Damascus was more frightening than the letter could make clear. The priest who had gone missing, Father Thomas, was a Capuchin monk born in Sardinia. He was a well-known figure in the city. The monk was trained in medicine and had healed people of all faiths. His disappearance excited comment everywhere. He had been going around the city putting up notices for a charity auction. Rumor spread throughout the city that he'd last been seen alive putting up one of the posters in the Jewish quarter.

Damascus in 1840 was a cosmopolitan city, a trading center with sizable Christian and Jewish minorities living in adjacent neighborhoods. It was a dusty metropolis of walls within walls. People lived discreetly behind these barriers, and so you never knew whether on the other side of a gate you would encounter a poor home or a sumptuous one. It was a perfect environment for maintaining the secrets on which a family business depended, but it also provided the environment in which rumors could grow. From one end of the city to the other the rumor quickly spread that the Jews had killed the monk.

Among the Muslims, Christians, and Jews living in the city, there were, however, a few facts. Everybody knew that the Sabbath was the quiet day in the Jewish quarter; its silence was woven into the pattern of Damascus's life. So the authorities chose that day to turn all the Jews out of their houses and begin a search for the priest or evidence of where he might be. They knew everyone would be behind their walls resting and unawares. Nothing was found but the Sabbath search had its intended effect: the community was terrified. The next day the police returned to the Jewish quarter, this time with a representative of the French consul, Count Ratti-Menton, in tow. The French diplomat had an interest in the case. As a Catholic, Father Thomas was under French protection. The police arrested a barber, Solomon al-Hallaq. They had found one of Father Thomas's notices posted above the entry to his shop. They took al-Hallaq to Count Ratti-Menton for interrogation. When Solomon did not provide suitable answers to the consul's questions he was taken away to the palace of Sherif Pasha, the city's governor, who used different methods to persuade the barber to talk.

Torture works. That is an incontestable truth and the main reason that most information obtained by torture is useless. People may try to be courageous but in the end virtually everyone breaks and to stop the pain says what their torturers want to hear. After receiving several hundred lashes on his feet and having his head crushed in a vise, the barber Solomon named the names his interrogators wanted:

the leaders of his community in Damascus were responsible for the priest's disappearance. The beleaguered Solomon confessed that Father Thomas had been murdered so that his blood could be used to make Passover matzo.

The Blood Libel—Jews slaughtered Christians and used their blood in religious rituals—was a lie dreamed up in medieval Europe to foment violence against the community. On the entry gate to the Frankfurt Judengasse was a picture representing a Christian boy who had allegedly been murdered for his blood in 1475. Now in 1840 the Blood Libel had returned. The French consul, Count Ratti-Menton, shook his head ruefully when he heard the barber's confession. Without a second thought as to how it had been obtained, he believed it and duly wrote in his dispatches to his government in Paris that the Jews were at it again—murdering Christians for their religious rites. The British consul in Damascus, Nathaniel Werry, accepted the barber's posttorture confession as well. It was as if accusations of witchcraft returned to Salem in 1840 and were taken seriously by the authorities.

On the basis of the barber's confession, seven of the most prominent citizens of the community and three rabbis were arrested and tortured. Two of the rabbis and one of the leaders died under the lash. For a while, about sixty Jewish children were also detained. The search for the priest's body continued. House after house was demolished in a fruitless search for Father Thomas's and his servant's bodies. Terror among Damascus's Jewish population was absolute.

While the descent into a pit of medieval fear continued day by day, the community desperately tried to get help from the outside world. But the speed of communication from the city was also medieval. Weeks went by before messages began to reach first Constantinople and then Europe about the outrage. This worked both for and against the unfortunate men languishing in the pasha's dungeon. Damascus and the rest of Syria were part of the Ottoman Empire. When it came to law enforcement, Sherif Pasha had the right to torture confessions out of them but he did not have the authority to execute them.

One other thing kept the men alive: The Ottoman Empire was in end-stage decline. It was splitting in half. Sultan Abdülmecid I in Constantinople had lost control of Syria and Damascus to Muhammad Ali, his viceroy in Egypt. In theory Ali owed allegiance to the sultan, but in practice he was trying to take over the empire. Moreover, Sherif Pasha in Damascus was his adopted son. The pasha was obligated to ask his father for instructions on what to do with his prisoners.

Weeks passed as dispatches wended their way through the deserts of Syria and Palestine toward Egypt and his father's court. Diplomatic pouches destined for Europe with news of the affair traveled by caravan over the mountains of Lebanon to Beirut and then were put on ships to sail across the Mediterranean to France. Rumor travels faster than official mail. Word of what was happening in Damascus spread around the eastern Mediterranean. On the island of Rhodes a young Christian man disappeared and like some fast-traveling plague the Blood Libel accusation appeared there. More Jews were arrested and tortured.

In Beirut, a Jewish merchant wrote to Hirsch Lehren in Amsterdam, who was the primary liaison between European Jewry and the handful of Jews who lived in Palestine. The letter summarized the rumors and facts and urged Lehren to contact the one family who could make the nightmare stop, the Rothschilds. "Let them sanctify themselves," read the letter. "Let them speak to the kings and to their ministers to persuade them to write to Ali" to intervene on the Damascus Jews' behalf.

Lehren sent a letter to Baron James de Rothschild in Paris. "The Jews will never be free of persecution until the Messiah comes," he wrote. "But the good Lord has always given us men of eminence with sufficient influence to ameliorate their misfortunes. And in our time, He has given us the renowned Rothschild family which has the power to save their brethren suffering persecution . . . Here is a chance to prove yourself the guardian angel of the oppressed and for you to open the doors of Paradise."

## ii.
## The Rothschilds

Sometimes the tide of history runs in the favor of even the most cruelly oppressed people. Legally emancipated or not, this was happening now for Jews as the industrial revolution took hold of Europe. In the centuries of ghettoization Jews were forced by circumstance into becoming experts on low and high finance. They had been hated and abused for dealing in money but they had no choice, their survival depended on it. During that time family networks of business connections had grown throughout the world of Ashkenaz. They extended across borders of principalities and states. Now the times demanded large amounts of capital to be shifted over borders to build projects, to give the industrial revolution its head. With a head start of centuries, Jews were best placed to provide financial services to the entrepreneurs creating the new industrialized economy of Europe. And no family was more successful at providing these services than the Rothschilds.

They had, in the words of that failed businessman Heinrich Heine, "destroyed the predominance of land by raising the system of state bonds to supreme power, thereby . . . endowing money with the previous privileges of the land." Feudalism empowered those who owned the land. That era was finished and now money ruled.

The family's rise had paralleled the Emancipation era. Fifty years before the Damascus Affair, Baron James's father, Mayer Amschel Rothschild, was a rare coin dealer and small-time banker in Frankfurt's Judengasse. The family's history had been bound with that ghetto ever since an ancestor had moved onto that dark, squalid street several centuries earlier and lived in a house with a red shield painted on the door. He adopted the symbol as the family surname, Rothschild. No matter the cruel restrictions, the Rothschild family stayed in Frankfurt. Mayer Amschel conducted business and lived above his shop at number 7.

The Rothschild rise to influence began in the 1780s when Wilhelm, Crown Prince of Hesse, son of the local ruler the Landgrave of Hesse, and also an avid coin collector, bought some rare items from Mayer Amschel. The men developed a relationship and Amschel discreetly petitioned Wilhelm for the title of "court factor." He understood that titles acquired added an unquantifiable value to his family's reputation. Wilhelm granted his request and, more importantly, the status of "protected Jew." This gave Rothschild certain freedom of movement that other Jews did not have. He used it to branch out beyond coin dealing and into general trading.

As the old order mobilized against the French Revolution, the next step came in the creation of the family fortune. Wilhelm had inherited the title of Landgrave of Hesse and Mayer Amschel was one of several bankers he employed. The landgrave was rich. His fortune came from land and peasants—lots and lots of peasants. He hired them out as soldiers to other monarchs like his cousin, Britain's King George III. Hessians had fought for the British in America's War of Independence and now they would fight the French. Rothschild handled the business end of that transaction. Then the Austrian Army arrived in the vicinity of Frankfurt as it made its way toward France. Rothschild used the trading networks he had developed to become the provisioner for the army as well as its paymaster.

The next step toward their massive fortune came from something immeasurable: the power of family. Mayer Amschel had nine children, and all worked within the business he was building. There were five sons and the third of them, Nathan, chafing to get out from under his older brothers' rule, was sent to England to look after the family's interests. The family were big importers of British textiles into Germany just as the Napoleonic wars were getting under way. All around Europe massive armies were being raised and they needed to be outfitted. Britain, which was already industrializing, turned out vast amounts of cloth for military uniforms. Nathan moved to Manchester to oversee the export of these textiles back to Germany.

Nathan's success was phenomenal and one of its by-products was the creation of human networks of communication and distribution that were unparalleled by any business group in Europe. Mayer Amschel wanted daily dispatches on business: Nathan's mother wanted to know how he was eating and whether his wardrobe was holding up. When the other sons were on the road, they too had to communicate back to Frankfurt regularly. Ordinary postal services were not efficient enough for the family so they developed their own courier service.

With continental Europe conquered in the first decade of the nineteenth century, Napoleon declared economic war on Britain. When all ports on the continent were closed to British manufacture, Nathan and his family simply used their couriers to organize a highly successful blockade-running operation.

These networks would come in handy at the critical final step in establishing the Rothschild family as indispensable to Europe's governments. By now the family had established a branch in Paris run by the youngest son, Jakob. At the height of the Napoleonic wars, the Duke of Wellington was fighting a campaign in Spain, trying to push the French out of the Iberian Peninsula. The British government, through its own ineptitude, was unable to get Wellington money to pay his troops. Nathan was able to purchase a large sum of gold, got the government to buy it from him, and, as part of the deal, he agreed to deliver the gold to Wellington. Using Rothschild family networks the brothers managed to ship the gold in chests, which were landed on the French coast and then transported across France to Wellington in Spain without Napoleon even knowing about it.

As he watched his sons build on the foundations he had laid, Mayer Amschel continued to give them examples of how to live. While other prominent Jewish patriarchs watched their children convert, and sometimes even encouraged them to become Christians, Mayer Amschel bound his children fast to their community. In 1806, with Frankfurt now under effective French control, he asked that Frankfurt's Jews be given the same rights as their coreligionists in France. Instead he was offered the rights of citizenship in Frankfurt by the prince-primate, Karl Dalberg. He respectfully declined until all Jews received the same right.

As the family fortune grew and restrictions on where Jews could reside evaporated, Mayer Amschel and his wife, Gutle, remained on the Judengasse. It was the world they knew. It was a sign of loyalty to their community. Old Rothschild died in 1812 as Nathan and James were pulling off their great coup. The prowess with which he had managed to lay the foundations of a dynasty was matched by the emotional skill he and his wife displayed in raising a family with no black sheep, bound to the business and to Judaism.

The five sons continued to prosper. By 1820, the second son, Salomon, set up operations in Vienna; two years later the fourth son, Calmann, set up a branch in Naples. Just as their father did, the brothers sought titles and privileges and these were granted by grateful rulers around Europe. The emperor of Austria ennobled the family. All the brothers were now Austrian barons. The barons "von Rothschild" were now Europe's most important bankers.

Yet the family business remained headquartered in and around the Judengasse. The oldest son, Amschel, looked after his mother. Gutle continued to live in the house where she had raised her children in such a way that there were no black sheep. They consciously made a different choice than most other Jews of their class in the early days of Emancipation. They did not get involved with reformed worship much less consider conversion. Their commitment to orthodox religion and Jewish identity remained strong. They would go no further than Christianizing their names. In 1816, Jakob, who had changed his name to James, wrote to his brothers, "We work as much for the sake of our prestige as Jews, as for any other reason."

They gave to Jewish charities and set up schools. Son Amschel, remembering the days when Jews were forbidden to walk in Frankfurt's public gardens, bought a plot of land and built a park for his community to enjoy at any time. He gave specific instructions that it be landscaped so the citizens of Frankfurt understood that Jews also knew how to cultivate beauty in nature.

At the start of the Emancipation era it was the philosopher Moses Mendelssohn to whom Jews turned to intercede with their rulers in times of trouble. By the time of the Damascus Blood Libel, philosophy had been replaced by money. It was the Rothschilds who were now the good shepherds of their coreligionists.

# iii.
# Mobilization

Events in Damascus cut across many lines of Rothschild influence. Among those detained in the initial roundup of Jews was a trader from Tuscany, Isaac Cacciatto. That part of Italy had reverted to Austrian control after the Congress of Vienna and so Cacciatto was under the protection of the Austrian consul in Damascus, who saved him from torture but not arrest.

The detention of someone under its protection gave Austria's government a reason to get involved in the case. Prince Metternich, now well into his sixties, was still chancellor of Austria. For the best part of a quarter of a century he had relied on the friendship and business acumen of Mayer Amschel's third son, Salomon, to finance the reconstruction of his country after the Napoleonic wars and help modernize its infrastructure. The Damascus Affair was one more mutual interest for them. They discussed the situation. Metternich was dismissive of the Blood Libel accusation. How to proceed required careful thought, however.

Metternich's decades in power had confirmed in his own mind the theory of international relations based on the balance of power among nations. The Ottoman Empire's northern borders were adjacent to Austria. Its rapid decline threatened to bring instability to Austria's borderlands as well as Europe's balance of power. For the moment Austria and England propped up the sultan's court in Constantinople. France backed the Egyptian viceroy, Muhammad Ali. Metternich saw an opportunity in the situation to strengthen his own country and his allies' hands in relation to its policy in the Middle East. The fate of the Damascus Jews now became part of a larger diplomatic game. He wrote to Austria's consul general in Alexandria, Anton Laurin, instructing him to at the very least get Muhammad Ali to order the torture stopped.

Anton Laurin was the very best kind of diplomat, the type who anticipates his superior's intentions and acts without waiting for instruction. He had already met with Muhammad Ali and asked him to instruct his son, Sherif Pasha, to stop torturing confessions out of Damascus's Jews. Ali thought of himself as an enlightened man in the European sense. His arguments with Constantinople were about reforming the Ottoman Empire's governance so it could survive in the modern world. He knew that torture was as much about punishment as about gaining evidence and so he ordered an immediate end to the abuse of the Jewish prisoners.

The consul duly sent a report back to Metternich with a blind copy going to the Austrian consul general in Paris, who just happened to be Baron James de Rothschild. All the brothers had been made honorary consuls general of Austria. Among the titles collected by the family this was among the most useful. It gave them quasi-official diplomatic standing. In a cover note sent with the report to Baron James, Laurin suggested that the information be circulated in the press.

By now, seven weeks after Father Thomas's disappearance and the start of the Damascus reign of terror, news of the affair was circulating around Europe via the press. The story was causing a sensation. Facts, or the attempt to report them from both sides of a dispute, played little part in journalism in 1840. Any rumor would do, so long as it pandered to the prejudices of readers, and the Blood Libel story offered so many prejudiced rumors it was irresistible. Overt acts of Jew hatred were in decline around Europe, but the old suspicions weren't too far under the surface. The news from Damascus, flowing via Count Ratti-Menton, contained the most gory speculation about the fate of Father Thomas and the use Jews made of his blood. Even though the Blood Libel belonged to the Middle Ages, not modern society, many people reading the lurid accounts were inclined not to question the accusation. Believing the worst of Jews was an ingrained habit from the centuries of ghettoization.

This was true at an official level as well. France's Prime Minister Adolphe Thiers was a man of impeccable intellectual and liberal credentials yet he did not look at Ratti-Menton's report with skepticism. He took it at face value and backed his envoy's assessment.

The Jewish community needed to fight back in the press and elsewhere on behalf of the Damascus community and themselves. But this wasn't a battle that could be waged entirely by the phenomenal Rothschild clan. James understood that other members of the community would have to be involved in influencing public opinion. This represented an important change. Even in the recent past, in a crisis born of prejudice, Jews in Europe would have relied on allies outside the community, such as Mirabeau or Abbé Grégoire or Lessing, to sway public opinion. But now they had greater access to the press. The Damascus Affair was turning into a measure of how successfully Jews had integrated in the Emancipation era.

From Paris, Heinrich Heine tried to influence opinion in Germany through his newspaper column in the leading liberal newspaper, *Augsburg General Gazette*. He even dug up "The Rabbi of Bacharach" from the bottom of his desk drawer and allowed the fragment to be published. Members of the community in Britain began a steady letter-writing campaign to the *Times*.

It did help that the Rothschilds had friends in the highest places. Metternich had set up the aggressive regime of press censorship that had driven Heine and Börne into exile in Paris, and that ultimately led to Heine's books being banned, but now the prince used his control of the Austrian press on behalf of the Damascus Jews.

But the greatest burden of public persuasion fell on the French community. It was the French consul in Damascus who had set the whole crisis in motion and it would not be resolved short of the French government repudiating him.

France had granted Jews civil rights in 1791. Napoleon had circumscribed them with his laws of 1808 but when they expired in 1818 those laws had not been renewed. A generation of Jews had grown up in France with civil rights and integrated into the growing French middle class. They served as officers in the army and as senior bureaucrats in the civil service. They studied law and were permitted to practice their profession. They could be elected to the National Assembly.

Adolphe Crémieux was arguably the most well known of these men. Born in the south of the country, he had made his reputation early. One of the unresolved bits of emancipatory legislation concerned the taking of oaths in court. No Jew could be expected to swear in the name of Jesus Christ or place his hand on the New Testament when speaking the words. Instead, if they had to swear an oath, Jews continued to take the Oath More Judaico. This was a humiliating medieval ritual in which Jews were forced to go to the nearest synagogue to swear their oaths, not just in judicial matters, but also when taking up positions in the professions.

When young Crémieux was first called to the bar as a lawyer in the Rhône valley city of Nîmes, he was asked to take his professional Oath More Judaico. He refused. "Am I in a synagogue?" he asked the authorities. "Am I in Jerusalem, in Palestine? No, I am in Nîmes in France. And am I only a Jew? No, I am also a French citizen. So I will take the oath as Jewish Frenchman."

Subsequently Crémieux successfully represented other Jews who refused to submit to the Oath More Judaico and this brought an end to the ritual in practice if not in law. But the lawyer was not primarily an advocate for Jewish causes, nor was he particularly religious. He was a forceful criminal defense attorney and advocate for liberal causes such as a free press. When King Louis Philippe attempted to shut down a newspaper that displeased him, Crémieux challenged the monarch in court. Crémieux was a thoroughly integrated Jewish Frenchman. He was voted onto the Consistory, the official body set up by Napoleon to run the community's affairs and liaise with the government, because of his renown as a lawyer as much as from his identity as a Jew.

By 1840, at age forty-four, he was one of the best-known lawyers in France. His collected courtroom arguments were published as books, which were avidly read, and he had a good sideline as a commentator in newspapers. It was logical that James de Rothschild would turn to Crémieux to start making the case against the Blood Libel accusation.

On April 6, with the baron's help, the *Gazette des Tribunaux* and *Journal des Debats* published a letter from Crémieux. There was no cringe in his words. His tone was one of outrage and sadness at the incredulity of the French press: "Is it really true that in France, in Paris, the newspapers which are most devoted to the ideas of progress and liberalism . . . have accepted the absurd and monstrous stories . . . about Father Thomas and his servant?" Jews are your fellow citizens, he reminds the papers' editors. "Did you not give any thought of the anguish which would be caused" the community by reporting these absurd allegations?

The voice of the successful courtroom lawyer came through in this letter, and its publication proved a rallying point not just for his coreligionists but for those simply disinclined to believe the medieval nonsense that had been tortured out of the men in Damascus.

Crémieux was now the public face of the fightback. Shortly after his letter was published he was invited to London to meet with the Board of Deputies of British Jews. This group had been established in the 1750s to look after their community's interests. The community in Britain was tiny, centered almost exclusively on London, and its influence was not particularly great. The Jewish Emancipation fight had never been as large a part of life in Britain as it had been in France or Germany. Emancipation of Catholics had been the big civil rights battle of the early nineteenth century in Britain. It wasn't until 1829 that laws had been passed that allowed Catholics to step out of the shadow of discriminatory statutes, some of which had been put in place during the Reformation.

The Board of Deputies wanted to join forces with the French Consistory to bring pressure on their governments. A two-pronged plan emerged from the meeting. First, the two communities would seek meetings at the highest levels of their respective governments to ask that they intervene in the situation. Then a joint mission of Anglo-French Jewry would be dispatched to Damascus to interview their imprisoned coreligionists and ascertain the truth of why they were tortured.

In France the first part of the plan proved problematic. Crémieux requested a meeting with Thiers, a man he knew personally, but the French prime minister declined the offer. In England the plan went more smoothly. The British foreign secretary, Lord Palmerston, like Metternich found the whole situation in Damascus grotesque. When he heard that his consul in Damascus, Nathaniel Werry, supported Ratti-Menton, he sent a terse memo noting that Werry had been too long in strange countries and ordering him home by Christmas. Beyond his own moral repugnance, Palmerston also saw an opportunity for influence. Britain had no particular group in the Middle East it could represent in the way that the French looked after Catholic interests. Taking up the cause of the Jews of Syria and Palestine offered that sort of entree into the workings of the region. Palmerston happily agreed to meet the Board of Deputies representatives.

Now the Damascus situation was so thoroughly intertwined with foreign policy and popular public opinion that it was inevitable that the legislatures in France and Britain would have to debate the crisis. In France the fate of the Damascus Jews was brought up by Benoit Fould, the only Jewish member of the National Assembly's Chamber of Deputies. Opening the debate, Fould accused Ratti-Menton of exceeding his authority and the bounds of decency and common sense by accusing not just an individual of murder "but an entire nation." He accused the count of inciting torture despite the fact that France was an enlightened nation that believed in "equality before the law, and religious equality."

Thiers for his part had to defend his envoy. If we are going to be fair to the Damascus Jews, he responded to Fould, then we need to be fair to the French envoy. One liberal deputy demanded the right to speak and excoriated Ratti-Menton for condoning torture and demanded to know why, as a representative of France, he did not oppose it on the spot.

Thiers responded by attacking Jews at their most vulnerable point. He raised the old questions about whether Jews could ever be citizens of one country, loyal to its government, or whether they were their own nation, whose primary allegiance was to its affairs. Thiers looked at Fould and said, "You protest in the name of the Jews, I protest in the name of the French." He pointed out that Jews were mobilizing governments all around Europe. This gave them tremendous power. "It takes courage to stand up to such zealous ardor." But he, Thiers, was loyal to France alone and to France's brave and isolated diplomat in Damascus.

On behalf of the Consistory, Crémieux visited Thiers shortly after this debate to discuss his mission to the Middle East. The lawyer questioned the prime minister closely. Was he supporting Ratti-Menton because he was obligated by political rules to back his envoy in public? Or did he actually agree with his man in Damascus that the Jews had killed Father Thomas for his blood? Thiers's answer left him in no doubt, "Those people are guilty . . . You do not know how far the fanaticism of the eastern Jews goes. This is not the first instance of such a crime."

The Rothschilds and the rest of the community's leadership were stunned by Thiers's public performance as well as his private words to Crémieux. It was time to get the second part of the plan moving. Crémieux would have to go to the Middle East as soon as possible. In Britain, the next generation of the Rothschild family had taken over the business but remained bound to Mayer Amschel's code. Their bonds to each other and their community were unshakable. The family organized a subscription to fund the "diplomatic" mission and contributed one thousand pounds to the cause. They also suggested that Sir Moses Montefiore be the British representative on the mission. This was not just because Montefiore could pay his own way, but because he was related to the family by marriage. Keeping it in the family was the way the Rothschilds did everything.

• • •

As the Rothschilds began planning and publicizing the Crémieux/ Montefiore mission, not coincidentally Damascus was discussed in Parliament. The British government wanted to make it clear to their public and the wider world that they took a very different view of the situation than the government of France did.

In what was more a choreographed piece of theater than it was a debate, on Monday, June 23, Britain's foreign secretary, Lord Palmerston of the Whig Party, agreed to take questions on the situation. According to the *Times* account, the leader of the opposition, Sir Robert Peel, a Tory, rose in the House of Commons and began by apologizing. He had no question to ask as the rules of debate required, but, he assured the House of Commons, when they knew his subject they would allow him to speak. Peel said he had been in conversation with notable people of "the Jewish persuasion" who along with the members of the House believed in the "great ends of Justice and liberality." He recounted their concerns that the charges that excited such prejudice in Damascus if left unchecked could "affect the entire body of Jews throughout the world" and lead to a general outbreak of hostility against them.

Palmerston concurred and made it absolutely clear that justice for the men who had been tortured was his great concern. Indeed he had already taken action, telling his consul in Alexandria to make it clear to the viceroy, Muhammad Ali, that it would be in his interests to investigate the situation thoroughly and repudiate any confessions obtained under torture. Palmerston knew his words would find their way to Egypt.

The most interesting point of the debate was made by Daniel O'Connell, an Irishman, who had led the successful fight for Catholic Emancipation. He noted that one way of vindicating the Jews would be to give them the same rights as Catholics—including the right to run for election to Parliament. O'Connell noted that Peel's statement would have carried more force if it had been made by a "Hebrew gentleman in the House."

Following the debate on June 25, the *Times,* the paper of record, published its largest issue ever, giving reams of space to the controversy. It printed the original letters sent by the Damascus community to Europe and Constantinople. But shockingly, it printed across a third of a page extracts from a notorious book called *Mystery of the Blood,* purportedly written by a priest who had been brought up a Jew. The author goes into detail about the uses to which Christian blood is put in Jewish rituals. Blood is not just for making matzo, says the author. At circumcision, the rabbi officiating mixes a drop of the circumcised child's blood and a drop of Christian blood in a goblet of wine and then "puts a drop on the babe's lips twice, each time saying, 'I have given thee thy blood and thy life.'" Four pages later, in an editorial, the paper congratulated itself for providing the space to air all sides of the issue and bringing to the notice of the civilized world a case "upon which the very existence of the Jewish religion and the Jews, as a separate class of the community may be said to depend."

The public campaign moved on ten days later to the Mansion House in the City of London. (The City is the financial district of London in the way that Wall Street is a designation for New York's financial district, but the City has a self-governing autonomy that Wall Street's moneymen can only dream about.) The Mansion House is the financial district's City Hall, so the meeting had an official quality.

The building was absolutely packed with politicians, leading businessmen, and Christian ministers. The lord mayor opened proceedings with a simple declaration: "The Jews of Damascus are as worthy of respect as those who dwell among us in England." After three hours of testimonials and demands for the release of the tortured victims in Damascus, punctuated by shouts of "Hear! Hear!" O'Connell closed proceedings. "After the testimony given to demonstrate the moral worth of the Jews could any man be so insane as to believe they use blood in their rites?"

A motion deploring the affair was the small result of the meeting. The larger one was this: at no time in their modern history had any group of worthies shown such solidarity with Jews. As reports of the

Mansion House meeting made their way around Britain and then Europe, the message taken by Jews was this: despite the rights given and taken away, the Emancipation era was leading to a social acceptance of the community that had never existed before in Europe.

The events in Britain filled Montefiore and Crémieux with confidence as they set off for Egypt. They made a good progress under the aegis of the Rothschild family. Stopping in Naples, where Calmann Rothschild ran operations, they received supplies. Then the men sailed off to Alexandria and the court of Muhammad Ali.

## iv.
## Resolution

By the time the two envoys arrived in Egypt the larger diplomatic picture had come into sharp focus for the viceroy. Muhammad Ali knew the French government was his greatest supporter, but he also knew France was increasingly isolated from the other European nations not just on the Damascus question but on his struggle with the sultan in Constantinople. When Crémieux and Montefiore were preparing their mission in mid-July, Britain, Russia, Prussia, and Austria had signed the Treaty of London committing the four countries to restoring Syria to the sultan by whatever means necessary.

The rebellious Egyptian viceroy had two hundred thousand men under arms and a good line in bellicose rhetoric but the reality was that Ali didn't want war if a negotiated settlement was possible. So he needed to keep all sides calm. Ali received Montefiore and Crémieux on August 5, almost as soon as they arrived in Alexandria. The pair asked for immediate safe conduct to Damascus so they could interview the prisoners themselves.

The viceroy gave no direct reply to the request, which was a perfectly normal way to conduct business in the Middle East. Days went by with no formal reply. Again, perfectly normal. But there was another reason for the delay. The international situation was coming to a head. He had received an ultimatum from the allied powers: give up Syria now and you can maintain control of Egypt. To underline their seriousness a British fleet was sailing toward Beirut.

Ali was desperately preoccupied trying to save what he could without a full-scale war. At the same time he was ill, suffering from an extremely large, very painful boil right on his buttocks. He was receiving treatment from a French doctor and an Italian one, both of whom had become friendly with Crémieux after his arrival in the capital. Now the envoy enlisted the doctors to the cause. As the physicians attended the ugly sore on the viceroy's behind, both argued for the release of the Damascus Jews. According to Crémieux's diaries, the doctors repeatedly reminded Muhammad Ali that there was no better way to impress on the world his credentials as a modernizer and enlightened man than to free the Damascus Jews from their dungeon. "The voice of six million Jews around the world" would be raised in his favor.

On August 28, as the doctors were lancing his boil, the viceroy told them he would be setting the prisoners free. As soon as the wound was dressed the physicians hurried to Crémieux with the extraordinary news.

However, there was one final step before the Damascus Jews were set free from their dungeon. The viceroy's initial orders said the release was an act of "mercy." Crémieux, vigilant lawyer that he was, understood that "mercy" implied that somehow the men were guilty and being given a generous reprieve. He went to the viceroy and asked for a change in the language that would allow the world to understand that the charge of ritual murder had not been proved. This was done.

In Damascus, the survivors were restored to their families although all of them were maimed for life. Crémieux and Montefiore returned to their respective homes and were honored as heroes. In October war came and the viceroy was forced to withdraw from Syria. Adolphe Thiers had backed two wrong horses: Muhammad Ali and Ratti-Menton. He was forced to resign as prime minister.

For the Rothschilds the successful resolution of the Damascus Blood Libel affair projected them even more thoroughly into European public life. They were the unquestioned global leaders of their community.

What the Damascus Affair meant to other Jews is hard to summarize. Fifty years had passed since the National Assembly emancipated France's Jews. Full civil rights still eluded the rest of the community in Europe. Despite that fact, through their own efforts, the community was well on its way to integration. The fact that governments had taken up the Damascus case at the urging of the community showed how far they had come into the mainstream.

The price for this had been radical changes in their community's customs and religious practice. The Jewish part of their lives would have been unrecognizable to their grandfathers. For centuries they had been walled off from the events of European history. Now the overwhelming majority of Jews were living the same history as everyone else. Their lives were being shaped by rapid industrialization and the shift of population from the countryside to the cities. Even with the danger emanating from Damascus averted, for most Jews there was no time to breathe easy before returning to the reality of earning a living in the new economy. Indeed, when there was time to reflect, some in the community felt a profound unease.

Toward the end of 1840, one German Jew looked back on the events in Damascus and how they had played out in Europe. He saw the crisis as "a new point of departure in the Jewish life." He had reached his conclusion based on the fact that so many in Europe, from Adolphe Thiers to newspaper editors to ordinary people in the street, had been willing to accept the Blood Libel charge without question. This man wrote, "In spite of the degree of education which European Jews have attained there exists a barrier between them and the surrounding nations, almost as formidable as in the days of religious fanaticism . . . They don't understand how it is possible such a stupid medieval legend should be given credence even for a moment."

The author, Moses Hess, continued, "We shall always remain strangers among the nations. They may tolerate us and even grant us

emancipation but they will never respect us . . . In spite of enlightenment and emancipation, the Jew in exile who denies his nationality
will never earn the respect of the nations among whom he dwells."
When Hess wrote those words he was a committed communist busy
working on behalf of the "European proletariat." But he continued
to look for an answer to his "Jewish Question," and eventually Moses
Hess found it: the Jews would never be allowed to fully integrate into
European societies and therefore had to return to their own country,
to Palestine.

# PART 3

# REVOLUTION

## CHAPTER THIRTEEN

# We Have a Solemn
# Mission to Perform

THE LATE WINTER SKY EMPTIED ITSELF ON THE HEADS OF mourners as the funeral procession threaded its way among the tombstones in Vienna's Schmelzer-Friedhof cemetery. The only sounds that could be heard in the throng were footsteps on wet pavement and the quiet drip of rain guttering off overcoats. Something terrible had happened on March 13, 1848, and now, four days later, respect was being paid. At the head of the procession were five coffins. Inside each one was the body of a young man gunned down when a detachment of soldiers overreacted to a protest outside Austria's parliament. The men, students and workers, had been demanding a democratic constitution for their country when the troops arrived.

Following the coffins were the clergy who would officiate at the funeral: a Catholic priest, a Protestant pastor, and a rabbi. A single grave had been cut out of the muddy ground where all the dead would be laid to rest. When the procession reached the site, the coffins were laid before it. The priest, Anton Fuster, made an almost imperceptible gesture to the rabbi, Isaac Noah Mannheimer, inviting him to speak first. It was a quiet show of ecumenical brotherhood. Two of the five to be buried were Jewish. In a city where Jewish residence was still severely restricted—officially no more than four thousand Jews lived in Vienna—the fact that two community members had fallen in the cause of Austrian freedom had more than earned this gesture of respect. Rabbi Mannheimer stepped forward and spoke to his dead.

"You have sanctified the name of the Lord, you have redeemed the glorious name of Israel from the disgrace attached to it by the world." Then he looked out at the throng, "You have wished that these dead Jews should rest with you in your earth, in the same earth. Do not begrudge it that those who have fought the same battle with you, a hard battle, should *live* with you on the same earth, free and untroubled as yourselves." Then the rabbi pledged that the living would emulate the dead: "Someday Christians and Jews will live with you on one soil, free and unhampered like yourselves."

A reporter from the *Oesterreicher Rundschau,* or *Austrian Review* newspaper, noted for his readers, "All the speeches were brief and delivered in a conciliatory vein. The speech of the Jewish preacher Mannheimer was particularly impressive because of its precision, clarity and the passage that noted thenceforth a Jew will rest together with Christians in the consecrated soil."

It is wrong to judge revolutions by whether they succeed or fail. Virtually all revolutions fail. Either they fail literally and are reversed by forces of reaction or they fail metaphorically by compromising their lofty goals. The fairest way to assess the impact of a revolution is by the fact that it happens at all. Revolutions represent tectonic shifts in society, terrible rupturings that create decisive breaks with the past. That is what was happening in Austria and all over Europe in early 1848.

The system set up at the Congress of Vienna in 1815 was finally and irrevocably shattered. It was shattered because all the national questions that Metternich and his colleagues had ignored in trying to re-create the world as it was before the French Revolution had not gone away. Underneath the surface the pressure for national and individual rights had built up until it could no longer be contained.

Metternich's system was shattered because Europe's economy had changed. The structures of commerce were transnational now and the old system prevented the free flow of capital around the continent. It was shattered because people were less and less connected to the places where their families had lived for generations. They were leaving the countryside and moving to the city. This movement had been hastened by a catastrophic failure of the harvest in 1845 and 1846, leading to famine in some places.

It was shattered because it was not fair. The Metternich bargain of stability in exchange for severely restricted personal freedom benefited only the rulers.

The year of revolutions started on February 22, 1848, in Paris. The fading government of King Louis Philippe tried to suppress a movement for universal suffrage and the city exploded. Before the seismic spasm was finished there would be fifty revolutions and counterrevolutions around the continent. There were early rumblings of what was coming on the other side of the Alps in Italy at the start of the year, but it was the Paris event that triggered everything else. The city was not just the capital of France; six decades on from 1789 it remained the symbol of revolutionary promise all over Europe. As news filtered around the continent that the citizens of Paris had overthrown their king and his government in less than two days, young students and workers everywhere saw it as confirmation that their moment was at hand.

Revolutionary pressure immediately fell on Austria. From Vienna, the Habsburg family ruled a vast multiethnic, polyglot empire that stretched from Italy deep into what is today Ukraine. At the same time Austria remained the biggest player inside the German Confederation. And still running the show for the current emperor, Ferdinand I, was Prince Klemens Wenzel von Metternich. Now seventy-five years old, the chancellor continued to administer the vast realm with the same theories he had established thirty years earlier. In the name of maintaining a Europe-wide balance of power, he ruthlessly suppressed the national urges of Italians, Hungarians, Poles, Czechs, Slovaks, Ukrainians, and smaller ethnic groups through rigorous press censorship and draconian regulation of political activity. He had to be especially vigilant. Ferdinand was not a figure to inspire or command. He was physically weak, not very bright, and occasionally, it was rumored, not sane.

Two weeks after Parisians had risen, the citizens of Budapest demanded an independent parliament for Hungary and a written constitution for all the Habsburg lands. The threat of violent action if these demands were refused was implicit.

Throughout the following week news filtered up the Danube from Budapest to Vienna. At Vienna's university and polytechnic institute, students formed committees and frantically discussed what to do. First Paris, now Budapest. Like prisoners observing a jailbreak, the students had to quickly decide whether to risk going through the breach in the wall or wait in their cells for order to be restored. It was not a question they lingered over. A decisive break with the past was required. The Austrian Parliament was due to meet on Monday, March 13. The students decided to put their demands in writing and present the petition to Parliament on that day.

Throughout the weekend groups from the university met to hammer out the language of the petition. Once the language was agreed they set up tables near the university and went about getting signatures. Vienna's coffeehouses rumbled with excited and anxious talk about what was going to happen on Monday. Their grievances were clear so it was easy to draw up a list of demands. They wanted an end to censorship, increased academic freedom, and a written constitution. But throughout the frantic forty-eight hours no single leader of the students asserted himself.

On Monday morning, a mass meeting was called in the university assembly hall and from there thousands set off to the Landtag where the lower Austrian Parliament was in session. Upon arriving at the grand building the students found a supportive crowd of workers as well as people curious to witness history. The march had gotten everyone's blood up but the students found the doors to the Landtag locked. Since there was no leader, no one knew what to do next.

Among those in the crowd were two doctors in their mid-twenties, Adolf Fischhof and Joseph Goldmark. The pair was typical of their generation: politically aware and deeply frustrated by the restrictions of life in Metternich's Austria. Their political views were well-known in the medical faculty, one of the most liberal in the university. That they were also Jewish had less meaning at this moment. The mass of people was crammed inside a courtyard, and the closeness coupled with the lack of direction for their energy was growing dangerous. There was murmuring in the throng, but no clear voice taking command.

Fischhof sensed something ebbing out of the crowd; the moment was slipping away. The young doctor had never made a speech in his life and now without thinking about what he was doing he heard himself calling for the crowd's attention. Before Fischhof knew it he had been hoisted onto the shoulders of a couple of men he did not know. He shouted out, "This is a great day . . . We have a solemn mission to perform; he who on this day has no courage belongs in the nursery." Laughter and cheers. Now the crowd was recovering its focus. "What we need, what we ask, what we demand is first of all freedom of the press." Loud cheers. Now Fischhof ticked off the other demands— freedom of religion and academic freedom—and finally made a direct assault on the Metternich system: "Ill advised statesmanship has kept the peoples of Austria apart. They find a common ground and increase their strength by union." He shouted out in conclusion, "Long live the federated peoples of Austria. Long live freedom!"

By now members of Parliament were looking into the courtyard. The crowd was looking up at the legislators. Again there was a brief moment of hesitation. Then Joseph Goldmark managed to make himself heard. "Listen, friends, if we stay on here in this courtyard making speeches, that will not help us or our fellow-citizens. We have had enough talk among ourselves. Now is the time to get parliament to act."

With Fischhof at the front, the doors of the Landtag were forced open and the crowd rolled into the debating chamber. Fischhof handed the petition to the legislators and expressed the demonstrators' wish that it be conveyed to Hofburg Palace, where the emperor held court. After some private discussion, the demand was accepted and a deputation of legislators, followed by the growing crowd of students, workers, and people just arrived in town from the nearby countryside, headed for the Hofburg.

A *Vienna Gazette* reporter described what happened next: "The whole city was in an attitude of eager expectation; greatest uneasiness prevailed everywhere. That the dissatisfaction of the people has increased to a great degree is proved by the circumstance that the windows of Prince Metternich have been broken by the crowd. The military precautions for the maintenance of tranquility are very comprehensive, even cannon have been brought out." The dispatch ends, "Shots are being fired as I write."

In the melee the five young men were gunned down. Suddenly, placid and bourgeois Vienna was out of control. Students raced to the arsenal to grab weapons. Living out the stories they had read of revolutions in France, students and workers erected barricades across streets. For forty-eight hours the whole city was on edge. Then came word from the Hofburg. Emperor Ferdinand agreed to grant freedom of the press immediately and to work toward creating a constitution. The emperor also accepted Prince Metternich's resignation. A mob returned to Metternich's town house and burned it down but the prince was not at home. Wearing a disguise, he had slunk away from the city in a laundry wagon for exile in London.

On Friday the whole city turned out to bury Monday's dead. It was a chance to take stock of what the week meant. As in America after the shootings at Kent State, there was a sense of shock. Whatever the students had been doing, the state's response had been out of all proportion. But there was also real hope. A constitution had been promised, and old Metternich, who just a week earlier seemed likely to rule over all of them forever, was gone. On Monday evening the insurgents had manned barricades around the capital. Among them was a Jewish poet named Ludwig August Frankl. While standing guard during the night Frankl had composed an ode, "The University," praising the students as freedom fighters. Flyers containing the words were distributed to the crowds watching the funeral procession. At the bottom was a line noting that this was the first poem printed without censorship in Austria.

Among Jews there was an electric energy. Emancipation seemed close at hand. The emperor, a prisoner to the prejudices of his class, was no great friend of Emancipation but now he had begun to refer respectfully to the "Israelitish community" rather than the "Jews" when discussing civil rights. In his Sabbath sermon that week, Isaac Noah Mannheimer preached tactical patience to his congregation. "Say not a word about Jewish emancipation, unless others speak it for us." Emancipation was at hand because of the new political situation, but as Jews they were not to demand it. Equal rights for all the peoples of the empire was now their request.

Events moved quickly. On March 17, Venice broke away from Austria, and the following day Milan revolted against the Habsburgs. Meanwhile, in Prussia, Berlin erupted. As in Vienna, troops unused to facing their fellow citizens defying authority en masse became nervous and opened fire. Hundreds were killed, ten of them Jews. The king of Prussia, Frederick William IV, also promised a written constitution to his subjects.

## ii.
## Active Participants

These were not revolutions where monarchs were dragged off in tumbrels to the guillotine or lined up against a wall and shot. No matter how violent the initial insurrections, these revolts fought by law students, medical students, artisans, and that new kind of man, the factory worker, were supported by the growing urban middle class. The rebellions were very much about creating modern, legal frameworks that would allow the middle class to prosper. Many, particularly in Austria, were quite happy to maintain the monarchy, provided the monarch adhered to constitutional rules. So around Europe, the next phase of 1848 was the establishment of provisional governments to restore order, organize elections, and get to work writing constitutions. This wasn't always easy. Politically active students had studied the French Revolution of 1789, and in some places they wanted to move quickly to a Jacobin phase. A little reign of terror might make it clear to kings and emperors that they meant business.

In the Austrian capital, now dubbed "Red Vienna," this was the case. But Adolf Fischhof was appointed head of the provisional government's security committee and was able to prevent things getting out of hand. Similarly, in France, Adolphe Crémieux had been appointed justice minister. His prestige had only grown since the Damascus events, and his presence in the government soothed fears in the ruling class that they would be victims of retaliation and gave hope to the more radical elements that there would be no sellout of the revolution's key goal: one man, one vote.

They were not the only two Jews who were suddenly prominent in this destabilized Europe. Across the political spectrum, Jews, emancipated or not, took part in the events out of all proportion to their numbers in the population. In France, Crémieux was joined in the provisional government by Michel Goudchaux, as minister of finance. In Austria, Fischhof, Goldmark, and Mannheimer were all elected to the new Parliament. And, even though they lacked full civil rights, Jews were elected to several of the parliaments of the German Confederation. The Venice insurrection was led by Daniel Manin, a convert to Catholicism, who like most converts was still regarded as a Jew. The revolutions even reached Rome, where once again the ghetto doors were knocked down and several Jews were elected to the new city council.

This highly visible participation represented a break with the past as seismic as the revolutions themselves. For centuries, when the world around them was in upheaval, the denizens of the world of Ashkenaz stayed behind their ghetto walls. They knew from bitter experience that when law and order broke down, violence would find them sooner rather than later. Inevitably, during the early part of the 1848 revolutions there was an increase in Jew-hating violence in Alsace and rural parts of Germany, Hungary, and Slovakia. In 1789, only the Jews of Paris and the Sephardim of Bordeaux were active in the revolution. In 1848, all over the continent, despite the threat of violence, Jews were openly involved in trying to reshape their nations' destinies.

There were many reasons for this. The process of legal and self-emancipation had been going on for a half century and it had created a deeper bond between the community and the wider society. One of those bonds was a growing interest in politics. By 1848 perhaps half the community had developed a conservative political outlook. A third were moderate liberals. Around 14 percent were radical democrats. Just 1 percent was socialist.

The 1848 revolutions took place in the rapidly growing cities and large towns. More and more Jews were living in these urban spaces, having moved away from their villages either to seek work or to study. Probably the tightest bonds between Jews and others could be found in higher education. A generation of young Jews had found their way to university and it was university students who led the rebellions. But the main reason Jews became active in the revolutions was that most saw that the general purpose of the uprisings—creating constitutional, democratic states—offered the best chance for establishing governments that would guarantee Jewish civil rights in the broader context of granting national rights and workers' rights.

The large participation by the community in revolutionary activities was a phenomenon noted by Jew haters. A group of Viennese shopkeepers petitioned the provisional government to remove Fischhof and other Jews from the city's security committee. One minister of Ferdinand's Imperial Court, a fellow named Schwarzer, dismissed the upheaval of the time as "nothing but a Jew revolution."

• • •

The liberal Jews of Vienna listened to Rabbi Mannheimer. They did not agitate for Jewish Emancipation on its own; it had to be part of a wider program. Mannheimer was echoing the view of Heinrich Heine as written twenty years earlier. The task of the age was Emancipation, period. And not just of the Jews, but also of the Irish, the Poles, and the slaves in the West Indies. Indeed, a month after taking power, Crémieux led the French provisional government into abolishing slavery in France's Caribbean colonies.

Heine's idea of subsuming Jewish Emancipation into the general struggle for equality guided activists from the community in the early days of the revolution. To sympathizers outside the community it was notable. For years Jews had been lobbying the various parliaments of the German Confederation for civil rights. Now, with provisional governments in place and constitutions being drafted, that specific request seemed to have fallen out of public debate. In May 1848, *Spenersche Zeitung*, or *Spener's Gazette*, Berlin's leading liberal paper, noted that "the 'Jewish Question' which had raised strong feelings just one year ago, now belongs to the political antique chamber."

Heinrich Heine had missed the revolution of 1830 because he was on holiday. He would participate only by chance in the events of 1848. On the second and last day of the Paris insurrection he was riding in a special wooden coach, a kind of ambulance, to a small private hospital, in what is today the top of the Fifth Arrondissement, just off the Boulevard de Port-Royal. His body was slowly being tortured to death by what is thought to have been some kind of venereal disease, probably syphilis. The poet had always suffered from debilitating headaches; now they had rendered him partially blind. His spine was a long, thin line of pain and suppurating sores. He could no longer walk and had retreated to what he called his "mattress grave."

As his coach rolled slowly up the hill over the cobblestones, Heine heard the commotion drifting over the city and then the noise grew louder and more direct. A thump on the carriage door. A crowd of insurgents commandeered his ambulance and deposited the poet revolutionary and his long-suffering wife, Mathilde, on the pavement. They then smashed the coach to bits and used it to erect a barricade.

Eventually, the couple found a cab to take them the rest of the way to the nursing home. Heine's body was ruined but his mind wasn't. Within two weeks he had begun a series of articles on the events for his old newspaper, the *Augsburg Allgemeine Zeitung*. He was also capable of receiving visitors and would soon be reunited with his young friend Karl Marx, who was also missing out on all the excitement. Marx was living in his own political asylum a hundred and sixty miles away in Brussels. After a night in the cells at Brussels central police station, Marx and his family headed for the action. Everything he and Heine had been talking about for years seemed to be happening at once.

## CHAPTER FOURTEEN

# The Tradition of Dead Generations Weighs on the Brains of the Living

BEFORE THERE IS REVOLUTION THERE IS TALK. BEFORE THE old regime is overthrown there must be discussion about what is to replace it.

For almost two decades prior to 1848, Paris had been the world's center for discussions about the future shape of society. There was urgency and confusion in the conversations. The future, like an early arriving weekend guest, was knocking on the front door while the house was still a mess and no provisions had been laid in. Day by day industrialization was changing the physical and social ecology of Europe. Canals were being cut and railroads were being laid across land that had been used for farming since Roman times. The new reality of factory work was changing everyone's life. Cities were growing rapidly, too rapidly to provide anything like decent housing. The centuries-old obligations that existed in the countryside between landlords and their tenant farmers had found no parallel in the towns. People were paid poorly and treated without any regard to the unmeasurable value of their work: the cohesion it provided to society.

There were periodic riots by the new urban dwellers in the great cities of Europe but no coherent political and economic program they could ally themselves with. Political theorists were desperate to figure out a set of rules that would make sense of where this mad activity was taking people.

Many of the conversations in Paris were in languages other than French. They were in Italian, Polish, Russian, and most of all, German. There were an estimated seventy thousand Germans living in the French capital by the early 1840s. Most of them were in exile from the repression that defined life in the German Confederation. Paris, cosmopolitan center of Europe, was a congenial refuge for every revolutionary theoretician on the continent, particularly those from the German Confederation. Every time the censors in one part of the confederation closed down a journal and the police came calling on its editor, a new arrival would turn up in the French capital. That was the reason twenty-five-year-old Karl Marx first moved to the city in October 1843. For almost a year he had been in charge of the *Rheinische Zeitung,* the *Rhineland Gazette,* and when it was shut down by the government he moved to Paris to begin work on a new journal, the *Deutsche-Französiche Jahrbücher,* or *German-French Yearbook.*

Once Marx was settled he got himself introduced to Heinrich Heine. Young German radicals on the make sought introductions to Heine in the way that young German philosophers on the make in Enlightenment Berlin sought meetings with Moses Mendelssohn. It was a way of gaining credibility. Marx and Heine hit it off immediately. On Marx's side there was a bit of hero worship going on in the initial stages of the relationship. The young philosopher had grown up reading Heine's verse and political writing in the *Augsburg Gazette* and now he was hanging out and being treated as an equal by the famous man.

For Heine, who never stopped writing in German, it was a chance to hear his language out loud. He reveled in the sound and cadences of

German and in Marx he found someone who had a prodigious talent with the language, albeit far less lyrical than his own. The pair didn't lack for topics of conversation. Both came from the Rhineland and reminisced about the broad, meandering river and the hillsides covered with vineyards. They had distant relations in common. Heine was childless and Marx was about to become a father for the first time. For all the brutishness with which he treated those around him, there was a genuine tenderness to Marx as a husband and father. The poet was deeply moved by it. Some months after the men began their friendship, Heine turned up at Marx's apartment for an afternoon of chat and found the philosopher and his wife, Jenny, in a state of hysterics. Their first child, also called Jenny, was turning colors and doubled over with cramps. Heine took over the situation, drew a warm bath for the infant, and gave her a wash. The baby calmed down, the parents regained their equilibrium, and Heine was forever after an honorary uncle to the family Marx.

Then there was Hegel. Heine had personally studied with the philosopher and had a stock of amusing anecdotes—some of them actually true—to tell about their conversations. Marx had studied with Hegel's disciple, Heine's old colleague, Eduard Gans. The pair could pick apart the philosophy of the great thinker if they were feeling serious, or dissect the pretensions of his followers if they wanted to have a joke.

Another thing the two men had in common was a lordly sense of self-importance. Heine had always acted like a prince, but if the world of Ashkenaz had true, royal blood it flowed in the veins of Karl Marx. On his father's side he was a direct descendant of Rashi, the eleventh-century rabbi still acknowledged as the greatest interpreter of Talmud the Ashkenazic branch of Judaism has known. On his mother's side he counted Rabbi Judah Loew, the Lion of Prague, among his ancestors. Loew was famous inside and outside the community as the creator of the mythical Golem. According to the legend, the Golem was a creature of clay the rabbi brought to life through mystical knowledge. It was built to defend the community against attacks by Jew haters.

There were many other well-known rabbis in Marx's family tree and more than a few important Court Jews. Marx was the product of the cultivation of bloodlines. For centuries the wealthiest in the community had allied through marriage with the most prominent rabbis. The children of these unions formed the Ashkenazic elite. Marx, argumentative and imperious, a prince without a kingdom to inherit, was as elite as they came.

His father, Heinrich, né Hirschel, was an entrepreneur based in the ancient city of Trier. Heinrich Marx had stakes in many enterprises, notably vineyards in the Moselle valley. He was of that generation of German Jews who experienced Emancipation briefly under Napoleonic rule and decided that when exclusionary laws returned they were not worth resisting. So he broke the connection to Judaism and converted. Karl, born in 1818, was baptized at the age of six. The long connection to these illustrious ancestors could not have been broken without some residual bitterness.

Marx, who was very close to his father, had a precocious understanding of the limits society put on perfect freedom. In an essay written while he was still in high school he notes that in finding one's way to a career we learn from "our parents, who have already traveled life's road and experienced the severity of fate." He doesn't specify what that fate is but then adds, "We cannot always attain the position to which we believe we are called; our relations in society have to some extent already begun to be established before we are in a position to determine them." It isn't a stretch to think that he is referring to the accident of birth that makes one person a Jew and another a Christian: one born with all doors locked to his talents, the other facing no barrier at all.

In the millions of words he wrote, Marx constantly came back to this theme: The past determines who we are. It inhibits our ability to act freely. It needs to be thrown off. When the aftershocks of 1848 had subsided he would write, "Men make their own history, but they do not make it as they please . . . but under circumstances directly found, given and transmitted from the past. The tradition of all the dead generations weighs like a mountain on the brains of the living."

Preceding Marx to Paris and contact with Heine was another of the young men the poet called "the doctors of revolution." This was Moses Hess. The Hess family history read like Marx's: descendant of rabbis, father self-emancipated entrepreneur. The rabbinical lineage was not as grand as Marx's but it wasn't far off. The big difference was that Hess's father had not broken with Judaism. The father was an observant Orthodox Jew and ultimately the leader of the community in Cologne.

Moses Hess was born in 1812 in Bonn's Judengasse. In that brief moment of Emancipation, his father had moved his business just down the Rhine to Cologne and left his son in the care of his grandfather, the rabbi. Hess was educated in the traditional way at a yeshiva and did not have happy memories of his time there. "Until I was fifteen, they tried to beat the Talmud into me," he would later remember. "My teachers were inhuman, my schoolmates bad company."

As Heine had done, he worked briefly in the family business before it became clear to all concerned that he had no talent for commerce and should go to university and study for one of the professions. He knocked around the University of Bonn but never graduated. Like one of the perpetual students found near university campuses in the 1960s, Hess was a chaotic seeker of moral truth. In Hess's own view the main achievement of his studies was to cut himself free from the restraints of religion. "I did not possess a personal God anymore, but I had a moral world order, which satisfied me."

Hess's yeshiva education had deeply ingrained the prophetic mode of thinking. He had a clear sense of himself being a precursor to an era of great historical change and identified very closely with John the Baptist. His writing is full of declamation about the future, what will and what must come to pass. The young man read Spinoza avidly, mingled the Enlightenment philosopher's ideas with those of Hegel, and wrote his first book, *The Holy History of Mankind,* at the age of twenty-five. He published the work anonymously. The name on the title page said the book was written "by a young Spinozist."

Hess's *Holy History* warns of the consequences if this new era's problem of "the growing wealth of one section of society and the increasing poverty of the rest of the population" is not addressed. Among Hess's prescriptions for dealing with this unjust situation are full equality for women and the creation of a welfare state. Written in 1836, the book is acknowledged as the first socialist work written in German, although it's unlikely Hess knew anything about the socialist theories only just being invented around Europe. His socialism was instinctive. Hess may have left Judaism behind but he had not walked away from its central idea of community. He spent his whole life trying to invent a political system that would re-create in the wider society the communal life of the ghetto world.

His second book was published four years later. *The European Triarchy* proposed that Britain, France, and Germany unite to create a European superstate. This state would be a synthesis of the very best achievements of its members: the German intellectual love of independence exemplified by the Reformation; the French love of liberty and equality defined by the Revolution; the pragmatism of the English to solve the problems created by the extremes of wealth and poverty in society. In this superstate the most liberal ideals were bound to flourish. Among them would be the idea expressed in Rahel Varnhagen von Ense's salon, sociability. "Sociability is the essence of humanity," wrote Hess. "Man cannot act as an individual. The essence of his life activity is cooperation with other individuals."

The book was a success among the Rhineland's liberal elite and Hess was appointed to the staff of a new newspaper set up by members of this group in Cologne, the *Rheinische Zeitung,* or *Rhineland Gazette.*

Hess quickly became the de facto editor and was constantly on the lookout for new contributors. Marx was already making a name for himself writing articles and arguing until closing time in the Cologne pubs where young radicals hung out. The two met and Hess brought him onto the journal's staff. He formed an intellectual crush on the younger man. Hess wrote a letter of introduction for Marx to Berthold Auerbach, a Jewish folklorist who had already made a reputation outside the community as a "German" writer.

"You will be glad to make the acquaintance of a man who belongs to our friends, though he lives in Bonn. He is a phenomenon who made the deepest impression on me. Be prepared to meet the greatest, perhaps the only real philosopher living now.

"Dr. Marx—this is the name of my idol—is still a very young man, hardly 24 years old but he will give the final blow to all medieval religion and politics. Can you imagine Rousseau, Voltaire, Holbach, Lessing, Heine and Hegel combined into one person? If you can, you have Dr. Marx."

The relationship between the two wasn't entirely based on puppy love. Hess had by now spent time in Paris and was more thoroughly versed in modern theories of socialism. At the offices of the *Rhineland Gazette,* Moses Hess and Karl Marx talked ideas. They took apart Hegel. The great philosopher of history had been dead for a decade and every intellectual in the German-speaking world was wrestling with his legacy. Hegel dominated the young men's discussions in the way Marx's ideas would dominate the conversations of postgraduates on either side of the Iron Curtain a century later. Hegel wrote about man in his ideal state of being. The younger men wanted to drag Hegel out of the ether and find ways of applying his concepts to the material world. Hegel pointed out that history was a dialectical process of competing forces. The Hegelian model of how history reached new stages of development through conflict and the eventual synthesis of these forces appealed to them. They were on the threshold of a new era, clearly. What were its hallmarks? What was the best synthesis of old and new that could come out of this time? Despite the wild praise Hess lavished on Marx, it was the older man who took the lead in these discussions.

Hess understood that egoism and individualism were the hallmark of the new age and that this led to social problems. Hess picked up on a word used by Hegel, *alienation*. The simplest way to explain the term is that an alienated person feels estranged from his true nature. I used to know who I was but who am I now? This was the question that hovered around the life of the generation of Jews to which Hess and Marx belonged. They had been cut loose from ghetto restrictions but not given full citizenship. They were estranged from their past but had not been welcomed into a new society.

The idea of alienation is a keystone of modern thought. It would be the end of the nineteenth century before it found its way into more general use. In psychology, sociology, and cultural criticism the term *alienation* would be popularized primarily by Jewish thinkers. But in the early 1840s, as Hess told Marx about French ideas, he focused on the way radicals in Paris used the term. Alienation was what happened when people became caught up in the new industrial economy. Man was alienated from his true nature by modern commerce. Society was being organized in a way that put people in competition and forced men into service to those with money.

Hess brought another person into their conversations, the son of a wealthy factory owner. Friedrich Engels was not from the Jewish community but he had a strong affinity for society's outcasts and so had no problem spending hours with two assimilated Jews discussing the future. When the talk in the office or the wine cellar was finished Marx and Hess went to their respective lodgings and made notes that became articles for the newspaper. They had the outsiders' ability to see society as it truly is. Their understanding was not clouded by nostalgia for old Germany because they came from a people who for centuries had not been allowed to live in that society. Moreover, when it came to their own community's role in this rapidly evolving new world they tried to be equally objective. The pair scoured away any longing for their Jewish past. Whatever sweet memories might have lingered from childhood of holiday feasts and visits of favorite uncles were cleared out. In his poetry Heine returned to the themes of Sabbath meals and family ties, but he was from an older generation. The younger men were harder on their own community.

The irony of these discussions about man's fate in the new industrial era was that the German lands were hardly taking part in it. In the early 1840s no more than 4 percent of German workers actually toiled in factories, so Marx had no real knowledge of what life in an industrial city was like. But Hess had traveled. In 1836, he had run away with a chambermaid, a poor Jewish girl, and spent time in England with her. There he had seen what the industrial revolution was doing to those who had been forced by economic necessity into the cities from their rural communities.

Hess, like most of the radical intellectuals in the German-speaking world, shuddered when he thought of what life would be like when the industrial revolution came to his country. There needed to be a social system developed to handle this historic change. The young intellectual read the same French socialists that Heine and Börne read. His language was peppered with French terms like *proletariat* to describe the new urban community of workers. Hess explained to Marx that commerce crossed borders and that the conditions of those who worked in factories were the same whether in France or Britain. The solution to the social problems of the proletariat would have to be international.

Hess locked on to the most idealistic of French socialist theories, communism, and introduced Marx to the term. He spoke of the future with a wide-eyed hope that men would once again share all their possessions communally. Marx could only laugh. This idealism and simple belief in community led Marx to dub his older colleague the "Communist Rabbi."

Hess was given a chance to do more research on socialism when the *Rhineland Gazette* assigned him to Paris in 1842. Early in his stay he too met Heine. The pair had acquaintances in common. Leopold Zunz, Heine's old colleague from the Society for the Culture and Science of the Jews, was Hess's cousin.

The following year Marx arrived to begin work on the *German-French Yearbook*. All three became involved in writing for the new magazine.

## ii.
## Words, Words, Words

They talked and they wrote. Heine, Marx, and Hess focused on three main topics: religion, money, and Germany. Chief among these topics was religion. Organized religion was a key source of alienation. Why, even after the Enlightenment, did it continue to remain a social force? Man's need for it had to be understood.

Heine offered this explanation: it was a drug. The poet first came up with the image of religion as a painkiller in his critique of Ludwig Börne, published in 1840: "Welcome be a religion that pours into the bitter chalice of the suffering human species some sweet soporific drops of spiritual opium, some drops of love, hope and faith."

Moses Hess borrowed the thought for an essay published in 1843: "Religion can make bearable the unhappy consciousness of serfdom in the same way as opium is of good help in painful disease."

The following year Marx wrote in a critique of Hegel's *Philosophy of Right,* "Religion is the sigh of the oppressed creature . . . It is the opiate of the people."

Weakening the hold of this addiction became a primary focus of Hess and Marx's writing. The pair, armed with Hegel's ideas, decided to attack what they saw as the relationship between religion and the new economy. Hess went on the offensive against Lutheran Christianity. It was too egotistical. For Luther it was the individual, not the community, that was paramount, according to Hess. The new economy expressed this perfectly; it endorsed the individual pursuit of wealth at the expense of community. He called Jews who had left the ghetto behind and embraced modern moneymaking "Jewish Christians."

Marx scoffed. Christians have become Jews, he wrote. He felt Hess was avoiding the real question, the Jewish Question.

The Jewish community had taken no part in the days of talk before the great revolution of 1789. Jews had been the blank canvas on which the French philosophes painted their image of what liberty, equality, and fraternity could bring to the most wretched and alien of people. The Revolution's leadership answered their own question about what to do with the community by emancipating it. The philosophes also saw Emancipation as a way of breaking organized religion's stranglehold on society. Now, half a century later, a handful of young Jewish men from Germany were taking the leading role in theoretical discussions, and preparing a new revolutionary canvas. At the same time they were asking their own questions about what to do with their community in the continued struggle against religion.

Emancipation of German Jews had become a hot topic again around Europe. In the wake of the Damascus affair the question about Jewish loyalties, whether they were a "nation within the nation," had been revived. For Germans against giving Jews civil rights, the community seemed more like members of an international pressure group than natives of one place. One skeptic, Bruno Bauer, wrote an essay called "The Jewish Question," in which he laid out the case for denying German Jews citizenship. Bauer, a theologian, philosopher, and onetime collaborator of Marx, played word games. No one in Germany was emancipated, he asked, so why should Jews get special privileges? The German states are Christian anyway. So by definition Jews could not be citizens. For the first issue of the *German-French Yearbook* Marx decided to reply.

He demolished his erstwhile collaborator's ideas. Bauer demands that Jews stop being Jews if they want to be emancipated citizens of a Christian state. But Bauer doesn't define what "emancipation" really means, according to Marx. Does political emancipation mean the purer idea of human emancipation? For Marx, the key to the answer lies in religion. "The political emancipation of the Jew, the Christian and, in general, of religious man, is the emancipation of the state from Judaism, from Christianity, from religion in general." This is a restating in barbed terms of the basic principles that led to the guarantees of freedom of worship and separation of church and state in America's Constitution and France's Declaration of the Rights of Man.

Marx quotes the French document extensively and asks a question of its long-dead authors, similar to the one asked by Hess of Luther. What is the value of a right that allows a man to separate himself from his community? In a way, that was the same question that had been asked by leaders of the Orthodox Jewish community since the time of Mendelssohn. What value, the rabbis asked, was there in living outside the ghetto? What do the rights of "emancipation" mean if they lead to the disintegration of the community?

Marx's answer to the Jewish Question begins by looking at the reality of post-ghetto life. Jews were now less defined by their Sabbath worship and more by their activities in the secular world. In the early 1840s the stereotype of the Jewish usurer had shifted shape. The German word for Judaism, *Judentums,* became used in conversation to mean business or commerce. "What does he do for a living?" someone might ask. "Oh, he does Judaism" meant he was in business. Marx plays on this usage. "What is the secular basis of Judaism? Practical need, self-interest. What is the worldly religion of the Jew? Huckstering. What is his worldly God? Money."

*Judentums* is a practical creed and it is now the creed of Christians as well. Marx jokes that Jews have emancipated themselves insofar as the Christians have become Jews. Everyone bows down before money, "the jealous God of Israel," and money is "the alienated essence of man's work and existence; this essence dominates him and he worships it." Man had been alienated from himself by the new world of commerce and it is necessary to be emancipated from this economic life to achieve something like perfect freedom. Marx concludes that history must evolve beyond the current capitalist era of buying and selling. Jewish Emancipation can only happen once "society is emancipated from *Judentums.*"

While Marx worked on this essay on the Jewish question for the *Yearbook,* Hess was also writing on similar themes. His essay was titled "The Essence of Money."

After a long preamble Hess comes to the point, "Money is the product of mutually alienated man . . . Money is no longer the 'noble metal'—we now have paper money, state money and bank money rather than metallic money. Money is what has come to pass for human creative power . . ."

The Jewish-Christian shopkeeper was the final phase of one era of historical development. Soon through dialectical processes a new era would begin. "The mechanism of the money-machine has run down and it is in vain that our progressive and reactionary statesmen seek to keep it turning . . ."

Karl Marx and Moses Hess were opposites who attracted in their early years in Paris. People commented on the obvious, their physical difference. Marx was a burly man, with a great round head covered all around in hair. His wife called him "my little wild boar." His animal energy overwhelmed everyone with whom he came into contact. Hess was tall and thin, and gave the impression of constantly being involved in the deepest contemplation, absent-minded and ascetic at the same time. Marx inspired awe and a bit of fear. Hess was loved.

Hess lived life as he preached it. Born into comfort, he lived his entire adult life in chaotic poverty with a woman of the slums named Sybille Pesch. It was whispered that she had been a prostitute at one point. Marx, on the other hand, married up. His wife, Jenny von Westphalen, was the daughter of a baron in Marx's hometown of Trier. In Paris, Marx and family lived an existence of bourgeois comfort on the Rue Vanneau in Saint-Germain on Paris's Left Bank. For him, poverty would come later.

Hess's socialism was idealistic. Marx's socialism was "scientific." Hess's politics were based in moral knowledge. Changing men's hearts, not their material circumstances, was in his view the key to successful socialism. Based in the study of economics, Marx's politics were harsher. They were utterly without sentiment. The pair parsed their arguments until they sounded like Solomon Maimon's description of Talmud students using *pilpul* to argue "without end or aim."

For Hess the era of massive change in which they lived was heralded by the writings of Spinoza and then the act of Emancipation.

His study of history told him Jews were the "fermenting" element in Western humanity and had been destined from the earliest times to provide the elements of movement and change in Western civilization. But once humanity reached the next stage of development, Judaism would have to shrivel and disappear. That was the law of Hegelian synthesis. Hess wrote, "The emancipation of the Jews is an integral element of the emancipation of the spirit." And once emancipated, the human spirit would be guided toward an embrace of the communal. Communism would reign.

Marx was having none of this sentimentality. He thought it was too soon to declare allegiance to a single system. In a foreshadowing of the censorship that would be a hallmark of Marxist regimes, he froze Hess out of the *German-French Yearbook* and refused to publish the Communist Rabbi's article on money.

In the end, the fussing and falling out came to very little. Most of the copies of the *German-French Yearbook* were seized at the Prussian border. It wasn't Marx's writing that brought on their confiscation. It was a poem by Heine. In it he satirized the verse style of Bavaria's King Ludwig I, a despot who fancied himself a bit of a poet as well. Prussia's King Frederick William IV was incensed. Monarchs have to stand up for one another against the mockery of poets and so Frederick William ordered all copies of the *Yearbook* seized. It was only in retrospect, when the ideas being brewed up in Paris in 1843 had taken a grip on the world, that historians of Marxism went back through the papers of the time and brought Marx and Hess's founding essays of the movement to light.

## iii.
## Actions

The collapse of the *Yearbook* was shrugged off. There were other start-up journals to write and edit. There was proselytizing to do in the German fatherland. There was a world to be won.

Hess went back to Cologne. Marx stayed in Paris for a while working on a magazine called *Vorwärts,* or *Forward.* He was expelled in
1845 at the express request of King Frederick William IV of Prussia.
Once again a satirical joke made in print was the reason. It wasn't all
that funny at the time and is virtually meaningless now. What mat-
tered was that the king took offense and through his ambassador in
Paris, Rahel Varnhagen von Ense's old friend Alexander von Humboldt, he requested that his French counterpart, King Louis Philippe,
throw Marx out. The French king obliged. The would-be revolutionary made his way to Brussels.

All they had were words. This was their contribution to the nascent
political philosophy of socialism. They were members of a minority
community giving voice to a group of which they were not really a
part. There were many German artisans living in Paris learning French
socialist theories and forming primitive communist associations, such
as the League of the Just. Most of the members were not Jewish, nor
did they come from money or have easy access to it.

Hess before Marx realized that they needed to change the target of
their words. Too much energy was devoted to theoretical arguments
and not enough was being given to making their ideas clear to the proletariat. The Communist Rabbi began giving sermons at clandestine
meetings in Cologne. Like an early Christian apostle addressing small
groups in catacombs and secret places away from the eyes of the emperor, he spread the message: a new day is at hand, the money machine
is winding down. "Communism is not a theory," it is the inevitable
end of historical processes that have been in train for a very long time.

He traveled to Germany's most industrialized region, the Ruhr
valley, and joined Engels for public debates in the latter's hometown
of Elberfeld. The audience was comprised of the town's elite: indus-
trialists, judges, and lawyers. When local workers tried to attend, the
meetings were suspended. Hess protested. He was forced to leave the
area and also made his way to Brussels. He joined up again with Marx,
who continued to pour torrents of words onto the pages of his latest

newspaper venture, the *Deutsche-Brüsseler Zeitung,* or *German Brussels Gazette.*

In the midst of the proselytizing, Hess found time to write "A Communist Credo," a catechism of the new faith. In seventy-two questions and answers he lays out a protocommunist vision in what he hopes is language the ordinary worker can understand:

### 1. What is the meaning of working?

Every transformation of matter for the life of mankind means working.

. . .

### 14. What is Money?

It is human activity expressed in numbers, the buying price or exchange value of our life.

. . .

### 32. What is Freedom?

A being is free when he can . . . live and act according to his nature and express his essence without hindrance.

. . .

### 51. Which religion should we all confess?

The religion of love and humanity.

. . .

### 70. What is life?

It is love itself . . .

With Hess and Marx off trying to recruit German workers to their movement, Heine became friendly with yet another wealthy young

Jew from Germany who was in Paris to fight for the proletariat. Ferdinand Lassalle was a bit more Heine's style. He was handsome and articulate, not a hurricane like Marx or ethereal like Hess. Lassalle enjoyed the good life and was especially fond of the ladies. The poet enjoyed them as well and he took the young man to Paris's finest places to meet them.

Heine felt relaxed in Lassalle's company. He could joke with him. After reading yet more of Marx's analysis of the role of Jews in the creation of the money world, Heine wrote to Lassalle that it all came down to the ancient Hebrews' invention of one God. "Jews worshipped a higher being, who rules invisible from heaven, while the heathen, incapable of raising themselves towards the purely spiritual, made all sorts of gods of gold and silver which they worshipped on earth. If these blind heathen had turned all this gold and silver into money and invested it at interest, then they would have become as rich as the Jews."

There was a serious side to their conversations. Lassalle, just twenty when he arrived in Paris, was already a committed communist. He was also thinking in more pragmatic terms than Marx and Hess. He did not see how a mass movement of industrial workers could be built around arcane analyses of political economy. Heine saw that the young man possessed something he did not have: a will to act and back up his fine words. The poet called him a gladiator.

After a year the time for Lassalle's Paris adventure came to an end. He planned to return to Berlin and finish a doctorate in philosophy. Heine supplied him with a letter of recommendation to Rahel's widower, Karl August Varnhagen von Ense. The note acknowledged the young man's "acute knowledge" and "amazing energy of will and aptitude for action." The note would open Berlin's most important doors for Lassalle. Moreover, when he walked through them he was not seduced by the opportunities to join the Prussian elite.

More than any of the young revolutionary acolytes who sought out Heine, Lassalle was the one who might have been the son he had never had. The time he spent with the young man put the poet in a reflective paternal mood. In the recommendation letter to his old friend Karl August, Heine reminisced about the compromises he had made at the same age, "the renunciation . . . with which we hypocritically came to terms with our world." A quarter of a century had passed since Heine had turned up at the Varnhagen von Enses' salon and discussed with Rahel the price of integration, assimilation, and the sacrifice of the Jewish part of oneself in order to achieve a place in the world. "We of the older generation prostrated ourselves before the invisible . . . We renounced much and lamented it . . ." He admired the generation of Lassalle, Marx, and Hess because it would not run away from a fight. But he feared for them as well. "We were perhaps happier than these tough gladiators who so proudly march to death in battle."

## iv.
## Communism

A tiny movement was growing around the idea of communism. The artisans' and workingmen's associations in France, Germany, and Britain began to coalesce. Marx, working closely with Engels, began to maneuver to take over the most important of these groups, the League of the Just. His methods were as brutal as his polemics. Early leaders of the clandestine group were driven out by harsh words and underhanded maneuvers. Hess protested and broke with Marx. The younger man sought a reconciliation, possibly out of respect for their friendship, but more likely because he feared that Hess, who was now living in Paris, might end up starting his own party.

The Communist Rabbi returned to the fold. He realized he had a lot to learn from the "little wild boar." Hess had introduced Marx to the term *communism,* and now Marx had convinced Hess that the definition of *communism* had to come out of an understanding of political economy. The pair, with Engels, continued to agonize over a clear definition of what they meant by the term *communism* and over a statement of principles—a mission statement—for a communist party. The definition of what was and wasn't communism had to be parsed down to the last clause and punctuation mark. The "Communist Credo" was just a start.

While they argued and wrote, Engels worked to undermine Hess's growing popularity with the Paris branch of the League of the Just's rank and file. The defining moment in Engels's campaign came when he managed to get himself rather than Hess sent to London in June 1847 for a meeting of radical groups from around the continent. At that meeting, Engels, representing Marx, managed to take over the organization. Its motto was changed from "All men are brothers" to "Working men of all countries unite!" Its name was changed to the Communist League.

Adding to the tensions among the men was their social life together. They dined out with their wives and mistresses. Hess's partner, Sybille Pesch, and Jenny Marx became friends. But Marx's wife disapproved of Engels's libertine lifestyle. She refused to have anything to do with his mistress, Mary Burns. For his part, Engels claimed that Pesch was constantly trying to seduce him behind Hess's back. How much this added to the growing tension between Marx and Hess is not clear, but as the search for a definition intensified, Hess was being driven further and further away from Marx by Engels.

At the end of November 1847 there was a meeting in London of the Communist League. Marx and Engels attended. Hess did not. The league's Central Committee officially deputized Marx and Engels to write a party manifesto. The pair promised to get to work on the document immediately and returned to Brussels. But the holiday season intervened. Then there were domestic concerns that needed attention. Work proceeded fitfully. By the third week of January the committee in London had had enough of waiting for the manifesto and sent Marx a letter threatening to assign someone else the task of writing the document. He finally knuckled down to finishing *The Communist Manifesto*.

• • •

The conversation in writing that had existed throughout the decade among Marx, Hess, and Heine carried on in the *Manifesto*. In 1847 Hess had published an article titled "Consequences of the Proletarian Revolution." In it he wrote, "A specter is haunting Europe—the specter of Communism." Marx used the sentence to open his *Manifesto*.

Heine had written that "every day national boundaries are disappearing." Marx wrote in the *Manifesto:* "National differences and antagonisms between peoples are vanishing, owing to the development of the bourgeoisie, to freedom of commerce, to the world market, to uniformity in the mode of production."

Proletarians would end national strife. "Working men have no country," Marx declared. "We cannot take from them what they don't have." That point would be one more stick for Jew haters to beat back at Marx. What could be more sinister and sly and Jewish than this idea of internationalism? The people who have no national soil of their own are maneuvering to make the nation-state obsolete. Marx never responded to the Jew haters' attacks. He did not see himself as a Jew, so in his mind there was no need. But it seemed like everyone else with a political view and access to pen and ink did see the revolutionary's work as influenced by his ancestry. Marxism and communism would quickly and inaccurately become synonymous in the public mind and the fact that Marx was of Jewish ancestry meant that the movement was seen as being some extension of Judaism.

Even fellow revolutionaries used Marx's Jewish origins as a platform for attack. Mikhail Bakunin, a Russian anarchist born to even greater privilege than Marx, Hess, or Heine, had turned up in Paris and joined the staff of *Forward*. He wrote of Marx, "He is by birth a Jew. He combines within his person all the advantages and disadvantages of this gifted race . . . He is unbelievably vicious, vain, quarrelsome, as intolerant and domineering as the God of his fathers and like him, vengeful to the point of insanity." In another broadside the Russian writes, "He attracts whether in London or in France, but especially in Germany, whole heaps of Yids, more or less intelligent, intriguers, busybodies and speculators, as the Jews are likely to be . . . who stand one foot in the world of finance and the other in socialism."

The irony was that for most of the nineteenth century the Jewish community was far from radical. Evolving from ghetto life to bourgeois life marked a revolutionary change in the ordinary Jew's status, but to achieve that status most Jews were small-*c* conservatives or small-*l* liberals. They were supporters of a stable society. Even during the revolutions of 1848 the majority supported constitutional resolutions of problems.

Heine knew what was coming out of the fierce debate over communism. He knew even before Hess and Marx got to Paris the power of the communal idea. In 1841, he wrote, "Communism speaks a universal language as simple and elementary as hunger, as envy, as death." The poet divined where the all-encompassing nature of communist theories must lead: it would become the new religion and its leaders would set up a doctrine of infallibility that would be the equal to that of the founders of any church.

He prophesied that in the inevitable battle against nationalism, especially German nationalism, the communist movement would furnish the troops that beat down the "Teutomaniacs." But it wasn't a joyous vision. Heine understood he was a product of privilege and an older world. Where would a freethinking poet find space to imagine in a system where the individual is curtailed by the community? "I'm filled with immeasurable sadness when I think of the ruin with which the victorious proletariat threatens my verses," he wrote. But he was also a soldier of Emancipation. "Let justice be done! Let the old world be smashed . . ."

Marx sent the manuscript of *The Communist Manifesto* back to London in early February. It was transcribed and typeset in German and sent to a printer. The pamphlet rolled off the presses on February 24, 1848, too late to have any influence on the dramatic events that had already overthrown the French monarchy and would soon topple governments across Europe. Marx was in Brussels waiting for its delivery while Paris was convulsed, and so the godfather of world revolution missed out on the one chance in his life to take part in one. By the time he got to Paris the revolution was finished. The real action was taking place back in Germany.

CHAPTER FIFTEEN

# Do Not Presume Discriminatory Laws Can Be Tolerated

FROM THE MOMENT IN MID-MARCH WHEN THE REBELLIONS began inside the German-speaking lands, Germany's very efficient postal service was inundated with letters being exchanged by the liberal intelligentsia. Professors, lawyers, and journalists who had been waiting all their lives for a chance to create their dream—a constitutional, united Germany—knew this was their time. By the end of March a group of them had taken it upon themselves to move to Frankfurt and set up a new parliament.

Among those moving to the city was the lawyer Gabriel Riesser, who had achieved a bit of notoriety for publishing the magazine *Der Jude*. His name had been put forward by a group from Baden, who remembered his eloquence in debating Jewish rights fifteen years earlier. Riesser was pleased and a little surprised to be asked.

This "pre-Parliament" met for two weeks to discuss the basics of selecting representatives. One of the primary demands of the uprisings around Europe had been for freely elected parliaments based on universal suffrage. At the pre-Parliament Riesser was the lead voice advocating the parliament be elected by "one man, one vote." Elections were organized quickly. By the end of May a parliament with more than five hundred members had been elected, including seven Jews and ten recent converts, who would still have been identified as being Jewish.

Riesser was elected for the duchy of Lauenberg, a city just north of Hamburg. Following the vote he immediately wrote a note full of exclamation points to his sister describing his "brilliant success." He had won easily by a vote of 64 to 31! Those against him represented a perfect cross-section of the reactionaries: senior civil servants, aristocrats, and the pietist clergy! But the enlightened bourgeoisie had no problem with sending him to Frankfurt to represent their interest! That they outnumbered the old forces by two to one is a true reflection of why the revolution had traction once the barricades were torn down. The political events of 1848 were, more than anything, about the new middle class trying to modernize their societies.

Riesser's elation was beyond political; for him a period in the wilderness was coming to an end. He was in his early forties and had achieved nowhere near as much as he should have. The decision not to convert or leave the soil on which he had been born had cost him. By remaining a Jew there had been no professorship of law, something his academic record had warranted. By not emigrating there had been no international career as a commentator writing from a foreign capital to German readers, as Ludwig Börne and Heinrich Heine had been able to build. Riesser had been stuck doing menial legal tasks, working as a notary, endlessly authenticating and witnessing documents just to earn a living. There was no career for him before the bar as there was for Adolphe Crémieux in France, no opportunity to make case law in Germany as his French counterpart had done defending the rights of free speech.

His one moment of notoriety came when Heine challenged him to a duel after Riesser had written a scathing review of the poet's book on Börne. But throughout the Damascus Affair the lawyer had been silent. He was suffering from ill health, probably symptomatic of depression. The state of Hesse had indicated that he could become a citizen and thus be eligible to practice law there, but at the last minute that opportunity evaporated without a word of explanation. Riesser was condemned to more notarial work.

His magazine, *Der Jude,* appeared less frequently. He published articles on Jewish issues sporadically. When he did, he found himself involved in enervating arguments among Jewish reformers and the Orthodox part of the community. The bright spot was that his reputation extended to younger members of the community who took inspiration from his writings on how to maintain pride when integrating into society, for example, when he wrote, "Nobody has ever obtained the esteem of others by begging for it. The prerequisite for the esteem of others is self-esteem."

Now Gabriel Riesser was stepping up to the place his talents merited and he was completely revitalized. He arrived in Frankfurt and quietly made himself indispensable.

The Frankfurt Parliament met in the city's Saint Paul's Church. The assembly that gathered there was noble and naïve. They were a well-educated crew: professors, lawyers, doctors, and the entrepreneurs of the new society. But the members had no real political experience, since there had been no opportunity in the German-speaking lands to acquire it. Nor did they have any statutory authority to do what they were doing. The parliaments and diets of the member states of the German Confederation continued to meet. The assembled worthies at the church honestly believed that if they could write a constitution for a united Germany it would be accepted as written because it would be a "good" thing.

But they had no agreed definition of what Germany was. Were they talking about all the German-speaking lands, including Austria? If you include Austria, does that include the rest of the Habsburg lands, where people were not ethnic Germans? And once they agreed on what they meant by Germany, there were no procedures for defining who its citizens were and what the extent of their social contract would be. When Heine and Marx mocked Germans for their excessive attention to ideas rather than reality they were attacking a noticeable phenomenon. Many of those in Saint Paul's Church really hadn't a clue about the practical scale of the task they had taken on.

In the early days of the Parliament most of the representatives spent their time in smaller discussion groups that evolved into committees. A plump, bespectacled man with a square of gravity-defying curly hair, Riesser looked what he was in those early days: a backroom figure, an adviser rather than a leader. His opinion was sought on rules of procedure because his legal training gave him a head for those kinds of details. He had spent years studying other countries' constitutions and more and more people asked his opinion on what would work for Germany. When asked, he quietly but forcefully advocated that all of Germany, including Austria, be united under a constitutional monarch.

For the first few months of the gathering he made no public addresses. But in mid-August he entered a debate on the right to privacy. The government routinely intercepted private letters and read them. He spoke out against this practice and made a strong impression. A few weeks later, as it inevitably had to, the Jewish Question came up. Should Jews have the right to vote? If they have the right to vote are they entitled to full citizenship? On August 29, a representative from Stuttgart, Moritz Mohl, demanded the "Israelite tribe" be given no more than the right to vote. Mohl was a left-wing deputy, a nationalist and a socialist, one of the earliest examples of that deadly combination of political beliefs. There was no physical possibility that Jews could ever become Germans, he assured the assembly. "The Hebrew population will forever and ever swim like a drop of oil upon the waters of German nationality." Riesser had to respond.

Saint Paul's Church is an odd-looking building. It's a great rotunda with a single tower jammed onto the side, like a giant cookie jar with a bell tower attached. The massive circular interior is a challenging place to make a speech, but public speaking was one of Riesser's greatest gifts. Combining wounded passion, forensic logic, and words that for years had reached only a small audience, he demolished Mohl's case for excluding Jews from citizenship.

Did the representative from Stuttgart remember when the local government in his home region passed an ordinance forbidding Jews from buying and selling rural land? the lawyer asked. Eight years later the local parliament had to hold a debate about the situation because the Christians who had taken over the trade in property "were far more ruthless" and treated peasants in an "abominable fashion." Riesser did not linger long over the comparison. He returned to the great theme of his life: he was a native of German soil and he and his community should have all the rights of citizenship. The benefit was to the nation. "Jews would be the most ardent patriots of Germany; they will become Germans along with, as well as among, Germans." In conclusion, he warned, "Do not presume that discriminatory laws can be tolerated without dealing a disastrous blow to the entire system of freedom, and without introducing demoralization into it!"

The speech stunned the assembly and made Riesser's career within it. Riesser was no longer a backroom politician but a leading figure of the Parliament. Now Riesser was appointed to the Constitutional Committee and assigned to write the declaration of rights that would be part of the document.

Riesser had a curious ally. Karl Marx had followed his career for a long time and had written earlier in the decade, "Herr Riesser correctly expresses the meaning of the Jews' desire for recognition of their free humanity when he demands among other things, the freedom of movement, sojourn, travel, earning one's living etc. These manifestations of 'free humanity' are explicitly recognized in the French Declaration of the Rights of Man. The Jew has all the more right to the recognition of 'free humanity' as the 'free civil society' is thoroughly commercial and Jewish and the Jew is a necessary link in it."

By now Marx was back in Germany. After a brief competition with

Hess, he had been the first to secure funding to start a newspaper, the *Neue Rheinische Zeitung,* or *New Rhineland Gazette.* As events unfolded in Frankfurt, the paper kept up a sniping commentary in its pages. Did the assembly open its business with a great statement of principles? No. "But it has ensured the salvation of Germany by the following great deeds. The National Assembly realized that it must have rules, for it knew that when two or three Germans get together they must have a set of rules," read a report published on June 1. It went on, "They ventilate the thing, talk, get stuck, raise a din, waste time and postpone voting from the 19th to the 22nd of May. The matter is brought up again on the 22nd, there is a deluge of new amendments and new digressions, and after longwinded speeches and endless confusion they decide that the question, which was already placed on the agenda, is to be referred back to the sections . . . On May 23 they first wrangle about the minutes, then have innumerable motions read out again."

## ii.
## Failure

By the time the Frankfurt Parliament finally got to grips with its real task, time was running out on the revolutions around Europe. In June, the hopeful phase in France ended. To deal with unemployment the provisional government had started "national workshops." The government was now employing hundreds of thousands of people in everything from make-work projects to necessary public works, but as money ran out the scheme was shut down. Inevitably the workers of Paris began violent riots in protest. Troops were sent in to put down the disturbances. It was a brutal suppression.

Hess sent a dispatch back to one of the Frankfurt papers: "The Place de la Bastille is covered with blood and looks more like a slaughterhouse than a battlefield . . . There is hardly a doubt that the miserable proletariat will in the end be defeated. Tomorrow Paris will be quiet again. But what quiet! and what consequences!" Thousands were dead. Adolphe Crémieux and his colleagues in the provisional government resigned.

Now conservative forces began to reassert themselves around Europe. Vienna had seen more riots in May. Emperor Ferdinand I had fled his capital, but as autumn approached the Austrian Army began to bring the Habsburg Empire's rebellious territories back under control. In Frankfurt, riots came in September over the rights of ethnic Germans in the disputed territory of Schleswig-Holstein and the Parliament, which had until that point been acting independently, had to ask Prussian King Frederick William IV to send troops to restore order outside the doors of Saint Paul's Church. It was a reminder to the whole of Germany where real authority resided.

Blissfully unaware of their diminished stature, the members of Parliament continued their deliberations. Riesser was now a major player. He was elected vice president of the assembly, a job that required him to preside over general sessions. It was not a position that suited him. As big as his voice was, he could not control the unruly debates. The lawyer was more effective in the committee room, representing his constituency and his conscience. He more or less wrote the section of the constitution that stated the basic rights of citizens, rights that would allow his enlightened bourgeois electors to pursue their livelihoods with security and a minimum of state interference and his community to live without discrimination. He continued to argue that Austria be included in this new German constitutional order not just as a matter of patriotism but because he knew that this would extend civil rights to a much greater number of people in the community.

But events were moving in a direction that made this impossible. In early October the Austrian Army went into action to prevent Hungary from breaking away from the empire. To show solidarity with the Hungarians, the revolutionary core in Vienna, students and workers, took to the barricades for the third time in 1848. The Austrian Army surrounded their capital. At the very end of October they were given permission to march into Vienna and put down the revolt. The soldiers fought their way in district by district. To make a point about who was in charge, a number of radical intellectuals were executed. As it was at the beginning so it was at the end. Almost half the dead were Jewish.

The revolutionary rollback continued. In December the provisional government in France oversaw elections for president of the Second Republic. The French are not immune to nostalgia and with the country convulsed and once more on the brink of anarchy they voted overwhelmingly for Napoleon's nephew, Louis-Napoleon. Louis had spent most of his life in exile and had even dabbled a bit in revolutionary politics. Like his uncle he was trying to balance imperial arrogance with a vaguely socialist desire to improve the lot of the people.

Even Adolphe Crémieux backed Louis-Napoleon in the election, hoping that this Napoleon would not slide away from democratic republican principles and into dictatorship.

As a new year began Riesser was involved in the final stages of drafting the constitution. It was clear to him that the Parliament had been overtaken by events. Austria had a new emperor. He was young, a military man, and most importantly, mentally fit. There was no incentive for the Habsburgs to join in the great modernizing movement, so Austria's representatives in Frankfurt returned home. A greater Germany would not happen. The only option left was to create a modern state in the rest of the confederation.

Riesser had always had his doubts about whether pure democracy as it existed in the United States could work in his country. He thought that his fellow Germans might fall into irreconcilable regional factionalism in a system like America's. Centuries of fragmentation was a dark legacy in German politics, and the only way to overcome it was through a unifying figure of authority. Perhaps Riesser also shared Metternich's view that while Jews could handle Emancipation it was their fellow citizens who couldn't. There needed to be some higher authority embodying constitutional rights to prevent pockets of discrimination from continuing.

The lawyer preferred a constitutional monarchy similar to the one in Britain. An enlightened ruler, symbol of the nation, would preserve unity. There was a purely republican faction in the Parliament who wanted an end to the rule of kings and aristocrats. They needed to be persuaded. That task fell to Riesser. In March the lawyer presented the committee's draft of the constitution. It called for a monarch as head of state. In one last stirring speech in the great rotunda of Saint Paul's, Riesser called on the assembly to ratify the constitution and authorize an invitation to Prussia's King Frederick William IV to become the Kaiser, the Emperor, of Germany. Whatever dissent there might have been before the speech disappeared in the tumultuous cheers when Riesser sat down.

In April, Riesser and a small deputation traveled to Berlin. They were received by Frederick William with due ceremony. The group invited the king to take up their offer and become Kaiser of a united Germany. Frederick had already decided his answer. Without hesitation the king refused. Emperors do not accept their crowns from the hands of ordinary people. The delegation was shocked and surprised by the immediate refusal. They shouldn't have been. A simple sounding out of Frederick's advisers would have told them the Prussian king would never accept such an offer. But that would have required a fundamental political shrewdness the members of the Parliament lacked. Even after being in session for a year they remained surprisingly naïve about the way politics worked.

Riesser and the others returned to Frankfurt. The collective spell of self-delusion fell away from the members of the Parliament. They had failed. Unity disintegrated. However, the hard-core republicans and socialists were not willing to give up the fight for the unifying constitution. They claimed that more than twenty states inside the confederation did support the document. Forget Prussia—the time had come to return to the barricades in support of democratic principles. This was not language Riesser and his fellow centrists were prepared to follow. They left Frankfurt. Prussian troops approached the city and the rump of the Parliament fled to Stuttgart. There, a few weeks later, the remaining members turned up at their meeting place to find it occupied by soldiers. Without a shot being fired, what was left of the Parliament dissolved. The revolution in Germany was over.

It was finished as well in Austria, as Emperor Franz Joseph and his troops reasserted their authority in Hungary, northern Italy, and everywhere else inside the Habsburg Empire where there had been an uprising. In Rome, yet again, Jews were forced back inside the ghetto and the gates were locked.

In France, Louis-Napoleon very quickly emulated his great-uncle and turned into an autocrat, a thinking man's autocrat to be sure, but nevertheless someone who had no time for democratic procedure. In the autumn of 1849 he dismissed the elected government. The following year he disenfranchised three million voters, mostly from the working poor, the proletariat. In December 1851 he declared himself dictator.

Adolphe Crémieux published a letter criticizing Louis's action. For his trouble he was thrown into prison.

This ended the political revolutions that had begun in February 1848. A second era of political reaction settled across Europe but its roots would not be as deep as in Metternich's time. The economic revolution was too entrenched and eventually would force modernization in political structures around the continent.

## iii.
## And then . . .

To reactionaries looking to diminish the events of 1848, the easiest thing to do was to describe them as "Jew revolutions." They weren't. But it is true that many of the words that made and subsequently analyzed the events were written by Jews. Because of this, socialist revolution would always be colored by the view that it was somehow a Jewish thing. Socialism would thus be a hard sell in many cities in the German-speaking world. However, none of these Jewish theorists and reporters of socialism would live long enough to experience the racist resistance of the proletariat to the ideas they hoped would liberate that class.

Marx spent most of the revolutionary period editing the *New Rhineland Gazette*. In mid-May 1849, following the collapse of the Frankfurt Assembly, the paper was shut down. The banner headline of the final issue read, "Our last word everywhere and always will be: Emancipation of the Working Class!"

Marx was evicted from Prussia and went to Paris under an assumed name. He did not live in pleasant bourgeois accommodations this time around. He was completely broke and on the run. It took the French security service two months to find where he was living. When they did he was ordered out of the city. He fled to London and worked at journalism, writing regularly for the *New York Daily Tribune*, among other outlets. It was a pauper's existence. The Marx family descended into wretchedness. Three of his children died in those first years in London. Only after coming into a small inheritance a decade later was he able to provide some stability to his wife and children. The money also allowed him to begin work on *Das Kapital*. Throughout this time he never stopped maneuvering to control the international communist movement. He died in 1883.

Gabriel Riesser returned to Hamburg. In the disunited states of Germany, Hamburg was an independent political unit. The government there endorsed the constitution written in Frankfurt, so Riesser became a citizen and was finally able to practice all aspects of the law. In 1860, the law in Hamburg was amended to allow Jews to become judges. Riesser was installed as the chief judge on the city's court and so became the first member of the community to be appointed to the bench anywhere in the German Confederation. He was in poor health by then but enjoyed the work and the honor of his position for three years before his death in 1863.

Riesser very quickly fell from the public's memory. Perhaps if he had been a better writer, possessed of Heine's wit or Marx's bludgeoning passion, Riesser's work might have been long remembered. But he was a lawyer and wrote like one. His verbal gift was for spoken arguments. But few people had heard his speeches outside Saint Paul's Church and those words were not as alive when transcribed on the page. The failure of the Parliament tainted all its leaders, including Riesser, and this too contributed to his disappearance from historical memory.

Moses Hess continued to proselytize and study. He was no longer close to Marx but he was not estranged from him, either. He remained a seeker, open to new ideas. He was never a prisoner of doctrine and that fact would allow him one more great idea.

Ferdinand Lassalle did better after 1848 than the others. He became famous and the reason was a woman, a very rich woman. He had taken up the divorce case of Countess Sophie von Hatzfeldt. A member of the Prussian nobility, the countess had been married off at a young age to a cousin whose cruelty would be considered psychotic today but was merely regarded as unfortunate back then. The count locked her up in their castle and refused to let her out. He took their children away from her and forced her to watch him have sex with his many mistresses. Count von Hatzfeldt could do this because his wife was subjugated by law to his rule. Lassalle turned the countess into a radical martyr, a symbol of how women were reduced from human beings to mere property in Prussia's outmoded feudal social system. Lassalle pursued her rights even though he knew that as a Jew success would come at a price. He was in fact in a German prison for the first part of 1848 because of his activity on behalf of Sophie von Hatzfeldt. On his release, he and the "Red Countess" moved to Heine's hometown of Düsseldorf and became involved in organizing the town's working class.

For a decade Lassalle was banned from Berlin. When the ban was lifted he stepped through the doors Heine had opened for him and became a political figure operating at the highest levels in Prussia. By 1862, Prussia's Chancellor Otto von Bismarck was consulting him regularly. A pragmatic revolutionary rather than a radical one like Marx, Lassalle believed in working within the existing political system. He founded the General German Workers Party in 1862, the first socialist political party in Germany. It would later become the Social Democratic Party, a great force in German politics. But Lassalle would not live to see that. He was killed in a duel over a lady's honor in 1863.

Heinrich Heine had been a young man when the Metternich period of reaction was established. At that time he had been confronted by the reality of second-class citizenship imposed on him by his Jewishness. Under pressure from his own family, he converted. By the time the new reaction gripped Europe he was one of the continent's foremost citizens, although whether his conversion had anything to do with it is open to debate.

In private salons and workers' assembly halls, his lyrics set to music were constantly being sung. A massive back catalogue of work was reissued and translated into many languages. In the midst of this increased acclaim the poet reassessed his relationship to Judaism and returned to it; not the practice of the religion but the acknowledgment of one God and the place of his people in the world's history. Heine reread the Hebrew Bible and called it the Jews' "portable homeland." He wrote a cycle of poems about Judah Halevi, a great medieval Sephardic poet. He also reassessed his view of Marx and the other doctors of revolution who had sought him out. "Godless self-Gods" is how he described them and he warned against the triumph of their work. Throughout this final burst of mental activity he was a complete invalid, bedridden, nearly blind, in profound pain.

Heinrich Heine died in 1856. His death marked the end of the Emancipation story's second phase. It would no longer be about the sons of a handful of wealthy families, connected by rabbinical bloodlines, frustrated to find they were still, despite the law, second-class citizens. Conversion or revolution had been the choice open to them if they wanted to claim equal status. Emancipating all the world's oppressed had been their fight because they sensed it was the only way that their community could achieve equality. But now Emancipation was a more general phenomenon, and the story would become more diffuse.

# PART 4

# CONSOLIDATION

# CHAPTER SIXTEEN

# The Jews Are a Nation

THEY WERE IMMIGRANTS IN THEIR OWN COUNTRY. THEY MAY have traveled no farther than the other side of the village or twenty miles up the road to a larger town, but their psychological journeys were every bit as foreign and intense as the journeys made by their brothers and sisters who went down into the bowels of ships in Hamburg and Rotterdam and emerged on the other side of the Atlantic in New York.

Their lives mirrored the immigrant lives familiar to Americans. The struggle of the first generation out of the ghetto to put together a little money to start a small business, the drive to educate the second generation so they could qualify for the professions and not have to labor as hard as their parents. It was already an old joke in Germany by the middle of the 1830s that "Doctor" was a Jewish first name. When it came to learning, gender was no barrier. By the 1860s an astonishing 40 percent of Jewish women were graduates of the gymnasium. The push for education was not just in book learning but in social learning as well. They had to acquire the skills to fit in. Like Lot, Europe's emancipated Jews were always looking forward, afraid to look back from where they came.

They were helped because after 1848, the tide of history ran in their favor. As the cities and towns grew, the skills for success in these harsh, bricked-in environments belonged to those who had been forbidden the land, kept confined behind walls, and forced into small trade for centuries.

Years later Eduard Silbermann remembered, "Clothmakers became dry goods merchants, tailors became clothing manufacturers, shoe makers became dealers in footwear." Silbermann's family had lived the story. When Jews were granted freedom of movement in Bavaria in 1861, his father, a former clothmaker, moved his dry-goods business to the large town of Bamberg. The place was big enough to support a highly respected gymnasium. Ten-year-old Eduard was enrolled there and performed brilliantly. He went on to university, studied law, and by the age of twenty-eight was named a state prosecuting attorney, the first Jew in Germany to attain that status.

Eighteen forty-eight did not lead to a united Germany but it at least kick-started the German lands into the industrialized economy. Over the next quarter of a century German exports grew 500 percent. Germany became the place we know today: the industrial powerhouse of Europe.

No single group within German society was better placed to take part in this surge of economic growth. In Berlin by the 1850s at least half the city's entrepreneurs were Jews. Most former ghetto dwellers did not become rich but did own their own businesses.

The centuries of enforced wandering from place to place in order to earn a living meant that they already had well-developed networks of contacts throughout the country. Within two generations, the descendants of rag peddlers ran the entire supply chain for clothes from the textile mill to the shop where apparel was sold. The children of itinerant cattle dealers could connect all the points of the economic compass touched by cows, from selling their owners feed grain to obtaining them for slaughter and production of meat to the tanning of their hides. They set up enterprises in everything from food to shoe manufacture. Inevitably in specific areas of business, such as retail shops, Jewish families dominated. As cities became swollen with people of different means, the idea of great department stores where everything under the sun could be purchased was a natural development. Throughout Europe these monumental emporia were set up by Jewish families.

Another advantage was the unquantifiable psychological ability to withstand the economic uncertainty of life in this new capitalist industrial society. When it came to insecurity—having something today and overnight, for reasons beyond your control, having nothing—no group in Germany or for that matter Europe had more experience than the Jews. Starting over from zero was a Jewish specialty.

In Germany they were still excluded from the civil service, so their only path to influence in the society was through economic success. In 1871 in Hamburg, 43 percent of residents earned less than 840 marks a year, but only 3.4 percent of Jews lived at this poverty level.

The single most critical measure of the degree of well-being and acceptance of the community is this: people stopped converting. In Berlin in the 1840s, 7 of every 1,000 Jews converted. By the 1870s that was down to less than 1 out of every 1,000.

But there is one other factor that needs to be considered in looking at these statistics showing dramatic improvement in Jews' economic and social status. The poorest, those who failed to rise on this economic tide in Germany, left the country. Between 1843 and 1871, a third of Prussia's Jews emigrated, mostly to the United States.

The economic story was similar in France, with the advantage that restrictions on where Jews could live had disappeared in 1791. The community led the population rush from villages to towns. By the middle of the nineteenth century, 45 percent of Jews lived in district capitals compared to a mere 18 percent of the general population. Strasbourg, which had closed its gates to a man as wealthy as Cerf Berr, now became a major Jewish population center.

And the population was growing. A half century after gaining their civil rights, France's Jewish population had doubled. But even with more mouths to feed, the speed with which Jews became bourgeois was astonishing. In the city of Lyon in 1810, three-quarters of Jewish men were peddlers; by 1830 that figure was down to one-half and by 1860 it was down to a mere 13 percent. In Paris, as in Berlin, close to half of the Jews were entrepreneurs. For French Jews this path to the middle class came because as French citizens they could not be prevented from joining craft guilds. They learned arts and crafts and then founded enterprises to manufacture the things they learned to make or opened shops to sell the finished products.

Not everything was perfect. As it had been in Zalkind Hourwitz's time, Paris was the preferred destination for poor, single men emigrating from the eastern reaches of the Ashkenazic world. Even as French Jews were becoming middle-class, 20 percent of the capital's community was indigent. Most of those people were immigrants from the east. In Alsace, Jews were more likely to be indigent than Christians.

The biggest difference between France and Germany was in a state-sponsored process of integration. Conversion was never a price extracted from the French community for greater access to education or jobs. The consistory system meant the community had administrative ties to the government. Certain government rules had to be obeyed. For example, rabbis had to take tests to prove they were fluent in French. Jewish schools set up by the consistory had to meet government requirements. Instruction was in French. Secondary schools in France provided Jewish prayer spaces and kosher meals. There was a feeling of security in France that did not exist elsewhere. Jewish schools taught their pupils that being chosen was a mission, a call to leadership in French society and for the Diaspora community around the world.

## ii.
## The Mortara Case

The memory of the successful fight against the Damascus Blood Libel remained strong in the French community, so in 1858, when another threat to the security of a Jewish community outside their country arose, the French took the lead in confronting it.

The threat began as a bizarre tabloid story of abduction and child exploitation and soon involved international and revolutionary politics.

Edgardo Mortara was the six-year-old son of a Jewish merchant in Bologna. He was the fourth of six children. When he was still a baby, Edgardo had become seriously ill and the family's fourteen-year-old housemaid, an illiterate peasant girl named Anna Morisi, had baptized him. She had taken a small glass of water, sprinkled it on the baby's head, and said the brief, necessary words, "I baptize you in the name of the Father and the Son and the Holy Ghost." From Anna's point of view it was a devout act of Christian kindness. The boy might be dying and she feared for his soul. It would do no harm to bring him to the true faith in this way. His parents need not know, and if the worst happened, then his innocent soul would reside in heaven for eternity rather than be consigned to eternal flames with the rest of the Jews.

The boy recovered from his illness and Anna continued to work for the family. Years later, in passing, she mentioned to a girlfriend what she had done. On the evening of June 23, 1858, the police arrived at the door of the Mortara apartment and seized Edgardo. They took him to the Convent of San Domenico, where the local representative of the Holy Inquisition had his office. To the church's authorities, Anna Morisi's action made the boy a Catholic and that meant he could not be raised by Jews. The inquisitor's job was to make sure canon law was strictly observed. His power in Bologna was profound because the city was part of the Papal States, ruled by the Vatican.

The abduction of Edgardo Mortara was not the first case of its kind. Secret baptism followed by child abduction was just one more terror of Jewish life in Italy. There had been a number of young Jewish children in Italy secretly baptized and taken away from their parents in the previous decade. Still, this did not make the situation any more bearable for the Mortara family. The boy's mother, Marianna, immediately had a complete nervous breakdown. The boy's father, Momolo, was found unconscious in the street after a day of fruitlessly trying to find out where his son was.

It took some weeks but eventually Edgardo's father found out that his son had been taken to Rome and was lodged in the House of the Catechumens. The Catechumens had achieved a special sense of horror for Italy's Jews. In the three centuries since it was set up by Ignatius Loyola, the founder of the Jesuit order, hundreds of the community's members had been taken there and forced to convert. Now that Edgardo was inside, the chances of getting him back were very small. Momolo went to the ghetto in Rome to work with the local community to try to at least gain access to his little boy. For a few months the parents were allowed supervised visits with Edgardo. Then all contact was cut off.

In the meantime, word of the abduction began to leak out around Italy. The political situation on the Italian Peninsula had not changed much in the decade since 1848. Italy was still a fragmented series of kingdoms, principalities, and the Papal States. Camillo Cavour, the prime minister of the Kingdom of the Piedmont, was still trying to create a unified, modern state. Since 1848 he had managed to ally the Piedmont with Sardinia's king, Victor Emanuel II, but there was much more to do. For Cavour, leader of the unity movement called the Risorgimento, the biggest stumbling block to achieving his political goal was the Catholic Church. Pope Pius IX was deeply resistant to political change in Italy. A constitutional Italian state would see the church lose its territories across the peninsula and with it influence in the temporal affairs of Italians. A modern political concept such as separation of church and state was most definitely not an idea that had been endorsed in the Vatican, even in the middle of the nineteenth century.

The Mortara case offended Cavour and his supporters. It was an embarrassing example of just how out of touch with modern times the church was. From his base around Turin, Cavour made the plight of the Mortara family into a political issue. In his view it was not possible to create a constitutional Italian state so long as the pope exercised such medieval power. Once again, as in France and Germany, the Jewish Question had become tangled up with the creation of a modern nation-state.

For complicated reasons going back to 1848, French troops garrisoned Rome and provided security for the pope. The arrangement provided France a base to counter Austria's long-standing influence on the peninsula, particularly in the north. This gave the French ambassador in Rome, the Duke of Gramont, special importance. The French government had come a long way since the Damascus Affair. It saw the abduction of the boy for the medieval folly it was. Napoleon III (Louis-Napoleon), France's monarch, had, like his uncle, started out as a republican modernizer and, like the first Napoleon, had a very problematic relationship with the Vatican.

He instructed Gramont to visit Pope Pius IX and make clear that France wanted the boy released. The pope told the duke there was nothing he could do. The baptism was valid and the boy would remain inside the House of the Catechumens. Gramont was livid and spoke to confidants about using French soldiers to seize Edgardo and take him to Genoa—outside the control of the papacy—where he could be reunited with his parents.

The French government was not interested in using its power in this way but it did want to use its influence to finally modernize the political structure of the Italian Peninsula. For Napoleon III the time had come to end the anachronism of the Papal States. Catholicism was no longer a monolithic faith ruled from Rome. There were Catholics all over Europe desperately trying to reconcile their beliefs and practice with modern life. The Mortara case showed that Pope Pius IX was incapable of bringing the church into the modern era. Europe's great powers would have to do it for him.

As the year drew to a close, the case of Edgardo Mortara had become the kind of international cause célèbre that the Damascus Affair had been two decades before. The difference was that around Europe, the Jewish community was now in a better position to fight against this kind of injustice rather than wait for events to get out of hand. Forty rabbis from Germany petitioned the pope for the boy's release, but to no effect. Jewish leaders effectively engaged with Protestant clergymen to bring pressure from non-Catholic countries on the Vatican.

In France, the Jewish press made its case in tones of measured bewilderment. The *Archives Israélites* noted that the abduction was more astonishing than other outrages precisely because it was not the work of mad fanatics in isolation but was "the calculated work of intelligent men." The Mortara case was "a scene from the Middle Ages enacted in 1858, a scene of pure Inquisition!" In a modernizing Europe the image of a revived Inquisition had a negative power that cut across sectarian and national lines.

The situation quickly turned into a public relations disaster for the pope. This time around, newspapers were in no doubt about who the injured party was. The *Times of London* described the pontiff as "strong in his weakness" and called for the secularization of the Italian Peninsula. It also warned that it was dangerous for any but Catholic families to visit Rome, since their children could be baptized "by the first comer and seized," never to be returned.

In early 1859, one of the old guard from the Damascus struggle joined the fight to get the boy back. Sir Moses Montefiore, now seventy-four, circulated a letter among American Jews, most of whom were only recently arrived from Europe and still very interested in news from the world they had left behind. This stirred up passion among the 150,000-strong community. They linked with Protestant groups, always looking for a reason to bash the Vatican, to add a North American element to the international pressure mounting on the pope. Then the elderly British eminence and his wife, with the blessings of the British Board of Deputies, the Rothschild family, and Britain's Protestant Evangelical Alliance, set off for Rome.

It was spring, the time of the Passover. However, whatever confidence Montefiore felt based on his earlier success with Muhammad Ali in Cairo evaporated in the first days he was in the city. Neither the pope nor his secretary of state, Cardinal Antonelli, would meet him.

Eventually, through the intercession of the Duke of Gramont, the latter did grant him an audience as an act of courtesy. The meeting itself was deeply frustrating. The boy Edgardo was now a Catholic, explained Antonelli. The pope was his father. End of discussion.

As the two men met, war was breaking out in the north of the country. Camillo Cavour's Piedmont forces were fighting Austria's army over control of Lombardy. The battle to unite Italy had begun. Montefiore and his wife joined a hasty exodus of foreigners from Rome. The old man noted in his diary, "This mission has been . . . a painful and sad trial of patience." It was God's will, however: "he has permitted . . . disappointment and grief for the best and wisest purposes."

The failure of Montefiore's mission was a further example of how much things had changed for Jews in the Emancipation era. During the centuries of ghetto life, the community's relationship with authorities had been negotiated by its very few men of great wealth. Montefiore, phenomenally rich, related by marriage to the even wealthier Rothschild clan, represented a continuation of that tradition. He had failed in his mission, and even two decades earlier that would have been the end of the story. But in France, Jews were more integrated into the society so it was possible to try a different approach.

In the nation that had first emancipated them, a critical mass of educated professionals now existed. They were secure in their work and could lobby for their interests like any other constituency in the country. The community also possessed a lively press, dedicated to reporting on religious and political issues that affected the rapidly changing role of Jews in modern society.

From the beginning of the Mortara affair, the *Archives Israélites,* a monthly magazine, had been calling for group action. Success seemed assured because, as the magazine noted with pride, the community had come a long way in its influence since the ghettos were opened. "In every country, the voice of the Israelites occupy positions within the councils of government." Even in England, where swearing a

Christian oath had made it impossible for Jews to become members of Parliament, the law had recently been changed so that Baron Lionel de Rothschild, wearing a yarmulke and swearing his oath on the Hebrew Bible, had become the first Jewish member of Parliament.

After Montefiore's failure, a group of young professionals began to meet in Paris to plan an organization that would fight for Jews affected by injustice and oppression anywhere in the world. The group planning this new organization included a structural engineer, the inevitable couple of lawyers, and the private secretary of Adolphe Crémieux. They approached Crémieux to join in. After his brief imprisonment, he had resumed his legal practice. The lawyer was certainly interested in setting up an organization to lobby on behalf of Jewish communities under threat anywhere in the world. Crémieux also relished the opportunity to demonstrate how Emancipation had liberated Jews from the Montefiore approach to solving their problems. There would be no more hat-in-hand private negotiating—groveling, in Crémieux's view—for favors, with the promise of money changing hands if the favor was granted. French Jews embodied the ideal of equality. They did not have to kowtow before anyone.

In May 1860, the group announced the founding of the Alliance Israélite Universelle. They issued a manifesto, distinctly French in its rhetorical style but its call to solidarity reflecting the post-ghetto reality of life for European Jews. It began with an acknowledgment that assimilation had frayed the connections of individuals to their community.

> If, dispersed to all corners of the globe and mixed with the nations, you remain attached with your heart to the ancient religion of your fathers, however weak the link . . . If you believe the most ancient and simple of spiritual religions must . . . fulfill its mission and manifest its vitality in the great movements of ideas . . . If you believe that a large number of your coreligionists overwhelmed by twenty centuries of misery can recover their dignity as men . . . If, finally, you believe the influence of the principles of 1789 is all

powerful in the world, that the example of peoples who enjoy absolute religious equality is a force, then Israelites of the entire world, come give us your membership.

This kind of Jewish self-help organization had never existed before. The Alliance had a twofold purpose: to work for Emancipation around the world, particularly in Eastern Europe and North Africa, and to support those Jews who "suffer because they are Jews." Crémieux and the other founders meant individuals like Momolo Mortara, who had visited Paris in the months before the manifesto was published.

While the Alliance was being founded, over the Alps in Italy the borders of the Papal States were being methodically beaten back. By the spring of 1860, Cavour through force and statecraft had united most of northern Italy. The military commander, Giuseppe Garibaldi, at the head of an army of a thousand men, was doing the same in the southern part of the peninsula. The pope's political domain was shrinking to Rome and its immediate environs. Edgardo Mortara was still in the House of the Catechumens and his parents were still desperately trying to get him back. As the forces of the Risorgimento came closer and closer to Rome, their hopes grew that they would finally be reunited with him.

The Alliance went to work on Edgardo's parents' behalf. In the early autumn of 1860 letters were exchanged between the organization and Cavour. It was clear that Cavour wanted Edgardo returned to his parents but the moment was not right. Rome was not about to be taken by his forces and so there was nothing he could practically do. The Alliance's leadership then contacted Momolo Mortara, who was now living in Turin. They urged him to be patient but to stay alert to the news from Rome. There was a contact inside the ghetto who would arrange to return the boy the day the pope was driven out. They offered these words of encouragement: "Getting your child back is the cause of all Israel."

• • •

A *lost* cause, as it turned out. In early spring 1861, most of Italy was united under King Victor Emmanuel II, with Cavour named prime minister. But Rome remained under papal control. Cavour continued to take an interest in the Mortara case and met Momolo. Then, suddenly, Cavour died and the possibility of getting Edgardo back died with him.

But the Mortara tragedy did not end there. On September 20, 1870, Rome finally fell to Italian forces and Momolo returned to the city to look for the son he had not seen in a dozen years. But Edgardo was now a nineteen-year-old man, thoroughly indoctrinated in the Catholic faith, studying for the priesthood. As Momolo went around Rome trying to find him, Edgardo snuck out of the city to avoid meeting his father.

Momolo had lost everything in the world: his son, his livelihood, his health. He lived on the charity of the Rothschild family and other members of the community. But fate had one more torture to inflict on him. The following year, he was falsely accused of murder and spent more than six months in prison before being tried and acquitted. Momolo Mortara was released from his life's suffering one month after leaving jail.

Edgardo, now Father Pio Edgardo, was eventually reconciled with his mother and attended her on her deathbed. From time to time his name appeared in the Catholic press but soon the whole saga faded from public memory. He long outlived his notoriety, and in fact lived to see Kristallnacht and the opening of the first concentration camps. He died in 1940 at a Belgian monastery.

The Alliance Israélite Universelle had failed to gain the boy's release, yet it flourished. As European nations entered their age of imperialism, the Alliance became a proselytizing arm for French-style emancipation and regeneration among the Jewish communities in North Africa and other parts of Napoleon III's empire. It became the model for other Jewish self-help organizations and an active player in fighting the terrible waves of persecution that would mark the end of the nineteenth century in places where Emancipation had never taken place.

## iii.
## A Jewish State .

Back in Germany, old Moses Hess followed the events in Italy and decided he had had enough. While the Risorgimento worked its way around the Italian Peninsula, creating a new nation, he listened to educated Germans mocking the whole enterprise. He was offended by a lack of outrage over the abduction of Edgardo Mortara. The "Communist Rabbi" could no longer suppress an idea that had been gnawing at him since the Damascus days. Hess was convinced there was no possibility that Jews could ever live safely among Europeans. There would always be a large element in the European population whose worldview was founded on Jew hatred. Hess had agitated for political systems based on universal theories of the brotherhood of man. Workers of all the world were supposed to unite regardless of which country they lived in. Now he was beginning to doubt that such an internationalist view was correct.

Race science was becoming an intellectual trend around the continent and Hess was not immune to some of its ideas. There really were different national or racial characteristics among people, he decided. Equality was a matter of respecting the differences between different national groups. The Jews were a nation. Two millennia after Jerusalem was sacked by the forces of Rome and the community scattered around the world, the Jewish people still maintained their national characteristics. There was no reason for Jews to deny this. Until they were established in their own state they could never hope to be recognized as equals.

In 1862, Hess published a book, *Rome and Jerusalem: The Last National Question*. It is written as a series of epistles to an unnamed reader. Some of what Hess prophesied in 1862 can make a modern reader gasp. "Germany as a whole, in spite of its collective intellectuality, is in its practical social life far behind the rest of the civilized nations of Europe." This, according to the author, is because of the

German belief in the superiority of the *Volk,* in comparison to other races, especially as regards Jews. "The German hates the Jewish religion less than the race; he objects less to the Jews' peculiar beliefs than to their peculiar noses." Hess sees clearly where German Jew hatred must lead: "The race war must first be fought out and definitely settled before social and humane ideas become part and parcel of the German people."

In the midst of social analysis masquerading as prophecy, *Rome and Jerusalem* contains the seeds of an idea to overcome the situation: "Judaism is rooted in the love of the family; patriotism and nationalism are the flowers of its spirit . . . It is primarily the expression of a nationality whose history, for thousands of years coincides with the history of the development of humanity; and the Jews are a nation which, having once acted as the leaven of the social world, is destined to be resurrected with the rest of the civilized nations."

Then Hess steps back from prophecy to advocate a political solution to the dilemmas of Emancipation: the creation of a Jewish state in Palestine. His idea is not based in religion but rather in the logic of the modern world in which Jews are living. Jews are reforming themselves out of existence in order to obtain a civil equality that in Germany at least, they can never attain. If there was a Jewish state, accepted as an equal member of the company of nations, they could have their citizenship and still live anywhere they liked, just as a Frenchman could live in England, if he chose.

He advocated buying up parcels of land in Palestine and resettling Jews there; not emancipated Jews from Western Europe but those of North Africa and Russia and Poland, places where Emancipation had not occurred and where oppression and poverty scarred their lives. In Palestine they could be farmers again, as they had in biblical times. They would turn the place as green as Lebanon. The new Jewish state would be a light to the nations showing them how to live in socialist harmony.

Since the days of Spinoza there had been occasional calls for reestablishing a Jewish state in Palestine, but they had been made by millenarian Protestants eager to live out the prophecies of Revelation. This was an entirely different concept. Hess proposed a modern secular Jewish state, not a religious one, a nation like any other. It would be several decades before the idea became a political movement and was given a name: Zionism.

## CHAPTER SEVENTEEN

# Throw Out the Jew Itzig, Because He Takes Whatever He Sees

WHILE THE MORTARA SAGA FLARED UP, HELD EUROPE'S INterest, and died away, the final steps leading to a unified Germany took place. In 1866, Prussia went to war with Austria and in seven weeks managed to break apart the last chunk of the Metternich mosaic. After half a century the German Confederation was no more. The Prussian government, led by Chancellor Otto von Bismarck, created a North German Confederation to replace it. In 1869 it ratified a constitution based on the ill-fated one written in Frankfurt by Gabriel Riesser twenty years previously. On July 3, in a separate act, a single paragraph long, rights of citizenship were granted to all, "independent of religious denomination." The words lacked music but their intent was clear. The Jews of this new state were emancipated.

Two years later, following Prussia's crushing defeat of France in the Franco-Prussian War, the German Reich was created. Finally, the abstract idea of a single German nation had been turned into political reality. The emancipatory law of the North German Confederation now became the law of the whole Reich.

There were no wild celebrations; Jewish leaders did not offer up prayers of thanks to Bismarck as they once had to Napoleon. But there was, as lawyer Martin Lovinson would remember fifty years later, "joy and hope almost beyond description . . . The fact that the feeling of basic disenfranchisement had been taken from us lifted our spirits and spurred us on to accomplishments in the service of our fatherland . . ." Lovinson was twelve at the time of Emancipation. Many adults in his world might have been slightly less effusive. Satisfaction was the main feeling. The struggle for civil rights had long been overshadowed by the de facto social emancipation the community had achieved. Words written by Ludwig Philippson, editor of the *General Jewish Gazette,* after the failure of the Frankfurt Parliament perfectly summarized the general view of the community.

> It is not you who emancipate the Jews; they have long since eman-
> cipated themselves; you are merely completing their outward
> emancipation. From the time when Jews step out of the ghetto,
> when they take part in all of the industrial and intellectual aspira-
> tions of mankind . . . when their men participate in the sciences,
> art, industry, and the crafts, when their women pursue a general
> education—from that moment forward they are emancipated and
> have no need to wait for a few words in the constitution.

Of course, in the intervening years Jews had continued to work toward creating a unified, constitutional Germany. Whatever the vari-ous limitations placed on them for employment in the civil service and the judiciary in the individual parts of the confederation, there was nothing limiting their political and business activity. They joined parties across the political spectrum and ran for election to the doz-ens of parliaments inside the confederation. But the most successful activists congregated around the liberal end of the spectrum because liberalism meant supporting free trade and a secular state. This suited a minority sect primarily involved in businesses that crossed borders.

They had a public platform to advocate these positions throughout the German Confederation because in the big cities—Berlin, Frankfurt, and Vienna—Jews owned and edited most of the press. In Berlin, for example, there were twenty-one daily newspapers, and only four had no Jewish connections at all. The three political satire magazines, another popular way to shape opinion, were all owned by Jews. When the liberal supporting press was referred to by the man in the street as the Jewish press it was a completely accurate description.

Privately, members of the community were able to advocate for free-trade policies based on their position in the rapidly changing world of finance. Although Jews made up a little more than 1 percent of the population, more than 40 percent of the owners and directors of Germany's banking and credit institutions were Jews or of Jewish origin.

The final push for legal emancipation was a collaborative effort between liberal political parties and German Chancellor Otto von Bismarck. It was an odd relationship, a union born of political pragmatism and close personal contacts.

Otto von Bismarck was the center of the German universe in his time. For all his image as a purveyor of brute force politics, the Iron Chancellor was more than anything a pragmatic politician interested in doing whatever deal was necessary to achieve his goals and maintain power. This pragmatism was not innate. Bismarck was a Junker to the core. The Junkers were Prussia's landed gentry. It was a class whose sons became officers in the army and whose hereditary privileges were threatened by the new economy. Their gut-level political instincts were always reactionary. But Bismarck's personal ideology never got in the way of making a temporary alliance. He had lived through 1848 and learned that revolutions were best defused by expedient accommodations.

Bismarck had other things going for him. Junkers were not famous for their intellectual curiosity but the chancellor was a first-class thinker. He also possessed the authority, the charisma, for leadership. Bismarck's public career began in Prussia's diplomatic service. By the early 1860s he had been appointed prime minister by King William I. The government over which he presided was a hodgepodge of political forms. Monarchical-parliamentary authoritarianism is the best way to describe it. Bismarck served at the king's pleasure and the Prussian Parliament existed to pass budgets. Bismarck really ran the country by fiat, yet he was not a dictator. The Iron Chancellor needed political allies within the legislature.

As he began to maneuver toward war with Austria he courted the liberal grouping in Parliament. It was the largest bloc in the legislature and its support would make it easier to drum up support for war. The liberals were interested in doing a deal. They would support war so long as Bismarck pushed for unification and a constitution once the war was over. As the representatives of the free-trading business and professional classes, the liberal parties understood the need to do away with the dozens of internal borders that still hampered German economic development. Their supporters also wanted a clear set of rules and definition of political powers—a constitution—so that there was political stability in which to plan for their businesses. Bismarck was not particularly interested in German unification—he was a Prussian patriot—nor did he see a constitution as indispensable to a modern nation. But he struck a bargain: unification after the war with a written constitution. But the constitution was to give him maximum power.

Heinrich von Treitschke, a leading historian and National Liberal Party member of the Reichstag, the largest and most diverse of this center-left bloc, wrote, "We must become more radical in questions of unity and more conservative in questions of liberty." The German Constitution was a trade-off between political liberalization and economic liberalization.

One Junker tradition Bismarck did not dispense with was having a personal Jewish banker. Accompanying Bismarck on his ascent to power was the fantastic figure of Gerson Bleichroder. The banker was a man uniquely of his time but also someone from the long-established tradition of Court Jews.

Bleichroder's father had established a bank in Berlin in the very early days of the nineteenth century, around the time that Mayer Amschel Rothschild was building his bank in Frankfurt. The two enterprises worked together, and by the time Gerson entered his father's business, Bleichroder's bank was the agent for the Rothschilds in Berlin. The connection brought wealth and influence to the firm.

In 1851, Bismarck was given his first important posting. He was sent to Frankfurt as envoy for Frederick William IV at the German Confederation. He was already marked as a man of rising importance and the Rothschilds cultivated such men. A respectful relationship grew between eighty-year-old Amschel, head of the Frankfurt house; his son Mayer Carl; and the young Prussian envoy. Toward the end of the decade, Bismarck was posted to Saint Petersburg. He asked Mayer Carl to suggest someone to help him make banking arrangements and look after his estates during his Russian sojourn. Rothschild was pleased to suggest Bleichroder.

It was a good match. Bleichroder did not fit any of the physical stereotypes associated with Jewish bankers. The banker was a man of stature, tall and strong-jawed. His facial hair conformed to German rather than religious fashion: long muttonchop sideburns and mustache. He was eminently conservative, conservative as a Junker or a Rothschild. Bleichroder was also a staunch monarchist. His business skills, however, did fit the stereotype that had grown up around the Rothschilds. He was an alchemist of money, able to move currencies across borders and make their value grow. Bleichroder unlocked the liquidity in Bismarck's property, invested it, and made the chancellor rich. He also created finance for affairs of state, including wars.

In his work for Bismarck, Bleichroder may have continued the function of the Court Jew but he was also a modern Emancipation-era Jew. He had never known ghetto isolation, as Mayer Amschel Rothschild had. Bleichroder didn't feel the compulsion for discretion and self-effacement—invisibility—that earlier Jewish financiers to power felt. He conducted himself in the circles close to Bismarck as an equal, and when the chancellor dined at the banker's mansion in Berlin it underscored just how close the two were; Bismarck hardly ever socialized in public. The banker spent his money without regard to whether he was being overly ostentatious. The outward flamboyance was at odds with his political and professional conservatism. In the liberal press Gerson Bleichroder became the paradigm for the new man of the age of money: the parvenu, the uppity nouveau riche.

His triumph came in the aftermath of Prussia's defeat of France in 1871. For months, Bismarck was in residence in Versailles negotiating terms with Adolphe Thiers. Napoleon III had fled following the war's end and now, thirty years after the Damascus fiasco, Thiers was once again in power as president of the provisional French government. Bismarck was not overwhelmed by merciful sentiments as he sat down to negotiate. He forced Thiers to cede Alsace and Lorraine to the Reich. German troops surrounded Paris and the city was to be ransomed. Thiers agreed to pay 200 million francs to get Paris back. Bismarck asked Bleichroder to organize the payment, which was done quickly. Although he was not a civil servant, the chancellor's personal banker was now the key treasury functionary of the German state. Six months later, at Bismarck's request, King William I gave Bleichroder the hereditary title of Baron. He was only the second Jew to be given that honor and the first with children to inherit it. Baron von Bleichroder had acquired the status to be received at court and could pass secure social status on to the next generation. Nothing could be taken from him.

Having forged the Reich through war and statecraft, Bismarck now had to make the political system work. He needed to centralize power in the Reichstag. This was easier said than done, even for Bismarck. The long, fractured history of German states had not been erased by unification. The Catholic south of the country around Bavaria resented the dominance of Protestant Prussia in the Reich. The local legislative bodies urged on by the Catholic Church resisted Bismarck. This was never a wise thing to do. The chancellor instituted the Kulturkampf, the culture war, against the church and its political allies. He used the liberal press as a prime vehicle for shaping public opinion in this struggle.

The chancellor also needed to create a uniform legal and monetary system. In the Reichstag, or parliament, he turned to two Jewish members of the National Liberal Party, Eduard Lasker and Ludwig Bamberger, to perform these tasks. Both men were veterans of the 1848 revolutions. Both had the by now familiar Jewish résumé of education in the law, then a period in either banking or journalism to make ends meet, since they were not allowed to practice before the bar. Lasker went to work drafting a civil code of law for the Reich, while Bamberger took the lead in creating a single currency, the mark, for the empire.

The result of all this activity was precisely what the National Liberals and Bismarck had hoped when they joined forces: rapid economic expansion. It was a golden age. The foundation of a new German Empire was being laid and every person with a bit of capital wanted to be part of it. Between 1870 and 1873 as many ironworks and machine factories opened in Germany as had done so in the previous seventy years.

The Liberal-Bismarck alliance seemed set to dominate German life for a long time. Then it all came apart very quickly. The exuberance of investors became irrational. The excess money in the system from French reparations led to inflated stock prices all around the German-speaking world. On May 9, 1873, the Vienna stock market crashed. Several banks collapsed shortly thereafter. The dominoes started falling in Germany. A major railroad company went bust and soon a general panic was in full swing. The contagion spread around the globe. In America, Jay Cooke's bank, the largest in the country, filed for bankruptcy. The global economy was plunged into a depression. There was no liquidity anywhere. Karl Marx, who was busy working on volume 2 of *Das Kapital,* noted it was a "universal crisis" and was convinced it would "drum dialectics" even into the heads of Germans.

## ii.
## Anti-Semitism

Marxist dialectics did find a few new heads to inhabit in the years that followed the crash. But something else more insidious began to come out. Jew hatred returned to German life. It wasn't the old-fashioned kind. Hep! Hep! riots didn't break out all over the country. This was a modernized and spruced-up kind of hatred. The concept of the Jew had changed during the decades of the community's reformation. Judaism and Jewishness had become almost distinct concepts. Similarly, Jew hatred had changed. The raw sectarian rage against Christ killers had been replaced by something more "scientific," a "perceived" biological fact of racial difference, and by social criticism—a hatred of modern secular society with its emphasis on making money at the expense of traditional German "spiritualism."

"The Germans are idealists even in their hatred," Heinrich Heine once noted. Now a new abstract idea was taking hold. Money was not a German invention. It was being imposed on the *Volk* by Jews and the Jewish people were from a different race, the Semites. So this new hatred was given the name, anti-Semitism, and its first proponents weren't rabble-rousers in beer halls but members of the intellectual elite. In newspapers, learned journals, and public lecture halls they constructed a new theory of the incompatibility of Jews and German society.

One of the early apostles of anti-Semitism was Paul de Lagarde, a leading scholar of theology and ancient biblical languages, including Aramaic and Syriac. He was internationally renowned as a translator of the Bible and that reputation carried weight with the public when he made his public pronouncements. "We are anti-Semites, not enemies of the Jews, because in the midst of a Christian world Jews are Asiatic pagans. Every objectionable Jew is a grave reproach to the genuineness of our Germandom."

Lagarde's genuine "Germandom" was based in spiritual Christianity. The Jews "destroy all faith and spread materialism and liberalism." They exercise mind control through "the Palestinization of the universities, of the law, of medicine and the theater." He placed this rise in Jewish power into a historical context. "The principles of 1789 have been transplanted to Germany by those representatives we call liberals." The most insidious of the principles of 1789 was tolerance. "Tolerance is fatal to everything serious."

The theme of the French Revolution was constantly repeated as the movement grew. "The Victorious ideals of the French Revolution: Liberty, Equality, Fraternity have torn down the barriers against the Jewish race that had been erected for the protection of the Christian peoples," read the manifesto of the First Anti-Jewish Congress, in 1882.

Amid the smoldering ruins of the stock markets, the destructive power of unbridled capitalism was attacked by Otto Glagau, a leading financial journalist. Glagau wrote a series of exposés on swindles but the swindlers were always Jews. Glagau had speculated heavily during the boom and had been wiped out in the bust. Now he repented of his involvement in the whole system and wrote nostalgically of the old days in Germany, when every person knew his place, all social relations were fixed, and Jews were kept apart from the guild system. "The abolition of guild privileges has torn every bond between master, mate and apprentice and ruined the artisan class which once formed the core of the bourgeoisie."

Glagau's views were echoed by Konstantin Frantz, a former Prussian consular official: "I see in unrestrained capitalism the evil of our epoch and am naturally also an opponent of modern Judaism on account of my view." In the popular press Jews became the symbol of capitalism. They were never the majority in business or anything else but it didn't matter. A long nose is easy for a political cartoonist to satirize.

Capitalism was Jewishness for Frantz but so was the new constitutional Reich. "It need hardly be said that nothing suits the Jewish point of view better than the idea of the so-called constitutional state which ignores the character and political position on which states are founded and replaces it by abstract concepts . . . The constitutional state recognizes neither Jews nor Christians, only citizens."

Much of anti-Semitism's appeal came out of nostalgia. Despite the chaotic economic situation, a young Jew starting a family in the mid-1870s could look back at the ghetto life his grandfather led and be certain his own was much, much better. A young German the same age, whether from Bavaria in the south or Prussia in the north, looked back and was not so sure. Feudalism, a time when everyone knew their place, the obligations between the landed aristocrat and his tenants were clear, and guilds, not markets, set prices and controlled who could perform specific jobs, seemed a better system than this new one of terrible economic freedom and uncertainty. The modern world was frightening and insecure and Jews seemed to have invented it. Since they had been allowed out of their ghettos they were thriving, and ordinary Germans weren't doing so well.

That Bismarck relied for advice on Jews—Bleichroder, Lasker, and Bamberger—was a relevant fact. That the chancellor was equally reliant for counsel on his fellow Junkers, as well as diplomats and academics who weren't Jewish, was not mentioned. The Kulturkampf was a fact. It was a policy devised by Bismarck, but who benefited most from anti-Catholicism? Never mind the centuries of enmity between Protestant Prussia and Catholic Bavaria—for anti-Semites in the modern world the Kulturkampf benefited Jews more than any other group.

It took a few years for the anti-Semitic agitation to turn into a political movement. By the end of the decade, Wilhelm Marr, a schoolteacher, had formed the League of Anti-Semites. In a pamphlet called *The Victory of Jewry over Germandom* he warned, "The end of Germany is at hand." The league's mission was "saving our fatherland from complete Judaization."

The court preacher of William I, Adolf Stoecker, formed the Christian Social Workers Party. Its original purpose was to steer the urban working class away from socialism. Depending on one's point of view, it was either ironic or proof of the all-pervasiveness of Jewish influence that both capitalism and socialism, the political movement that sought to destroy capitalism, were seen by Stoecker as being completely Jew-ish. Stoecker tried to cloak his prejudice in "full Christian love but also in full social truthfulness." He called for realism in the Jewish community about their changed religious status: "Jewish orthodoxy with its circumcision has outlived itself. Reform Judaism is not even a Jewish religion. When Israel has recognized this, it will give up its so-called mission and cease trying to rob the nations that have given it domicile." He asked for regulation of the stock markets and more transparency in the credit system, both of which he regarded as being wholly Jewish enterprises. Then he demanded a census based on re-ligious confession so that "the disproportion between Jewish wealth and Christian work can be established." He ended on a note of "woe betide" if these measures are not enacted: "Our German spirit will be Jewified."

But neither Stoecker nor Marr was able to build a strong politi-cal party out of anti-Semitism. While they were huffing and puffing, Bismarck had come to realize that free trade, the essential economic philosophy of the Liberal Party, was no longer a viable position for a German political leader to hold. The depression that followed the crash made protecting German manufacturing and jobs the smart move. The chancellor turned away from his alliance with the National Liberals and joined forces with the Conservative Party, whose mem-bers firmly believed in the power of tariffs to protect industry. He also suspended the Kulturkampf and mended fences with the Centre Party, a Catholic party that was also protectionist. Both these political groups had a polite level of anti-Semitism implicit in their worldview because both had a profound sense of unease about capitalism and in-dustrialization. Bismarck pandered to their fears. Stoecker and Marr's Jew hatred was simply not enough of an issue in hard economic times to create a mass movement.

But that didn't mean an end to anti-Semitic agitation. Of all the intellectual proponents of anti-Semitism, none was more dangerous than Lasker and Bamberger's colleague in the National Liberal Party, Heinrich von Treitschke. He was a true intellectual. A professor of history at the University of Berlin, Treitschke was also editor of the influential magazine the *Preussische Jahrbücher,* or *Prussian Yearbook.* When he wrote, "The fatherland of modern anti-Semitism is Germany where the systems were thought out and the slogans coined. The German literature is the richest in anti-Jewish writing," it was with obvious pride.

Treitschke brought a degree of geopolitical thinking to his prejudice. In the November 1879 issue of the *Yearbook,* he responded to his colleagues in France and Britain who found German anti-Semitism distasteful. "The Jews are our misfortune," he wrote. It isn't just that Germany has more of them than France and Britain combined. Just look to the east, over the German border with Poland and deep into Russia—there are millions of them desperate to sneak into Germany. "Year after year out of the inexhaustible Polish cradle there streams over our eastern border a host of hustling, pants-peddling youths, whose children and children's children will someday command Germany's stock exchanges and newspapers."

## iii.
## Influence

Treitschke wasn't the only public figure in Germany looking eastward. Even as Bismarck tacked to the right in domestic politics, he was fully engaged in projecting German power abroad. The slow-motion collapse of the Ottoman Empire and Russian expansion into its territories had the chancellor looking east long before Treitschke wrote his article. In the middle of this area of instability, just on the eastern edge of the German-speaking world, Romania was asserting its right to national sovereignty. Though the borders of the country were unclear, Romania had a Jewish population of around 250,000 living in conditions of squalor and violent insecurity. Their situation was a terrible concern for the bourgeois Jews of Germany, France, and Austria-Hungary. It was also a worry for the leaders of those countries who feared being overrun by refugees.

Early in 1877, Gerson Bleichroder wrote to Otto von Bismarck, "For twenty-two years I have served your majesty faithfully without compensation. Now the time has come to request such a compensation. What I ask is equality for the Jews of Romania."

It was not an unreasonable request. Germany had an interest in Romania's smooth transition to nationhood. So did the other great powers of Europe. Yet again, the Jewish Question was bound up in a national question and the leaders of Europe sat down to answer it in July 1878 at the Congress of Berlin. The congress was supposed to settle the boundaries of the entire Balkan region and was attended by Europe's leaders from Britain to Russia as well as by representatives of the Ottoman Empire.

Recognizing Romania's sovereign rights was an important agenda item for Bismarck. However, his motives were not entirely high-minded. A number of his Junker friends had invested heavily in Romanian railroad companies that had gone bust when the worldwide bubble burst. Through the efforts of Bleichroder, the chancellor was trying to recover some of their money. The moral case for defending an oppressed minority was not one of his considerations in putting the fate of Romania's Jews on the negotiating table. Bismarck did not need Bleichroder to explain to him that a secure Jewish community in Romania would be better placed to regenerate the nation's economy and might get the railroad venture back up and running.

For months Bleichroder worked ceaselessly on a campaign to get civil rights for the Romanian community. It dominated his discussions with Bismarck and his contacts at the court. He discussed strategy with the Rothschilds and was visited by Moses Montefiore. The old man, approaching his hundredth birthday, was still traveling around Europe as a plenipotentiary of his community.

As the dignitaries arrived in Berlin for their negotiations, Bleichroder was a man to take a meeting with. He occupied a unique position not just in German but European life. He was the organizer of financial diplomacy for the Reich and the good shepherd of the personal fortune of not just the most powerful man in Europe, Bismarck, but a wide range of senior diplomats and politicians. The British delegation was led by Prime Minister Benjamin Disraeli. He sought out Bleichroder and the pair struck up a friendship of exceptional warmth.

Disraeli came from a family of Sephardic Jews who had wandered over centuries from Spain to Venice and then to Britain. His father, Isaac, was an author, a man of no great religious faith but one who had identity with the community. He transferred this attitude to his son. On his thirteenth birthday, Benjamin Disraeli was baptized instead of bar mitzvahed. Yet throughout his life, Disraeli was identified by others as Jewish and acknowledged himself the strong Jewish component of his personality.

He shared with Bleichroder an inclination to serve his monarch and so was a natural political conservative. But Disraeli demonstrated a liberal social awareness that fellow members of Britain's Conservative Party did not share. Another difference he had with many in his party was that he had no inheritance to live on. He had to support himself, and this he did by writing bestselling fiction and biographies. The books demonstrate this social awareness.

One of his most popular novels, *Sybil,* was subtitled *Two Nations.* The politician and author saw Britain as a country of two nations, rich and poor, "between whom there is no sympathy." The work has more in common with the writing of a left-wing social realist novelist than someone moving up through the ranks of the Tory Party. Despite his conversion, his writing shows a profound pride in his heritage and urges his own political allies to give up their knee-jerk prejudices against his community. Disraeli was convinced this was costing his party support: "The presentation of the Jewish race has deprived European society of an important conservative element and added to the destructive party an influential ally."

Bleichroder shared that sentiment. The respect and affection between the two was genuine. Disraeli had a keen appreciation of the way Bleichroder lived. When the Congress of Berlin had finished its business, Bleichroder invited all the leaders to a farewell banquet at his Berlin town palace. Disraeli couldn't wait to regale Queen Victoria with a description of the event. He sent her a chatty letter saying the German banker was the equal of the Rothschilds, and that "the banqueting hall is very vast . . . Indeed the whole of the mansion is built of very rare marble, and where it is not marble it is gold." Musicians at the banquet played "Wagner and Wagner only, which I was very glad of as I have rarely had an opportunity of hearing that master." After dinner the assembly promenaded through the mansion looking at Bleichroder's art collection. Only one person made a negative impression on Disraeli, "a mean little woman covered with pearls and diamonds" sitting by herself. That was Mrs. Bleichroder, who Disraeli felt did not quite rise to her station as the wife of the most important financier in Europe.

The main business of the congress, for Bleichroder at least, was securing the rights of Romanian Jews. The head of Romania's delegation was Ion Bratianu, leader of Romania's governing Liberal Party. In the case of Romania, *liberal* is a very elastic term. Bratianu's party was avowedly nationalist and anti-Semitic. Perhaps for him *liberal* meant no more than good manners. He met with Jewish leaders from around Europe and the meetings were cordial. Later Bratianu said, "If all Jews were Rothschilds and Crémieux, then the situation would be different."

The Berlin Congress's deliberations took a month before the assembled great men signed a treaty. Article 44 of the treaty was aimed specifically at Bratianu and his government. "In Romania the distinction of religion, creed or confession cannot be brought up against anyone as a motive of exclusion . . . The freedom and open practice of all religions shall be assured to all citizens of the Romanian state, and also to foreigners." The last phrase was included to make sure that Protestant Germans who might be working in Catholic Romania would not suffer the kind of discrimination that Jews suffered everywhere. It was clear to all, however, that article 44 had been inserted to alleviate the plight of the community.

Bratianu accepted the requirement graciously. How could he not? But he was a clever enough politician to know that failure to implement the demand would not trouble Bismarck. Bleichroder would be troubled, yes. But Bismarck? With all he had to manage? As the decades rolled on, Jews remained excluded from Romanian society. It was as if article 44 did not exist.

It was obvious from the outset that this would be the case. Gerson Bleichroder was despondent.

## iv.
## A Riot

While the highest statecraft was being applied on behalf of Romania's Jews, the battle over organized anti-Semitism was crystallizing in Berlin. The polite tone of Treitschke and the intellectual godfathers of anti-Semitism was transformed at street level into racist demagoguery and action. This provoked a response. In the summer of 1880 a petition calling for a repeal of emancipatory laws was circulated in Berlin. A quarter of a million signatures were gathered. This goaded Theodor Mommsen, Treitschke's rival for the title of Germany's outstanding historian, into circulating a petition of notables calling for an end to anti-Semitic agitation. A debate in the Reichstag followed but it was merely one of those occasions when legislators vent on a subject in order to demonstrate they are aware of the concerns of the people who vote them into office. No action was taken. Reason had spoken and this seemed to defuse the situation among the elites. But there were local elections scheduled for Berlin the following spring and the street agitators focused their attention on destroying the city's liberal consensus.

A schoolteacher named Ernst Henrici decided to set up a political party, the Social Imperial Party. Its program was entirely based on Jew hatred. On a Friday night in December Henrici organized a rally at the Reichshallen theater. For weeks before the event newspapers gave publicity to the "Meeting of the Anti-Semitic Liberal Party" and the "Liberal Citizens of the Christian Religion" to hear a lecture on the "Means for Maintaining Christian-German Interests." There was ample time for Jew haters and Jews and their allies to plan how to react.

The Reichshallen was a vast, ornate theater in the heart of Berlin with a horseshoe balcony overlooking the orchestra seats. Three thousand people packed into the place and the crowd was already agitated when Henrici, accompanied by two police officers, took the stage. According to the *Tribune* newspaper, the schoolteacher did not get beyond declaring the meeting open before the barracking began by Jewish supporters. They were shouted down with cries of "Jews, shut your mouths." Henrici called on a colleague named Ruppel to chair the meeting and the man agreed, provided there were only Christian men of German descent in the hall. There was a riotous clapping and pounding of feet and shouting that there were "Jews here. Yiddish wheeler-dealers." Fistfights broke out and escalated into full-scale brawls. Some Jews were forcibly evicted. Then Ruppel tried to settle the meeting down. He failed. Shrugging off the chaos in the hall, Henrici launched into a recital of the usual litany of anti-Semitic allegations.

"These days you see a lot of black-haired Christians in Germany. You see because of their plentiful money the Jews are in a position to buy Christian girls to satisfy their desires, thus the black hair of many Christians." There was bitter laughter and the continued sound of chairs being overturned and punches being thrown. Henrici continued: "Three quarters of the poets and writers in Germany belong to the Jewish people. It is widely known that our daily press is completely dominated by the Jews." He mocked the liberal newspapers' constant refrain of social progress, social progress, social progress. "Progress— means Jewish steps."

The meeting escalated from brawl to mild riot with protesters thrown out violently and using equal force to fight their way back in. Through it all Henrici hammered away before winding up: "It is necessary to isolate the Jews socially. So I call on you, Do away with the Jewish newspapers! Do not buy from Jews and do not vote for any Jew or Jewish crony, for the liberal parties are closely connected with the

Jews." The applause rose to a new crescendo. Then Henrici proposed a resolution for the founding of a new "liberal" party "independent of Judaism." It passed with only seven votes against. After what seemed like hours of cheering and clapping, the crowd left the hall singing, "Throw him out, the Jew Itzig, because he takes whatever he sees."

Whatever glow of triumph Henrici felt that night as he trooped out of the hall was short-lived. Reports of the riot caused a scandal. In Bismarck's Germany events that disrupted public order were condemned. The coarseness of the way Henrici expressed his ideas offended many even if they agreed with the central prejudice behind them. Henrici's party failed in the Berlin city elections. The German capital remained a political stronghold of the Social Democrats and Liberals. The arguments between those two parties would dominate local politics for decades. Anti-Semitism as the sole basis of a political party never caught on although as a political philosophy it never went away.

v.

## Looking East

For the Jews of Germany, anti-Semitic rabble-rousing was a profound annoyance. Their legal status was now secure. They had strong ties to the society and could count on others to show support whenever the anti-Semitic threat looked like getting out of hand. The Jewish community and its liberal allies had much graver events to be concerned about than Henrici's band of bigots.

In March 1881, Russia's Tsar Alexander II was assassinated. The event led to sustained anti-Jewish violence in Russia. Many hundreds were killed, thousands of women were raped, and more thousands were burned out of their homes. The Russian word for this kind of anti-Semitic violence, *pogrom,* crossed over into all the languages of Western Europe. The reports from Russia shocked the continent. The oppression of the community in Romania had been worrying, but the

Russian violence threatened widespread destabilization on the borders between the west and the autocratic east.

History had ceded the tsar vast swaths of the Ashkenazic heartland in Poland, Lithuania, and Ukraine. These territories and others made up a vast geographical area called the Pale of Settlement. Inside the Pale lived the largest concentration of Jews in the world. A finger of the Austro-Hungarian Empire was stuck into the middle of this mass of Jewry: the province of Galicia, which was slowly being overrun with refugees.

Humanitarian interest and government policy neatly intersected. Everyone feared that the pogroms would create a massive refugee crisis as the Russian Jews fled west from Galicia into Germany, France, and Britain. Governments didn't want to absorb this mass of aliens nor did the integrated, modern Jews of Western Europe. It was better to organize relief efforts at the border and then help the victims over the ocean rather than allow the refugees to settle in Western Europe and undo the gains of Emancipation.

As news of the scale of violence spread around Europe, the now veteran networks established during the Damascus and Mortara affairs roared back into life. In Paris, the Alliance Israélite Universelle formulated a plan to repatriate Russian Jews in the Americas. As it had on earlier occasions when Jews were being persecuted, London's Mansion House filled with prominent members of the liberal English establishment, including the aging poet Robert Browning; Cardinal Henry Manning, leader of the Catholic Church in Britain; and the Earl of Shaftesbury, a proponent of resettling Jews in Palestine.

At the time of the Damascus Affair, the *Times,* voice of the British establishment, had been equivocal in its support for the Jewish victims of persecution. As Britain's empire had grown so had the newspaper's stature. It was now the most important paper in the English-speaking world and there was no question about where it stood. On February 15, 1882, it thundered against the tsar and called for resettling Jews preferably away from Europe. "Austria and Germany, which is itself not without blemish in its mode of looking upon the Jewish race, have cause to dread a vast Jewish inroad across the frontier. Tens of thousands, not to speak of millions, are not added at a stroke to a present population without stress . . ." The editorial went on to say that Jews with their "oriental blood" might find it simpler to take root in hot and sunny climes like South Africa or Australia or South America. "The Jew is in many countries not a stranger. In Syria and Palestine he is at home."

But mainly the editorial called for emancipation of Jews in Russia. "It will be to that country's enormous benefit. A tsar can banish three millions of his subjects for the crime of being richer and more versatile than the rest. He cannot keep them in legal ghettos. They may suffer by having to accept the alternative of exile in preference to degradation. He and his country must suffer tenfold by the loss of their services and from the humiliation of the weakness, bigotry, and lawlessness from whence it will have arisen."

Throughout the 1880s, self-help organizations of the post-ghetto Jewish community consolidated the gains of Emancipation by helping the Jews of the Pale of Settlement leave Russia and settle around the world.

Sometime around 1884, at the southern end of the Pale, in the city of Odessa, a young man named Mordechai Katz left his father and mother behind and began the journey northwest toward Austria-Hungary. Arriving at the empire's border in Galicia, he had to obtain travel papers. The documents weren't legal. The forger who made fake passports told the young man he needed a more German-sounding name to gain entry to Austria. Mordechai Katz chose or was given the name Goldenfarb. Under his new alias Mordechai Goldenfarb finally made it to Hamburg and took ship. When he arrived in America the immigration clerk wrote my great-grandfather's name down as Goldfarb.

# PART 5

# RENAISSANCE

CHAPTER EIGHTEEN

# I Want to Get Out . . .
# Out! Out of the Ghetto

JANUARY 5, 1895

Place de Fontenoy, the heart of France's military establishment. The Ecole Militaire, the War College, is located here. A few hundred yards up Avenue de Lowendal is the Invalides, where Napoleon lies in his massive tomb. On the other side of the War College grounds is the Champ de Mars, where cavalry regiments parade and maneuver. Looming over all: the tallest structure in the world, the recently completed Eiffel Tower. On this cold January day the Place de Fontenoy is full of soldiers in dress uniform for a solemn ceremony. A traitor will be expelled from their ranks. The traitor is Captain Alfred Dreyfus; the Jew, Alfred Dreyfus.

At the edge of the Place de Fontenoy a small mob is shouting. In modern countries the real nation within the nation is the military. It has different laws and a different social code. The military operates in a separate world and the general public has very limited access to it, but not today. Although the charges against Dreyfus were made in secret and the public was kept out of his trial, thousands of civilians are being allowed to watch his ritual humiliation. To keep warm they exercise their lungs, calling out anti-Semitic slogans. They remind each other that even when Jews are taken into the heart of France—Dreyfus was the only Jew serving on the army's general staff—these people cannot be trusted. They serve only one cause, the cause of international Jewish domination.

Finally, at 9 A.M., the man himself is led out in full uniform with all the insignia of his rank in its correct place. Four brother officers and a noncommissioned officer take him to the center of the square. Slim and holding himself ramrod straight, Dreyfus looks much older than his thirty-six years. He has always looked more mature than his age. His hairline has been receding for years and he wears glasses at all times, but the shock of the last few months makes him look like someone deep in middle age. Since his arrest he has sometimes wished his life would end but he has controlled those thoughts. He is not so ground down that he has forgotten his military training.

The charge of which he has been convicted is read out. He has passed high military secrets to France's great enemy, Germany. His sentence is called out. He is to be imprisoned for the rest of his life at the penal colony on Devil's Island, off the coast of French Guiana. Then the ritual humiliation begins. An adjutant of the Republican Guard, an enormously tall and wide fellow, approaches the bespectacled man. Towering over Dreyfus, he tears the epaulets from his shoulders; the insignia of rank follow, and the buttons of his uniform, the braid along his dress trousers. The insignia on his *kepi,* the hat unique to the French military, is torn away and thrown into the dirt. Finally his sword is snapped in two. Then he is marched around the parade ground in front of the assembled ranks of his former comrades. Throughout the ordeal, he calls out over and over again, "I am innocent. I swear by my wife and children I am innocent. Vive la France!" His military bearing throughout never wavers.

It was this demeanor that observers remembered, although they interpreted its meaning depending on their own points of view. For the anti-Semites watching the show his unwillingness to shed a tear at his disgrace was proof that Dreyfus had no love for his country. If he loved France then surely he would weep to see the symbols of the nation ripped from his uniform. "The wretch was not a Frenchman," went the report in *Le Figaro.* "We all understood it from his deed, his demeanor, and from his face."

To the few Jews who observed this ceremony the man's restraint was proof of a noble and innocent heart standing up to injustice. To some of his fellow officers, it was a demonstration of a man living by their code, and his fidelity to that code was a sure sign of his innocence.

The public humiliation finished, Dreyfus was taken to prison to await transport to Devil's Island. The curtain of military separateness descended once more; documents pertaining to the case were destroyed and those who had taken part in the investigation and tribunal swore to secrecy.

That night in his cell at La Santé Prison, former captain Alfred Dreyfus wrote to his wife, Lucie, "I have not the heart to tell you what I have gone through today . . . When I promised you to live, when I promised to bear up until my name had been vindicated, I made the greatest sacrifice possible for a man of feeling and integrity . . . Leave no stone unturned my dearest to find the real culprit; don't slacken your efforts for a minute. This is my only hope in the midst of this horrible tragedy of which I am the victim."

If the Abbé Grégoire, Count Mirabeau, and the other revolutionary advocates of Emancipation had been asked what the Jews of France might become in a hundred years, they would have invented Alfred Dreyfus. He was the perfect product of their great social experiment.

The Dreyfus family was from the eastern hills of Alsace. At the beginning of the Emancipation era Dreyfus's grandfather was a peddler in Alsace, and his grandmother a seamstress. The couple worked hard, saved what they earned, and took advantage of their new civil rights to move to a larger town and buy a local mill that produced cloth. Dreyfus's father, Raphael, went into the family business and under his guidance, in the great economic expansion of the middle nineteenth century, the family became rich.

Raphael Dreyfus's family expanded along with the business. There were nine children, seven of whom survived infancy. Alfred was the youngest. By the time of his birth the family was established in Mulhouse, in the southern part of Alsace, where they lived the lives of perfectly assimilated Jewish Frenchmen. There was sufficient money for Alfred's private education. He was not needed in the family business, so, like other Jews of his generation and wealthy background, he prepared for a career in public service. The French state had given Jews unparalleled opportunities and among the community's upper bourgeoisie there was a sense that that gift should be repaid by encouraging at least one child to work in some capacity for their country.

The aftershocks of the great Revolution of 1789 had rumbled for a century. France had lived through two further revolutions, countless insurrections in Paris, one stunning military defeat, two empires and, at the time of Dreyfus's arrest, was on its Third Republic. One constant in this turmoil had been the fidelity of French-born Jews to the nation. Other Frenchmen might question the value of what followed the overthrow of Louis XVI but the Jewish community did not.

In 1870, Bismarck's German Army overran France. The treaty that ended the conflict ceded Alsace and Lorraine to the Reich. Rather than live under German rule, the Dreyfus family, like true French patriots, left their business behind and moved to Paris. Eleven-year-old Alfred decided there and then to join the French Army. He singlemindedly pursued an education via the elite Ecole Polytechnique, which ultimately led to a commission as an artillery officer. He was not the only young Jew in the officer corps. France's chief rabbi, Zadoc Kahn, encouraged young Jewish men to join the military. The army is the place where "beats the heart of France; it is there that are blended as in a crucible, the sentiments which are the soul of the nation."

Just as France's Jewish community had changed and adapted to their status as citizens in the century since their Emancipation, so too had the forces of the right in the revolutionary National Assembly. If Abbé Maury and Jean-François Reubell and others who fought against Emancipation had been asked who would carry their argument forward they might have invented a man like Edouard Drumont. A son of the artisan class, Drumont had a brief career as a civil servant before turning to journalism to air out his grievances against the group that in his mind had destroyed the French artisan class and whose machinations had led to the defeat by Germany: the Jews.

Ironically, much of Drumont's theorizing on anti-Semitism borrowed heavily from German thinking, not least the concept of an Aryan race to which Jews could not scientifically belong. In 1886 he published an analysis of the Jewish takeover of France, *La France Juive,* or *Jewish France.* The book begins with an explicit statement. Drumont tells his readers, "I will write of the Jews' conquest" of France, and "the only person to profit from the Revolution is the Jew." According to the author, the French Revolution marked the conquest of France by this tiny but cohesive minority, and Drumont takes almost six hundred pages to recount the story of how it was done. No stereotype hatched in Germany by the founding theorists of political anti-Semitism is missed by Drumont. But he adds his own spin. He mocks the man in the street's stereotype of the Jew as cowardly. Surely any people who survived eighteen centuries of oppression has a strong spirit of resistance, Drumont reminds his readers. This is an enemy to be respected and against whom a fierce campaign must be waged to reclaim France.

*La France Juive* sold a million copies and became a bible for organized political anti-Semitism.

By the end of the nineteenth century, Jew hatred provided an umbrella for a coalition of monarchists, traditional Catholics, and workers who were trying to undo the Third Republic and see France restored to its former glory as a monarchy. The success of his book led Drumont to start the Anti-Semitic League in 1889, and as the movement grew he started a newspaper, *La Libre Parole,* or *Free Speech,* in 1892. From its pages he launched relentless attacks on Jews in public life. Because of Emancipation there were many targets. The Rothschild family was an obvious one, although since 1848 the family's banking business had been eclipsed by massive joint stock companies that now dominated French finance. Most had no Jewish connections at all, but that didn't matter to Drumont. There had been a number of prominent Jews in politics and Drumont took aim at them. He was even able to invent a Jewish prime minister, Leon Gambetta. A staunch republican and someone who spoke out against the power of the church in French life, Gambetta was of Italian-French parentage. That fact didn't matter to Drumont and his followers. In their eyes he was a Jew.

After bankers and politicians, Drumont decided to publish a series of anonymous attacks on the courage of Jewish army officers. It was an insult too far. In June 1892 Drumont was challenged to a duel by André Crémieu-Foa, a Jewish cavalryman. The duel took place and both were lightly wounded. But that was not the end of the affair. A notorious anti-Semite, the Marquis de Morès, was suspected of being the author of the attacks and Armand Mayer, a cavalry captain, issued a challenge to him a few days later. They met on the Ile de la Grande Jatte, an island in the Seine just outside Paris. Swords were the weapons of choice. Rather than fighting to inflict a light wound and satisfy honor, as was the custom, the marquis attacked with deadly intent. Mayer was killed.

The death shocked France to its senses. *La Libre Parole*'s attack on Jewish officers' courage was an attack on the entire institution of the army. The minister of war noted that in the army no one's religion was recognized; all were brother officers. Mayer's funeral became an occasion for Paris to turn out en masse. He was buried with full military honors. Rabbi Zadoc Kahn preached a eulogy that noted the wide public and institutional sympathy for the young officer. "Never has the holy unity of the fatherland more dramatically manifested itself, recognizing equally all of its beloved sons who defend its flag and who are inspired with its spirit."

The next edition of the *Archives Israélites* ran an editorial, "No to anti-Semitism: this Germanic import will not take root in our land!

No, France will not deny the work of the Emancipation and the French Revolution!!"

Kahn and the editorial writer's words spoke to a hope rather than the reality. Despite widespread condemnation in the Chamber of Deputies and in much of the mainstream press, *La Libre Parole* flourished and was read avidly by members of the officer corps of the army.

So, in the autumn of 1894, when Alfred Dreyfus was arrested, the initial reaction among his brother officers was one of no surprise. Of course, the Jew was a traitor.

## ii.
## First Response

As Dreyfus was shipped off to his life sentence, the silence among French Jews was noticeable. The community that had organized on behalf of their coreligionists in Damascus, Edgardo Mortara, and the victims of pogroms in Russia and Romania had very little to say about the case of one of its own members trapped in an anti-Semitic web of lies.

At the edges of the community not everyone was so sanguine. Bernard Lazare came from a background very similar to Alfred Dreyfus's. His father was a wealthy textile manufacturer in southern France. The family was assimilated although it did observe the big religious feast days. The same opportunities for elite education drew Lazare to Paris in the mid-1880s. But service to the state was never on his mind. Destruction of the state was his intention. He became an anarchist propagandist, a friend of avant-garde poets and artists congregating in Paris. If his life and thought resembled anyone's it was that of Moses Hess. He spent his twenties distancing himself from his community, being critical of it and at the same time exploring every one of the new intellectual movements sweeping across Paris. He was a socialist yet an anti-Marxist, an occasional playwright but more than anything an author of exceptionally caustic and amusing political analysis. As he observed the growing popularity of Drumont's movement he found himself thinking about his own Jewishness.

In the spring of 1894 he published a book-length history of the phenomenon of modern Jew-hatred. *Anti-Semitism: Its History and Causes* was a comprehensive refutation of Drumont without being an endorsement of his own community. The meaning of the ghetto in his community's past became important to him. In November of that year, as his contemporary Dreyfus was being interrogated, Lazare published an essay on the subject in a magazine called *La Justice*. "The Jews are no longer cloistered, the streets in which they live are no longer cordoned off by chains," he noted, yet the atmosphere of suspicion and latent hatred being drummed up by Drumont and his cohorts was a "ghetto more terrible than that from which they could escape by revolt or exile."

The reality of ghetto days was a century past in France and restrictions elsewhere had been gone for at least three decades in the rest of Europe, but for Jews of Dreyfus and Lazare's generation the ghetto seemed to linger in a psychological space.

That same autumn of 1894, Theodor Herzl, the Paris correspondent of the Viennese newspaper *Neue Freie Presse*, or *New Free Press*, took some time off to write a play. He called it "The New Ghetto." The play came out of the same set of circumstances as Lazare's essay in *La Justice*. Herzl was also the product of successful emancipation: an assimilated Jew whose family had prospered once restrictions had been lifted. Now he found himself being forced to consider the meaning of his Jewishness by the anti-Semitic movement. During his recent summer holidays back home in Austria he had been called a Jew pig. It probably wasn't the first time he had been insulted but this time, in the context of burgeoning political anti-Semitism in Austria, France, and elsewhere, it made Herzl begin to think that the ghetto would always cling to him even if the gates had long since been torn down.

The play exploded out of him. It was finished in a three-week blitz. The drama includes all the ingredients of the moment for men like

Lazare and Herzl. There is a willingness to accept some anti-Semitic criticism about unpleasant Jewish characteristics, so some of the Jewish characters are not very nice. There is a sense of confusion about where Jews fit into society and they express hurt at social rejection. Herzl borrows from the headlines. The play concludes with a duel in which Samuel, the Jewish protagonist, like Armand Mayer, is killed by an anti-Semitic nobleman. Samuel's dying words are, "I want to get out . . . Out! Out of the ghetto!"

The author immediately sent the manuscript to his playwright friend in Vienna, Arthur Schnitzler. Herzl asked Schnitzler to help him get the play put on. Schnitzler was also Jewish, and had some very strong reservations about the piece. "Your play is bold," he wrote Herzl. "I should like it to be defiant as well."

Herzl had many verbal gifts but playwriting was not one of them. He was a speechmaker, polemicist, critic, and a passable novelist. He would later prove to be a very capable editor. But a dramatist he was not. Schnitzler was one of the fastest rising young theater writers in Vienna, incredibly well-connected, but he was unable to get any theater to produce *The New Ghetto*.

While Herzl rushed his play to completion, he actually had a news story on his hands. His editors demanded coverage of the Dreyfus trial. The author did this in a cursory fashion. He noted without question the result of the trial and accepted at face value the statement of War Ministry officials that Dreyfus was a spy. He did not note his ancestry. In his report on the ritual humiliation of Dreyfus he quoted the mob baying "Death to the traitor!" rather than anything overtly anti-Semitic.

Newspaper deadlines don't always allow for insights. It took a few months for the impact of watching the ritual humiliation of Alfred Dreyfus to affect Herzl. He turned over the events of that day and in thinking about them he achieved clarity about how to deal with the psychological ghetto. His conclusion was the same reached by Moses Hess in *Rome and Jerusalem*, although the younger man claimed never to have read the book. Jews needed to reestablish themselves in Palestine. For Herzl there would be no more dabbling in writing plays. He returned to Vienna and went to work on a larger project: creating a Jewish state.

## iii.
## Slowly Fighting Back

Events surrounding Dreyfus unfolded at an excruciatingly slow pace. Bernard Lazare was approached by a publisher friend and asked to take up the case. Lazare initially demurred. The Dreyfus family was wealthy and had its own connections, so what did they need his anarchist's rhetoric for? But the pressure on Lazare continued to build from all sides. While Dreyfus was in the Santé Prison, the prison's director developed sympathy for the disgraced officer's claims of innocence. Some anarchist prisoners suggested to the director that Lazare was someone who might take up the cause and so he passed the name along to Dreyfus's wife. Her family came from the same part of southern France as Lazare and through mutual friends another approach was made.

Lazare studied more of the details of the case and saw quite quickly what no one else had yet seen, not even the victim himself. This was not some judicial error. Dreyfus had been set up by anti-Semites on the general staff carrying on the campaign against Jewish army officers begun by Drumont in *La Libre Parole*.

Dreyfus's older brother, Mathieu, met with Lazare. Mathieu was a persuasive man. Soon the anarchist author got to work on an investigation of the facts. By the summer of 1895 Lazare had prepared a blistering pamphlet forensically arguing the full case for the captain's innocence. He turned the tables on Dreyfus's accusers to make it seem like a plot of anti-Semites against the French Army rather than a plot of international Jewry against the institution.

But Mathieu Dreyfus was convinced the time was not right to publish. There were quiet words being spoken into the ears of important men, the possibility of a new trial was mooted; now was not the time to stir things up. The older brother's attitude was similar to that of the Jewish community leadership in Rome during the Mortara case. The leadership urged Momolo to keep a low profile. A just resolution of the situation could only come via back-channel negotiation.

So Lazare waited at Mathieu's request. Meanwhile the French community remained quiet, kept its collective head down, and acted as if nothing had happened. It was one thing to demonstrate on behalf of the Jews of Damascus or Edgardo Mortara or the shtetl communities being subject to terrible pogroms in Russia. But about a similar outrage on their own territory the overwhelming number preferred to keep a low profile. Lazare turned his fire on them. "There are a great number of Jews who have retained a deplorable habit from the old persecutions—that of receiving blows and of not protesting . . . of playing dead so as not to attract lightning." There needed to be massive public protest. That would not be forthcoming for a few years yet.

In the meantime, as 1895 wore on, Dreyfus languished on Devil's Island, a barren rock three-quarters of a mile long and a quarter of a mile wide. It had been used as a lepers' colony at one time, but the extreme heat and humidity and general foulness of the place had made it unsuitable for even those pariahs. The disgraced officer lived in a tiny stone hut of around one hundred and thirty square feet. For a time he had access to a treeless exercise area, but shuffling around under the relentless tropical sun was a form of slow torture. A guardroom was adjacent to his little hut and the prisoner was under twenty-four-hour observation, although the guards were under strict orders not to talk to him. That was Dreyfus's fate: constant observation, total isolation in the middle of a filthy tropical island. He was not even allowed to see the sea.

## CHAPTER NINETEEN

# The Jewish Question:
# Anxiety About My Children

T HAT SAME YEAR OF 1895, IN VIENNA, DR. SIGMUND FREUD was making notes about his dreams. He was looking for a key to their meaning. A neurologist by training, Freud had built a medical practice dealing with people who suffered physical problems that seemed to have no physical basis. He had been treating these patients by analyzing their words and descriptions of their dreams, and he was certain that by understanding how the mind works at night he might find the way to understand its disturbances during the day. So he began to work on his own dreams.

Dr. Freud dreamt of all manner of things. Some of his sleep stories were easy to understand: a man is standing on a rock in the sea. To him it was obvious this was Alfred Dreyfus. Other dreams were very complicated and he needed to analyze them more deeply.

Like all good Viennese professionals, Freud sent his family to the hills outside the city during the summer and joined them for a few weeks of vacation when he could. On Wednesday, July 24, he was seated alone at a table at the northeast corner of the restaurant terrace at Bellevue guesthouse looking out at the sloping hillsides of vineyards and wooded hilltops, puzzling through a dream of the previous night.

It involved several colleagues and a patient, Irma, who was also a friend of his wife. As with most dreams, Freud realized that this one had offhand moments from the previous day reshaped into a new narrative. Irma had visited the Freud family the day before and in passing mentioned that something he had been treating her for was still bothering her.

That was the starting point of the dream. But in this story, Irma reveals that despite Freud's treatments she had strange new symptoms troubling her. On examination they turn out to be very strange indeed. Freud calls his colleagues for consultation and this leads to disagreements between Freud and them as to how to treat the symptoms. In the dream's arguments, the normal daytime relations among the colleagues are scrambled up, in particular, the relationship with a colleague named Otto. The dream ends with Freud thinking Otto has given Irma an injection with a dirty needle.

Sitting on the restaurant terrace, analyzing the dream's sequence of events, pausing over even the most ridiculous details, Freud remembered he had had a disagreement about Irma's treatment with Otto the previous day. In the dream Otto is responsible for the poor treatment of the patient, not Freud. Then suddenly he saw what the dream was about: "The dream represents a certain state of affairs, such as I might wish to exist; the content of the dream is the fulfillment of a wish; its motive is a wish."

It's not my fault, Otto is to blame, Freud realized was the wish being fulfilled, the secret to understanding it. Dreams possess meaning, he concluded. They aren't just chaotic sequences of images, as most people thought. He could now see a path via this insight to understanding the way his neurotic patients' minds worked when awake. There was much more research to do but this was the beginning of a new way of understanding and treating psychological disease.

He dashed off a letter to his closest friend in what was by Freud's standards a state of giddy good humor, and joked that someday there would be a marble tablet placed on the precise spot of the Bellevue terrace restaurant where the idea came to him, reading, HERE THE SECRET OF DREAMS WAS REVEALED TO DR. SIGM. FREUD ON 24 JULY 1895.

The satisfaction Freud felt at this moment was immense. He needed the boost because very little else in his professional life was going well. The doctor was becoming increasingly isolated from his medical colleagues. They didn't understand his dream obsession and they were troubled by another aspect of his work. He kept asking his patients about their sex lives. He did not ask in a prurient way; he was being quite clinical. The doctor had become convinced that sex was a primary force in shaping neurosis. He wrote and spoke about sex with increasing frequency and frankness. However, in late-nineteenth-century Vienna public discussion of the topic was taboo. Asking one's patients about their erotic feelings was quite shocking even to his fellow doctors.

For more than a decade Freud had been collaborating with Josef Breuer, one of the most famous medical researchers in Europe. Breuer had become a father figure to him but their collaboration came to a halt over Freud's insistence on the importance of sex in understanding the workings of the mind.

Now other colleagues had stopped attending his lectures. His career in the University of Vienna's medical faculty was stalled. This was dangerous territory for a man who needed a steady supply of clinical referrals to support a wife and five children, with a sixth on the way. A year shy of his fortieth birthday was not the time to be risking what had started out as a very promising career for a young man with no connections. There was another reason to be cautious. Political anti-Semitism was stronger in Vienna than in probably any other city in Europe. There were already formidable roadblocks in the way of a middle-aged Jewish man without engaging the interest of the Jew haters.

But the doctor was certain of his ideas and could not walk away from them. Freud continued to work at his theories of dreams, sex, and the motivations of the unconscious mind. His professional circle grew smaller, and smaller. No matter. He persevered with his insight into dreams. Freud understood it was his Jewishness that made this possible. He did not go to synagogue, because he did not have faith, but he never denied his ancestry. To Freud it would have been "undignified." He saw clearly that because he was a Jew, part of a minority community, he was free of many of the majority population's unchallenged assumptions and "prejudices that restrict others in the use of intellect." For a Jew it was actually easier to be in opposition and disagree with the majority. Thinking differently than others was his birthright. This simple recognition of what it means to be from a minority could be applied to understanding what motivated Heine, Marx, Börne, Hess, Riesser, and others to their own particular insights.

## ii.
## Early Life

Freud was of the same generation as Alfred Dreyfus, just two and a half years older than the luckless Frenchman. If Dreyfus's family history was a paradigm of the century of Emancipation in France, then Freud's family history was its mirror for the German-speaking world.

The family's roots were in Galicia. His father, Jacob Freud, was born in 1815, the son and grandson of Hasidic rabbis, and the young man grew up in their religious practice. He was contracted to marry at the age of seventeen and quickly fathered two sons. Jacob Freud was a small-time trader of anything and everything, from cloth to honey, and was constantly on the road. Most of his business was in Moravia, today part of the Czech Republic. As a Jew, Freud's father constantly had to apply for special *Wanderjuden* permits to travel there. While visiting customers he was confined to special Jewish quarters at night. It was a ghettoized life.

The year 1848 marked the beginning of the end of restrictions on Jewish residence around Austria-Hungary, and soon Jacob was able to permanently move west from the muddy backwardness of Galicia to the Moravian town of Freiberg, today Pribor, in the Czech Republic. In 1852 his first wife died and three years later he married Amalia Nathansohn. The following year, 1856, the couple's first child, Sigmund, was born. Jacob was forty-one and already a grandfather. The grandson lived close by and so Sigmund's earliest playmate was actually his nephew.

Three years after Sigmund's birth, Jacob and his family left Freiberg and joined the migration to Vienna. The city was experiencing the rapid expansion that all the other great capitals of Europe were undergoing in the middle of the nineteenth century. The last restrictions on Jewish residence in the city were coming to an end and Jews from all over the empire began to head there. When the Freud family arrived in 1860, Vienna's Jewish population was around 6,900. By the end of the decade it was 40,000. By 1880 it was 73,000.

Jacob Freud settled his family in the Leopoldstadt district along with the rest of the recent Jewish arrivals from Hungary, Moravia, Bohemia, and Galicia. The immigrants were crammed into tenements just across the Danube Canal from the plump, bourgeois imperial city. By day the new arrivals tramped across the short bridges to work in the established businesses of other community members. At night they walked back to the place everyone called Matzo Island and into the dark courtyards, up the stairwells with paint and plaster flaking off the walls like diseased skin. But the new arrivals loved Vienna, the way another group of Jewish immigrants from Galicia would come to adore New York: in spite of its reality. Discrimination was pervasive, the poverty brutal, but the city offered the best environment in which to assimilate. In the countryside they could never shake off the ghetto, but rapidly expanding, cosmopolitan Vienna was a place to redefine yourself.

Jacob Freud had already gone a considerable way toward remaking himself. He had left behind the Hasidic tradition into which he had been born. His Judaism became an increasingly private matter. It was not imposed on his children. Freud's father worked and studied

Talmud in his spare time. There was a Bible in the house, in German, not Hebrew, and Sigmund began reading it when he was seven or eight. He devoured the book for its stories, but detached from rituals and spirituality, the tales came across as adventures and parables. They were Homeric myths rather than holy texts. Faith in God was never something Freud possessed, but this never made him feel less Jewish.

Jewishness was in the air of the Freud household and for better or worse in the street outside. His boyhood friends were all Jewish, and that was a matter of happy choice. But one of the key differences between Emancipation in France and the German-speaking world was that in France Jews were encouraged by law to think of themselves as Frenchmen, whereas in the German-speaking world Jews were not allowed to think of themselves as anything other than Jews, even after gaining civil rights. From the time of his arrest through his trial and imprisonment, Alfred Dreyfus never expressed a thought that he was being victimized because he was a Jew. He thought of himself as French. Freud was a Jewish citizen of the Austro-Hungarian Empire, always aware of his background, ever alert to the mocking eyebrow, the sarcastic tone of voice hinting that a comment was motivated by prejudice.

As the years went by there were more and more hours available for Jacob Freud to study Talmud, because he was a man of very limited business skills. There were many times when business was slow. He was generous to a fault, or improvident, depending on how you looked at it. If there was money in his hand it was spent quickly, and his schemes for making more usually fell short. Cash was always a problem. The family moved a lot: five times in the first decade they were in Vienna. But whatever the economic strain, psychological if not physical space for Sigmund to study was part of home life. Jacob and Amalia recognized that their firstborn was gifted. The father did what he could to provide for the son's success, but it was never enough. By the time he was an adolescent, Sigmund had come to regard his father as somewhat hopeless, someone who was old and old-fashioned and too much of a dreamer. The son also resented the father's passivity in the face of anti-Semitism.

Jacob Freud had grown up in a different time and place. When he was a young man, if a Christian coming down the sidewalk shouted at him, "Jud mach mores!" "Jew show your manners!" he had to take off his hat and step into the muddy road, just as Moses Mendelssohn or Mayer Amschel Rothschild had had to. That was the way life was lived. Jacob learned early in his life to shrug off confrontation and laugh when luck inevitably turned bad, but Sigmund was a city boy, and his hometown was in the process of becoming the capital of the Jewish world. He had no interest in stepping aside.

In the time of his dream work, which carried on for several years past the summer of 1895, Freud's sleep reminded him of an incident from his boyhood:

> I might have been ten or twelve years old when my father began to take me with him on his walks, and in his conversation to reveal his views on the things of this world. Thus it was that he once told me the following incident, in order to show me that I had been born into happier times than he: "When I was a young man, I was walking one Saturday in the village where you were born; I was well-dressed with a new fur cap on my head. Up comes a Christian, who knocks my hat into the mud and shouts, 'Jew get off the pavement!'"
>
> "And what did you do?"
>
> "I went into the street and picked up the cap," he calmly replied. That did not seem heroic on the part of the big, strong man who was leading me, a little fellow, by the hand.

The son began to daydream about doing something heroic that would avenge the honor of the Jews. Hannibal became his hero. The ancient general was not a Jew but did come from a Semitic tribe and had brought Rome to its knees. The adolescent decided he would enhance Jewish honor by entering public life. There was a liberal government in Austria at the time, and some of the cabinet were actually Jews. Young Freud thought he might study law, go into politics, and become a government minister. Then the crash of 1873 turned Austrian politics upside down and the same dark forces that began to show up in Berlin appeared in Vienna. Political anti-Semitism took root and a political career was now out of the question.

Around the time of the crash, Sigmund graduated first in his class from the gymnasium and was admitted to the University of Vienna. Acquiring a credential that would allow a man to earn a living was the main purpose of going to university and so like many young Jewish men without family money, he had to choose between law or medicine as a field of study. By now the young man's real interest had shifted from government to, in his own words, trying to understand how the physical world worked. The study of medicine seemed closer to that intellectual pursuit than the law. He crossed the Danube Canal to become a doctor and would never live with the immigrants in Leopoldstadt again.

That Freud was the perfect combination of intellectual brilliance, work habits, and ambition, capable of making a significant contribution to science, became clear to his professors at the medical school from the start. That he had no money or social connections was equally apparent. The young man hoped to pursue a career as a researcher. He wanted to make some historic advance in science and spent much of his time in medical school working in a poorly paid position at Vienna's foremost research institute. But without private money a sustained career doing pure research was not possible. He would have to build a medical practice and hope at some point to achieve a tenured position as a clinical professor; then the time for research would be his.

Freud was fascinated by the brain and the nervous system and so specialized in neurology. A neurology practice was potentially very lucrative and he needed to earn money quickly because just after graduation he had become engaged. The young doctor was marrying up. His fiancée, Martha Bernays, was from the Ashkenazic aristocracy. Her grandfather, Isaac, had been chief rabbi of Hamburg and had become famous throughout the world of Ashkenaz as the great modernizer of Orthodox worship in Germany. In Freud's words Martha was born to be a "Frau Professor," entertaining colleagues and graduate students with charm and wit in a large, salubrious home near the university. The couple agreed to postpone their marriage until Sigmund could actually afford that kind of residence as well as take on the responsibilities of feeding a family.

It would take four long years of residency, publishing papers and taking slow steps on the ladder of professional advancement to reach that point. Freud's appetite for work was prodigious. He was made an adjunct lecturer at the university. There was little money in it and fewer privileges but it was the first hurdle crossed. He worked increasingly in psychiatric units with people whose cases were considered hopeless and attached himself to older mentors, ultimately becoming close to one of the best-known doctors in Vienna, Josef Breuer.

In the middle of this time he won a fellowship to study in Paris with Jean-Martin Charcot, the man recognized as the world's leading expert on nervous diseases. This was an important step. He would gain access to the latest knowledge in his field and have a headline for the top of his vitae. He promised to bring Martha something lovely from Paris and went off for six months.

In the French capital, he devoured Charcot for knowledge. But he made the time to do what all young intellectuals do on their first trip to Paris: he visited the city's cemeteries to pay homage at the graves of personal heroes. Freud visited two for private meditation. The first was that of Ludwig Börne at Père-Lachaise. The second was the resting place of Heinrich Heine at Montparnasse.

Börne's grave was of particular importance. At the age of fourteen, the young Freud had been given a set of his complete works. He eagerly consumed them and could quote long passages by heart. Freud's admiration for Börne was an acknowledgment from the third generation of emancipated Jews of the struggles of the first group to step out of the ghetto.

• • •

After Paris it was time to get to work. The ambitious young doctor with no money and connections opened an office in the most expensive part of Vienna, just behind the enormous City Hall. His time there was brief; a medical practice was not so easy to build. Soon he had to move to less grand premises. Realizing that the marriage might never be consummated if they waited for Freud to earn a decent living, one of Martha's aunts gave her a significant cash gift. The couple were married in the autumn of 1886.

Slowly but surely, by working shifts in clinics, giving interesting lectures, and cultivating the friendship of established colleagues, particularly Breuer, Freud built a reputation for treating "hysterical" patients. Referrals began to come his way. His methods skirted the edges of orthodoxy. He used hypnosis. He encouraged his patients to lie down on a sofa, concentrate on memories, and then talk about them.

Freud found that talking was the best way to get closer to an understanding of the place where his patients' minds had been traumatized. But he wondered, how much talking should the doctor do and how much should the patient hold the floor? Here his reading of Ludwig Börne helped Freud refine his method. Börne had written a light-hearted essay called "The Art of Becoming a Writer in Three Days." His prescription: "Take a few sheets of paper and three days in succession write down everything that comes into your head. Write what you think of yourself, of your women . . . of Goethe . . . of the Last Judgment—when the three days are over you will be amazed at what novel and startling thoughts have welled up in you." Freud adapted Börne's suggestion of free-associating thoughts into his work method.

By 1891, Freud's practice had grown. He took a massive apartment on the mezzanine floor at 19 Berggasse, a clean, new building located a few blocks from the university. With several thousand square feet of space there was more than ample room for his growing family and a professional suite at the back. The immigrants' son had done well for himself.

## iii.
## Vienna

During these decades as Freud single-mindedly pursued his career, the city of Vienna had undergone a metamorphosis. With bureaucratic restrictions on movement in the Austro-Hungarian Empire lifted, the city had seen a massive influx of not just Jews but all groups from within the empire. The city had become a melting pot and expanded rapidly.

Austria had dawdled behind other European nations on the way to modernity, but after its defeat by Bismarck in 1867 the empire had finally begun to move forward. The economic growth of the city was rapid but then, Vienna had a lot of catching up to do. Freud's arrival in the city as a little boy coincided with the tearing down of the city's medieval walls and construction of the great avenue, the Ringstrasse. Throughout his adolescence and years of medical training the city was constantly reshaping itself.

Yet there was still economic backwardness. Laws remained on the books to protect small artisans and businesses. The city had no factory for baking bread until 1895. Unlike every other great European capital, Vienna had no department stores, because of these restrictions. Many of these statutes remained on the books to keep the city's Jewish businessmen from dominating retail trade as they did in Berlin and Paris.

The civil service and the courts remained off-limits to Jews. Tenured positions at the university were extremely limited and the most important posts were still reserved for Christians. Conversion, which was no longer a factor in Germany, was still a choice faced by members of the community if they wanted to reach the highest levels. Yet the community, which by the mid-1890s accounted for about 12 percent of the expanded city's population, thrived where it was allowed to.

Freud was not the only son of provincial Jewish immigrants to reach the middle class quickly. A third of the University of Vienna's student body was Jewish. In 1890, 22 percent of the law faculty was Jewish or of Jewish origin and an astonishing 48 percent of the medical faculty came from the community. Many of these people were unpaid lecturers like Freud, but nevertheless, considering that the Jewish population of the city a mere three decades earlier was less than seven thousand, this represented a major shift in the social makeup of the Austro-Hungarian capital.

The one place of work where there were virtually no restrictions on Jews was in the world of the arts, particularly the performing arts. This was the area where the community most palpably changed the character of the city. To take just one example, from the early 1860s a new form of entertainment took hold: the operetta. The Viennese went out to dozens of theaters throughout the city to watch these shows and it was Jewish immigrants who provided much of the entertainment. They brought a new degree of specialization, professionalization, and commercialism to the world of the theater. They produced the shows, wrote the music, the lyrics, the books, directed the productions, designed them, starred in them, and played in the orchestras. The productions were reviewed by critics who, for the most part, were Jewish. They wrote with the acerbic wit whose identification with Jews was so common that no one commented on it anymore. Low and high culture was explained to the Viennese by these professors without portfolios. No section of the population was more dedicated to theatergoing than the Jewish community. A night at the theater was a more regular habit than going to the synagogue for the rapidly assimilating members of the community.

It seemed as if the entire world of culture was a closed circle of work created by Jews for a Jewish audience and interpreted for them by Jewish critics. That wasn't the case, of course. The art was of more universal interest than that, and by the middle of the 1890s, Vienna was acknowledged as the one city in Europe to rival Paris as a cultural capital.

While the community was changing the public character of Vienna, social anti-Semitism remained an accepted part of Viennese life and political anti-Semitism was growing in power. The leading political anti-Semite was Karl Lueger. He was a Jew baiter of the first rank but not a simple bigot.

Lueger was an opportunist: a typical, populist demagogue. A lawyer by training, he started out as a liberal Austrian politician. He was a Huey Long type, spending hours drinking with his Catholic working-class constituents, regaling them with jokes. Their hopes and fears were his hopes and fears. So were their prejudices. His people hated Jews and Hungarians. So he learned to talk that talk. He gave barnstorming speeches defaming both groups, although how deep his own prejudices ran is open to question. He had Jewish friends among the cultural elite, and when his own supporters questioned why he was drinking with the Yids he replied, "I get to decide who is a Jew around here."

In 1895 the position of mayor came up for a vote. Vienna's mayor was selected by the city council. The Christian Social Party, a Catholic working-class group, formed a majority on the council and Lueger was their choice for the post. The prospect of an avowed anti-Semite who was probably the most gifted public orator of the day becoming mayor filled Jewish Vienna with dread. But Emperor Franz Joseph had to approve the selection. The emperor had been on the throne for almost fifty years and had done everything he could to hold Austria-Hungary together. He was not prepared to let someone who had risen to prominence making incendiary speeches about Hungarians and Jews become mayor of the imperial capital city. He vetoed the appointment.

When Freud heard the news, he laughed out loud, and, despite a promise to his wife, Martha, that he would give up smoking, he lit up one of his favorite cigars to celebrate.

The city council held another vote. Lueger was elected once more and Franz Joseph once again vetoed the choice. The struggle over Lueger's appointment between the emperor and the city council underscored the ambivalence most of Viennese society felt about rabid anti-Semitism. There are degrees of prejudice. Finding Jewish manners offensive or worth mocking is one thing. Refusing to allow a Jew into your home or club is another. Wanting to violently remove them from your midst and lock them back up is something else entirely, and few middle-class Viennese were prepared to follow the rabid anti-Semites' down that path. One non-Jewish author, Hermann Bahr, called anti-Semitism "a new madness." The rich, he said, deadened themselves to modern life with morphine and hashish. "Those who cannot afford drugs become anti-Semites."

## iv.
## Herzl Returns

At around the same time that Lueger was being denied power and the secret code of dreams was being cracked, Freud's first major book came out. *Studies in Hysteria* was written with Breuer and summarized what the pair had learned treating patients by various forms of the talking cure over the last few years. Each man contributed individual chapters to the book. Freud insisted on including an essay on sex as a key to understanding neurosis. The book was lambasted in the medical press.

But the sensational subject matter stirred interest in the general public. Theodor Herzl had returned from Paris and was now the literary editor of the *New Free Press.* In December 1895 a review appeared in the paper that showed Freud's theories had profound interest to those outside the medical profession. "Surgery of the Soul" was the headline of the review written by the director of the Imperial Theatre, Alfred von Bergner. He predicted that through this new method it would be possible to discover "the innermost secret of human personality." But he added that Freud's psychology was following a path opened up by poets. Shakespeare had used the same knowledge of the human condition to create the character of Lady Macbeth, for example, Bergner wrote. But the director's review created a link to the doctor's work in Vienna's theater world.

Freud was aware of the connection of his work to artistic expression. He knew that Arthur Schnitzler was also exploring the power of erotic urges in his writing for the stage. The men moved in the same circles. Schnitzler, five years younger than Freud, had been a medical student at the university when Freud was doing postdoctoral research. Freud called him his doppelganger and for reasons he never fully explained spent years avoiding direct contact with the writer.

Herzl, however, was happy to be in touch with Schnitzler. He looked him up as soon as he got back from covering the Dreyfus trial in Paris. He had big news: the editor had decided he was going to establish a Jewish state, probably in Palestine, and already had met with some of the richest Jews in Europe to discuss the plan. The fact that he had no experience in politics or in organizing anything was not a concern. Herzl had an inheritance and so did his wife. He could afford to chase the dream.

Schnitzler encouraged Herzl, but he was one of the few members of the community to do so. Some old acquaintances, when they realized Herzl was serious, told him frankly that he had lost his mind. Others reminded the journalist of the last hundred years of progress that had been made since leaving the ghetto. The anti-Semitism would pass; there were plenty in the gentile community who were embarrassed by it, they said. Herzl chose not to listen.

In early 1896, Herzl's pamphlet, *The Jewish State: An Attempt at a Modern Solution of the Jewish Question,* was published. It wasn't the idea that was new. Moses Hess, acknowledging the persistence of Jew hatred in Europe, had had the idea before Herzl was born. Each prolonged period of anti-Semitic outrages had encouraged small groups within the community to think of reestablishing a Jewish state in the Ottoman province of Palestine. But no one from Herzl's background and with his platform—the august *New Free Press*—had broached the subject so loudly and clearly.

The response was equally intense. Publication of the pamphlet isolated Herzl in Vienna's Jewish community as thoroughly as Freud's essay on sex in *Studies in Hysteria* had in the medical community. But like Freud, Herzl was absolutely convinced that his idea was the way forward and he was going to stick with it. The Jewish press begged to differ and did so in the most withering terms. In a paradigm of the law of unintended consequences, it was the anti-Semitic press that praised Herzl.

If the Viennese community found Herzl's idea strange, there were others who wanted to meet and encourage him: Jewish students from the Pale of Settlement studying in Western Europe, Christian Millenarians from Britain, and leaders of pioneer groups who were trying to raise money to purchase land in Palestine. A steady stream of visitors turned up at Herzl's apartment, which was just down the Berggasse from Freud's office. The two men saw each other in the street, yet never became close. They operated in their own world of isolation and single-mindedness. Each was like a rail in a set of train tracks, running parallel to each other, fated never to meet except at some illusory vanishing point on the horizon.

For both men, 1896 represented a time of loss. Herzl was stunned by the degree to which his plan was rejected by his own class. He lost months to depression. Freud's father died in October of that year. Whatever disappointments he expressed about the old man, the loss left him in what he would call a "neurotic" state.

The year 1897, however, was a decisive time of work for the two of them. On August 29, in the Swiss city of Basel, Herzl presided at the opening of the First Zionist Congress. Zionism was very much a minority idea but those who attended were a cross section of the world of Ashkenaz a century into the Emancipation era. There were religious Jews and assimilated businessmen and socialist students. They spoke Yiddish, German, Russian, English, French. Some still knew how to pray in Hebrew and actually understood the words they were saying. Their manners and customs were as diverse as the countries they came from.

The three-day-long congress was occasionally chaotic and totally exhausting. It ended in a flurry of votes on resolutions. The critical ones were to continue strengthening Jewish national consciousness and begin the process of obtaining the necessary governmental consents to achieve the goal of Zionism: the creation of a Jewish state.

There was no guarantee that anything would come of this gathering but Herzl knew what he had done. "In Basel I founded the Jewish state," he confided to his diary. He added that it might take fifty years for the world to agree. He was off by one year.

Freud looked inward even further. Analyzing his dreams had shown him a work method. But he realized that to make full use of the method he needed to do a complete self-analysis. What is the self? What are its component parts? What is one's true identity? He began making notes for a book, *The Interpretation of Dreams,* that would incorporate his findings.

The death of his father had affected him profoundly, and his work focused increasingly on his relation to his parents. The sex drive was part of his thinking. His feelings toward his father were shaped by jealousy. As a child, at a level beyond his comprehension, he had been jealous of his father's relationship to his mother and wanted to take his place. What had happened to those feelings? Did they still live, deep inside, at a level below ordinary waking consciousness? He looked for a simile to explain the phenomenon he was talking about and found it in the world of the theater. *Oedipus Rex* still moved theatergoers after all these centuries because it touched on these common feelings of jealousy and a desire to take one parent's place in the affection of the other. He noted with satisfaction that the truth is revealed to Oedipus in Sophocles' play in a method similar to the questioning of psychoanalysis.

His professional isolation continued. He gave occasional talks at the B'nai B'rith lodge. He saw every patient he could, sometimes practicing psychoanalysis for eleven hours a day before adjourning to his study to work on his own self-analysis and his book.

In April 1897 an event alarming to both Herzl and Freud took place: for the fourth time the Vienna city council elected Karl Lueger mayor. This time Franz Joseph did not fight the selection. The anti-Semitic socialist demagogue was running the city.

• • •

At the end of the year, riding either the author's new fame or his no-toriety, Herzl's play *The New Ghetto* was finally given a production. Freud, who rarely attended the theater, decided to see his neighbor's work.

The production affected him profoundly. That night he dreamt a strange dream: He is in the Tuscan city of Siena, which his children must flee because of something happening in Rome. Freud is sitting at the side of a well, depressed to the point of tears. His sons are brought outside by their father, but the man is not him.

On waking, Freud immediately understood what underlay the strange imagery. Rome had been the symbol of the implacable foe since his boyhood. He had visited Italy the previous summer but had not gone to Rome. He had traveled south through Tuscany, visited Siena, and stopped his journey on the shores of Lake Trasimeno, scene of one of Hannibal's greatest triumphs against the Roman Army. Freud could not bring himself to go the mere eighty miles from the lake to the imperial city. That accounted for the setting of the dream. What was its meaning?

Herzl's play had reached deep into the place in the doctor's mind where "the Jewish Question, anxiety about the future of my children who cannot be given a fatherland, anxiety about educating them so that they may enjoy the privileges of citizens" all lived. These anxieties were not unique to Freud. To a greater or lesser degree they occupied many in the community. Anxiety, sometimes neurotic anxiety, about Jews' own identity remained unresolved even after all this time outside the ghetto.

Several years earlier, when he wrote the play, Theodor Herzl shared those anxieties but the Zionist Congress had resolved his feelings about the ghetto. It was the Russian Jews in attendance who changed the way Herzl viewed the ghetto. They were unemancipated and unas-similated yet they were modern and fierce. Shortly after the congress ended he wrote in his diary: "They are not tormented by the need to assimilate . . . they are upright and genuine. Yet they are ghetto Jews, the only ghetto Jews of our time. By looking at them we understood what gave our forefathers the strength to endure the most difficult time. They confronted us with our history."

In late 1897 and early 1898, while Freud was dreaming anxiously about his children's future and Herzl was manically fund-raising and organizing for his new movement, something was happening in France that would focus the whole world on anti-Semitism. The Alfred Dreyfus case was about to become an "affair."

## CHAPTER TWENTY

# The Truth Is on the March

O N THURSDAY, JANUARY 13, 1898, THE FRONT PAGE OF THE
Paris newspaper *L'Aurore* carried a single article under the banner headline J'ACCUSE. The author was the novelist Emile Zola.

The article took the form of an open letter to the president of
France, Félix Faure. In four thousand brilliantly organized words, Zola
laid out before the president the facts of the Dreyfus case, the menda-
cious reasons why the former captain continued to languish in prison,
and the potential harm this great miscarriage of justice could do to
French society and France's reputation abroad.

Having laid out his case, Zola concluded with a list of accusations. By name he accused the senior military figures who had created
or were complicit in the scheme. He accused others of the general
staff of fraud and bias. He accused the court-martial of convict-
ing Dreyfus on secret evidence to which his lawyer had never had
access.

Zola ended his essay with an acknowledgment: by making these
accusations he was exposing himself to the libel laws. So what? "I have
but one passion, that light be shed . . . My fiery protest is simply the
cry of my very soul." Then he issued a challenge to the men he named.

"Let them dare to bring me before a court of law and investigate in the full light of day! I am waiting."

He didn't have to wait long. Five days later, France's minister of war, General Jean-Baptiste Billot, sued Zola and *L'Aurore* for libel. A court date was set for February; Zola was confident all the facts would come out then. He had achieved his goal. He was well aware of his status as one of the world's most famous authors, and now he would use that celebrity to focus everyone's attention on the fate of an innocent man.

Zola's interest in the case was not something any of the handful of Dreyfus's supporters, mostly members of the innocent man's family, had reason to count on. The novelist was as likely to attend literary soirees with anti-Semitic authors, where the general conversation fashionably mocked Jews, as he was to attend get-togethers where members of the Jewish community were present. In this respect he was a normal member of France's elite. Anti-Semitism was socially acceptable. When it came to prejudice, members of the more rarefied strata of French society occupied a middle ground—not offended by the presence of Jews, not offended by extreme expressions of Jew hatred.

Socially Zola was in the middle but his fiction and essays had a fierce commitment to social justice. He was identified with writers of the left, where he had many Jewish colleagues. He was on good terms with Bernard Lazare, for example. Both men wrote for the left-wing newspaper *La Justice*.

In the years leading up to the publication of "J'Accuse," as Drumont and other writers gained more and more of a following, Zola found himself increasingly troubled by organized anti-Semitism, not out of great love for the community but because this movement was becoming an irrational and destabilizing force in France.

In the spring of 1896, the novelist published a lengthy essay in *Le Figaro*, France's newspaper of record. The piece was titled "A Plea for the Jews." In the first paragraph Zola confessed his mounting "surprise and disgust" at the "blind stupidity" of anti-Semitism. Throughout the essay the old arguments of a hundred years ago were dusted off, given an airing, and put back in their cases. He criticized the Catholic clericalism underpinning people like Drumont. The logic of anti-Semitism is a return to wars of religion. Zola attacked the view of the community as a "nation within the nation" that loves money above all other things. Noting the obvious, that it is not true that the Jews are all-powerful in matters of money, he concluded that anti-Semitism had no roots in the reasonableness of the French people but was the product of a few "fuzzy minds" creating the illusion of a political movement.

The style Zola used to attack the unreason of the bigots was less lofty than that of Mirabeau. He mocked anti-Semitic attitudes in terse, dismissive terms. Yet it is clear that at one time Zola held or at least understood these same attitudes. In the *Le Figaro* article he talks about friends of his "who can't bear the sight of their noses," or to shake hands with them "because the touch of their flesh makes their skin crawl." Zola had put similar words in the mouth of one of the characters in his novel *Money*, without any critical comment from another character. In his biggest bestseller, *The Debacle*, published in 1892, Zola had described people following the German Army after battle "to rob the corpses, a pack of base, preying Jews."

But now, four years later, the attacks on the community were out of hand. The article ends with an echo of 1789 with a call for brotherhood and a very specific demand that the breeders of hate withdraw from society. Christ has long since forgiven the Jews . . . so should they.

Following publication of the article, Bernard Lazare approached Zola for help in exonerating Dreyfus. Lazare was a polemicist by nature but had turned into an investigative reporter over the previous eighteen months and had dug out enough facts to put together an inflammatory pamphlet accusing high-ranking army officers of covering up a miscarriage of justice. As a Jew, he knew how important it was to find someone of prominence outside the community to take up the case. Zola declined.

A year passed. In November 1897, Lazare, now an editor of

*L'Aurore,* visited him again to discuss new facts coming to light. Once again Zola made no commitment to help, but his interest was now piqued. Two days later a lawyer, Louis Leblois, came to see the novelist. He represented the man who was ready to blow the whistle on the whole affair, Lieutenant Colonel Georges Picquart, and the lawyer had a most astonishing story to tell.

The whole case against Dreyfus had been built on a scrap of paper plucked out of a wastepaper basket by a cleaning lady at the German Embassy in Paris. The woman worked for the French intelligence services and recognized the paper as an official memorandum, or *bordereau,* from someone on the French army's general staff. The *bordereau's* author wrote that he would pass along information including a draft of the field artillery Manual of Fire. The court-martial decided the *bordereau* was in Dreyfus's handwriting. Case closed.

Time passed. The cleaning lady at the German Embassy continued to pick through the rubbish for items of interest. In March 1896, Colonel Picquart, head of the army's intelligence unit, was presented with the interesting remnants of a note collected by the cleaning lady. It had been sent by a member of the French general staff, Major Ferdinand Walsin Esterhazy, to a military figure at the embassy. Picquart was of course very familiar with Esterhazy. The major was the son of a general and a bit of a strange character whose old family connections had smoothed his career path despite repeated displays of incompetence during his quarter-century-long military career.

The torn-up note, which would come to be known as the *petit bleu,* was a perfect example of this incompetence. First of all it was headed by Esterhazy's name and address—no attempt at disguise in case the note should fall into the wrong hands. It tried to be oblique but was clearly the communication of someone who was doing something underhanded. Picquart began to discreetly gather more information on Major Esterhazy. It turned out Esterhazy spoke German and had worked at one time in the intelligence section translating German documents.

In June, Picquart received an intelligence report from Berlin that members of the German general staff were trying to find out who Dreyfus had been passing documents to, since no one in their military intelligence operation had ever had anything to do with the man. Their contact was a major on the general staff. Now the strands of new evidence began to come together for the colonel and he was increasingly convinced that this major, probably Esterhazy, was the real traitor, not Dreyfus. He faced a difficult decision now. Should he follow his hunch, which would mean reopening the Dreyfus case, or let things slide? He decided to act on the innocent man's behalf.

Picquart was an unlikely ally for Dreyfus. Like so many others on the general staff, he was a committed anti-Semite. He had been present at Dreyfus's arrest and first interrogation. At the time of the original trial he had reflexively assumed Dreyfus's guilt. But whatever his feelings about Jews, there was a more important point at stake here. Justice was being traduced and the facts of the case meant that the traitor was still at large. Once he was committed to finding out who the real traitor was, he had no choice. Toward the end of July, the colonel opened up the classified Dreyfus file. He picked up the torn and faded *bordereau,* and placed it side by side on his desk with the *petit bleu*. It was obvious that the same person had written the two documents.

The importance of this hit him immediately: not only was Dreyfus innocent, the real spy, Esterhazy, was still at work. This knowledge was dynamite. Who in the army could he tell? He decided to go straight to the top and requested a meeting with the chief of the General Staff, General Boisdeffre. What happened at that meeting can only be guessed at by what happened at a subsequent one a month later with the deputy chief of staff, General Gonse. He was advised to leave the Dreyfus file alone and pursue a separate investigation of Esterhazy. Another meeting between the two men followed and one account quotes the following dialogue:

"What is it to you, if that Jew stays on Devil's Island?"

"But General, he is innocent."

"It is a case we can't reopen. General Mercier and General Saussier are involved in it."

"But since he is innocent?!"

"If you say nothing, no one will be the wiser."

"What you have just said is an abomination, General! I will not carry this secret to my grave!"

Picquart understood what was happening. If the truth came out, all the senior staff members who had been involved in the original miscarriage of justice would have their careers ruined. For reasons of bigotry an innocent man had been sent to prison while a traitor continued to operate with impunity.

The real nation within the nation, the army, now went to war to defend its leaders' reputations. No whistle-blower would be allowed to call their honor into question. Black propaganda was spoon fed into the right-wing and anti-Semitic press. Picquart was relieved of his intelligence post and for good measure sent on assignment to North Africa, where insurgents were fighting against French colonial rule. It was an intentionally hazardous tour of duty.

At the same time two other officers, Lieutenant Colonel Armand Mercier du Paty de Clam and Major Joseph Henry, forged new incriminating documents and put them in the Dreyfus file. Both had been involved in the case from the beginning. Paty de Clam had supervised the captain after his arrest. On one occasion he had awakened Dreyfus in the middle of the night and forced him to provide handwriting samples. Paty de Clam testified in secret that the handwriting samples matched those of the *bordereau*. His word had been enough to convict Dreyfus. Henry's involvement was more sinister. Esterhazy was his friend and he had immediately recognized the handwriting on the *bordereau* as belonging to the major. To protect his friend, Henry had pointed the finger at the only Jew on the staff. Henry was the man who framed Dreyfus in the first place.

For nine months, the case—not quite an affair yet—hung in this balance. Then, in late June 1897, Colonel Picquart returned on leave from the North African war zone. He put together his own dossier and handed it to his lawyer, Louis Leblois, along with a cover letter to the president of France. It was to be handed over in the event of his death . . . a circumstance the colonel deemed eminently possible, given the lengths to which the general staff had mobilized against him.

The lawyer showed the file to someone already sympathetic to Dreyfus, the vice president of the French Senate, Auguste Scheurer-Kestner. The senator wanted to act, not just to free Dreyfus but also to bring the real traitor to justice. But he knew he had to proceed cautiously. Public opinion needed to be engaged but first the effect of the black propaganda had to be undone. Naming Esterhazy as the real traitor would provoke a storm in the anti-Dreyfus press. A heavy-hitting public intellectual had to be recruited. So in November, shortly after Zola had turned Lazare down, Leblois was sent to visit the author and invite him to the senator's house for lunch. Just for a chat.

Zola knew he didn't need this fight. He was at the height of his fame, secure in his position in French public life. Out of this success, he had created for himself the space to write as he pleased. He was just finishing the third book in a trilogy of novels on great cities and had plans to start another big book right away. But the Dreyfus situation offended him. It offended his Enlightenment sensibility. Reason was not being acknowledged here. Clearly, Dreyfus was being framed; the documents proved the case; to ignore the facts as they existed was to ignore reason. This is where the stupidity of anti-Semitism leads. It affronted his patriotism. The author truly believed France was the light of humanity, the place where equality and brotherhood reigned. This miscarriage of justice gave the lie to that belief. Not only that, but once the truth came out, as it inevitably would, the whole world would know that France had railroaded an innocent man because he was a member of a minority group. The reputation of his country internationally was at stake. Finally, he shared Picquart's anger that to save the personal reputations of a few senior officers, Dreyfus was imprisoned while the real spy was still at work. The novelist told the senator he would do whatever was necessary.

Two days later battle was joined. Scheurer-Kestner published an open letter declaring Dreyfus innocent. The next day Mathieu Dreyfus published an open letter to the minister of war naming Esterhazy as the real traitor. The expected storm erupted.

## ii.
## The Campaign

"The Truth is on the march"—thus concluded Zola's first article in *Le Figaro* on November 25. The tone of the essay was not polemical. It was lighthearted and certain. This was a tale that made a novelist's heart leap with admiration and excitement, he told readers; there were so many interesting characters. But, the author made clear, there was only one character he wanted to talk about, the good Senator Scheurer-Kestner. The article's intent was to give the senator's bona fides in the hope that the public would understand that the man was working from his own time-honored sense of justice.

Reasonableness ruled Zola's pen. The senator's actions weren't an attack on the integrity of the military. Miscarriages of justice can happen. "Judges do make mistakes; army officers can make mistakes as well . . . If such a mistake has occurred the only thing to do is correct it."

If he thought his essay would persuade the public he was wrong. Letters flooded into the newspaper excoriating the author and claiming Zola was acting at the behest of a syndicate of rich Jews. The author's response came less than a week later. "Who created the syndicate? . . . the false patriots and braying anti-Semites." He upped the stakes, "France—just and generous France—is being forced to commit a genuine crime." Zola acknowledges being part of a syndicate . . . a syndicate of decency.

More letters poured in to the paper. Zola wrote another article in which he stated where the guilt lay in what was now the Dreyfus Affair. "Anti-Semitism is the guilty party. I have already stated how this barbarous campaign which drags us back a thousand years in time goes against my craving for brotherhood and my passionate need for tolerance and the emancipation of the human mind," he told readers. The truth is on the march and the longer the army delays in letting it out, the more devastating its impact will be.

The editors of the paper decided their readers had had enough. There would be no more Zola essays in the paper of record.

Who needed *Le Figaro* anyway? The battle for justice was under way. But in the streets there was no reaction. Zola was puzzled and hurt. Where were the student activists of his youth? Why was the Latin Quarter not crammed by demonstrators demanding justice?

Toward the end of December, it was announced that a military tribunal would look into the case against Major Esterhazy. Senior officers and the man himself had decided the best way to face down the accusation was through a judicial proceeding. The court-martial convened in secret on January 10 and the next day reached its preplanned conclusion: Esterhazy was not the author of the *bordereau.* The same day Picquart was arrested for passing the secret military documents related to the case to civilians.

Zola, Scheurer-Kestner, and a few other converts to the cause, including Georges Clemenceau, editor in chief of *L'Aurore,* began circulating a petition calling for a retrial. Zola went to his office and wrote "J'Accuse." A libel trial was the only way to get the truth into the open.

As the drama came to a boil, two actors were missing. The first was Dreyfus himself. The previous year a report had appeared in a British newspaper claiming he had escaped from Devil's Island and was living in England. The report was obviously false and may well have been planted by anti-Semites as part of the black propaganda exercise. Regardless, on the basis of this rumor a new man was put in charge of Devil's Island with instructions to be extra harsh in his treatment of the prisoner. For two months Dreyfus was manacled even when he slept. His feet were placed in stocks installed at the foot of his bed; the chains on his wrists were fastened to the stocks. The physical punishment ended but not the psychological one. He was being held incommunicado. He had no knowledge of what was going on in Paris and could get no message out to help influence opinion.

The other actor missing from this great story was the French Jewish community, whose silence echoes through the historical record. Some individuals, such as Bernard Lazare, stepped forward early on, but most of the community kept to itself. The *Archives Israëlites* made no mention of Dreyfus's humiliation in January 1895 and over the ensuing two years before Zola's campaign began, the paper continued to take more note of attacks against Jews in Algeria and of Blood Libel accusations in Tatarstan than of the fate of Dreyfus. It did not take an activist stance and in this it reflected the attitudes of its readership. They were assimilated French citizens but the old ghetto psychology was deeply ingrained. In times of social upheaval keep your head down. Their concerns for Dreyfus remained private.

## iii.
## Trial and Consequences

In every respect but one, the trial was what Zola had hoped for. France was now completely focused on the fate of Dreyfus. So was the rest of the world. Just as the Dreyfusards had hoped, hundreds of foreign reporters came to Paris to watch the famous author have his day in court. World opinion would be engaged on behalf of the innocent man.

From day one, February 7, 1898, the reporters had plenty to write about. The setting was historic. The Palais de Justice, on the Ile de la Cité, is adjacent to Sainte-Chapelle. The great building is a masterpiece of Gothic architecture. It was built by King Louis IX, Saint Louis, to house his collection of relics, including the crown of thorns. French official life had carried on from this place for almost a thousand years. Zola arrived and stepped out of his cab, into a maelstrom. Thousands were thronging around the grand building and many hurled abuse as he walked calmly across the Cour d'Honneur, up the stairs, and through the colonnaded entry. Inside, the court of assizes gallery was packed and noisy.

The author affected an air of studied nonchalance in his performance for the spectators. The *Times* of London noted that throughout the first day's proceedings clerks brought him telegrams of support from all over the globe, four hundred in all, which he read quietly as the lawyers went through the preliminaries.

France was now split in two. There were no more political parties, just Dreyfusard and anti-Dreyfusard groups. The former represented progress, the latter reaction. The Dreyfus Affair was a social civil war, splitting families and friends. The rifts went on for generations.

It was a reenactment of the Emancipation battles of the Constitutional National Assembly during the French Revolution, only the stakes were higher. This wasn't an argument over abstract rights: a real man's life was in the balance. The anti-Dreyfusards were taking up the arguments of the monarchists and conservative clergy. The Dreyfusards harked back to the authors of the Declaration of the Rights of Man. Shortly after "J'Accuse" appeared, the Dreyfusards organized the French League for the Defense of the Rights of Man to lobby for his release. In response, anti-Dreyfusards organized the nationalist League of the French Homeland. Followers of Drumont had already organized the League of Anti-Semites. Both groups sought to undo the mistake of Emancipation and remove Jews from the French body politic. Their motto was "France for the French."

As in 1789, the Jewish community remained on the sidelines. This was an argument about the kind of country France would be as much as it was about the Jewish community.

Paris became a theater of Dreyfus and everyone was at one time or another either acting a part in the production or watching it performed. Small one-act plays were improvised at dinner parties. There were great set pieces in the street whenever something related to the case reached a courtroom.

Marcel Proust was transfixed by the whole story. To anyone who knew him that was a surprise. Proust was a young aesthete about town, not deeply engaged in politics. On the surface he was no different than many other comfortably well-off, would-be authors, painters, and musicians living a languorous bourgeois bohemian life in Paris.

Zola's articles in *Le Figaro* had roused him to action. Proust called himself, with some justification, the first Dreyfusard. He had attended the meeting at Scheurer-Kestner's house immediately following Esterhazy's exoneration and offered to get some of his well-known literary friends to sign the petition demanding a new trial for Dreyfus. Zola's name was on the petition, of course, but the organizers knew they needed one more important intellectual to sign. This would demonstrate to the public that the novelist was not riding his Dreyfus hobbyhorse for reasons of personal vanity. Proust took the petition to his friend Anatole France and convinced him to sign. France was an all-around man of letters, a novelist, poet, and critic, and at Zola's level on the intellectual celebrity scale. He was also a much more establishment figure than Zola, by reputation a conservative and a monarchist. Anatole France's name on the petition was the breath of wind that turns a fire into a conflagration, and Proust's obtaining it was no small achievement.

It earned him international notice of a sort. On January 16, 1898, the *New York Times* carried a 1,300-word article on the petition. The last paragraph noted that "M. Marcel Proust is probably the author, Marcel Prevost, or he may be Dr. Achille A. Proust, the well-known Professor of Hygiene and Commander of the Legion of Honor. There is no prominent Frenchman by the name of Marcel Proust."

Actually, Achille Proust was Marcel's father, an ambitious man who had risen by talent out of the provincial lower middle class. He was Catholic. Proust's mother was Jewish, from an extremely wealthy, prominent family—her uncle was Adolphe Crémieux. Proust was raised Catholic in a fairly desultory manner. He was exceptionally close to his mother and her relatives and so was a typical product of the assimilation by marriage that had also been a hope of Abbé Grégoire and others. He felt and understood what it meant to be Jewish in probably the same way as Dreyfus had.

As a good soldier in the cause, he attended every day of Zola's trial, arriving early each morning at the Palais de Justice with a thermos of coffee and enough sandwiches to last him all day. From a seat in the public gallery he watched the show. At night he made the rounds of salons where the day's proceedings were rehashed, gossip about who fought with whom over the affair was savored, and moral sensibilities were heated up and then cooled down by the fine art of conversation.

The tactic of forcing a libel trial to draw worldwide attention to the Dreyfus Affair succeeded beyond the Dreyfusards' wildest dreams. The foreign press was overwhelmingly sympathetic. It was one of those cases where the whole world could see quite clearly that a great nation was making a colossal judicial error but the official class of that country was blind to that fact. The French had gone a little mad over the case, was the general tone of the reporting.

The trial did very little to change the French people's minds. Their positions before it began pretty much stayed the same as it went on. That is due in part to the fact that Zola and his friends had been outflanked by the minister of war. The last accusation in Zola's article had related to the trial and acquittal of Esterhazy. General Billot had only sued the novelist and *L'Aurore* for libel in regard to that accusation. So no evidence on the Dreyfus case was presented.

The trial lasted two weeks and the verdict was not surprising. Guilty. Zola immediately appealed. The next day Picquart was dismissed from the army. Zola's lawyers were clever and fought good delaying tactics but after two appeals trials the conviction for libel still held. In July 1898 he was sentenced to one year in prison. Before he could be handed official notification he fled over the English Channel to London and went into hiding. However, it was not so easy for one of the most famous writers in the world to live incognito. The author moved around constantly from one suburban hotel to another. Like

Dreyfus, the man he never met but whose cause he had taken up, Zola could only wait for the truth to make its inevitable entry.

## iv.
## Resolution

The truth arrived by mistake. In June 1898, the government of France fell. A new government with a new war minister, General Jacques Cavaignac, took office. A month later, in the National Assembly, Cavaignac attempted to draw a line under the Dreyfus case. He declassified a particular piece of evidence that conclusively named Dreyfus as a German agent. Picquart knew for certain that this particular scrap of paper was a forgery. He met the Socialist Party leader Jean Jaurès and the pair went public with this knowledge. Far from drawing a line under the case, Cavaignac gave the affair new publicity.

Now Cavaignac needed to cover his back, so he asked an officer of the security section to go through the secret Dreyfus file one more time. The officer verified that the note Cavaignac had shown to the National Assembly was indeed a forgery. It was an easy task to identify the forger since so few people had had access to the file. It was Major Henry. He was arrested on August 30 and confessed to having forged the document. The next day he committed suicide in his cell by slitting his throat with a razor.

As Zola predicted, the truth would out and the longer it took the worse the consequences. Within two days, Army Chief of Staff General Boisdeffre resigned, followed by Cavaignac. Esterhazy fled the country altogether.

The anti-Dreyfusard, anti-Semitic movement hemorrhaged public support and its leadership became increasingly aggressive. Their newspapers whipped up anti-Jewish riots by its core supporters.

But events were inexorably moving away from Drumont's followers. Lucie Dreyfus was given leave to petition for a retrial that autumn. In the winter, a new president took office, Emile Loubet, who was sympathetic to the cause. In June 1899, Alfred Dreyfus was told he would be leaving Devil's Island and returning home to face a new trial. In his last letter to Lucie from his prison rock, Dreyfus wrote of his "trust in the justice of my country." He was still a French patriot after all.

The same week Dreyfus began the long voyage home, Zola returned to France. It's a nice coincidence but it does not lead to a neat dovetailing of story lines. Only in one of Zola's novels would something like that happen. The reality of the end of the affair was as messy and confused as the beginning.

On September 8, 1899, Alfred Dreyfus faced a court-martial for the second time. The next day he was convicted again, with "extenuating circumstances." The army had covered its back by refusing to admit it had made an error in the first place, but did open the door for the government to issue a pardon.

Now the innocent man dug in his heels. He filed an appeal. He would have justice. The truth must come out. The government sent Mathieu to visit his brother to try to make him see sense. Accept the pardon, take your freedom, another trial will only yield the same result. Reluctantly, Alfred Dreyfus accepted the deal. On September 19 he was pardoned. The next day's newspapers carried a statement from him: "Liberty is nothing to me without honor . . . I shall continue to seek amend for the shocking judicial wrong of which I am still the victim."

With Dreyfus free the country could look to the future. That was the government's hope. A new century was arriving and to mark it Paris was holding a world's fair, the largest exposition of its kind ever mounted. The threat of a boycott by a number of countries, if justice for Dreyfus was not done, had already been mooted. Now everyone could come to Paris and celebrate the future.

## CHAPTER TWENTY-ONE

# Everywhere an Intruder, Never Welcomed

FREUD'S BOOK ON DREAMS WAS PUBLISHED ON NOVEMBER 4, 1899. The printer put the publication date as January 1900. *The Interpretation of Dreams* was a book for the new century.

The century was not quite ready for it. The medical press drew a veil over their colleague's endeavor and just ignored it. Once again it was the general press that found the ideas in it worth discussing, even if only to criticize them. Dismissing the book's author, one reviewer in Berlin inadvertently put his finger on why *The Interpretation of Dreams* would become one of the most influential works of the twentieth century. "The imaginative thoughts of an artist have triumphed over the scientific investigator," wrote one Professor Liepmann. So much of what Freud explores in his book—dream meanings, the unconscious, repression, erotic feelings—pointed to new ways for artists to unlock their own imaginations, even if they didn't read the book, as was likely. *The Interpretation of Dreams* sold 351 copies in the first two years after publication. But the ideas quickly leaked out into the overheated atmosphere of Vienna.

• • •

The arrival of a new century heightens society's sense of time as people assess the hundred years that have just passed and look forward with greater intensity. These are periods of great nostalgia and blind faith. Millennial prophecies abound. Those inclined to believe prophecy confidently await their future among the saved.

Even people with no faith live as if there is no tomorrow because of the momentous change in the calendar. We can be certain from one day to the next what is in store, but from one century to another? Decadence and licentiousness are often social features of a changing century.

In some places a changing century is welcomed; in others it is dreaded. In Paris the end of the nineteenth and the beginning of the twentieth century is still called La Belle Epoque, the Beautiful Era, but in Vienna it is still called the Fin de Siècle, the End of the Century. In Paris, with its exposition illuminating the night sky with electric light, the future seemed limitless. In Vienna anxiety seeped into every corner of society because people could feel that something was coming to an end.

Emperor Franz Joseph had been on his throne for more than half a century. It was Franz Joseph who held what was left of his empire together, not through political cunning but simply by being beloved. Nationalism had been kept at bay to a great extent because the grandfatherly figurehead of the emperor seemed worthy of allegiance. But he was seventy years old and in photos looked wearier than that. His only son, Crown Prince Rudolph, had blown his brains out over an unhappy love affair many years earlier, and that had sapped the emperor's joy in life. The heir apparent, Archduke Franz Ferdinand, was not someone to inspire hope for the future. It was not likely the empire would hold together once the old man was gone. No one could be sure what would take its place.

The anxiety was reflected in the culture. Vienna was an "experimental station for the collapse of mankind," according to the era's most famous essayist, Karl Kraus, a Jew who would become a Catholic and in the end renounce all religion.

• • •

Looking back over the nineteenth and forward to the twentieth century, Vienna's Jews were filled with anxiety but also nostalgia. They weren't nostalgic for the old ghetto life. They were nostalgic for a life they had never known. As the new century arrived the community regarded itself as the keeper of the flame of Goethe. Culture was everything. It was the key to *Bildung,* the ideal of Goethe and Rahel Varnhagen von Ense: self-knowledge through education and life experience. Perhaps other parts of the German-speaking world had forgotten the value of this concept, but not the Jewish community.

The nobility had retreated from its role as patrons of art and the Jewish bourgeoisie had taken its place. Its members bought up the subscription tickets for concert series and commissioned rising artists like Gustav Klimt to paint their portraits. The spiritual descendants of Fanny von Arnstein held salons where writers and painters mingled with those who had money and *Bildung.*

The anxiety over what would come next was profound. No single group within Franz Joseph's realm embraced the idea of imperial citizenship with more enthusiasm than the Jews. Austrians thought of themselves as Germans and looked down on Hungarians with real racial animosity. Moravians and Slovaks and Poles and Bohemians all were rivals and looked forward to the day when they would throw off the Habsburg yoke and have their own nation-states. But Jews from the provinces thought of themselves as Austrians first. This identity offered them protection from local hatreds.

There was a good example of local hatred to reflect on as the century turned. Yet another Blood Libel trial was grabbing headlines. In rural Bohemia, today part of the Czech Republic, a Jewish vagabond, Leopold Hilsner, was on trial for the murder of a nineteen-year-old Christian woman. The prosecuting attorney alleged that the murder had been committed to obtain blood for Jewish ritual. It was a kangaroo court. Hilsner was imprisoned for life. The trial confirmed a lesson for members of the community: peasant hatreds would never go away, even in this modern era. That's why so many moved to the cities, and the bigger the better. In 1900, a quarter of Europe's Jews lived in cities with a population of more than one million.

The artistic and intellectual life of Vienna, so dominated by people connected to the Jewish community, reflected this nostalgia and anxiety. No wonder Freud's book, even if it wasn't selling, was influencing artists and framing everyday conversations among the bourgeoisie, a goodly number of whom were Freud's patients or knew people who were being analyzed by him. Nothing was certain; there was a surreal, dreamlike quality to life and people were trying to figure out its meaning. They weren't locking themselves away to do this; the gaiety of city life continued. There were dozens of theaters to visit and salons to attend and coffeehouses in which to waste an afternoon that ran over into the evening. Vienna's cozy and unhurried life carried on, but something was gnawing underneath.

Some artists wanted to clear away everything and start all over. A new century demanded new forms. In 1898 a group of them who met regularly at the salon of Berta Zuckerkandl announced they were "seceding" from the traditions of academic painting. The artists of the Vienna Secession wanted to show modern man his true face. The artists depicted sex as it really was: lush and feverish. Architects started hammering away at the extra ornaments that characterized the buildings of the imperial capital. The century to come would have no place for such foolishness. It would be austere and cold as the grave. Jewish or not, Freud's work spoke to them. Sex and death were the great life forces Freud had identified.

A critical mass of creative minds had assembled in Vienna from all over the empire and other parts of the German-speaking world. A preponderance of them were Jews from the third generation of Emancipation.

## ii.
# Mahler

Every year the Vienna Philharmonic gave a benefit concert for the musicians' pension fund. The event was a high point of the music calendar. In February 1900, the orchestra's conductor, Gustav Mahler, decided to greet the new century with a performance of Beethoven's Ninth Symphony. The concert immediately sold out, so a second was added. The audience cheered the first performance for a long time after orchestra and chorus had wrung the last bit of glory from the music. The brickbats came the next day: What had Mahler done to Beethoven? the critics demanded.

In the city where Beethoven lived and the Ninth Symphony had been premiered this was a profound question. Music is for the Viennese what painting is for Florentines: a secular religion. The city was home in the space of half a century to Haydn, Mozart, Beethoven, and Schubert. Brahms had lived there until his death a mere three years before Mahler's performance. The public guarded that heritage. Music in all its forms suffused their lives. Whether they could get tickets to performances or not, they picked apart, guided by the critics, the work of the conductors who led the great orchestras through the repertoire. It was not just their city's repertoire, it was their inheritance on display every time an orchestra played the great composers.

By the middle of the 1890s, Gustav Mahler was the man on the podium to watch. It wasn't only the music. People came to see the performance of Mahler himself. He had revolutionized the role of the modern conductor. Prior to Mahler, most conductors were human metronomes, keeping time for the orchestra and maintaining a low profile during performance. Mahler let the music play through his body. He moved to it, he was elevated and transfigured by it. His arm might fly up as if a passage had electrocuted him. He swayed with sadness or tenderness, his mop of wavy hair bouncing with the energy. In preparing for a performance, he psychologically analyzed the composer's intentions, shaped the performance to reflect those intentions, then acted out the meaning of the work even as his arm kept time.

His interpretations breathed modern life over pieces that were in danger of becoming frozen in time. Audiences and performers were for the most part enthralled by this but there were some critics who saw in the gestures and the intensity something else. Only a Jew would treat classical perfection with such nervousness and emotion and disdain for the heritage it represented. For many critics that was the problem with his performance of Beethoven's Ninth.

The irony was that Mahler had been born Jewish but no longer considered himself a Jew. He considered himself an individual, and an artist, unique in himself.

He was of the generation of Freud and like the psychoanalyst he hailed from the countryside. Mahler was born in 1860 in a small village on the Bohemia-Moravia border in what is today the Czech Republic. There were no rabbis in his background, just peddlers. From an early age he was aware that he was a double outsider. In this rural outpost of the Austro-Hungarian Empire, German speakers were a privileged minority, despised by the local Czech-speaking majority. He was also a Jew, although the family was far from observant.

Mahler's father had risen by hard work from being a driver of a goods wagon to being a private coach driver. Self-educated and strong-willed, Bernard Mahler had convinced a local Jewish soap manufacturer to allow him to marry the businessman's daughter. She didn't want to do it but was bent to her father's will. Coach driving was no profession for a son-in-law, so Bernard was set up in the liquor distilling business.

The marriage was miserable. "They were ill-matched as fire and water," Mahler later told a friend. "He was obstinate, she was gentle." But without this mismatch, "neither I nor my third symphony would exist."

There was plenty of other pain for Mahler to absorb. His mother bore twelve children, five of whom died in childhood. One Jewish ritual he knew was that of the Kaddish, the prayer for the dead. He was the oldest surviving child.

Despite the brutality and tragedy that scarred their marriage, another thing that Mahler's parents had in common with Freud's family was the recognition of extraordinary talent in their son. The Mahlers saw it in Gustav's lost sense of time when sitting at the piano and in the inside-out look with which he stared at the world, taking sound in instead of sights. He was a piano prodigy and started performing in public at the age of ten. At the age of fifteen he was sent off to Vienna to study music at the conservatory.

His talent was prodigious. He dazzled his teachers and fellow students. His name was committed to memory as someone who was likely to be heard from in the future. Mahler was a virtuoso pianist and clearly a man of conducting gifts, someone who could play an orchestra as if it were an instrument. But what he really wanted to do was give life to the musical sounds in his head. In the glory days of Viennese musical history he might have been able to pursue all three talents under the patronage of some member of the royal court. But the days of aristocratic patronage were long past. Music was a commercial enterprise. He had to earn a living and hope that it paid enough for him to have chunks of free time to compose. He set up shop as a piano teacher after finishing his studies and while teaching the children of Vienna's middle classes got to work on original compositions. But he didn't earn nearly enough to pay the rent.

A few years passed. Mahler was approaching his twentieth birthday and was already in danger of falling into a rut. His piano teacher at the conservatory, Julius Epstein, laid out the facts of life for him. Conducting was a way to earn a steady living; it would force him to improve his compositional skills. He then arranged for the twenty-year-old musician to acquire an agent, who in turn set up his first engagement as a conductor. Mahler spent the summer as music director of a theater in a second-class spa town in the Austrian countryside. Summer stock, in other words. It was just the first step in an apprenticeship that took him to many provincial cities in the German world.

• • •

The life found a rhythm: nine months a year of conducting, three months in a lakeside cottage in the Austrian Alps composing.

The conductor's reputation grew and grew. He was the prototype of the conductor as martinet, browbeating his orchestra players into finding musical ability they did not know they had. Sometimes he screamed, and occasionally they screamed back. But they followed him because they understood Mahler was bringing something out of the music that other conductors had not heard.

The conductor's organizational skills were perfect for the opera house. Richard Wagner's operas were the music of the moment in Europe, and Mahler became known as the outstanding conductor of those pieces. Of course, he was not allowed to conduct them at Wagner's personal music shrine at Bayreuth, because he was Jewish. This did not stop Wagner's widow, Cosima, from consulting with Mahler on points of interpretation.

Over a decade and a half of wandering, Mahler became famous. In 1896, when the music directorship of Vienna's Court Opera opened, he had the stature to seek the appointment. Music director of the Court Opera was the most important position in the music capital of the world. It was an imperial appointment. No Jew could attain the position. So Mahler was faced with the same choice that Mendelssohn, Börne, and Heine had been faced with, the same choice Freud would face if he wanted to get a tenured position at the university.

Mahler was baptized a Catholic in 1896. His wife, Alma, would later remember that Mahler did not see it as a renunciation of his Jewishness. The composer was enough of a realist to know that the rest of the world would always be there to remind him he was a Jew if he tried to forget the fact. But he did not convert simply for career advancement. Like many non-Catholics he found the liturgy and drama of Catholic ritual beautiful. It seemed possible to gain a greater understanding of the mystery at the center of human existence in the chanting, smells, and echoing bells that filled a church during Mass. His recent compositions had been reflecting this desire for religious transfiguration.

The year after he converted, Mahler was appointed music director of the Court Opera. The conductor took over a company that had been founded in the burst of modernizing energy that saw the building of the Ringstrasse but in the three decades since had already become musty with tradition. It was out of touch with an audience looking toward a new century. Mahler tore the company's productions apart and started over. New directors and designers were brought in. The public was delighted. So were most of the critics. To neither Mahler's surprise nor anyone else's, the anti-Semitic papers detected endless Jewishness in the way he interpreted the repertoire. The *Deutsche Zeitung,* or *German Gazette,* wrote, "In our view, in a German city, only a German appears qualified to interpret German music . . . This is a condition Mahler is just not able to fulfill."

It didn't matter. Mahler now became one of the most famous conductors in the world.

Two years later the Vienna Philharmonic's conductorship became open. The orchestra players themselves selected their chief. They voted to offer Mahler the job.

The musicians must have known what they were getting, but many were surprised the conductor set about reshaping their work as thoroughly as he had at every stop along his career. Mahler brought a modern sensibility to the Viennese classics. He analyzed the music psychologically to shape his interpretations. He noted to his confidante, Natalie Bauer-Lechner, that in preparing a performance of Beethoven's Third Symphony, the *Eroica,* that there are only "two places where Beethoven's subjective individuated feeling break through, and the whole symphony must be built up as a foundation for them."

Without knowing Freud or his ideas about dreams, the composer was searching in his own work to convey their power. In 1896, Mahler wrote, "When you wake out of this sad dream, and must re-enter life, confused as it is, it happens easily that this always-stirring, never-resting, never-comprehensible pushing that is life becomes horrible to you . . . Then life seems meaningless to you, like a horrible chimera, that you wrench yourself out of with a horrible cry of disgust."

Dream emotion underpins much of his music. The *New Free Press* noted that the music was like an "imaginary play" full of reminiscence. Sometimes the emotion is shameless, the harmonies attend to classical rules of composition and then break them; melodies come from all manner of places, there are echoes of klezmer, Richard Wagner, and Austrian marching bands. It is lush and shamelessly emotional.

By the time Mahler reached the pinnacle as a conductor, he had already composed four symphonies. The Second Symphony was the fullest musical summary of his life's experience. It was a massive piece for orchestra, vocal soloists, and chorus. In 1899 he decided to use the occasion of the annual pension fund benefit concert to give the symphony its Vienna premiere.

The concert audience was about to be overwhelmed. The Second Symphony is close to an hour and a half long. The emotion in the music seemed to be dragged out of the end-of-century moment Vienna was living through. The sound is nostalgic and anxious yet it concludes with a declaration of hope. A singer cries out that through suffering in this life you will find God. To make sure the point that heaven awaits was understood, Mahler stashed a small group of brass instruments backstage so their final call seemed to be coming from heaven. The Second Symphony quickly became known as the "Resurrection" symphony.

Mahler conducted the symphony in April 1899 at the Musikverein. It was one of those occasions where performers and audience inhale and exhale as one. As the final song declaring the certainty of seeing God rolled across the golden ceiling of the magnificent hall, the cheering began. It was so loud and insistent that Mahler repeated the whole movement as an encore. When the piece was over, the ovation continued. It never really stopped. The crowds waited for the composer-conductor after he left the theater. They cheered him in the street.

But there was a part of him that knew it couldn't last. The critics would have to have their say. The anti-Semitic *German Gazette* noted the cheering was from an almost exclusively Jewish audience "whose demonstrations 'defied all rules of decency.'"

But even critics from the music press found fault. The symphony was "sound effects," not music. It was simply too much, too soon for critical ears. It was too modern.

When Mahler stepped to the podium in February 1900 to conduct Beethoven's Ninth Symphony, the memory of all this was on top of him. The criticism he received was not unexpected but it hurt. He was well aware that he was overseeing an unprecedented revival of Viennese music. Yet in the city that he wanted to feel was his home there was a vocal minority reminding him that that could never be. Years later he said to his wife, "I am thrice homeless, as a Bohemian in Austria, as an Austrian among Germans, as a Jew throughout the world, everywhere an intruder, never welcomed."

For the moment, the controversy died away. Mahler was headed for Paris with Vienna's Philharmonic and Choral Societies. The *Times* noted that the planned concerts were the most eagerly anticipated musical events planned for the exposition. "Austria-Hungary is considered the cradle of modern music and each of its numerous nationalities is famous for its musicians." In Paris, Mahler didn't stay at a hotel. He was invited to stay at the Austrian Embassy. Whatever the sneers back in Vienna, on the road he was a quasi-official representative of the Austro-Hungarian Empire.

## iii.
## Schnitzler

Early in 1900, Arthur Schnitzler began circulating the manuscript of his newest play to a select group of friends. Several publishers had refused to print it, so he paid to have several hundred copies made and handed them out to people he trusted. He wasn't thinking of having it produced. It was absolute dynamite and could do to his career what Freud's work had done to his. The play was called *Reigen*, or *La Ronde*, and in its time was startling. It was as modern as a piece of dramatic writing could be.

*La Ronde* contains ten scenes. In the first a prostitute and a soldier meet, talk, have sex, talk some more. In the next scene, the soldier and a parlor maid meet, talk, have sex, talk some more. Then the parlor maid meets someone, and so on up Vienna's social ladder, until in the last scene an aristocrat visits the prostitute from the first scene. Along the way syphilis gets passed around. But the casual round-robin of coupling is just a mechanism for dissecting fin-de-siècle Viennese society. I know you, Schnitzler is saying. I know what is underneath the city's frantic pursuit of pleasure. You are hypocrites. You are diseased.

The author could say these things by birthright. Arthur Schnitzler was a son of the capital.

Schnitzler was born in 1862 in a house on the grand boulevard leading from the city through the Jewish neighborhood, Leopoldstadt, to the Prater, Vienna's great park. He was born with the door open to the two professions easiest for a Jewish boy to enter: medicine and the theater. His father was one of the city's most prominent physicians, a specialist in laryngology. When Vienna's professional singers had sore throats, Dr. Schnitzler was the man they went to see for treatments that would allow them to continue performing. From an early age, Arthur knew performers and became stagestruck.

His upbringing was comfortable and insulated. The Jewish immigrants from the provinces felt the anti-Semitism of the city, but not Schnitzler. He later remembered that he never encountered any expression of hatred as a boy or at school. Even at the University of Vienna it was more comical than dangerous. That changed when he entered medical school.

His Jewishness became a critical part of his identity. Years later he would write that for a Jew, "It was not possible . . . to ignore the fact that he was a Jew; nobody else was doing so, not the Gentiles and even less the Jews. You had the choice of being counted as insensitive, obtrusive and fresh; or of being over sensitive, shy and suffering from feelings of persecution."

But Schnitzler wore many identities. He was a full-time clinician, a commissioned medical officer in the Austrian Army. He was also a playwright, novelist, poet, and critic and acknowledged leader of a group of predominantly Jewish writers who called themselves Young Vienna. Their goal was simple: to lead the Austrian branch of German letters into the modern age. Literature was ready for the change. In subject matter, form, and technique, Schnitzler was leading his younger colleagues from the front.

In 1900, almost forty years old, Schnitzler was at the peak of his intellectual power. *La Ronde* became famous even though it wouldn't have its first theatrical performance for another twenty years. As the year ended he published one more trailblazing work. *Lieutenant Gustl,* a novella, appeared in the Christmas edition of the *New Free Press.* The story is simple. The night before he is to fight a duel, an army officer attends the opera, where he is insulted by a baker. The officer is enraged at the impertinence and ashamed that he doesn't deal with the baker more severely. He spends the rest of the night wandering the city. That's it. What makes the story extraordinary is that Schnitzler unfolds it as a set of free-associated thoughts and images inside Gustl's mind. It is one of the first examples of the technique of "stream-of-consciousness" writing that would dominate twentieth-century literature. Two decades later, as he worked on *Ulysses,* James Joyce had a copy of the novella in his work space.

The story touched a raw nerve in Austria-Hungary. A few months after the story appeared, Schnitzler was relieved of his commission in the imperial army.

## iv.
## Zionism

Theodor Herzl started the new century stretched to the limit. The Zionist movement needed his attention, his personal funds were running out, he needed to earn money while at the same time keeping up the work of organizing. He drove himself to write a new play, a comedy called *I Love You*. The show opened in January 1900. Herzl had high hopes for this play and thought it would run for a long time and he could live on the royalties. No chance. The critics slaughtered it and his relationship to the theater came to an end.

He returned to the *New Free Press* as literary editor. It was a role he played well. He had an eye for young talent and a generosity toward it. A nineteen-year-old named Stefan Zweig managed to get an appointment with him. The young man was a representative of the next generation of Jews, so at home in Vienna that Karl Lueger seemed no more annoying than a clattering wind, not a malign force to be monitored with care. Herzl began publishing Zweig's essays immediately.

Herzl continued to travel on behalf of his movement. He met with the wealthy and with foreign diplomats, trying to find money and a place to buy where he could build the homeland. At the same time he was writing a novel.

In 1902 *Alt-Neuland,* or *Old-Newland,* was published. It is a utopian fantasy, a wish fulfillment on a grand scale of what the Zionist state will look like.

Palestine is a true commonwealth. Everything is publicly owned and shared. All citizens are equal. Women even have the right to vote. The infrastructure is ultramodern, with a mass-transit system whizzing people from one place to the next and a tunnel connecting the Dead Sea to the Mediterranean so the minerals extracted from the former can be easily shipped off to markets.

The commonwealth is multiethnic. Its motto is "Man, thou art my brother." Even the local Arabs embrace their Zionist brothers. "Why shouldn't I love the Jew?" one Arab says. "He made me rich."

The book, like so many other of the man's attempts to proselytize for Zionism, came in for harsh criticism from his fellow Jews. Something began to go out of Herzl. He was essentially working at three full-time jobs, difficult for a healthy man, but foolhardy for someone in his mid-forties who suffered from heart problems.

One spring day in 1904, Stefan Zweig was strolling through a Vienna park and saw Herzl stooped over, walking very slowly. Zweig was shocked by how his editor had aged since their first meeting. He was on the verge of walking away when the older man noticed him; so there was nothing to do but have a chat. Herzl began to talk about the disappointment of his life. "It was my mistake that I started too late," he told the young writer. Starting a political movement took a young man's energy. He didn't have that now.

Within months Herzl died of congestive heart failure. Then something quite extraordinary happened. Thousands of people began to stream into Vienna for the funeral. No one expected it. No one had any idea how deeply the Zionist movement had reached in the world of Ashkenaz. The mourners came from wherever Jews were living, from west to east. The crowd followed the funeral cortege to Vienna's Central Cemetery, a massive necropolis where the whole city buried its dead. There was a separate section for Jews, a ghetto for the departed.

By the time the whole throng had pushed into the cemetery, emotions were uncontainable. Zweig noted there was "crying, sobbing, screaming in a wild explosion of despair. It was almost a riot, a fury . . . The thousands expressing grief came from the depths of millions of souls."

Herzl told Zweig at that meeting in the park, "If you knew how I suffer at the thought of the lost years . . ." He felt he had failed. But he had at least dreamed, and as he wrote in *Alt-Neuland*, "Dream and deed are not as different from one another as many believe. All deeds of men are dreams at first and in the end become dreams again."

Herzl's Zionist dream came to him in broad daylight shortly after watching Alfred Dreyfus publicly humiliated. As the founder was laid to rest, the last act of the Dreyfus Affair was about to play out in Paris.

## CHAPTER TWENTY-TWO

# My Honor Has Been Restored

I N 1899, ON RECEIVING HIS PARDON, ALFRED DREYFUS HAD pledged to continue fighting to clear his name. He was true to his word but he was running out of allies in the battle. Senator Scheurer-Kestner had died on the day the pardon was granted. Emile Zola died in 1902. Bernard Lazare was taken by cancer the following year at the age of thirty-eight.

No matter. Dreyfus had not survived Devil's Island all those years without a certain amount of pure stubbornness. He would wait out the system until he was completely exonerated.

France had changed because of his ordeal. The combined forces of monarchists, Catholic traditionalists, and nationalists held together by the glue of anti-Semitism had seen their influence wane, no matter how loud they shrieked in *La Libre Parole*. From the time of Dreyfus's return from prison they were in retreat. In the early years of the twentieth century, the Socialist Party had been formed and joined with other left-wing parties in a coalition government.

The time was right for a judicial review of the Dreyfus conviction. The socialists were led by Jean Jaurès, a former newspaper editor, who had been a major figure among Dreyfusards. In 1903 he called on the

Chamber of Deputies, the lower house of the National Assembly, to authorize a retrial . . . but in a civilian court. A few months later the army investigated the circumstances of the first trial and acknowledged there were good grounds to allow the case to be heard in a civilian court.

In 1905, the coalition passed a law in the National Assembly officially separating church and state. This was a return to the original intent of the constitutional National Assembly of 1789–91. Napoleon, for political reasons, had made the Catholic Church the official religion of the country. Inevitably the church had become a political anchor of the right and, in the view of the left-wing coalition ruling the country, had played an unseemly role during the Dreyfus Affair. The act was meant to take the church out of France's political life.

On June 15, 1906, the Court of Cassation, France's supreme court, met to hear Alfred Dreyfus's appeal against his conviction. On July 12 their judgment was read out. Dreyfus was innocent of all charges. The following day, both houses of the National Assembly voted to reinstate Dreyfus to the army. He was promoted to the rank of major. The legislation also reinstated Colonel Picquart, the whistle-blower who had saved his life, with the rank of brigadier general.

The following week, for good measure, Dreyfus was made a commander of the Legion of Honor. The minister of war said it was just amends for a soldier who had endured martyrdom without parallel.

That same day at the Ecole Militaire, in a courtyard not far from where they had been torn off, Dreyfus's stripes were restored to him. Years later Dreyfus remembered his feelings as the thundering sounds of military ceremony unfolded around him. "My heart beat as though it would break, the blood rushed to my temples, and my forehead was bathed in perspiration." Once again he had to exercise to the limit the self-control his military training had bred in him.

Then the ceremony was over. He was cheered by his once-again comrades with cries of "Vive Dreyfus!" No, he corrected them. "Vive La République!"

At the time Dreyfus told a reporter from *Le Temps,* "I am now at the end of my suffering. My honor has been restored." Then he was asked his opinion about what the decision meant for his future. "I am an officer and as such am obliged to refuse to express any opinion." In fact, a year later, he resigned from the army and returned to civilian life.

The news of this final act of the affair spread quickly. In Vienna, the *New Free Press* was jubilant: "The sense of justice in the French people must indeed be strong if with so unattractive a symbol as the Jewish officer it could overthrow the combined forces of clericalism, militarism, racial hatred and political reaction."

Its anti-Semitic counterparts sounded grudging and defeated. *Vaterland,* or the *Fatherland,* was typical: "A cry of jubilation rings today through the world wherever the Jewish Liberal tongue resounds."

The jubilation in the French community was as muted as its support for the victim had been throughout the years of the affair. It was deeply satisfied by this demonstration that the fundamental relationship of Emancipation, that of the Jewish community and the nation, was so strong. The *Archives Israélites* noted, "The Dreyfus Affair has concluded for the Israelites and its conclusions would make us love even more, were that possible, our own dear country."

Another weekly journal, *L'Univers Israelites,* was more triumphant. This had been the final battle of Emancipation, and the Jewish community had won. "In giving birth to the Dreyfus Affair," an editorial trumpeted, "anti-Semitism has died."

# EPILOGUE

# Every Jew Has His System

THE END OF THE DREYFUS AFFAIR CONFIRMED FOR THE emancipated Jews of Europe that they were living in an unprecedented moment in their history. Stefan Zweig in his memoirs, written in exile during World War II, recalled those times as a "golden age of security." Shortly after writing of the golden age, Zweig committed suicide. He had outlived his time.

But no one could have known what was coming in 1906. Anti-Semitism as a political force shriveled away around Europe. Social prejudice remained, the foul newspapers still published, but there had always been a way to work around such ignorance. For members of the community, religious or not, proofs of the triumph of Emancipation were everywhere. It truly seemed like a golden age, not just of security but also of achievement. Jews had been in the ghetto for the first renaissance. Now, after a century of Emancipation, Jews were leading Western European culture into a second rebirth.

"Every Jew has his system," wrote Bernard Lazare toward the end of his life. As cancer ate away at him he was working furiously on an analysis of the impact of Emancipation. It was published posthumously as *Job's Dungheap.* "Every Jew has his system, his idea of the world, his economic and social theory, his means of solving the problem of Jewish wretchedness, of anti-Semitism. He is a great builder of doctrines."

Lazare saw that even after a century of integration and assimilation, the need to find a unified theory of everything, whether in day-to-day life or the cosmos, was something that remained at the core of Jewishness. It was a hangover from the days when the Talmud, a theory of everything for a people scattered to the four corners of the earth, was at the center of education and life. Add Lazare's idea to Freud's insight about the way being an outsider frees a thinker from the accepted wisdom of the majority, then mix in Schnitzler's words about never being allowed to forget that you are different, and it is possible to glimpse an explanation for the intellectual explosion that was under way in a minority group that still made up less than 1 percent of Europe's population.

Every Jew has his system. In the anti-Semitic din surrounding the Dreyfus Affair, Emile Durkheim—son, grandson, and great-grandson of rabbis from Lorraine—sought to find a quantitative theory to explain the role of religion in society. From this study he developed a method of work that created the discipline of sociology in France. A century later his intellectual descendant Alain Touraine was able to see clearly what motivated him. "It was in part because anti-Semites rejected them that Jewish bourgeois intellectuals felt sufficiently distant from their society that they were able to analyze it. It is no accident that French sociology and for that matter American sociology were almost totally Jewish."

In Paris at precisely the same time, Durkheim's classmate from the Ecole Normale Supérieure, Henri Bergson, was establishing himself as one of the world's leading philosophers. Bergson was descended from a family of Polish Court Jews. He worked at the intersection of philosophy, biology, psychology, and the arts, synthesizing the thinking of the pre-Socratic philosophers, Charles Darwin, William James, and Freud's mentor Jean-Martin Charcot. The result was a sequence of philosophical essays that depict time, matter, and memory as fluid concepts. Physical perception is relative, Bergson concluded. Memory is not just the recall of past experience, it is the filter through which our physical perceptions of the present must pass. His friend and colleague, American psychologist William James, would later write that Bergson's speculations on the relative nature of time, matter, and memory marked something completely new in the history of philosophy. "Nothing in his work is shopworn or second hand."

In 1905, as the final judicial act in the Dreyfus case unfolded, Albert Einstein, a clerk in the patent office of the Swiss capital, Bern, published a series of four papers on physics. The implication of the third paper, titled "Special Theory of Relativity," was that time and space curved, and that time did not unfold at a constant rate in space. Its measurement was relative to the motion of whoever was observing it. The fourth proposed that there was a link between energy and the mass of an object: $E = mc^2$.

Einstein's work fundamentally upended the Enlightenment worldview of Isaac Newton. His background was similar to Freud's or Mahler's, except for the detail that the family's origins were in rural Germany rather than Austria-Hungary. On both sides of his family he was descended from peddlers who over the Emancipation era had graduated to running businesses.

Religious observance in Einstein's boyhood home was trumped by his parents' desire to assimilate. When his mother was pregnant with him the parents thought they would call their child, if it was a boy, Abraham, after the paternal grandfather, but they changed their minds because it sounded too Jewish. They settled on Albert instead. A pick and mix of Jewish traditions were observed in the household. One of them was that a poor scholar be invited to dine once a week. The recipient of the Einstein family's charity was an impoverished medical student with the remarkable name of Max Talmud. The student, noting Albert's precocious interest in science and mathematics, introduced the ten-year-old to everything from Euclid to the latest scientific publications. It was an unstructured beginning to Einstein's education.

The great thinker's failures at school are well-known. He paid for them when he entered the job market, was unable to secure a university teaching post, and ended up in the patent office. But that didn't stop him from creating his system.

In the same year that Einstein published his world-upending papers, Sigmund Freud published two books. The first was called *Jokes and Their Relation to the Unconscious*. Freud was as interested in applying his theories outside the consulting room as anyone else. He was certain that wit revealed something about unconscious states of mind. Since the wit he knew best was Jewish, he used a lot of Jewish jokes to illustrate his theory. Intentionally or not, the book is an explanation from a third-generation emancipated Jew to the critics who carped that Heine and Börne could never be fully German because of their reliance on irony and jokes. Indeed, the book is filled with examples of Heine's exceptional skill with puns.

The second book, *Three Essays on the Theory of Sexuality,* raised Freud to a new level of infamy. Years later he would look back on the controversy and with self-deprecating Jewish irony tell a friend, "It seems to be my fate to discover the obvious: that children have sexual feelings, which every nursemaid knows . . ."

It was the second essay, on infantile sexuality, that created the controversy. But the ideas it contained would filter out and become part of everyday conversations in the twentieth century: sublimation of sexual urges, castration complex, penis envy. The essay defined a framework for understanding the intense biological force that shapes the way our individual personalities and societies develop.

What Freud, Einstein, Bergson, Durkheim, and other products of Emancipation were doing was nothing less than reshaping Western man's understanding of himself, his society, and his place in the universe. These thinkers were not, as they might have been in the time before Emancipation, being arrested, tortured, and put to death for blasphemy. Nor were they being excommunicated and expelled from their own community. They were being acknowledged for this achievement and their work was being taken very seriously.

## ii.
## Jubilee

### Vienna, June 12, 1908

The imperial capital is celebrating Emperor Franz Joseph's Diamond Jubilee. It has been sixty years since Franz Joseph ascended the Habsburg throne in the aftermath of the failed 1848 revolutions. In the first decades of his reign, the old man had liberalized the laws throughout his empire regarding the Jews and had finally emancipated them. His imperial capital is throbbing with artistic and intellectual life because of those acts. The proof is all around.

The various imperial regimental bands, most of their players Jewish, march past the reviewing stand in a hallucination of color, gold braid, and ostrich feathers. They represent all the outposts of the empire. No one watching, not the emperor and his court nor the wealthy members of Viennese society, can imagine that in six years this whole world will end and all of these regiments and their gaudy uniforms will be ground into mud, blood, and bone on the Western Front, the Eastern Front, and the Italian Front.

No, the Diamond Jubilee is a day of happiness. Writing about the parade, the correspondent of the *New Free Press* was caught up in the patriotic fervor: "These weren't the various nationalities; this was Austria. The colorful melting pot of people in their cultural forms, held together by a unifying bond." That was the essence of the Jewish love of Vienna, summed up in a phrase: "the melting pot."

On this day, people visit the exhibition of contemporary art being held to mark the Diamond Jubilee in a new art gallery, at the foot of the Imperial Palace grounds. The show, organized by Gustav Klimt, is a spectacular demonstration of why Vienna is a rival to Paris in the visual arts and design. Vienna's bourgeois Jewish life is the unintentional theme of the exhibition. It is in Jewish homes that the most beautiful modern designs are found. Out of contacts made in Jewish salons come the collectors to buy the artists' work and commission them to paint portraits. The highlight of the exhibit is several rooms of paintings by Klimt, including portraits of some of Vienna's best-known Jewish art patrons, such as Adele Bloch-Bauer.

Franz Joseph's jubilee year began with the *Neue Rundschau,* or *New Review,* serializing Arthur Schnitzler's latest work, a novella called *The Road into the Open.*

The novella is very different from *La Ronde* or *Lieutenant Gustl.* There are no stylistic or structural experiments in his story. It is a straight dissection of society. He opens up his Vienna as neatly as an anatomy instructor opens a cadaver.

The hero of the novella is Georg von Wergenthin, Christian aristocrat and composer. The milieu in which he lives most of his life is Vienna's cultured Jewish bourgeoisie. There is not much plot. The story is about his relationships with his Jewish friends, and the changes they are going through at this uncertain time: the beginning of a new century.

Schnitzler's work is up to the minute. Zionism is as much a part of these wealthy young people's world as the concert hall or gossip about bad behavior. George questions why. "What does 'homeland' Palestine mean to you? A geographic concept. What does the Faith of your Fathers mean to you? A collection of customs that you have long ceased to practice, most of which you find as ridiculous and tasteless as I do."

What is trailblazing about this work is that a Jew is writing about contemporary Jewish life in a realistic manner. Schnitzler's story emancipates Jews in fiction, releasing them from a tradition where they were merely objects of satire and anti-Semitic caricature. He makes the Jewish presence in society worthy of exploration in serious literature.

• • •

By the spring of 1908, the infamy surrounding Sigmund Freud was morphing into international renown. The theories that less than a decade earlier had older colleagues shaking their heads and cutting off contact with him made sense to a younger generation of doctors. In Europe and America a movement was forming around Freud's psychoanalytic theories. At the end of April, these young doctors got together with the master in Salzburg for what the invitation called a "Meeting for Freudian Psychologists."

Freud was particularly gratified that the meeting's main organizers, Carl Gustav Jung and Ernest Jones, were not Jewish. He was very sensitive to the charge that his theories and practice were somehow just for Jews.

Freud was particularly flattered by Jung's endorsement. He saw in the charismatic Jung, a Zurich-based doctor, someone who could represent the movement to the wider world. One outcome of the Salzburg get-together was the decision to start a journal devoted to psychoanalysis. Jung was appointed editor and quickly rubbed many of the long-standing Freudian followers the wrong way. He particularly aggravated one of Freud's earliest and most devoted acolytes, Karl Abraham. Jung was arrogant and self-serving, in Abraham's eyes. The young psychoanalyst detected more than a hint of anti-Semitism in Jung's attitude to the Vienna followers of Freud and wrote to his mentor to tell him.

Freud wrote back, acknowledging that there might be some truth to Abraham's feelings about Jung but urging his younger colleague to try to work things out with the Swiss. "My opinion is that we Jews, if we want to cooperate with other people, have to develop a little masochism and be prepared to endure a certain amount of injustice. There is no other way of working together."

Gustav Mahler missed out on the Diamond Jubilee celebrations. He had had enough of Vienna and left the previous year. There were two reasons. His four-year-old daughter died of diphtheria and the composer was diagnosed with a serious heart condition. He could no longer maintain his punishing conducting schedule.

But he was also just tired and angry with the endless backbiting of critics and the relentless attacks of the anti-Semites. He would always be a Jew first in Vienna, despite his baptism, and because of his heritage he would certainly never be thought of as a musician of the first rank. He was angry about the anti-Semitism not just for himself but for all the other young men of Jewish origin, men of great musical talent whose careers were being stalled by prejudice even when they converted. When an invitation came to conduct a season of Mozart and Wagner at New York's Metropolitan Opera he leapt at the chance, and so in 1908 he was earning ovations conducting in New York.

Shortly before Mahler left Vienna, he nearly got into a fistfight at the premiere of his protégé Arnold Schoenberg's first string quartet. Schoenberg, like Schnitzler, was a son of Leopoldstadt and like Mahler he had converted, easing his passage to Christianity by his interest in church music. Mahler had opened a door to a new world of sound; Schoenberg walked through it and changed everything.

As 1908 drew to a close, Schoenberg decided to try the public's patience again with the premiere of his second string quartet, a musical study of raw anxiety. To find a sound that expressed this emotion Schoenberg had to break the rules of musical composition.

Schoenberg was not trying to express beauty in this piece. His wife had left him and their children for a painter, Richard Gerstl. After a short while she had returned to the composer. Gerstl then committed suicide. First he tried to drive a knife through his heart, but failed. So then, with the knife sticking out of his chest, he had hung himself. The quartet was composed during this time. No traditional sound could begin to capture what Schoenberg was feeling.

In the quartet he did not use a system of tonality, but rather one of atonality. In doing so he disoriented his audience, inducing in them a state of apprehension. They had no idea what this music was and they did not like the confusion. When a soprano came out and sang along with the quartet in the final two movements they stopped being polite. Hissing grew to booing and the music disappeared into the angry protestations of the audience.

Something happened for Schoenberg at that concert. The brutally emotional response of the audience to his work confirmed for him that he was on the right path in his composition. Atonality was the way to musically explore the complicated emotions of the new century. Schoenberg built a whole system around his discovery and laid the foundation for the twentieth century's classical music.

Not everyone in Vienna in 1908 was thrilled by this flowering of culture. In his journeys around the city Schnitzler absorbed the resentments of people who did not understand the work, who thought it was too Jewish. In *The Road into the Open* the author has one of his Jewish characters writing a play about a German art student who poisons himself with mushrooms from despair over the Emancipation of the Jews.

In 1908 a young German art student was living in Vienna preparing to try for a second time to pass the entrance exam for the Academy of Fine Art. He wandered the city from cultural landmark to cultural landmark. He sat in the galleries with his sketchbook and made copies of classical paintings. That autumn the young man once again was rejected by the academy. It hurt. What was it these Viennese liked? Clearly it was these degenerate modern works by Jews and Jew lovers, thought the young man, Adolf Hitler.

That same year, in addition to pursuing culture, Hitler attended rallies held by Karl Lueger. He appreciated the performing skill of Vienna's mayor. He noted that no matter how big the crowd was it fell completely silent when the man was talking. To lead a people required a great actor's skill.

When he eventually came to power, in part because of his considerable performing skills, Hitler waged a campaign against the degenerate art he had first seen and heard in Vienna in 1908.

## iii.
## Proust and Kafka

Every Jew has his system.

In 1905, Marcel Proust's mother died. Slowly the author began to withdraw from the world. From being one of the most social creatures in Paris he became a virtual recluse. The writer knew he had taken part in extraordinary events and wanted to write the whole story of his society in the time of the Dreyfus Affair. His inheritance allowed him to take his time and indulge his psychological quirks. He worked at night and slept by day, so Proust had his bedroom lined with cork to keep sound out. He spent several years trying to find a way to tell his story.

In 1909 he began again, and the multivolume book would not be completed until 1922. *Remembrance of Things Past,* or *In Search of Lost Time,* runs to six volumes. It is a synthesis not just of the events Proust lived through but of the intellectual theories of the day. Time and memory, as Bergson and Freud thought about them, inform the writing.

Shortly after the book begins the narrator describes a moment on a wintry day when, chilled to the bone, his mother brings him a cup of tea with a little cake called a madeleine on the side. He absentmindedly dips the cake in the tea. When he takes a sip of the drink with a spoon, the liquid sweetened by crumbs of the cake, some undefined joy overwhelms him. What is it? A memory of something buried so deep he cannot recall it, yet filling this moment with a tremendous emotion. The narrator puzzles through what it means and then he remembers. His aunt used to give him this cake with his tea when he visited her at her country home. The novel returns in time to that place. It is a small moment, spun out over several pages in delicate prose. This tiny incident is invested with the weight of the storyteller's entire life.

It is a moment of psychoanalytic insight. But where Freud worked in night dreams, Proust worked with daytime reverie. The author's speculation on the interplay of memory and perception echo Bergson, who had pointed out that physical perception is not pure, it is always filtered through memory.

When the first volume was published in 1913, one French critic spotted in his work a "rabbinical style" and objected to the "incessant flow of cultural reminiscences that call to mind a certain quasi-charlatanical Jewish erudition." That critic was in the minority. Proust showed the way for novelists to use the most minute details of daily life as entry points into the inner workings of their characters and became one of the pillars of modern literature.

At the same time Marcel Proust was isolating himself from the rest of Paris, Franz Kafka in Prague had dropped out of sight from the world of letters. In 1908, *Hyperion,* an upmarket literary magazine in Germany, had published eight of his pieces. They weren't stories so much as prose poems, verbal images, impressions. It was quite a debut for a twenty-five-year-old fresh out of law school. It should have encouraged him to keep writing, but then there was nothing.

The reason for Kafka's disappearance is simple. He carried a terrible burden in his life. He was hypersensitive and physically weak and lived in mortal fear of his physically domineering father. Hermann Kafka had traveled the same road as Freud's and Mahler's fathers without arriving at the same place of love and indulgence for a supremely gifted son. He was cruel and a bully, and this may have had something to do with the fact that he was a more successful businessman than the other two.

He was hard on his family. When Kafka finished law school, Hermann made clear to him that was the end of parental support. He would have to earn his own keep. The would-be writer decided he would not get involved in the literary halfway house of journalism. So Kafka took a series of jobs in insurance companies, expecting to write serious fiction in his spare time. But he underestimated how tiring the office work would be and so was writing nothing.

Kafka drifted, pursued love affairs, suffered when they ended, and thought about his father obsessively. If he had been in a more dynamic city—Vienna, Paris, or Berlin, places where you can move a few blocks away and leave your whole life behind—Kafka might not have been so isolated. There would have been more young people like himself. But he lived in a provincial capital of a dying empire. Not only that, he was a double-minority, German-speaking Jew in a Czech land. His isolation grew. Well into his twenties he still resided at his father's house and had to endure Hermann's mockery and anger about dawdling with writing—a stupid idea, work for a weakling—when he should have been married with a family of his own.

The young man found comfort in reading Freud's theories about the role of fathers in young children's lives. But he was no longer a child. He was in a no-man's-land of his own making. By late 1911 he was managing—badly—a factory recently opened by his father. At the age of twenty-nine he found himself still being berated like a little boy by Hermann Kafka. Yet he was not strong enough to break with him and go to a room and write. He trailed Hermann about the city like a dutiful Jewish son, attending synagogue with his father on Yom Kippur, noting the "muffled stock-exchange" murmuring of the prayers. Franz Kafka was at breaking point; suicidal thoughts filled him.

Then one day a Yiddish theater troupe took up residence in Prague. Friends took him along to a performance and he began to hang out with the actors. They were in town for many months trying to earn enough money to move on. Kafka spent most of his free time with them. The contact with these representatives of the ghetto world opened something up in the young writer. He had had a very modest contact with Judaism: a Bar Mitzvah and occasional references to the old way from his father. But these actors offered a key to an understanding of his identity.

He began to study Judaism and Jewish history and to take an interest in Zionism. His father was dismissive. His son couldn't possibly know the real Jewish life, the life Hermann grew up with in the countryside. But his father couldn't knock him off course now. Kafka was certain that in understanding the Jewish part of himself better he might be able to get past the huge psychological roadblock of his father. Understanding what it meant to be of two worlds—German and Jew—was the key.

In a letter to his friend Max Brod, he noted the problem of being a Jew whose working language was German. "Most Jews who began writing in German wanted to get away from Judaism . . . but their hind legs were still stuck to the Jewishness of their fathers, and with their front legs they could find no new ground. Their despair over this was their inspiration."

From despair came inspiration. One night in September 1912, Kafka began writing a story. He wrote through the night and by morning it was finished. It was like giving birth, he wrote in his diary, and noted, "Thoughts of Freud, of course."

The story was called "The Judgment." It was a little slice of autobiography about a young man with an elderly abusive father. The young man is telling his father about his intentions to get married, and an argument begins. Soon it is clear that the argument is just slightly unhinged from reality. This is a nightmare. It concludes with the father screaming, "I sentence you to death by drowning." The young man goes to a bridge by the river, climbs over the railings, and quietly throws himself in.

More than a story was born on the night "The Judgment" was written. Kafka became a writer. The problem of his father was never resolved, and his hypersensitive insecurity would never leave him, but now he could work. All artists are unique and the struggle to reach this point was singular to Kafka. But it shared a crucial element with the struggle of Freud, Schnitzler, and Mahler: the Jewish identity question. A century had gone by since the ghetto days ended and it was still being asked: Who am I now? It wasn't just members of the community asking, Who am I in this world? The nineteenth century had brought dramatic change to all levels of society, and many people were confused about where they belonged. The genius of Kafka, his system, was to take the confusion and uncertainty and create a world of nightmare anxiety that was not specifically Jewish. Anyone who took the time to read his stories, regardless of their background, could understand what he was saying.

In Kafka's world, ordinary men wake up after a bad night's sleep having turned into bugs. They are condemned to death for crimes they had no idea they committed.

World War I started and for a moment the second renaissance was suspended. The community did its patriotic duty for its respective countries. Alfred Dreyfus came out of retirement, was given the rank of lieutenant colonel, and spent the entire war at the front. He was joined there by his son, Pierre, who would be awarded the Croix de Guerre for his heroism. Freud was past military age but his son Martin carried the family name to the trenches.

Kafka responded to the guns of August 1914 by writing the first chapter of his great novel, *The Trial*. The book begins, "Someone must have maligned Joseph K., for without having done anything wrong, he was arrested one morning."

Did he even understand that with this one sentence he prophesied life as it was to be for so many in the century to come?

## iv.
## Wittgenstein

Despite the war it seemed as if something that started with Baruch Spinoza had followed the curving edge of space-time and landed in the middle of this second renaissance.

Every Jew has his system. During World War I an Austrian patriot, a philosopher by training, found himself languishing in a prisoner-of-war camp in Italy. Ludwig Wittgenstein had taken a manuscript of a book he was writing to the front and by chance he had it on him when he was captured. So he continued to work at ideas he had first discussed before the conflict began, while studying in England. Wittgenstein was the son of Austria's wealthiest industrialist. The father had made the decision before Ludwig was born to convert from Judaism to further his business interests. The philosopher grew up in Vienna, immersed in the world of culture described by Schnitzler and painted by Klimt. The artist had even painted a portrait of Wittgenstein's sister.

Wittgenstein's philosophical work was an extended investigation into the identity question through language. How can I be certain of what another person means by a word or a phrase? It was a reasonable question to ponder in a world where a man could call himself a Christian and be rebuked by others for being a Jew even if his father and grandfather had led the family to conversion. It was a fertile area to explore in a society where feelings of anxiety lay buried underneath elaborate rituals of gaiety.

Unlike Freud, Wittgenstein was not interested in finding the true meaning of words through interpretation. He wanted to understand them via rules of logic. What could not be known in this way could not be commented on. Wittgenstein wrote in a style that imitated Spinoza's geometrical method. This allowed him to express abstract ideas about language with an almost mathematical certainty.

With the help of the Red Cross he sent the manuscript from his prison to friends in England, the philosophers Bertrand Russell and George Moore. Moore suggested he title the book after Spinoza. So Wittgenstein called his work *Tractatus Logico-Philosophicus*. Like Spinoza's *Tractatus*, it would be the only book Wittgenstein published during his lifetime. Like Spinoza, Wittgenstein would influence the philosophy of his time enormously, even after his death. Throughout the English-speaking world in particular, Wittgenstein's thought dominated twentieth-century philosophy.

Spinoza hovers over and around the story of Emancipation. One day, in his American exile, Albert Einstein received a telegram from an Orthodox rabbi asking whether he believed in God. Einstein replied, "I believe in Spinoza's God, who reveals himself in the lawful harmony of all that exists, but not in a God who concerns himself with the fate of the doings of mankind."

Jewish Emancipation was a story whose prologue began in Spinoza's time, the Enlightenment, and burst into life during the French Revolution. Enlightenment and the ideals of 1789 drove the community forward against all resistance. Even after the Armistice ended World War I and the era of Emancipation was consigned to history, these ideals remained rooted in the community and motivated its thinkers and artists to great achievement. In the sciences, members of the community were receiving the ultimate measure of intellectual achievement, the Nobel Prize, in large numbers. Across the range of culture, the next generation was beginning to make a mark, particularly in the new art form, the cinema. It seemed as if the Jewish renaissance would go on and on.

But the Europe that had shaped Jewish life after the ghetto no longer existed on the map. The economy of the old nations that formed the world of Ashkenaz was shattered. In the dislocated social landscape, questions about nationhood raised by the French Revolution and Napoleon that many thought had been definitively answered were being violently asked again. This was particularly true in Germany. In 1923, the former art student and ardent admirer of Karl Lueger, Adolf Hitler, attempted to start a revolution, failed utterly, and was thrown in jail. So unstable was German society that a decade later he was the chancellor of Germany.

On February 27, 1933, Germany's Parliament building, the Reichstag, was gutted in an arson attack. Within days, Hitler was given emergency powers. In less than a month, he had consolidated these powers to become Germany's dictator. On the first of April, Joseph Goebbels, in a propaganda broadcast to the German people, explained that Nazi rule meant "the year 1789 is being expunged from history."

No one knew then that Hitler would also try to expunge from history the group in European society whose existence had been changed most by the French Revolution, the Jews. Before they revealed themselves to be mass murderers, the Nazis showed themselves to be obsessive bureaucrats. Step by step, they rolled back the legal framework of Emancipation and reimposed old rules on the community.

By the end of April 1933, Jews in Germany were once again banned from working in the civil service. Eighteen months later came the Nuremberg laws forbidding intermarriage while reclassifying the grandchildren of Christian converts as Jews and taking away their German citizenship. Year by year, new restrictions were imposed. Time began to curve back on itself as the Nazi government steadily pushed the community back into a segregated existence. It was a mere sixty-five years since Bismarck's Reich had granted full civil rights to the community, a grandfather's age. So there were people in the community who remembered it had been this way before and you could work around the restrictions. The same people knew that conversion had never fooled anyone. The most grotesque political anti-Semitism had always been countered by right-thinking Germans. This would happen again, surely. The Nazi era was a difficult moment but it would pass.

By now the early fighters for Emancipation had been forgotten. If the men had been remembered, their words might have moved people to act sooner in their own defense. What had Moses Hess written? "The race war must first be fought out and definitely settled before social and humane ideas become part and parcel of the German people." Gabriel Riesser said, "Hatred will find its man, just like the Angel of Death."

The community in the German-speaking lands had relied too heavily on its status under the law for security. No one except perhaps a few historians of the French Revolution would have remembered the words of Jérôme Pétion de Villeneuve in the debate on the religion clause of the Declaration of the Rights of Man and the Citizen back in 1789. "Rights are not laws. Rights are for all time and come before laws." A sad corollary of that point is that blind hatred of rights, especially human rights, also is a force outside of law.

But there was another aspect of Emancipation, one that involved laws of a different kind, the laws of social science. The process by which immigrant minorities integrate and assimilate, their struggles for acceptance and the cultural by-products of those struggles are the same everywhere. Even as the Nazis were crushing Jewish life in Europe, the social process of Emancipation was under way in America for millions of immigrants fresh from the shtetls of Russia, Poland, and the geographical extremes of the Austro-Hungarian Empire. Their lives in the United States re-created the pattern in Europe. An example: A young Orthodox Jewish woman from Galicia arrives in New York, drops out of school at fourteen, and goes to work in a sweatshop. Her son becomes a doctor. His son becomes a writer. Along the way, religious observance diminishes in importance, the identity of Jew does not. That happens to be my family's story, but in its broad outlines it is like millions of others.

Today, in the United States and across Europe, the process continues for different ethnic and religious groups. In our time, immigrants face struggles that are very similar to those faced by the people coming out of the ghetto. Always the same push for acceptance, the resistance from the majority, the surrender of tradition in the name of assimilation, the question between generations: "Is it worth it?" and the resulting identity question: "Who am I?"

The story of Jewish Emancipation offers no simple answers to those questions, but it provides an example. The first generation of emancipated Jews understood this: the great changes they were living through, the challenges to their identities as individuals and members of a group, would soon be experienced by all communities in Europe. Their mission was to set an example for those who would come after.

Sometime in the 1820s, in Lithuania, a man named Mordechai Ginzburg, under the pseudonym Aviezer, wrote the story of his life coming out of the ghetto. "Come here," he said to his readers. "Let me be a parable to you." At the same time, at the other end of Europe, Joseph Salvador, a French Jew already wrestling with the identity crisis—his father was Jewish, his mother was not—wrote, "Israel was not created and does not live for itself alone." Salvador added that his community had a task—"showing the way to the redemption of humanity as a whole."

# ACKNOWLEDGMENTS

I AM A JOURNALIST—A SUMMARIZER AND SIMPLIFIER BY TRADE. I could not have written this book without the help of scholars who have spent decades mining specific seams of the Emancipation story and who answered my e-mails out of the blue asking questions and requesting clarification on various points. In America, thanks go to Paula Hyman, John Jeep, Carol Krinsky, Frances Malino, Steven Nadler, George Peters, Jeffrey Sammons, Alyssa Sepinwall, Steven Smith, Fritz Stern, Heidi Thomann Tewarson, and Angelika Zilberman. In France, the late Richard Ayoun and Rita Herman-Belot answered my queries written in tortured French.

I was privileged in Britain to have tutorials when I started this project from Eric Hobsbawm and Peter Pulzer. Christian Wiese also took several hours out of a day to discuss *Wissenschaft des Judentums*. Three retired German academics who almost single-handedly excavated the history of the Emancipation era out of the postwar ruins of their country were unfailingly helpful: Reinhard Rürup, Monika Richarz, and especially Helga Krohn. In Vienna, William Godsey answered questions about the Congress of Vienna, and Christian Glanz gave me a private lesson on the Jewish impact on the city's music scene in the late nineteenth and early twentieth centuries.

No book that touches on Jewish German life is possible without

Acknowledgments

the Leo Baeck Institute. I am grateful to librarians Gabriele Raha-
man in London and Frank Mecklenburg in New York. Thanks also
to Aubrey Pomerance at the Leo Baeck Institute Archive at the Jewish
Museum in Berlin and Gerhard Milchram at the Jewish Museum in
Vienna. No book on Jewish French life is possible without the Alliance Israélite Universelle and its librarian, Jean-Claude Kuperminc.
The overworked staff of the British Library also deserve my gratitude.

My journalist colleagues Francis Wheen and Thomas Kielinger answered questions and offered encouragement. Susie Hondl translated
the words of Gabriel Riesser and others. Thanks also to the family of
Guillaume Parmentier and Adeline Gouarné.

At Simon & Schuster, Alice Mayhew understood from the beginning what this book was supposed to be and pushed me at the finish line
to make it better. Thanks to her and her team: Karen Thompson, Roger
Labrie, Gypsy da Silva, Tom Pitoniak, Victoria Meyer, and Alexis Welby.

Kathleen Anderson of Anderson Literary Management guided this
project through the shoals of a changing business. Thanks also to Anderson Literary Management.

My wife, Christin Cockerton, reads my pages before anyone else
and brings to the task a sharp eye and a good feel for what is necessary
and what is useless verbal display. My love and my thanks to her are
boundless.

Finally, I started researching this book the modern way: typing
combinations of words into Google and seeing what came up. Frequently, what came up were grossly anti-Semitic Web sites. But some
had their uses. These were the sites that posted large sections of Marx,
Freud, Kafka, and others' writings on what it meant to be Jewish. It
would seem that the haters saw in these works proof of a Jewish con-
spiracy to rule the world. I found in these writings proof that the work
of even the most assimilated and prominent members of the community were demonstrably shaped by the postghetto experience. Thus
these sites proved very useful, and so I suppose I should acknowledge
the anti-Semites who posted this work online. The reader will understand if I don't thank them or their Web sites by name.

# NOTES

## Preface

PAGE

xvi *"Jewish men of genius"*: Frederic V. Grunfeld, *Prophets Without Honour: A Background to Freud, Kafka, Einstein and Their World* (London: Hutchinson, London, 1979), 27.

xvi *"After many centuries"*: Eric Hobsbawm, "Benefits of Diaspora," *London Review of Books,* October 20, 2005.

xvi *"the internal crisis"*: Salo Baron, *Great Ages and Ideas of the Jewish People,* edited by Leo Schwarz (New York: Random House, 1956), 336.


## PART 1: EMANCIPATION

### Chapter One: Everything in the Universe Is Changing

PAGE

6 *"It is an astonishing spectacle"*: *Mercure de France,* February 11, 1786.

8 *"One would say to the descendants"*: Frances Malino, *A Jew in the French Revolution* (Oxford: Blackwell, 1996), 10.

8 *"There is a sweet, easy and infallible means"*: Ibid., 13.

10 *Something the author called "intellectus"*: A. G. Wernham, *Spinoza: The Political Works* (Oxford: Clarendon, 1958), 71, 99, 137.

14 *"The opponents of freedom exult"*: T. E. Jessop, *Spinoza on Freedom of Thought* (Montreal: Mario Casalini, 1962), 87.

15 *"produced by the renegade Jew"*: Lewis Samuel Feuer, *Spinoza and the Rise of Liberalism* (Boston: Beacon, 1958), 118.

16 *"The purpose of the state"*: Steven Smith, *Spinoza, Liberalism and the Question of Jewish Identity* (New Haven: Yale University Press, 1997), 160.

16 *"They do not force me"*: Feuer, *Spinoza and the Rise of Liberalism,* 22.

17 *"This was perhaps the first founder"*: Jacques Basnage, *History of the Jews from Jesus Christ to the Present Time,* translated by Thomas Taylor (London, 1708), 742.

19 *"The Jewish religion is an old trunk"*: Ronald Schechter, *Obstinate Hebrews: Representations of Jews in France, 1715–1815* (Berkeley: University of California Press, 2003), 40.

20 *"They are like the pegs and nails"*: Diderot and d'Alembert, *Encyclopédie, tome 9* (Geneva: Chez Cramer L'aîné, 1752), 25.

21 *"When I see Christians"*: Norman Torrey, *Voltaire's English Notebook* (Chicago: Modern Philology, 1929), 309.

21 *"You will only find in the Jews"*: Voltaire, *A Philosophical Dictionary* (London: W. Dugdale, 1843), 94.


### Chapter Two: Hold Fast to the Religion of Your Fathers

PAGE

24 *six oxen, seven pigs, and one Jew:* Amos Elon, *The Pity of It All* (London: Allen Lane, 2002), 2.

26 *"How can a man in whom a sense"*: Alexander Altmann, *Moses Mendelssohn* (London: Vallentine Mitchell, 1998), 41.

26 *"On Thursday the academy held"*: Ibid., 116.

26 *"Only few people have the good fortune"*: Immanuel Kant, *Philosophical Correspondence, 1759–1799,* translated by Arnulf Zweig (Chicago: University of Chicago Press, 1986), 106.

28 *"I dare to ask you"*: Altmann, *Moses Mendelssohn,* 209.

30 *"I must confess"*: Frank Talmage, *Disputation and Dialogue* (New York: KTAV, 1975), 269.

32 *"Adapt yourselves to the morals"*: Moses Mendelssohn, *Jerusalem,* translated by Alan Arkush (Boston: University Press of New England for Brandeis University, 1983), 133.

32 *The community was strewn:* Zosa Szajkowski, *Jews and the French Revolutions of 1789, 1830 and 1848* (New York: KTAV, 1970), 45.

36 *"The great and noble business"*: Peter Pulzer, *Jews and the German State* (Oxford: Blackwell, 1992), 31.

36 *"the Jew is a man more than a Jew"*: Paul Mendes-Flohr and Jehuda Reinharz, *The Jew in the Modern World* (Oxford: Oxford University Press, 1995), 30.


### Chapter Three: The Means to Render the Jews More Useful and Happy?

PAGE

38 *That was a sum of 20,000:* David Feuerwerker, *L'émancipation des Juifs en France* (Paris: Editions Albin Michel, 1976), 56.

39 *"They are soldiers, sailors and workers"*: Ibid., 71.

39 *"If one renders them more useful, one ruins artisans"*: Ibid., 72.

40 *"They are a troop of vile"*: Ibid., 84.

41 *"The means to make the Jews"*: Zalkind Hourwitz, *Apologie des Juifs* (Paris: Chez Gattey, Libraire, au Palais Royal, 1789), 2.

42 *"My crimes are yours"*: Feuerwerker, *L'émancipation des Juifs en France,* 74.

44 *"Since the time of Vespasian"*: Abbé Grégoire, *Essai sur la Régénération Physique, Morale et Politique des Juifs* (Metz: L'Imprimerie de Claude LaMort, 1789), 1.

44 *"Jewesses are subject to nymphomania"*: Alyssa Sepinwall, *The Abbé Grégoire and the French Revolution* (Berkeley: University of California Press, 2005), 72.

46 *"The Jews are members"*: Abbé Grégoire, *Essai sur la Régénération,* 194.

48 *"The majority of the essays"*: Feuerwerker, *L'émancipation des Juifs en France,* 119.

48 *"Monsieur de Malesherbes, you"*: Frances Malino, *Enlightenment, Reawakening and Revolution 1660–1815,* edited by Stewart J. Brown and Timothy Tackett (Cambridge, U.K.: Cambridge University Press, 2006), 219.

## Chapter Four: No One Shall Be Troubled for His Religion

PAGE

56 *"as a minister of a religion"*: David Feuerwerker, *L'émancipation des Juifs en France* (Paris: Editions Albin Michel, 1976), 292.

56 *"Rights are not laws"*: *Le Moniteur,* August 4, 1789.

57 *"Religion," the bishop told the Assembly*: *Le Moniteur,* August 22, 1789.

58 *The next day the discussion*: *Le Moniteur,* August 23–26, 1789.

## Chapter Five: The Name of "Active Citizen"

PAGE

63 *"A Portuguese Jew is English"*: Paula Hyman, *The Jews of Modern France* (Berkeley: University of California Press, 1998), 5.

64 *Their "Address to the National Assembly"*: "Adresses, Mémoires et Pétitions des Juifs," *La Révolution Française et L'émancipation des Juifs,* vol. 5 (Paris: EDHIS, 1968), 49.

65 *Five days later the Jews*: Ibid., 61.

68 *On September 28, Count Stanislas*: *Le Moniteur,* September 28, 1789.

69 *"In the name of"*: "Adresses, Mémoires et Pétitions des Juifs," 93.

72 *"Let me ask you to be clear"*: *Le Moniteur,* December 21, 23, 1789. All subsequent quotes and descriptions of this debate are from this source.

80 *On January 28*: *Le Moniteur,* January 29, 1790. All subsequent quotes and descriptions of this debate are from this source.

82 *The same day, Berr*: "Adresses, Mémoires et Pétitions des Juifs," 163.

83 *In the* Chronique: Frances Malino, *A Jew in the French Revolution* (Oxford: Blackwell, 1996), 86.

85 *Hourwitz carried on his campaign*: Ibid., 92.

87 *On September 27, with no preamble*: *Le Moniteur,* September 27–28, 1791.

88 *"Letter of a Citizen"*: "Lettres, Mémoires et Publications Diverses," *La Révolution Française et L'émancipation des Juifs,* vol. 8 (Paris: EDHIS, 1968), 201.

## Chapter Six: I Shall Maintain Your Freedom

PAGE

92 *The general wrote to his wife:* Napoleon I, *The Corsican: A Diary of Napoleon's Life in His Own Words,* http://napoleonic-literature.com/Book_22/1797.htm.

93 *In nearby Padua, he forced:* Paul Mendes-Flohr and Jehuda Reinharz, *The Jew in the Modern World* (Oxford: Oxford University Press, 1995), 129.

93 *By now he was known:* Simon Schwarzfuchs, *Napoleon, the Jews and the Sanhedrin* (London: Routledge & Kegan Paul, 1979), 23.

97 *The twelve questions the seventy-one:* Philippe Landau, *Bicentenaire du Grand Sanhedrin* (Paris: Consistoire de Paris, Ile de France, 2007).

101 *"I went and stood outside the front door":* Heinrich Heine, *The Harz Journey and Selected Prose,* translated by Ritchie Robertson (London: Penguin, 2006), 108, 113.

101 *Metternich tried to allay:* Schwarzfuchs, *Napoleon, the Jews and the Sanhedrin,* 166.

# PART 2: REFORMATION

## Chapter Seven: It Is Hateful to Be a Jewess

PAGE

107 *Later Rahel Varnhagen wrote:* Heidi Thomann Tewarson, *Rahel Levin Varnhagen: The Life and Work of a German Jewish Intellectual* (Lincoln: University of Nebraska Press, 1998), 142.

108 *At the beginning of the nineteenth:* Monika Richarz, *Jewish Life in Germany: Memoirs from Three Centuries* (Bloomington: Indiana University Press, 1991), 3.

111 *There were nine regular salons:* Deborah Hertz, "Salonières and Literary Women," *New German Critique* (Spring 1978), 103.

113 *"Just as I was born":* Tewarson, *Rahel Levin Varnhagen,* 61.

115 *She wrote to a friend, Rebecca Friedländer:* Ibid., 102.

115 *"I am as unique":* Ibid., 134.

115 *Wilhelm von Humboldt:* Ibid., 152.

115 *Rahel saw herself in:* Hannah Arendt, *Rahel Varnhagen: The Life of a Jewess* (Baltimore: Johns Hopkins University Press, 1997), 89.

116 *A few days before the ceremony:* Tewarson, *Rahel Levin Varnhagen,* 140.

118 *A leading rabbi of the early:* Paul Mendes-Flohr and Jehuda Reinharz, *The Jew in the Modern World* (Oxford: Oxford University Press, 1995), 172.

## Chapter Eight: Israel Must Be Exemplary for All Peoples

PAGE

120 *The highest level of Talmudic:* Solomon Maimon and J. Clark Murray, *Solomon Maimon: An Autobiography* (Boston: Cupples & Hurd, 1888; reprinted Whitefish, Mont.: Kessinger, 2006), 47.

121 *Maimon thought his fellow rabbis:* Ibid., 45.

121 *Maimon re-created Mendelssohn's arrival:* Ibid., 194.

123 *The magazine was being published:* Paul Mendes-Flohr and Jehuda Reinharz, *The Jew in the Modern World* (Oxford: Oxford University Press, 1995), 86.

126 *The answer, he wrote, came:* Simon Schwarzfuchs, *Napoleon, the Jews and the Sanhedrin* (London: Routledge & Kegan Paul, 1979), 176.

127 *"Just God, how easy":* Heidi Thomann Tewarson, *Rahel Levin Varnhagen: The Life and Work of a German Jewish Intellectual* (Lincoln: University of Nebraska Press, 1998), 129.

127 *He urged his coreligionists to reform:* Tsarphati (Olry Terquem), *Première Lettre d'un Israélite Français* (Paris: Chez Bachelier, 1821), 5.

128 *"It is forbidden to change":* Mendes-Flohr and Reinharz, *The Jew in the Modern World,* 167.

128 *The reforming Rabbi of Livorno:* Moshe Pelli, *Studies in Jewish Bibliography, History and Literature* (New York: KTAV, 1971), 382.

129 *One reforming rabbi, Mendel Hess:* David Jan Sorkin, *The Transformation of German Jewry 1780–1840* (New York: Oxford University Press), 103.

## Chapter Nine: Incite the People to Terror

PAGE

131 *At sunrise on the morning:* Karl Raumer and Frederic Beecher Perkins, *German Universities* (New York: F. C. Brownell, 1859), 82.

134 *The concept of emancipation:* Uriel Tal, *Salo Wittmayer Baron: Jubilee Volume on the Occasion of his Eightieth Birthday,* vol. 2 (Jerusalem: American Academy for Jewish Research, 1974), 933.

134 *One student of the time:* Ibid., 926.

135 *A week after Wartburg, one student:* Ibid., 33.

136 *"A man counts as a man":* Shlomo Avineri, "A Note on Hegel's Views on Jewish Emancipation," *Jewish Social Studies xxv,* no. 2 (1963), 146.

136 *wrote of the "Jewish-infested":* Ibid., 149.

139 *Rahel wrote back:* Heidi Thomann Tewarson, *Rahel Levin Varnhagen: The Life and Work of a German Jewish Intellectual* (Lincoln: University of Nebraska Press, 1998), 160.

139 *"Terror," she wrote her brother:* Ibid., 161.

## Chapter Ten: I Try to Tell My Grief and It All Becomes Comic

PAGE

141 *Heine saw on Rahel's face:* Heinrich Heine, *Ludwig Börne: A Memorial,* translated by Jeffrey Sammons (Rochester: Boydell & Brewer, 2006), 3.

146 *"History is not falsified":* S. S. Prawer, *Heine's Jewish Comedy* (Oxford: Clarendon, 1985), 1.

146 *"We no longer have the strength":* Jeffrey Sammons, *Heinrich Heine: A Modern Biography* (Princeton: Princeton University Press, 1979), 91.

147 *Hassan prophesies:* Hal Draper, *The Complete Poems of Heinrich Heine* (Cambridge, Mass.: Suhrkamp/Insel, 1982), 187. Note that all verse translations are from Draper.

148 *Heine admitted he hadn't been trying:* Prawer, *Heine's Jewish Comedy,* 79.

149 *"the thousand-year-old family affliction":* Draper, *The Complete Poems of Heinrich Heine,* 398.

149 *"The Polish Jew with":* Prawer, *Heine's Jewish Comedy,* 62.

152 *"He must have felt and lived":* Philip Kossoff, *Valiant Heart* (Cranbury, N.J.: Associated University Presses, 1983), 55.

153 *"You did as much":* Heidi Thomann Tewarson, *Rahel Levin Varnhagen: The Life and Work of a German Jewish Intellectual* (Lincoln: University of Nebraska Press, 1998), 193.

156 *Heine wrote to his old friend:* Sammons, *Heinrich Heine* (Princeton: Princeton University Press, 1979), 109.

## Chapter Eleven: Since I Was Born a Slave I Love Freedom More than You Do

PAGE

159 *He wrote to his friend Moses:* Amir Eshel and Todd Presner, "Introduction," *Modernism-Modernity* 13, no. 4 (November 2006), 608.

160 *"When the fatherland faded":* Heinrich Heine, *English Fragments,* http://www .fullbooks.com/The-German-Classics-of-The-Nineteenth-andx18393.html.

161 *"these are times when":* Jefferson Chase, *Inciting Laughter: The Development of Jewish Humour in 19th Century Germany* (Berlin: Walter De Gruyter, 2000), 247.

162 *Moritz Saphir, another theater critic:* Ibid., 58.

164 *"Gradually, day by day":* Heine, *English Fragments.*

166 *"When I say that all":* Chase, *Inciting Laughter,* 259.

166 *"It is miraculous!":* Paul Mendes-Flohr and Jehuda Reinharz, *The Jew in the Modern World* (Oxford: Oxford University Press, 1995), 259.

169 *Riesser concludes, "There is":* Gabriel Riesser, *Pamphlet on the Emancipation of Baden Jews,* http://germanhistorydocs.ghi-dc.org/sub_document .cfm?document_id=341.

169 *"Vain hope! Believe me":* Helga Krohn, *Dem Streiter fur Recht un Freiheit* (Frankfurt: Jewish Museum of Frankfurt am Main, 2000), 44.

170 *"Offer me with one hand":* Wilfried Fiedler, *Gabriel Riesser—a Famous Jewish "Father" of the German Constitution of 1849,* http://www.jura.uni-sb.de/FB/LS/ Fiedler/Fiedler/Aufsaetze/riesser.html.

## Chapter Twelve: Let the Rothschilds Sanctify Themselves. Let Them Speak to Kings

PAGE

171 *"On the first day of Adar":* *Times of London,* June 25, 1840.

174 *"Let them sanctify themselves":* Ronald Florence, *Blood Libel* (Madison: University of Wisconsin Press, 2004), 124.

174 *Lehren sent a letter to:* Ibid., 125.

175 *They had, in the words of that:* Niall Ferguson, *The House of Rothschild: Money's Prophets, 1798–1848* (London: Penguin, 2000), 16.

178 *In 1816, Jakob, who:* Ibid., 177.

182 *"Am I in a synagogue?":* S. Posener, *Adolphe Crémieux* (Paris: Librairie Felix Alcan, 1933), 45.

183 *His tone was one of outrage:* Ibid., 208.

185 *"You protest in the name of the Jews":* Jonathan Frankel, *The Damascus Affair* (Cambridge, U.K.: Cambridge University Press, 1997), 189.

185 *Thiers's answer left him:* Ibid., 191.

189 *According to Crémieux's diaries:* Florence, *Blood Libel,* 189.

190 *This man wrote, "In spite":* Moses Hess, *Rome and Jerusalem: The Last National Question,* http://www.zionismontheweb.org/Moses_Hess_Rome_and_Jerusalem.htm.


# PART 3: REVOLUTION

## Chapter Thirteen: We Have a Solemn Mission to Perform

PAGE

196 *"You have sanctified the name":* Salo W. Baron, "The Revolution of 1848 and Jewish Scholarship: Part II Austria," *American Academy for Jewish Research* 20 (1951), 2.

199 *"This is a great day":* Josephine Clara Goldmark, *Pilgrims of 1848* (New Haven: Yale University Press, 1930), 41.

199 *"Listen, friends":* Ibid., 42.

200 *A Vienna Gazette reporter: Times of London,* March 21, 1848.

201 *"Say not a word about Jewish":* Ismar Elbogen, *A Century of Jewish Life* (Philadelphia: Jewish Publication Society, 1944), 19.

203 *One minister of Ferdinand's Imperial:* Reinhard Rürup, *Revolution and Evolution: 1848 in German History,* ed. Werner Mosse et al. (Tubingen: J.C.B. Mohr, 1981), 27.

204 *In May 1848,* Spenersche Zeitung: Reinhard Rürup, *Europe in 1848: Revolution and Reform in German History,* ed. Dieter Dowe et al. (Oxford: Berghahn, 2001), 754.


## Chapter Fourteen: The Tradition of Dead Generations Weighs on the Brains of the Living

PAGE

208 *Their first child, also called Jenny:* Francis Wheen, *Karl Marx* (London: Fourth Estate, 1999), 64.

208 *On his father's side:* Shlomo Barer, *The Doctors of Revolution* (London: Thames & Hudson, 2000), 178.

209 *In an essay written while:* Karl Marx, "Reflections of a Young Man on the

Choice of a Profession," http://www.marxists.org/archive/marx/works/1837 -pre/marx/1835-ref.htm.

209 *When the aftershocks of 1848:* Karl Marx, *The 18th Brumaire of Louis Bonaparte,* http://www.marxists.org/archive/marx/works/1852/18th-brumaire/.

210 *"Until I was fifteen":* Shlomo Avineri, *Moses Hess: Prophet of Communism and Zionism* (New York: New York University Press, 1985), 9.

210 *"I did not possess":* Ibid., 11.

211 *"Sociability is the essence":* Ibid., 121.

212 *"You will be glad to make":* Moses Hess, *The Holy History of Mankind and Other Writings,* edited by Shlomo Avineri (Cambridge, U.K.: Cambridge University Press), xi.

215 *Man's need for it had to:* Michael Lowy, "Marxism and Religion," http:// newsocialist.org/newsite/index.php?id=243.

216 *"The political emancipation of the Jew":* Karl Marx, *On the Jewish Question,* http:// www.marxists.org/archive/marx/works/1844/jewish-question/index.htm.

217 *After a long preamble:* Moses Hess, *The Essence of Money,* http://www.marxists .org/archive/hess/1845/essence-money.htm.

221 *"1. What is the meaning":* Hess, *The Holy History of Mankind and Other Writings,* 116.

222 *"Jews worshipped a higher being":* Julius Carlebach, *Karl Marx and the Radical Critique of Judaism* (London: Routledge & Kegan Paul, 1978), 189.

223 *In the recommendation letter:* Barer, *The Doctors of Revolution,* 991.

225 *In it he wrote:* Ibid., 1035.

225 *He wrote of Marx:* Carlebach, *Karl Marx and the Radical Critique of Judaism,* 311, 312.

226 *In 1841, he wrote:* Barer, *The Doctors of Revolution,* 904.

## Chapter Fifteen: Do Not Presume Discriminatory Laws Can Be Tolerated

PAGE

230 *The bright spot was:* Moshe Rinott, *Gabriel Riesser: Fighter for Jewish Emancipation* (London: Leo Baeck Institute, Yearbook VII, 1962), 37.

231 *There was no physical possibility that Jews:* Salo W. Baron, "Revolution of 1848 and Jewish Emancipation," *Jewish Social Studies* 11 (1949), 229.

232 *"Jews would be the most ardent":* Helga Krohn, *Dem Streiter fur Recht und Freiheit* (Frankfurt: Jewish Museum of Frankfurt am Main, 2000), 3.

232 *"Herr Riesser correctly expresses the meaning":* Shlomo Avineri, "Marx and Jewish Emancipation," *Journal of the History of Ideas* (1964), 447.

233 *"But it has ensured":* Friedrich Engels, "The Assembly at Frankfurt, June 1848," http://www.marxists.org/archive/marx/works/1848/06/01b.htm.

233 *Hess sent a dispatch back:* Shlomo Barer, *The Doctors of Revolution* (London: Thames & Hudson, 2000), 1067.

238 *The banner headline of the:* Francis Wheen, *Karl Marx* (London: Fourth Estate, 1999), 146.

# PART 4: CONSOLIDATION

## Chapter Sixteen: The Jews Are a Nation

PAGE

246 *Years later Eduard Silbermann remembered:* Monika Richarz, *Jewish Life in Germany: Memoirs from Three Centuries* (Bloomington: Indiana University Press, 1991), 88.

247 *In 1871 in Hamburg:* Monika Richarz, "Jewish Social Mobility in Germany During the Time of Emancipation" (London: Leo Baeck Institute, Yearbook XX, 1975), 70.

247 *By the middle of the nineteenth:* Paula Hyman, *The Jews of Modern France* (Berkeley: University of California Press, 1998), 58, 60.

249 *She had taken a small:* David I. Kertzer, *The Kidnapping of Edgardo Mortara* (London: Picador, 1997), 40.

252 *The* Archives Israëlites *noted: Archives Israëlites* 19 (1859), 547.

253 *The old man noted in his diary:* Moses Montefiore, *The Diaries of Sir Moses and Lady Montefiore,* vol. 2 (London: Griffith, Farran, 1890), 99.

254 *If, dispersed to all corners:* Hyman, *The Jews of Modern France,* 77.

255 *"Getting your child back":* Kertzer, *The Kidnapping of Edgardo Mortara,* 252.

257 *"Germany as a whole":* Moses Hess, *Rome and Jerusalem: The Last National Question,* http://www.zionismontheweb.org/Moses_Hess_Rome_and_Jerusalem.htm.

## Chapter Seventeen: Throw Out the Jew Itzig, Because He Takes Whatever He Sees

PAGE

261 *But there was, as lawyer:* Monika Richarz, *Jewish Life in Germany: Memoirs from Three Centuries* (Bloomington: Indiana University Press, 1991), 110.

261 *It is not you who emancipate:* Reinhard Rürup, "Jewish Emancipation and the Vision of Civil Society in Germany," *Leo Baeck Institute Yearbook LI,* (2006), 50.

262 *In Berlin, for example:* Reinhard Rürup, interview with author.

263 *Heinrich von Treitschke, a leading historian:* Hans Kohn, "National Prophet," *Review of Politics* (1945), 426.

266 *Between 1870 and 1873:* Fritz Stern, *Gold and Iron: Bismarck, Bleichroder and the Building of the German Empire* (London: Allen & Unwin, 1977), 181.

266 *Karl Marx, who was busy:* Ibid., 182.

267 *"The Germans are idealists":* Fritz Stern, *The Politics of Cultural Despair* (Berkeley: University of California Press, 1974), 53.

267 *"We are anti-Semites":* Peter Pulzer, *The Rise of Political Anti-Semitism in Germany and Austria* (Cambridge, Mass.: Harvard University Press, 1988), 80.

268 *"The principles of 1789":* Stern, *The Politics of Cultural Despair,* 65.

268 *"The abolition of guild":* Pulzer, *The Rise of Political Anti-Semitism in Germany and Austria,* 85.

268 *"I see in unrestrained"*: Ibid., 74.

269 *In a pamphlet called:* Ibid., 49.

270 *Stoecker tried to cloak:* "Court Preacher Adolph Stoecker," http://germanhistorydocs.ghi-dc.org/sub_document.cfm?document_id=1798.

271 *"The Jews are our"*: Heinrich von Treitschke, "The Jews Are Our Misfortune," http://germanhistorydocs.ghi-dc.org/sub_document.cfm?document_id=1799.

272 *Early in 1877, Gerson:* Jonathan Frankel and Steven Zipperstein, *Assimilation and Community* (Cambridge, U.K.: Cambridge University Press, 2004), 172.

273 *Disraeli couldn't wait to regale:* Stern, *Gold and Iron,* 478.

274 *Later Bratianu said:* Albert S. Lindemann, *Esau's Tears: Modern Anti-Semitism and the Rise of the Jews* (Cambridge, U.K.: Cambridge University Press, 1997), 316.

275 *A schoolteacher named:* "Report from *Tribune* Newspaper," http://germanhistorydocs.ghi-dc.org/sub_document.cfm?document_id=562.

## PART 5: RENAISSANCE

### Chapter Eighteen: I Want to Get Out . . . Out!
### Out of the Ghetto

PAGE

285 *"The wretch was not"*: Amos Elon, *Herzl* (London: Weidenfeld & Nicolson, 1975), 129.

285 *That night in his cell:* Alfred Dreyfus and Pierre Dreyfus, *The Dreyfus Case,* translated by Donald McKay (New Haven: Yale University Press, 1937), 36.

286 *"The army is the place"*: Michael Marrus, *Politics of Assimilation: The French Jewish Community at the Time of the Dreyfus Affair* (Oxford: Clarendon, 1980), 201.

287 *Drumont tells his readers:* Edouard Drumont, *La France Juive* (Paris: Dijon, 1886), 1.

288 *Rabbi Zadoc Kahn preached:* Marrus, *Politics of Assimilation,* 198.

290 *"The Jews are no longer cloistered"*: Ibid., 178.

291 *Samuel's dying words are:* Elon, *Herzl,* 124.

291 *In his report on the ritual:* Yossi Sarid, "A Man of Action," *Ha'aretz,* December 11, 2007.

293 *"There are a great"*: Marrus, *Politics of Assimilation,* 182.

### Chapter Nineteen: The Jewish Question: Anxiety About
### My Children

PAGE

294 *On Wednesday, July 24:* Sigmund Freud, *The Interpretation of Dreams,* translated by A. A. Brill (Ware: Wordsworth, 1997), 20.

298 *When the Freud family arrived:* Julia Kaldori, *Jewish Vienna* (Vienna: Mandelbaum Verlag, 2004), 71.

300 *I might have been ten:* Freud, *The Interpretation of Dreams,* 97.

302 *Börne's grave was of particular importance:* Ernest Jones, *The Life and Work of*

*Sigmund Freud,* edited by Lionel Trilling and Steven Marcus (London: Penguin, 1962), 219.

303 *"Take a few sheets":* Ibid., 219.

304 *A third of the University:* Steven Beller, *Vienna and the Jews, 1867–1938* (Cambridge, U.K.: Cambridge University Press, 1989), 34.

307 *One non-Jewish author:* Amos Elon, *Herzl* (London: Weidenfeld & Nicolson, 1975), 162.

307 *"Surgery of the Soul":* Jones, *The Life and Work of Sigmund Freud,* 224.

310 *There was no guarantee:* Elon, *Herzl,* 247.

311 *Herzl's play had reached deep:* Freud, *The Interpretation of Dreams,* 294.

311 *"They are not tormented":* Elon, *Herzl,* 246.


## Chapter Twenty: The Truth Is on the March

PAGE

313 *"I have but one":* Emile Zola, *The Dreyfus Affair: J'Accuse and Other Writings,* translated by Eleanor Levieux (New Haven: Yale University Press), 53.

315 *In the* Le Figaro: Ibid., 23.

315 *In his biggest bestseller:* Ibid., 2.

317 *Another meeting between the two:* Alfred Dreyfus and Pierre Dreyfus, *The Dreyfus Case,* translated by Donald McKay (New Haven: Yale University Press, 1937), 47.

320 *"Judges do make mistakes":* Zola, *The Dreyfus Affair,* 13.

320 *"Who created the syndicate?":* Ibid., 19.

320 *"Anti-Semitism is the guilty":* Ibid., 23.

327 *In his last letter to Lucie:* Dreyfus and Dreyfus, *The Dreyfus Case,* 105.

327 *The next day's newspapers:* Ibid., 142.


## Chapter Twenty-one: Everywhere an Intruder, Never Welcomed

PAGE

328 *"The imaginative thoughts of":* Ernest Jones, *The Life and Work of Sigmund Freud,* edited by Lionel Trilling and Steven Marcus (London: Penguin, 1962), 307.

329 *Vienna was an "experimental":* Ernest Grunfeld, *Vienna* (London: Readers Digest Association/Newsweek Books, 1981), 94.

331 *In 1900, a quarter:* Salo W. Baron, "The Jewish Question in the 19th Century," *Journal of Modern History* (1938), 53.

333 *"They were ill-matched as":* Donald Mitchell, *Gustav Mahler: The Early Years* (London: Barrie & Rockliff, 1958), 5.

336 *He noted to his confidante:* Natalie Bauer-Lechner, *Recollections of Gustav Mahler,* translated by Dika Newlin (London: Faber Music, 1980), 136.

336 *In 1896, Mahler wrote:* Francesca Draughon and Raymond Knapp, "Gustav Mahler and the Crisis of Jewish Identity," http://www.echo.ucla.edu/Volume3 -issue2/knapp_draughon/knapp_draughon1.html.

337 *The anti-Semitic* German Gazette: Henry Louis de la Grange, *Gustav Mahler,* vol. 2 (Oxford: Oxford University Press, 1995), 151.

338 *Years later he said:* Draughon and Knapp, "Gustav Mahler and the Crisis of Jewish Identity."

339 *Years later he would write:* Arthur Schnitzler, *My Youth in Vienna,* translated by Catharine Hutter (London: Weidenfeld & Nicolson, 1971), 6.

341 *The commonwealth is multiethnic:* Theodor Herzl, *Alt-Neuland,* http://www .wzo.org.il/en/resources/view.asp?id=1600.

342 *"It was my mistake":* Stefan Zweig, *The World of Yesterday* (London: Cassell, 1943), 90.


## Chapter Twenty-two: My Honor Has Been Restored

PAGE

344 *The minister of war said:* Alfred Dreyfus and Pierre Dreyfus, *The Dreyfus Case,* translated by Donald McKay (New Haven: Yale University Press, 1937), 239.

344 *"My heart beat":* Ibid., 240.

345 *At the time Dreyfus: The Times,* Friday, July 13, 1906.

345 *"In giving birth to the Dreyfus Affair":* Paula Hyman, *Jews of Modern France* (New Haven: Yale University Press, 1991), 113.


## Epilogue: Every Jew Has His System

PAGE

347 *Stefan Zweig in his memoirs:* Stefan Zweig, *The World of Yesterday* (London: Cassell, 1943), 13.

347 *"Every Jew has his system":* Bernard Lazare, *Job's Dungheap,* translated by Harry Lorin Binsse (New York: Schocken, 1948), 45.

348 *"It was in part because":* Pierre Birnbaum and Ira Katznelson, *Paths of Emancipation* (Princeton: Princeton University Press, 1995), 67.

349 *His friend and colleague, American:* John Alexander Gunn, "Bergson and his Philosophy," http://www.ibiblio.org/HTMLTexts/John_Alexander_Gunn/.

350 *Years later he would look back:* Ernest Jones, *The Life and Work of Sigmund Freud,* edited by Lionel Trilling and Steven Marcus (London: Penguin, 1962), 299.

352 *"What does 'homeland' Palestine":* Arthur Schnitzler, *The Road into the Open,* translated by Roger Byers (Berkeley: University of California Press, 1992), 82.

353 *"My opinion is that we":* Jones, *The Life and Work of Sigmund Freud,* 339.

357 *When the first volume:* Isabelle Monette Ebert, "Le Premier Dreyfusard," *French Review* (1993), 208.

359 *"Most Jews who began writing":* Ritchie Robertson, *The Jewish Question in German Literature, 1749–1939* (Oxford: Oxford University Press, 1999), 290.

359 *It was like giving birth:* Ronald Hayman, *K: A Biography of Franz Kafka* (London: Abacus, 1983), 1.

361 *Einstein replied, "I believe":* Walter Isaacson, *Einstein: His Life and Universe* (London: Simon & Schuster, 2007), 389.

362 *On the first of April:* Peter Pulzer, Eli Kedourie Memorial Lecture, British Academy, London, May 22, 2002.

364 *"Come here," he said:* Moshe Pelli, "The Literary Genre of the Autobiography in Hebrew Enlightenment Literature," *Journal of Jewish Studies* XXVII, no. 1 (Spring 1976).

364 *"Israel was not created":* Michael Graetz, *The Jews in 19th Century France* (Stanford: Stanford University Press, 1996), 9.

# BIBLIOGRAPHY

## BOOKS IN ENGLISH

Altmann, Alexander. *Moses Mendelssohn*. London: Vallentine Mitchell, 1998.

Arendt, Hannah. *The Origins of Totalitarianism*. London: André Deutsch, 1986.

———. *Rahel Varnhagen: The Life of a Jewess*. Translated by Richard and Clara Winston. Baltimore: Johns Hopkins University Press, 1997.

Asprey, Robert. *The Rise and Fall of Napoleon Bonaparte*. London: Abacus, 2001.

Avineri, Shlomo. *Hess: Holy History of Mankind and Other Writings*. Cambridge, U.K.: Cambridge University Press, 2004.

———. *Moses Hess: Prophet of Communism and Zionism*. New York: New York University Press, 1985.

———. *The Social and Political Thought of Karl Marx*. Cambridge, U.K.: Cambridge University Press, 1970.

Barer, Shlomo. *The Doctors of Revolution: 19th-Century Thinkers Who Changed the World*. London: Thames & Hudson, 2000.

Barker, Richard. *Marcel Proust: A Biography*. London: Faber & Faber, 1958.

Basnage, Jacques. *History of the Jews from Jesus Christ to the Present Time*. Translated by Thomas Taylor. London, 1708.

Bauer-Lechner, Natalie. *Recollections of Gustav Mahler*. Translated by Dika Newlin. London: Faber & Faber, 1980.

Bein, Alex. *The Jewish Question: Biography of a World Problem*. Madison, N.J.: Fairleigh Dickinson University Press, 1990.

Beller, Steven. *Vienna and the Jews, 1867–1938*. Cambridge, U.K.: Cambridge University Press, 1989.

Berk, Stephen M. *Year of Crisis, Year of Hope: Russian Jews and the Pogroms of 1881–1882*. Westport, Conn.: Greenwood Press, 1985.

Berkovitz, Jay. *Rites and Passages*. Philadelphia: University of Pennsylvania Press, 2004.

Berlin, Isaiah. *The Life and Opinions of Moses Hess.* London: Jewish Historical Society of England, 1959.

Bettelheim, Bruno. *Freud's Vienna and Other Essays.* New York: Knopf, 1990.

Beutin, Hoffacker, et al. *A History of German Literature.* London: Routledge, 1993.

Birnbaum, Pierre. *Jewish Destinies.* Translated by Arthur Goldhammer. New York: Hill & Wang, 2000.

———. *Paths of Emancipation.* Princeton: Princeton University Press, 1995.

Bonaparte, Napoleon. *The Corsican.* Edited by R. M. Johnston. Boston: Houghton Mifflin, 1910.

Borchsenius, Poul. *The Chains Are Broken: The Story of Jewish Emancipation.* Translated by Michael Heron. London: Allen & Unwin, 1964.

Brod, Max. *Heinrich Heine: The Artist in Revolt.* Translated by Joseph Witriol. London: Vallentine, Mitchell, 1956.

Burton, R. G. *Napoleon's Campaigns in Italy.* London: George Allen & Unwin, 1912.

Cahnman, Werner. *German Jewry: Its History and Sociology, Selected Essays.* Brunswick, N.J.: Transaction Publishers, 1989.

Carlebach, Julius. *Karl Marx and the Radical Critique of Judaism.* London: Routledge & Kegan Paul, 1978.

Chase, Jefferson. *Inciting Laughter: The Development of Jewish Humour in 19th Century Germany.* Berlin and New York: Walter de Gruyter, 2000.

Cook, Nicholas. *The Schenker Project: Culture, Race, and Music Theory in Fin-de-Siècle Vienna.* New York: Oxford University Press, 2007.

Craig, Gordon Alexander. *Germany, 1866–1945.* Oxford: Oxford University Press, 1999.

Cuddihy, John Murray. *The Ordeal of Civility: Freud, Marx, Lévi-Strauss, and the Jewish Struggle with Modernity.* Boston: Beacon Press, 1987.

Deutscher, Isaac. *The Non-Jewish Jew.* Oxford: Oxford University Press, 1968.

Diderot, Denis, and Jean le Rond d'Alembert. *The Plan of the French Encyclopedia or Universal Dictionary, Translated from the Preface.* London, 1752.

Diller, Jerry Victor. *Freud's Jewish Identity: A Case Study in the Impact of Ethnicity.* Rutherford, N.J.: Fairleigh Dickinson University Press, 1991.

Dowe, Dieter, et al. *Europe in 1848: Revolution and Reform.* Oxford: Berghahn Books, 2001.

Draper, Hal. *The Complete Poems of Heinrich Heine: A Modern English Version.* Oxford: Oxford University Press, 1982.

Dreyfus, Alfred, and Pierre Dreyfus. *The Dreyfus Case.* Translated by Donald McKay. New Haven: Yale University Press, 1937.

Elbogen, Ismar. *A Century of Jewish Life.* Philadelphia: Jewish Publication Society, 1944.

Elon, Amos. *Founder: Meyer Amschel Rothschild and His Time.* London: HarperCollins, 1996.

———. *Herzl.* London: Weidenfeld & Nicolson, 1976.

———. *The Pity of It All: A Portrait of German Jews, 1743–1933.* London: Allen Lane, 2002.

Fejto, Francois, ed. *The Opening of an Era: 1848.* London: Allan Wingate, 1948.

Ferguson, Niall. *The World's Banker*. London: Weidenfeld & Nicolson, 1998.

Feuer, Lewis. *Spinoza and the Rise of Liberalism*. Boston: Beacon Press, 1964.

Florence, Ronald. *Blood Libel: The Damascus Affair of 1840*. Madison: University of Wisconsin Press, 2004.

Frankel, Jonathan. *The Damascus Affair: "Ritual Murder," Politics, and the Jews in 1840*. Cambridge: Cambridge University Press, 1997.

Freud, Sigmund. *An Autobiographical Study*. London: Hogarth Press, 1935.

———. *Interpretation of Dreams*. Translated by A. A. Brill. Ware, U.K.: Wordsworth Editions, 1997.

Gay, Peter. *Freud, Jews, and Other Germans: Masters and Victims in Modernist Culture*. New York: Oxford University Press.

Goldmark, Josephine Clara. *Pilgrims of 1848*. New Haven: Yale University Press, 1930.

Golomb, Jacob, ed. *Nietzsche and Jewish Culture*. London: Routledge, 1997.

Graetz, Michael. *The Jews in Nineteenth-Century France*. Translated by Jane Marie Todd. Stanford: Stanford University Press, 1996.

Grunfeld, Frederic. *Prophets Without Honour: A Background to Freud, Kafka, Einstein, and Their World*. London: Hutchinson, 1979.

Guedalla, Philip. *Napoleon and Palestine*. London: George Allen & Unwin, 1925.

Halasz, Nicholas. *Captain Dreyfus: The Story of a Mass Hysteria*. New York: Grove Press, 1955.

Hayman, Ronald. *K: A Biography of Kafka*. London: Abacus, 1983.

Heine, Heinrich. *Complete Poems*. Translated by Hal Draper. Cambridge, Mass.: Suhrkamp/Insel Publishers, 1982.

———. *Harz Journey and Selected Prose*. Translated by Ritchie Robertson. London: Penguin, 1993.

———. *Memoirs*. Edited by Gustav Karpeles; translated by Gilbert Canaan. London: Wm. Heinemann, 1910.

———. *Pictures of Travel*. Translated by Charles Godfrey Leland. Philadelphia: Schafer & Koradi, 1879.

———. *The Sword and the Flame*. Edited by Alfred Werner. New York: Thomas Yoseloff, 1960.

Heller, Henry. *Bourgeois Revolution in France*. Oxford: Berghahn Books, 2006.

Hertzberg, Arthur. *The French Enlightenment and the Jews: The Origins of Modern Anti-Semitism*. New York: Columbia University Press, 1990.

Hess, Moses. *Rome and Jerusalem*. Translated by Meyer Waxman. New York: Bloch Publishing Co., 1918.

Hunt, Lynn. *Politics, Culture, and Class in the French Revolution*. London: Methuen, 1984.

Hyman, Paula. *Emancipation of the Jews of Alsace*. New Haven: Yale University Press, 1991.

———. *The Jews of Modern France*. Berkeley: University of California Press, 1998.

Isaacson, Walter. *Einstein: His Life and Universe*. London: Simon & Schuster, 2007.

Johnson, Douglas. *France and the Dreyfus Affair*. London: Blandford Press, 1966.

Jones, Ernest. *The Life and Work of Sigmund Freud*. London: Penguin Books, 1993.

Kant, Immanuel. *Philosophical Correspondence, 1759–1799.* Translated by Arnulf Zweig. Chicago: University of Chicago Press, 1986.

Kaplan, Marion. *Jewish Daily Life in Germany, 1618–1945.* New York: Oxford University Press, 2005.

Katz, Jacob. *Out of the Ghetto: The Social Background of Jewish Emancipation, 1770–1870.* Cambridge, Mass.: Harvard University Press, 1973.

Kertzer, David I. *The Kidnapping of Edgardo Mortara.* New York: Knopf, 1997.

Kirwan, F. D. *Transactions of the Paris Sanhedrin.* London: Charles Taylor, 1801.

Kobler, Franz. *Napoleon and the Jews.* New York: Schocken Books, 1976.

Kohler, Max. *Jewish Rights at the Congress of Vienna.* New York: American Jewish Historical Society, 1941.

La Grange, Henry-Louis de. *Gustav Mahler.* Oxford and New York: Oxford University Press, 1995.

Lazare, Bernard. *Job's Dungheap.* Translated by Harry Lorin Binsse. New York: Schocken Books, 1948.

Lemay, Edna, and Alison Patrick. *Revolutionaries at Work: The Constituent Assembly, 1789–91.* Oxford: Voltaire Foundation, 1996.

Lessing, Gotthold. *Nathan the Wise.* Translated by Walter Frank Charles Ade. New York: Barron's Education Series, 1972.

Lindemann, Albert. *Esau's Tears: Modern Anti-Semitism and the Rise of the Jews.* Cambridge, U.K.: Cambridge University Press, 1997.

Magnus, Shulamit. *Jewish Emancipation in a German City: Cologne, 1798–1871.* Stanford: Stanford University Press, 1997.

Maimon, Solomon. *Solomon Maimon: An Autobiography.* Translated by J. Clark Murray. Whitefish, Mont.: Kessinger Publishing, 2006.

Malino, Frances. *A Jew in the French Revolution.* Oxford: Basil Blackwell, 1996.

———. *The Sephardic Jews of Bordeaux.* Birmingham: University of Alabama Press, 1978.

Malino, Frances, and David Sorkin. *Profiles in Diversity.* Detroit: Wayne State University Press, 1998.

Marrus, Michael. *Politics of Assimilation: The French Jewish Community at the Time of the Dreyfus Affair.* Oxford: Clarendon House, 1971.

Marx, Karl. *Early Writings.* Translated by Tom Bottomorey. London: C. A. Watts, 1963.

Mayer, Gustav. *Friedrich Engels.* London: Chapman & Hall, 1936.

McCagg, William O. *A History of the Habsburg Jews.* Bloomington: Indiana University Press, 1989.

Mendelssohn, Moses. *Jerusalem and Other Jewish Writings.* Translated by Alfred Jospe. New York: Schocken Books, 1969.

Mendes-Flohr, Paul. *German Jews: A Dual Identity.* New Haven: Yale University Press, 1999.

Mendes-Flohr, Paul, and Jehuda Reinharz. *The Jew in the Modern World.* New York: Oxford University Press, 1995.

Meyer, Michael. *Judaism Within Modernity: Essays on Jewish History and Religion.* Detroit: Wayne State University Press, 2001.

———. *The Origins of the Modern Jew.* Detroit: Wayne State University Press, 1979.

Mitchell, Donald. *Gustav Mahler: The Early Years*. London: Faber & Faber, 1958.

Mosse, George L. *German Jews Beyond Judaism*. Boston: Brill, 2002.

Mosse, Werner. *The German-Jewish Economic Elite, 1820–1935*. Oxford: Oxford University Press, 1989.

Mosse, Werner, et al. *Revolution and Evolution: 1848 in German-Jewish History*. Tübingen: JCB Mohr, 1981.

Nadler, Steven. *Spinoza: A Life*. Cambridge, U.K.: Cambridge University Press, 1999.

Necheles, Ruth I. *The Abbé Grégoire, 1787–1831*. Westport, Conn.: Greenwood Publishing, 1971.

Newton, Peter M. *Freud: From Youthful Dream to Mid-Life Crisis*. New York: Guilford Press, 1995.

Oxaal, Ivar, et al. *Jews, Anti-Semitism, and Culture in Vienna*. London: Taylor & Francis, 1987.

Pawel, Ernst. *The Nightmare of Reason: A Life of Franz Kafka*. London: Collins Harvill, 1988.

Peters, George F. *Poet as Provocateur: Heinrich Heine and His Critics*. Rochester, N.Y.: Camden House, 2000.

Popkin, Jeremy. *Revolutionary News: The Press in France, 1789–1799*. Durham, N.C.: Duke University Press, 1990.

Popkin, Jeremy, and Richard Popkin. *The Abbé Grégoire and His World*. London: Kluwer Academic Publishers, 2000.

Prawer, S. S. *Heine's Jewish Comedy*. Oxford: Clarendon Press, 1983.

Pulzer, Peter. *Jews and the German State: The Political History of a Minority*. Oxford: Basil Blackwell, 1992.

———. *The Rise of Political Anti-Semitism in Germany and Austria*. Cambridge, Mass.: Harvard University Press, 1988.

Raphael, Chaim. *A Coat of Many Colours: Memoirs of a Jewish Experience*. London: Chatto & Windus, 1979.

Reinhardt, K. F., and Frederic Tuback. *Germany: 2000 Years*. New York: Frederick Ungar Publishing Co., 1961.

Reinharz, Jehuda, ed. *Living with Anti-Semitism*. Hanover, N.H.: University Press of New England, 1987.

Richarz, Monika. *Jewish Life in Germany: Memoirs from Three Centuries*. Bloomington: Indiana University Press, 1991.

Riess, H. S. *Political Thought of the German Romantics*. Oxford: Basil Blackwell, 1955.

Rose, William. *Heinrich Heine: Two Studies of His Thought and Feeling*. Oxford: Clarendon Press, 1956.

*Salo Wittmayer Baron Jubilee*. Cambridge, U.K.: Proceedings of the American Academy for Jewish Research, Cambridge University Press, 1974.

Sammons, Jeffrey. *Heinrich Heine: The Elusive Poet*. New Haven: Yale University Press, 1969.

———. *Heinrich Heine: A Modern Biography*. Manchester: Carcanet Press, 1979.

———. *Ludwig Börne: A Memorial*. Rochester, N.Y.: Camden House, 2006.

Schechter, Ronald. *Obstinate Hebrews: Representations of Jews in France, 1715–1815.* Berkeley: University of California Press, 2003.

Schnitzler, Arthur. *My Youth in Vienna.* London: Weidenfeld & Nicolson, 1971.

———. *None but the Brave* [Lieutenant Gustl]. Translated by R. L. Simon. New York: AMS Press, 1971.

———. *The Road into the Open* [Der Weg ins Freie]. Translated by Roger Byers. Berkeley: University of California Press, 1992.

Schwarz, Leo, ed. *Great Ages and Ideas of the Jewish People.* New York: Random House, 1956.

Schwarzfuchs, Simon. *Napoleon, the Jews, and the Sanhedrin.* London: Routledge & Kegan Paul, 1979.

Scott, Walter. *Life of Napoleon Buonaparte.* Edinburgh: Ballantyne, 1827.

Sepinwall, Alyssa. *The Abbé Grégoire and the French Revolution.* Berkeley: University of California Press, 2005.

Smith, Steven. *Spinoza, Liberalism, and the Question of Jewish Identity.* New Haven: Yale University Press, 1997.

Sombart, Werner. *Jews and Modern Capitalism.* London: T. F. Unwin, 1913.

Sorkin, David. *Transformation of German Jewry, 1780–1840.* Oxford: Oxford University Press, 1987.

Spinoza, Benedict. *Correspondence.* Translated by A. Wolf. London: Frank Cass & Co., 1928.

———. *Ethics.* Translated by G. H. R. Parkinson. London: Everyman's Library, 1989.

———. *Tractatus Theologico-Politicus.* Translated by R. H. M. Elwes. London: Dover, 2004.

Stern, Fritz. *Einstein's German World: Historical Reflections.* Princeton: Princeton University Press, 1999.

———. *Gold and Iron: Bismarck, Bleichroder, and the Building of the German Empire.* London: Allen & Unwin, 1977.

———. *The Politics of Cultural Despair.* Berkeley: University of California Press, 1974.

Stern, Selma. *The Court Jew: A Contribution to the History of the Period of Absolutism in Central Europe.* New Brunswick: Transaction Books, 1985.

Sutcliffe, Adam. *Judaism and Enlightenment.* Cambridge, U.K.: Cambridge University Press, 2003.

Szajkowski, Zosa. *The Jews and the French Revolutions of 1789, 1830, and 1848.* New York: KTAV Publishing House, 1970.

Talmage, Frank. *Disputation and Dialogue.* New York: KTAV Publishing House, 1975.

Tewarson, Heidi Thomann. *Rahel Levin Varnhagen: The Life and Work of a German Jewish Intellectual.* Lincoln: University of Nebraska Press, 1998.

Vallentin, Antonina. *Mirabeau: Voice of the Revolution.* London: Hamish Hamilton, 1948.

Weiss, John. *Moses Hess, Utopian Socialist.* Detroit: Wayne State University Press, 1960.

Wellesz, Egon. *Arnold Schoenberg.* London: Galliard Paperbacks, 1971.

Wheen, Francis. *Karl Marx.* London: Fourth Estate, 1999.

Wistrich, Robert. *Socialism and the Jews.* Madison: Fairleigh Dickinson University Press, 1982.

Zola, Emile. *The Dreyfus Affair.* Translated by Eleanor Levieux. New Haven: Yale University Press, 1996.

Zweig, Stefan. *The World of Yesterday.* London: Cassell & Co., 1987.

## WORKS IN FRENCH

Ayoun, Richard. *Les Juifs de France: de l'Emancipation à l'Intégration.* Paris: L'Harmattan, 1997.

Cahen, A. B. *L'Emancipation des Juifs Devant la Société Royale des Sciences et Arts.* Paris: Archives Israélites, 1880.

Carmoly, Eliacin. *Biographie des Israélites de France.* Frankfurt: G. Hess, 1868.

Comte de Mirabeau, Honore Gabriel Riquetti. *Sur Moses Mendelssohn et le Reforme Politique des Juifs.* Paris: EDHIS (Editions d'Histoire Sociale), 1968.

Diderot, Denis, and Jean le Rond d'Alembert. *Encyclopédie ou Dictionnaire Universel.* 1752.

Feuerwerker, David. *L'émancipation des Juifs en France. De l'Ancien Régime à la Fin du Second Empire.* Paris: Albin Michel, 1976.

Grégoire, Henri. *Essai sur la Régénération Physique, Morale et Politique des Juifs,* 1791.

Hourwitz, Zalkind. *Apologie des Juifs.* Paris, 1789.

Lazare, Bernard. *Contre l'Anti-Semitisme.* Paris: P-V Stock, 1896.

Lemay, Edna. *Dictionnaire des Constituantes.* Oxford: Voltaire Foundation, 1991.

Salvador, Joseph. *Histoire des Institutions de Moise.* Brussels: M. Dupin, 1829.

Spire, André. *Quelques Juifs et Demi-Juifs.* Paris: Bernard Grasset, 1928.

Tsarphati (pseudonym of Olry Terquem). *Première et Troisième Lettres d'un Israélite Français.* Paris, 1821.

### Miscellaneous

*Adresses, Mémoires et Pétitions des Juifs.* Paris: EDHIS (Editions d'Histoire Sociale), 1968.

*Archives Parlementaires: l'Assemblée Nationale Constituante, 1789–1791.*

*Journal de Paris,* various editions, 1789–1791.

*Mercure de France,* various editions, 1786 and 1789.

*Moniteur Universel,* proceedings of l'Assemblée Nationale Constituante, 1789–1791.

*Revue des Etudes Juives,* 1880.

# SCHOLARLY ARTICLES

Avineri, Shlomo. "Marx & Jewish Emancipation." *Journal of the History of Ideas,* 1964.

———. "A Note on Hegel's Views on Jewish Emancipation." *Jewish Social Studies* XXV, no. 2 (1963).

Baron, Salo W. "The Jewish Question in the 19th Century." *Journal of Modern History* 10, no. 1 (March 1938).

———. "The Revolution of 1848 and Jewish Scholarship, Part II: Austria." *American Academy for Jewish Research* 20 (1951).

Draughton, Francesca, and Raymond Knapp. "Gustav Mahler and the Crisis of Jewish Identity." *ECHO* 3 no. 2.

Ebert, Isabelle Monette. "Le Premier Dreyfusard." *French Review,* 1993.

Feuer, Lewis. "The Influence of the American Communist Colonies on Engels and Marx." *Western Political Quarterly* 19 (1966).

Fiedler, Wilfried. "Gabriel Riesser—A Famous Jewish 'Father' of the German Constitution of 1849." archiv.jura.uni-saarland.de/FB/LS/Fiedler/Fiedler/Aufsaetze/riesser.html.

Gilman, Sander. "Karl Marx and the Secret Language of Jews." *Modern Judaism,* 1984.

Glick, Leonard. "Types Distinct from Our Own: Franz Boas on Jewish Identity and Assimilation." *American Anthropologist* 84, no. 3 (September 1982).

Hertz, Deborah. "Salonières and Literary Women." *New German Critique,* Spring 1978.

Hook, Sidney. "Karl Marx and Moses Hess." *New International* 1, no. 5 (December 1934).

Jacobs, Joseph. "Comparative Distribution of Jewish Ability." *Journal of the Anthropological Institute of Great Britain and Ireland,* 1886.

Kahn, Lothar, "Moritz Gottlieb Saphir." *Leo Baeck Institute Yearbook* XX (1975).

Knittel, K. M. "Ein Hypermoderner Dirigent: Mahler and Anti-Semitism in Fin-de-Siècle Vienna." *19th-Century Music* 18, no. 3 (Spring 1995).

Linsky, Leonard. "Wittgenstein's Vienna." *Journal of Modern History* 47, no. 4 (December 1975).

Malino, Frances. "Resistance and Rebellion: The Jews in 18th Century France." *Jewish Historical Studies* XXX (1989).

Oelsner, Toni. "Ghetto of the Past." *YIVO* 1.

Philipson, David. "The Beginnings of the Reform Movement in Judaism." *Jewish Review* 15, no. 3 (April 1903).

Pulzer, Peter. "Emancipation and its Discontents." Centre for German-Jewish Studies, University of Sussex, Research Paper No. 1 (Spring 1997).

Rürup, Reinhard. "Emancipation and Crisis: The Jewish Question in Germany, 1850–1890." *Leo Baeck Institute Yearbook* XX (1975).

———. "Jewish Emancipation and the Vision of the Civil Society in Germany." *Leo Baeck Institute Yearbook* LI (2006).

———. "The Tortuous and Thorny Path to Legal Equality." *Leo Baeck Institute Yearbook* XXXI (1986).

Schechter, Ronald. "Translating the Marseillaise." *Past and Present,* May 1994.

Simon, Ernst. "Sigmund Freud, the Jew." *Leo Baeck Institute Yearbook* II (1957).

Sorkin, David. "The Case for Comparison: Moses Mendelssohn and Religious Enlightenment." *Modern Judaism* 14, no. 2 (1998).

———. "The Ideology of Emancipation." *Leo Baeck Institute Yearbook* XXXII (1987).

Sterling, Eleanor. "Jewish Reaction to Jew-Hatred." *Leo Baeck Institute Yearbook* III (1958).

Wieseltier, Leon. "Etwas Über die Judische Historik: Leopold Zunz and the Inception of Modern Jewish Historiography," *History and Theory,* Vol. 20, No. 2, May 1981.

# INDEX

# ABOUT THE AUTHOR

Michael Goldfarb was National Public Radio's voice in London for almost twenty years, first as NPR's London Correspondent, then Bureau Chief, and finally as Senior Correspondent of *Inside Out,* the award-winning public radio documentary program. He has been the recipient of the DuPont-Columbia Award, the Overseas Press Club Award, and British radio's highest honor, the Sony Award. The author of *Ahmad's War, Ahmad's Peace: Surviving Under Saddam, Dying in the New Iraq,* Goldfarb lives in London.